Collins gem

# French
## phrasebook

**Consultant**
Sophie Karnavos

First published 1993
This edition published 2010

Reprint 10 9 8 7 6 5
Typeset by Davidson Publishing Solutions, Glasgow
Printed in China

www.collinslanguage.com

ISBN 978-0-00-735858-8

## Using your phrasebook

Your *Collins Gem Phrasebook* is designed to help you locate the exact phrase you need, when you need it, whether on holiday or for business. If you want to adapt the phrases, you can easily see where to substitute your own words using the dictionary section, and the clear, full-colour layout gives you direct access to the different topics.

**The Gem Phrasebook includes:**

- Over 70 topics arranged thematically. Each phrase is accompanied by a simple pronunciation guide which eliminates any problems pronouncing foreign words.

- A Top ten tips section to safeguard against any cultural faux pas, giving essential dos and don'ts for situations involving local customs or etiquette.

- Practical hints to make your stay trouble free, showing you where to go and what to do when dealing with everyday matters such as travel or hotels and offering valuable tourist information.

- Face to face sections so that you understand what it is being said to you. These example mini-dialogues give you a good idea of what to expect from a real conversation.

- Common announcements and messages you may hear, ensuring that you never miss the important information you need to know when out and about.

- A clearly laid-out 3000-word dictionary means you will never be stuck for words.

- A basic grammar section which will enable you to build on your phrases.

- A list of public holidays to avoid being caught out by unexpected opening and closing hours, and to make sure you don't miss the celebrations!

It's worth spending time before you embark on your travels just looking through the topics to see what is covered and becoming familiar with what might be said to you.

Whatever the situation, your *Gem Phrasebook* is sure to help!

# Contents

# Pronouncing French

In this book we have used a simple system to help you pronounce the phrases. We have designed the book so that as you read the pronunciation of the phrases you can follow the French. This will help you to recognize the different sounds and enable you to read French without relying on the guide. Here are a few rules you should know:

| French | sounds like | example | pronunciation |
|---|---|---|---|
| **au** | oh | **autobus** | oh-toh-bews |
| **c (+ a, o, u)** | ka, ko, ku | **cas, col, cure** | ka, kol, kewr |
| **c (+ e, i), ç** | s | **ceci, ça** | suh-see, sa |
| **ch** | sh | **chat** | sha |
| **é** | ay | **été** | aytay |
| **è** | eh | **très** | treh |
| **eau** | oh | **beau** | boh |
| **eu** | uh | **neuf** | nuhf |
| **g (+ e, i)** | zhe, zhee | **gel, gîte** | zhel, zheet |
| **gn** | ny | **agneau** | a-nyoh |
| **oi** | wa | **roi** | rwa |
| **u** | ew | **sur** | sewr |
| **ui** | wee | **huit** | weet |

**e** is sometimes weak and sounds like uh. This happens either in very short words (**je** zhuh, **le** luh, **se** suh, etc.) or when the **e** falls at the end of a syllable: **retard** ruh-tar, **depuis** duh-pwee.

**h** is not pronounced: **hôtel** oh-tel, **haricot** a-ree-koh.

There are nasal vowels in French (represented by **ñ**):
**un** uñ
**fin/bain** fañ/bañ
**on** oñ
**dans/en** dahñ/ahñ

Word endings are often silent: **Paris** pa-ree, **Londres** loñdr, **parlent** parl. However, the ending is sometimes pronounced if it is followed by a word which begins with a vowel:

**avez-vous** a-vay voo **but vous avez** voo za-vay.

In French, unlike English, there is normally no strong accent on any syllable, but instead a slight emphasis on the final syllable of each word, phrase and sentence, which takes the form of a rising intonation rather than an increase in volume.

# Top ten tips

1. Use **vous** instead of **tu** until you are asked to use the familiar form. Do not use first names until you are invited.

2. Foreign visitors should not bring wine as a gift unless certain of its high quality.

3. Do not forget to stamp your train ticket before getting on the train – otherwise it will not be valid.

4. By law, French people must carry their ID cards all the time, and there might be ID inspections in the street (especially in big cities). The police will ask '**Vos papiers, s'il vous plait**'.

5. Flowers should be given in odd numbers (but not 13). Do not send chrysanthemums (they are funeral flowers) or red roses (they have romantic connotations).

6. Keep your hands on the table at all times during a meal, do not place them on your lap. Elbows, however, should be kept off the table!

7 A glass of wine is filled to three-quarters, never to the brim.

8 When addressing a stranger, always add **Monsieur** or **Madame**, even if you are only asking for directions.

9 In some areas (especially the countryside) people do not speak a word of English, so have your phrasebook ready!

10 It is usually much appreciated when guests bring a bouquet for the lady of the house or chocolates for their hosts.

# Talking to people



## Hello/goodbye, yes/no

You will find the French quite formal in their greetings, shaking hands both on meeting and on parting. **Bonjour, madame** or **bonjour, monsieur** are the politest ways to greet someone. **Mademoiselle** is becoming less frequently used. **Salut** is more informal than **bonjour**. If someone offers you something, perhaps an extra serving of food, and you simply reply **merci**, they will take this to mean 'no'. You must say **oui, merci** or you will go hungry!

| | |
|---|---|
| Please | **S'il vous plaît**<br>seel voo pleh |
| Thanks (very much) | **Merci (beaucoup)**<br>mehr-see (boh-koo) |
| You're welcome! | **De rien!**<br>duh ryañ! |
| Yes | **Oui**<br>wee |
| No | **Non**<br>noñ |

| | |
|---|---|
| Yes, please | **Oui, merci**<br>wee, mehr-see |
| No, thanks | **Non, merci**<br>noñ, mehr-see |
| OK! | **D'accord!**<br>da-kor! |
| Sir/Mr | **Monsieur/M.**<br>muh-syuh |
| Madam/Mrs/Ms | **Madame/Mme**<br>ma-dam |
| Miss | **Mademoiselle/Mlle**<br>mad-mwa-zel |
| Hello/Hi | **Bonjour/Salut**<br>boñ-zhoor/sa-lew |
| Goodbye/Bye | **Au revoir/Salut**<br>oh ruh-vwar/sa-lew |
| Bye for now | **À bientôt**<br>a byañ-toh |
| Good evening | **Bonsoir**<br>boñ-swar |
| Goodnight | **Bonne nuit**<br>bon nwee |
| See you tomorrow | **À demain**<br>a duh-mañ |
| Excuse me! (to catch attention) | **Pardon, monsieur/madame!**<br>par-doñ, muh-syuh/ma-dam! |
| Sorry! | **Pardon!**<br>par-doñ! |

| | |
|---|---|
| I'm sorry | **Je suis désolé(e)**<br>zhuh swee day-zo-lay |
| How are you? | **Comment allez-vous?**<br>ko-mahñ ta-lay voo? |
| Fine, thanks | **Très bien, merci**<br>treh byañ, mehr-see |
| And you? | **Et vous?**<br>ay voo? |
| I don't understand | **Je ne comprends pas**<br>zhuh nuh koñ-prahñ pa |
| I speak very little French | **Je parle très peu le français**<br>zhuh parl treh puh luh frahñ-seh |



# Key phrases

You don't need to say complicated things to get what you want. Often simply naming the thing and adding **s'il vous plaît** will do the trick, even when asking for directions.

| | |
|---|---|
| the (masculine) | **le**<br>luh |
| (feminine) | **la**<br>la |
| (plural) | **les**<br>lay |

| | |
|---|---|
| the museum | **le musée**<br>luh mew-zay |
| the station | **la gare**<br>la gar |
| the shops | **les magasins**<br>lay ma-ga-zañ |
| a/one (masculine) | **un**<br>uñ |
| (feminine) | **une**<br>ewn |
| a ticket/ one stamp | **un billet/un timbre**<br>uñ bee-yeh/uñ tañbr |
| a room/ one bottle | **une chambre/une bouteille**<br>ewn shahñbr/ewn boo-tay-yuh |
| some (masculine) | **du**<br>dew |
| (feminine) | **de la**<br>duh la |
| (plural) | **des**<br>day |
| some wine | **du vin**<br>dew vañ |
| some jam | **de la confiture**<br>duh la koñ-fee-tewr |
| some chips | **des frites**<br>day freet |
| Do you have...? | **Est-ce que vous avez...?/ Vous avez...?**<br>es kuh voo za-vay...?/voo za-vay...? |

| | |
|---|---|
| Do you have a room? | **Est-ce que vous avez une chambre?**<br>es kuh voo za-vay ewn shahñbr? |
| Do you have some milk? | **Vous avez du lait?**<br>voo za-vay dew leh? |
| I'd like... | **Je voudrais...**<br>zhuh voo-dreh... |
| We'd like... | **Nous voudrions...**<br>noo voo-dree-oñ... |
| I'd like an ice cream | **Je voudrais une glace**<br>zhuh voo-dreh ewn glas |
| We'd like to visit Paris | **Nous voudrions visiter Paris**<br>noo voo-dree-oñ vee-zee-tay pa-ree |
| Some more... | **Encore du/de la/des...**<br>ahñ-kor dew/duh la/day... |
| Another... | **Un/Une autre...**<br>uñ/ewn ohtr... |
| Some more bread | **Encore du pain**<br>ahñ-kor dew pañ |
| Some more soup | **Encore de la soupe**<br>ahñ-kor duh la soop |
| Some more glasses | **Encore des verres**<br>ahñ-kor day vehr |
| Another coffee | **Un autre café**<br>uñ nohtr ka-fay |
| Another beer | **Une autre bière**<br>ewn ohtr byehr |
| How much is it? | **C'est combien?**<br>say koñ-byañ? |

| | |
|---|---|
| How much is the room? | **C'est combien la chambre?**<br>say koñ-byañ la shahñbr? |
| large/small | **grand/petit**<br>grahñ/puh-tee |
| with/without | **avec/sans**<br>a-vek/sahñ |
| Where is/are...? | **Où est/sont...?**<br>oo ay/soñ...? |
| the nearest | **le/la plus proche**<br>luh/la plew prosh |
| How do I get...? | **Pour aller...?**<br>poor a-lay...? |
| to the museum | **au musée**<br>oh mew-zay |
| to the station | **à la gare**<br>a la gar |
| to Brioude | **à Brioude**<br>a bree-ood |
| There is/are... | **Il y a...**<br>eel ya... |
| There isn't/ aren't any... | **Il n'y a pas de...**<br>eel nya pa duh... |
| When...? | **Quand...?**<br>kahñ...? |
| At what time...? | **À quelle heure...?**<br>a kel ur...? |
| today | **aujourd'hui**<br>oh-zhoor-dwee |

| | |
|---|---|
| tomorrow | **demain**<br>duh-mañ |
| Can I...? | **Est-ce que je peux...?**<br>es kuh zhuh puh...? |
| smoke | **fumer**<br>few-may |
| What does this mean? | **Qu'est-ce que ça veut dire?**<br>kes kuh sa vuh deer? |

# Signs and notices

| | |
|---|---|
| **entrée** | entrance |
| **sortie** | exit |
| **ouvert** | open |
| **fermé** | closed |
| **chaud** | hot |
| **froid** | cold |
| **tirez** | pull |
| **poussez** | push |
| **à droite** | right |
| **à gauche** | left |
| **eau potable** | drinking water |
| **à emporter** | take-away |
| **dégustation de vin** | wine tasting |
| **prière de...** | please... |
| **libre** | free, vacant |
| **occupé** | engaged |

| caisse | cash desk |
|---|---|
| libre-service | self-service |
| toilettes | toilets |
| dames | ladies |
| hommes, messieurs | gents |
| hors service | out of order |
| à louer | for hire/to rent |
| à vendre | for sale |
| soldes | sale |
| baignade interdite | no bathing |
| sous-sol | basement |
| rez-de-chaussée | ground floor |
| ascenseur | lift |
| accès aux trains | to the trains |
| chambres | rooms available |
| complet | no vacancies |
| sortie de secours | emergency exit |
| sonnez | ring |
| appuyez | press |
| privé | private |
| arrêt | stop |
| billets | tickets |
| accueil | information |
| composter votre billet | validate your ticket |
| buffet | snacks |
| consigne | left luggage |
| non fumeurs | non-smoking |
| fumeurs | smoking |
| défense de fumer | no smoking |

# Polite expressions

There are two forms of address in French, formal (**vous**) and informal (**tu**). You should always stick to the formal until you are invited to **tutoyer** (use the informal **tu**).

| | |
|---|---|
| The meal was delicious | **Le repas était délicieux**<br>luh ruh-pa ay-teh day-lee-syuh |
| Thank you very much | **Je vous remercie**<br>zhuh voo ruh-mehr-see |
| Delighted to meet you | **Enchanté(e)**<br>ahñ-shahñ-tay |
| This is... | **Voici...**<br>vwa-see... |
| my husband/ my wife | **mon mari/ma femme**<br>moñ ma-ree/ma fam |
| Enjoy your holiday! | **Passez de bonnes vacances!**<br>pa-say duh bon va-kahñs! |

# Celebrations

Christmas celebrations revolve more around food than presents. They start on Christmas Eve (**réveillon de Noël**) with a lavish meal (often seafood) lasting many hours. The main course for the actual Christmas lunch is usually goose or turkey followed by the traditional dessert, a **bûche de Noël** (Christmas log). Families start the celebrations with an **apéritif** before the meal accompanied by elaborate **amuse-bouche** (nibbles). Champagne sometimes replaces the usual **apéritif** drinks.

| | |
|---|---|
| I'd like to wish you a... | **Je vous souhaite un/une...**<br>zhuh voo soo-eht uñ/ewn... |
| Merry Christmas! | **Joyeux Noël!**<br>zhwa-yuh noh-el! |
| Happy New Year! | **Bonne Année!**<br>bon a-nay! |
| Happy Easter! | **Joyeuses Pâques!**<br>zhwa-yuz pak! |
| Happy birthday! | **Bon anniversaire!**<br>boñ na-nee-vehr-sehr! |
| Have a good trip! | **Bon voyage!**<br>boñ vwa-yazh! |
| Enjoy your meal! | **Bon appétit!**<br>boñ na-pay-tee! |

# Making friends

In this section we have used the informal **tu** for the questions.

| FACE TO FACE | |
|---|---|
| A | **Comment tu t'appelles?**<br>ko-mahñ tew ta-pel?<br>What's your name? |
| B | **Je m'appelle...**<br>zhuh ma-pel...<br>My name is... |
| A | **Tu es d'où?**<br>tew ay doo?<br>Where are you from? |
| B | **Je suis anglais(e), de Londres**<br>zhuh swee zahñ-gleh(z), duh loñdr<br>I am English, from London |
| A | **Enchanté(e)!**<br>ahñ-shahñ-tay!<br>Pleased to meet you! |

| | |
|---|---|
| How old are you? | **Quel âge as-tu?**<br>kel azh a tew? |
| I'm ... years old | **J'ai ... ans**<br>zhay ... ahñ |
| Are you French? | **Tu es français(e)?**<br>tew ay frahñ-seh(z)? |

| | |
|---|---|
| I'm English/ Scottish/ American | **Je suis anglais(e)/ écossais(e)/américain(e)**<br>zhuh swee zahñ-gleh(z)/ zay-ko-seh(z)/za-mayree-kañ/ken |
| Where do you live? | **Où est-ce que tu habites?**<br>oo es kuh tew a-beet? |
| Where do you live? (plural) | **Où est-ce que vous habitez?**<br>oo es kuh voo za-bee-tay? |
| I live in London | **J'habite à Londres**<br>zha-beet a loñdr |
| We live in Glasgow | **Nous habitons à Glasgow**<br>noo za-bee-toñ a glaz-goh |
| I'm... | **Je suis...**<br>zhuh swee... |
| single | **célibataire**<br>say-lee-ba-tehr |
| married | **marié(e)**<br>mar-yay |
| divorced | **divorcé(e)**<br>dee-vor-say |
| I have... | **J'ai...**<br>zhay... |
| a boyfriend | **un petit ami**<br>uñ puh-tee-ta-mee |
| a girlfriend | **une petite amie**<br>ewn puh-teet a-mee |

| | |
|---|---|
| I have a partner (male/female) | **J'ai un compagnon/ une compagne**<br>zhay uñ kom-pa-nyoñ/ ewn koñ-panyuh |
| I have ... children | **J'ai ... enfants**<br>zhay ... ahñ-fahñ |
| I have no children | **Je n'ai pas d'enfants**<br>zhuh nay pas dahñ-fahñ |
| I'm here on holiday/on business/for the weekend | **Je suis ici en vacances/ en voyage d'affaires/ en week-end**<br>zhuh swee zee-see ahñ va-kahñs/ ahñ vwa-yazh da-fehr/ ahñ wee-kend |



# Work

| | |
|---|---|
| What work do you do? | **Qu'est-ce que vous faites comme travail?**<br>kes kuh voo fet kom tra-va-yuh? |
| I'm... | **Je suis...**<br>zhuh swee... |
| a doctor | **médecin**<br>may-dsañ |

> **Leisure/interests** (p 71) > **Sport** (p 76)

| | |
|---|---|
| a manager | **directeur**<br>dee-rek-tur |
| a secretary | **secrétaire**<br>suh-kray-tehr |
| I work from home | **Je travaille à domicile**<br>zhuh tra-va-yuh a do-mee-seel |
| I'm self-employed | **Je travaille à mon compte**<br>zhuh tra-va-yuh a moñ koñt |

## Weather

| | |
|---|---|
| **temps variable**<br>tahñ va-ree-abl | changeable weather |
| **beau** boh | fine |
| **temps orageux**<br>tahñ o-ra-zhuh | thundery weather |

| | |
|---|---|
| It's sunny | **Il y a du soleil**<br>eel ya dew so-lay |
| It's raining | **Il pleut**<br>eel pluh |
| It's snowing | **Il neige**<br>eel nezh |
| It's windy | **Il y a du vent**<br>eel ya dew vahñ |

| | |
|---|---|
| What a lovely day! | **Quelle belle journée!** kel bel zhoor-nay! |
| What awful weather! | **Quel mauvais temps!** kel moh-veh tahñ! |
| What will the weather be like tomorrow? | **Quel temps fera-t-il demain?** kel tahñ fuh-ra-teel duh-mañ? |
| Do you think it's going to rain? | **Vous croyez qu'il va pleuvoir?** voo krwa-yay keel va pluh-vwar? |
| It's very hot/cold | **Il fait très chaud/froid** eel feh treh shoh/frwa |

# Getting around

## Asking the way



| | |
|---|---|
| **en face de** ahñ fas duh | opposite |
| **à côté de** a ko-tay duh | next to |
| **près de** preh duh | near to |
| **le carrefour** luh kar-foor | crossroad |
| **le rond-point** luh roñ-pwañ | roundabout |

**FACE TO FACE**

**A** **Pardon, pour aller à la gare?**
par-doñ, poor a-lay a la gar?
Excuse me, how do I get to the station?

**B** **Continuez tout droit, après l'église tournez à gauche/à droite**
koñ-tee-new-ay too drwa, a-preh lay-gleez toor-nay a gohsh/a drwat
Keep straight on, after the church turn left/right

**A** **C'est loin?**
say lwañ?
Is it far?

**B** **Non, c'est à deux cents mètres/à cinq minutes**
noñ, say ta duh sahñ metr/a sañk mee-newt
No, 200 yards/five minutes

**A** **Merci!**
mehr-see!
Thank you!

**B** **De rien!**
duh ryañ!
You're welcome!



| | |
|---|---|
| We're looking for... | **Nous cherchons...**<br>noo shehr-shoñ... |
| Can we walk there? | **On peut y aller à pied?**<br>oñ puh ee a-lay a pyay? |
| We're lost | **Nous nous sommes perdu(e)s**<br>noo noo som pehr-dew |
| Is this the right way to...? | **C'est la bonne direction pour...?**<br>say la bon dee-rek-syoñ poor...? |
| Can you show me on the map? | **Pouvez-vous me montrer sur la carte?**<br>poo-vay voo me moñ-tray sewr la kart? |

| YOU MAY HEAR... | |
|---|---|
| **C'est indiqué**<br>say tañ-dee-kay | It's signposted |
| **C'est au coin de la rue**<br>say toh kwañ duh la rew | It's on the corner of the street |
| **C'est là-bas**<br>say la-ba | It's over there |

# Bus and coach

**FACE TO FACE**

A **Pardon, quel bus pour le centre-ville?**
par-doñ, kel bews poor luh sahñtr veel?
Excuse me, which bus goes to the centre?

B **Le 15**
luh kañz
Number 15

A **Où est l'arrêt?**
oo ay la-reh?
Where is the bus stop?

B **Là-bas, à gauche**
la-ba, a gohsh
There, on the left

**A** **Où est-ce que je peux acheter des tickets de bus?**
oo es kuh zhuh puh ash-tay day tee-keh duh bews?
Where can I buy bus tickets?

**B** **Là-bas, au distributeur**
la-ba, oh dees-tree-bew-tur
Over there, at the ticket machine

| | |
|---|---|
| Is there a bus to...? | **Est-ce qu'il y a un bus pour...?**<br>es keel ya uñ bews poor...? |
| Where do I catch the bus to go to...? | **Où est-ce qu'on prend le bus pour aller à/au (etc.)...?**<br>oo es koñ prahñ luh bews poor a-lay a/oh...? |
| How much is it to...? | **C'est combien pour aller à/au (etc.)...?**<br>say koñ-byañ poor a-lay a/oh...? |
| to the centre | **au centre**<br>oh sahñtr |
| to the beach | **à la plage**<br>a la plazh |
| to the shops | **aux magasins**<br>oh ma-ga-zañ |
| to Montmartre | **à Montmartre**<br>a moñ-martr |
| How frequent are the buses to...? | **Les bus pour ... passent tous les combien?**<br>lay bews poor ... pas too lay koñ-byañ? |

| | |
|---|---|
| When is the first/ the last bus to...? | **À quelle heure part le premier/le dernier bus pour...?** a kel ur par luh pruh-myay/ luh dehr-nyay bews poor...? |
| Could you tell me when to get off? | **Pourriez-vous me dire quand descendre?** poo-ree-ay-voo muh deer kahñ deh-sahñdr? |
| This is my stop | **C'est mon arrêt** say moñ na-reh |



| YOU MAY HEAR... | |
|---|---|
| **Prenez le métro, c'est plus rapide** pruh-nay luh may-troh, say plew ra-peed | Take the metro, it's quicker |



> **Luggage** (p 92)

# Metro

In Paris ticket options include **un carnet de dix tickets** (a book of ten tickets), which can be used on metro, bus and RER (suburban metro), or **un billet de tourisme**, which covers seven days' travel.

| | |
|---|---|
| **entrée** ahñ-tray | entrance |
| **sortie** sor-tee | way out/exit |
| **la ligne de métro** la lee-nyuh duh may-troh | metro line |
| **en direction de...** ahñ dee-rek-syoñ duh... | in the direction of... |
| **correspondance** ko-reh-spoñ-dahñs | connecting line |

Where is the nearest metro? **Où est la station de métro la plus proche?** oo ay la sta-syoñ duh may-troh la plew prosh?

I'm going to... **Je vais à...** zhuh veh a...

How does the ticket machine work? **Comment marche le guichet automatique?** ko-mahñ marsh luh gee-sheh oh-toh-ma-teek?

| | |
|---|---|
| Do you have a map of the metro? | **Vous avez un plan du métro?** voo za-vay uñ plahñ dew may-troh? |
| How do I get to...? | **Pour aller à/au (etc.)...?** poor a-lay a/oh...? |
| Do I have to change? | **Est-ce qu'il faut changer?** es keel foh shañ-zhay? |
| Which line is it for...? | **C'est quelle ligne pour...?** say kel lee-nyuh poor...? |
| In which direction? | **Dans quelle direction?** dahñ kel dee-rek-syoñ? |
| What is the next stop? | **Quel est le prochain arrêt?** kel ay luh pro-shañ na-reh? |

# Train

Before you catch your train, you must validate your ticket in the machines situated on the platforms, which carry the warning **n'oubliez pas de composter votre billet**. Failing to do so could result in a fine that is more than the cost of the ticket. You can book tickets on the French Railways website **www.sncf.com**.


> **Luggage** (p 92)

| | |
|---|---|
| **horaire** o-rehr | timetable |
| **circuler** seer-kew-lay | to operate |
| **dimanches et fêtes** dee-mahñsh ay fet | Sundays and holidays |
| **accès aux quais** ak-seh oh keh | to the platforms |

**FACE TO FACE**

A **Quand part le prochain train pour...?**
kahñ par luh pro-shañ trañ poor...?
When is the next train to...?

B **A 17 heures 10**
a dee-set ur dees
At ten past five

A **Deux billets pour...**
duh bee-yeh poor...
Two tickets to...

B **Aller simple ou aller-retour?**
a-lay sañpl oo a-lay-ruh-toor?
Single or return?

| | |
|---|---|
| First class/ Second class | **Première classe/ Deuxième classe** pruh myehr klas/duh-zyem klas |
| Smoking/ Non-smoking | **Fumeur/Non fumeur** few-mur/noñ few-mur |

| | |
|---|---|
| Is there a supplement to pay? | **Y a-t-il un supplément à payer?**<br>ee a-teel uñ sew-play-mahñ a pay-yay? |
| I want to book a seat on the TGV to Nîmes | **Je voudrais réserver une place dans le TGV pour Nîmes**<br>zhuh voo-dreh ray-zehr-vay ewn plas dahñ luh tay-zhay-vay poor neem |
| When is the train to...? | **Le train pour ... est à quelle heure?**<br>luh trañ poor ... ay ta kel ur? |
| the first/the last | **le premier/le dernier**<br>luh pruh myay/luh dehr-nyay |
| When does it arrive in...? | **À quelle heure arrive-t-il à...?**<br>a kel ur a-reev-teel a...? |
| Do I have to change? | **Est-ce qu'il faut changer?**<br>es keel foh shañ-zhay? |
| Which platform does it leave from? | **Il part de quel quai?**<br>eel par duh kel kay? |
| Is this the right platform for the train to Paris? | **C'est le bon quai pour le train de Paris?**<br>say luh boñ kay poor luh trañ duh pa-ree? |
| Is this the train for...? | **C'est le train pour...?**<br>say luh trañ poor...? |
| When does it leave? | **Il part à quelle heure?**<br>eel par a kel ur? |



> **Luggage** (p 92)

| | |
|---|---|
| Does the train stop at...? | **Est-ce que le train s'arrête à...?** es kuh luh trañ sa-ret a...? |
| Where do I change for...? | **Où dois-je changer pour...?** oo dwa-zhuh shahñ-zhay poor...? |
| Please tell me when we get to... | **S'il vous plaît, prévenez-moi quand nous serons à...** seel voo pleh, pray-vnay mwa kañ noo suh-roñ za... |
| Is this seat free? | **Cette place est-elle libre?** set plas ay-tel leebr? |
| Excuse me | **Excusez-moi** eks-kew-zay-mwa |
| Sorry! | **Pardon!** par-doñ! |



# Taxi

| | |
|---|---|
| **la station de taxis** la sta-syoñ duh tak-see | taxi rank |

| | |
|---|---|
| I want a taxi | **Je voudrais un taxi** zhuh voo-dreh uñ tak-see |
| Where can I get a taxi? | **Où est-ce que je peux prendre un taxi?** oo es kuh zhuh puh prahñdr uñ tak-see? |

| | |
|---|---|
| Could you order me a taxi? | **Pouvez-vous m'appeler un taxi?**<br>poo-vay voo ma-play uñ tak-see? |
| How much is it going to cost to go to...? | **Combien ça va coûter pour aller à/au (etc.)...?**<br>koñ-byañ sa va koo-tay poor a-lay a/oh...? |
| to the town centre | **au centre-ville**<br>oh sahñtr-veel |
| to the station | **à la gare**<br>a la gar |
| to the airport | **à l'aéroport**<br>a la-ay-ro-por |
| to this address | **à cette adresse**<br>a set a-dres |
| How much is it? | **C'est combien?**<br>say koñ-byañ? |
| It's more than on the meter | **C'est plus qu'au compteur**<br>say plew skoh koñ-tur |
| Keep the change | **Gardez la monnaie**<br>gar-day la mo-neh |
| Sorry, I don't have any change | **Je suis désolé(e), je n'ai pas de monnaie**<br>zhuh swee day-zo-lay, zhuh nay pa duh mo-neh |
| I'm in a hurry | **Je suis pressé(e)**<br>zhuh swee preh-say |
| Is it far? | **C'est loin?**<br>say lwañ? |


> **Luggage** (p 92)

# Boat and ferry

When is the next boat/ferry to...? **À quelle heure part le prochain bateau/ferry pour...?**
a kel ur par luh pro-shañ ba-toh/ feh-ree poor...?

Have you a timetable? **Vous avez un horaire?**
voo za-vay uñ noh-rehr?

Is there a car ferry to...? **Est-ce qu'il y a un car ferry pour...?**
es keel ya uñ car feh-ree poor...?

How much is...? **C'est combien...?**
seh koñ-byañ...?

a single **un aller simple**
uñ na-lay sañpl

a return **un aller-retour**
uñ na-lay-ruh-toor

A tourist ticket **Un billet touristique**
uñ bee-yeh too-rees-teek

How much is it for a car and ... people? **C'est combien pour une voiture et ... personnes?**
say koñ-byañ poor ewn vwa-tewr ay ... pehr-son?

How long is the crossing? **La traversée dure combien de temps?**
la tra-vehr-say dewr koñ-byañ duh tahñ?

Where does the boat leave from? **D'où part le bateau?**
doo par luh ba-toh?

| | |
|---|---|
| When is the first/ last boat? | **Le premier/dernier bateau part quand?** luh pruh-myay/dehr-nyay ba-toh par kahñ? |
| What time do we get to...? | **On arrive à quelle heure à...?** on a-reev a kel ur a...? |
| Is there somewhere to eat on the boat? | **Est-ce qu'on peut manger sur le bateau?** es koñ puh mahñ-zhay sewr luh ba-toh? |

## Air travel

| | |
|---|---|
| How do I get to the airport? | **Comment fait-on pour aller à l'aéroport?** ko-mahñ fay toñ poor a-lay a la-ay-ro-por? |
| How long does it take to get to the airport? | **On met combien de temps pour aller à l'aéroport?** oñ meh koñ-byañ duh tahñ poor a-lay a la-ay-ro-por? |
| How much is the taxi fare...? | **C'est combien le taxi pour aller...?** say koñ-byañ luh tak-see poor a-lay...? |
| into town | **en ville** ahñ veel |
| to the hotel | **à l'hôtel** a loh-tel |

| | |
|---|---|
| Is there an airport bus to the city centre? | **Est-ce qu'il y a une navette pour aller au centre-ville?**<br>es keel ya ewn na-vet poor a-lay oh sahñtr-veel? |
| Where do I check in for...? | **Où est l'enregistrement pour...?**<br>oo ay lahñ-ruh-zhee-struh-mahñ poor...? |
| Where is the luggage for the flight from...? | **Où sont les bagages du vol en provenance de...?**<br>oo soñ lay ba-gazh dew vol ahñ pro-vnahñs duh...? |
| Which is the departure gate for the flight to...? | **Quelle est la porte d'embarquement pour le vol à destination de...?**<br>kel ay la port dahñ-bar-kuh-mahñ poor luh vol a des-tee-na-syoñ duh...? |

| YOU MAY HEAR... | |
|---|---|
| **L'embarquement aura lieu porte numéro...**<br>lahñ-bar-kuh-mahñ oh-ra lyuh port new-may-ro... | Boarding will take place at gate number... |
| **Présentez-vous immédiatement porte numéro...**<br>pray-zahñ-tay voo ee-may-dyat-mahñ port new-may-ro... | Go immediately to gate number... |
| **Votre vol a du retard**<br>votr vol a dew ruh-tar | Your flight is delayed |

> **Luggage** (p 92)

# Customs control

With the Single European Market, European Union (EU) citizens are subject only to spot checks and can go through the blue customs channel (unless they have goods to declare). There is no restriction, in either quantity or value, on goods purchased by EU travellers in another EU country provided that they are for personal use.

| | |
|---|---|
| **contrôle des passeports** koñ-trol day pas-por | passport control |
| **UE (Union Européenne)** ew uh | EU (European Union) |
| **autres passeports** ohtr pas-por | other passports |
| **douane** dwan | customs |

Do I have to pay duty on this? **Est-ce que je dois payer des droits de douane sur ça?**
es kuh zhuh dwa pay-yay day drwa duh dwan sewr sa?

It is for my own personal use **C'est pour mon usage personnel**
say poor moñ new-zazh pehr-so-nel

We are on our way to... (if in transit through a country) **Nous allons en/au/aux...**
noo za-loñ ahñ/oh/oh...

# Driving

## Car hire

| | |
|---|---|
| **le permis de conduire** luh pehr-mee duh koñ-dweer | driving licence |
| **l'assurance** la-sew-rahñs | insurance |

| | |
|---|---|
| I want to hire a car | **Je voudrais louer une voiture** zhuh voo-dreh loo-ay ewn vwa-tewr |
| for ... days | **pour ... jours** poor ... zhoor |
| for the weekend | **pour le week-end** poor luh wee-kend |
| What are your rates...? | **Quels sont vos tarifs...?** kel soñ voh ta-reef...? |
| per day | **par jour** par zhoor |
| per week | **par semaine** par suh-men |

| | |
|---|---|
| Is there a mileage (kilometre) charge? | **Est-ce que le kilométrage est en plus?**<br>es kuh luh kee-lo-may-trazh ay tahñ plews? |
| How much is it? | **C'est combien?**<br>say koñ-byañ? |
| Does the price include comprehensive insurance? | **Est-ce que le prix comprend l'assurance tous-risques?**<br>es kuh luh pree koñ-prahñ la-sew-rahñs too reesk? |
| Must I return the car here? | **Est-ce que je dois rendre la voiture ici?**<br>es kuh zhuh dwa rahñdr la vwa-tewr ee-see? |
| By what time? | **Vers quelle heure?**<br>vehr kel ur? |
| I'd like to leave it in... | **Je voudrais la laisser à...**<br>zhuh voo-dreh la leh-say a... |
| What do I do if we break down? | **Que dois-je faire en cas de panne?**<br>kuh dwa-zhuh fehr ahñ ka duh pan? |

**YOU MAY HEAR...**

| | |
|---|---|
| **Veuillez rendre la voiture avec un plein d'essence**<br>vuh-yay rahñdr la vwa-tewr a-vek uñ plañ deh-sahñs | Please return the car with a full tank |

# Driving

| | |
|---|---|
| I am looking for a car park | **Je cherche un parking**<br>zhuh shehrsh uñ par-keeng |
| Do I need to pay? | **Il faut payer?**<br>eel foh pay-ay? |
| Can I park here? | **On peut se garer ici?**<br>oñ puh suh ga-ray ee-see? |
| How long can I park for? | **Combien de temps peut-on se garer ici?**<br>koñ-byañ duh tahñ puh-toñ suh ga-ray ee-see? |
| Is the road good? | **Est-ce que la route est bonne?**<br>es kuh la root ay bon? |
| Can you show me on the map? | **Pouvez-vous me montrer sur la carte?**<br>poo-vay voo muh moñ-tray sewr la kart? |

## Petrol

| | |
|---|---|
| **sans plomb** sahñ ploñ | unleaded |
| **diesel/gasoil** dee-eh-zel/ga-zwal | diesel |

| | |
|---|---|
| Fill it up, please | **Le plein, s'il vous plaît**<br>luh plañ, seel voo pleh |
| Please check the oil/the water | **Pouvez-vous vérifier l'huile/l'eau?**<br>poo-vay voo vay-ree-fyay lweel/loh? |
| ...euros' worth of unleaded petrol | **...euros d'essence sans plomb**<br>...uh-roh deh-sahñs sahñ ploñ |
| Pump number... | **La pompe numéro...**<br>la pomp new-may-roh... |
| Can you check the tyre pressure? | **Pouvez-vous vérifier la pression des pneus?**<br>Poo-vay voo vay-ree-fyay la preh-syoñ day pnuh? |
| Where do I pay? | **Où dois-je payer?**<br>oo dwa-zhuh pay-yay? |
| Do you take credit cards? | **Vous acceptez les cartes de crédit?**<br>voo zak-sep-tay lay kart duh kray-dee? |

# Breakdown

| assistance automobile<br>a-sees-tahñs oh-toh-mo-beel | breakdown assistance |
|---|---|

| | |
|---|---|
| Can you help me? | **Pouvez-vous m'aider?**<br>poo-vay voo may-day? |
| My car has broken down | **Ma voiture est en panne**<br>ma vwa-tewr ay tahñ pan |
| I can't start the car | **Je n'arrive pas à démarrer**<br>zhuh na-reev pa a day-ma-ray |
| I've run out of petrol | **Je suis en panne d'essence**<br>zhuh swee ahñ pan deh-sahñs |
| Is there a garage near here? | **Il y a un garage près d'ici?**<br>eel ya uñ ga-razh preh dee-see? |
| Can you tow me to the nearest garage? | **Pouvez-vous me remorquer jusqu'au garage le plus proche?**<br>Poo-vay voo muh ruh-mor-kay zhew-skoh ga-razh luh plew prosh? |
| Do you have parts for a (make of car)? | **Avez-vous des pièces de rechange pour une...?**<br>a-vay voo day pyes duh ruh-shahñzh poor ewn...? |
| There's something wrong with the... | **J'ai un problème avec le/la/les...**<br>zhay uñ prob-lem a-vek luh/la/lay... |

Breakdown

# Car parts

| | |
|---|---|
| The ... doesn't work | **Le/La/L' ... ne marche pas**<br>luh/la/l ... nuh marsh pa |
| The ... don't work | **Les ... ne marchent pas**<br>lay ... nuh marsh pa |

| | | |
|---|---|---|
| accelerator | **l'accélérateur** | ak-say-lay-ra-tur |
| battery | **la batterie** | ba-tree |
| bonnet | **le capot** | ka-poh |
| brakes | **les freins** | frañ |
| choke | **le starter** | star-tehr |
| clutch | **l'embrayage** | ahñ-bray-yazh |
| distributor | **le delco** | del-koh |
| engine | **le moteur** | mo-tur |
| exhaust pipe | **le pot d'échappement** | poh day-shap-mahñ |
| fuse | **le fusible** | few-zeebl |
| gears | **les vitesses** | vee-tes |
| handbrake | **le frein à main** | frañ a mañ |
| headlights | **les phares** | far |
| ignition | **l'allumage** | a-lew-mazh |
| indicator | **le clignotant** | klee-nyo-tahñ |
| points | **les vis platinées** | vees pla-tee-nay |
| radiator | **le radiateur** | ra-dya-tur |
| reversing lights | **les phares de recul** | far duh ruh-kewl |

| | | |
|---|---|---|
| seat belt | **la ceinture de sécurité** | sañ-tewr duh say-kewr-eetay |
| sidelights | **les veilleuses** | vay-yuhz |
| spare wheel | **la roue de secours** | roo duh skoor |
| spark plugs | **les bougies** | boo-zhee |
| steering | **la direction** | dee-rek-syoñ |
| steering wheel | **le volant** | vo-lahñ |
| tyre | **le pneu** | pnuh |
| wheel | **la roue** | roo |
| windscreen | **le pare-brise** | par-breez |
| windscreen washers | **le lave-glace** | lav-glas |
| windscreen wiper | **l'essuie-glace** | es-wee-glas |

# Road signs

customs

toll station for motorway

CÉDEZ LE PASSAGE

give way

RALENTIR

slow down

SENS UNIQUE

one way

Déviation

diversion

priority road

north

Nord

west

Ouest

Est

east

Sud

south

libre

spaces

complet

full

STATIONNEMENT INTERDIT

no parking

switch on your lights

speeds are in kilometers per hour

AUTOROUTE

motorway

# Staying somewhere



## Hotel (booking)

You can book accommodation over the internet using the French Tourist Office website, **www.franceguide.com**.

| | |
|---|---|
| a single room | **une chambre pour une personne**<br>ewn shañbr poor ewn pehr-son |
| a double room | **une chambre pour deux personnes**<br>ewn shañbr poor duh pehr-son |
| with bath | **avec bain**<br>a-vek bañ |
| with shower | **avec douche**<br>a-vek doosh |
| with a double bed | **à un lit**<br>a uñ lee |
| twin-bedded | **à deux lits**<br>a duh lee |
| with an extra bed for a child | **avec un autre lit pour un enfant**<br>avek uñ nohtr lee poor uñ nahñ-fahñ |

**FACE TO FACE**

**A** **Je voudrais (réserver) une chambre pour une/deux personnes**
zhuh voo-dreh (ray-zehr-vay) ewn shahñbr poor ewn/duh pehr-son
I'd like (to book) a single/double room

**B** **C'est pour combien de nuits?**
say poor koñ-byañ duh nwee?
For how many nights?

**A** **Pour une nuit/... nuits**
poor ewn nwee/... nwee
For one night/... nights

**B** **Du... au...**
dew... oh...
From... till...

**A** **C'est pour combien de personnes?**
say poor koñ-byañ duh pehr-son?
For how many people?

**B** **Pour une personne/... personnes**
poor ewn pehr-son/... pehr-son
For one person/... people

Do you have a room for tonight? **Est-ce que vous avez une chambre pour ce soir?**
es kuh voo za-vay ewn shahñbr poor suh swar?

How much is it per night/ per week? **C'est combien par nuit/ par semaine?**
say koñ-byañ par nwee/par suh-men?

| | |
|---|---|
| I'll arrive at... | **J'arriverai à...**<br>zha-ree-vuh-ray a... |
| Do you have a list of hotels with prices? | **Vous avez une liste des hôtels avec leurs prix?**<br>Voo za-vay ewn leest day zoh-tel a-vek lur pree? |
| Could you recommend a good hotel? | **Pouvez-vous me conseiller un bon hôtel?**<br>poo-vay voo muh koñ-say-yay uñ boñ noh-tel? |
| not too expensive | **pas trop cher**<br>pa troh shehr |

| YOU MAY HEAR... | |
|---|---|
| **C'est complet**<br>say koñ-pleh | We're full |
| **Votre nom, s'il vous plaît?**<br>votr noñ, seel voo pleh? | Your name, please? |
| **Veuillez confirmer...**<br>vuh-yay koñ-feer-may... | Please confirm... |
| **par e-mail**<br>par ee-mehl | by e-mail |
| **par fax**<br>par fax | by fax |
| **Vous arriverez à quelle heure?**<br>voo za-reev-ray a kel ur? | What time will you arrive? |

# Hotel desk

You generally have to fill in a registration form (**fiche d'étranger**) and give your passport number on arrival.

| | |
|---|---|
| I booked a room | **J'ai réservé une chambre**<br>zhay ray-zehr-vay ewn shahñbr |
| My name is... | **Je m'appelle...**<br>zhuh ma-pel... |
| Have you anything else? | **Vous avez autre chose?**<br>voo za-vay ohtr shoz? |
| Where can I park the car? | **Où est-ce que je peux garer la voiture?**<br>oo es kuh zhuh puh ga-ray la vwa-tewr? |
| What time is...? | **À quelle heure est...?**<br>a kel ur eh...? |
| dinner | **le dîner**<br>luh dee-nay |
| breakfast | **le petit-déjeuner**<br>luh puh-tee day-zhuh-nay |
| The key, please | **La clé/clef, s'il vous plaît**<br>la klay, seel voo pleh |
| Room number... | **Chambre numéro...**<br>shahñbr new-may-ro... |
| I'm leaving tomorrow | **Je pars demain**<br>zhuh par duh-mañ |
| Please prepare the bill | **Pouvez-vous préparer la note?**<br>poo-vay voo pray-pa-ray la not? |

# Camping

| | |
|---|---|
| **ordures** or-dewr | rubbish |
| **eau potable** oh po-tabl | drinking water |
| **bloc sanitaire** blok sa-nee-tehr | washing facilities |

| | |
|---|---|
| Is there a restaurant on the campsite? | **Y a-t-il un restaurant dans le camping?** ee a-teel uñ re-sto-rahñ dahñ luh kahñ-peeng? |
| Do you have any vacancies? | **Vous avez des emplacements de libre?** Voo za-vay day zahñ-plas-mahñ duh leebr? |
| Does the price include...? | **Est-ce que le prix comprend...?** es kuh luh pree koñ-prahñ...? |
| hot water | **l'eau chaude** loh shohd |
| electricity | **l'électricité** lay-lek-tree-see-tay |
| We'd like to stay for ... nights | **Nous voudrions rester ... nuits** noo voo-dree-yoñ res-tay ... nwee |
| How much is it per night...? | **C'est combien la nuit...?** say koñ-byañ la nwee...? |
| for a tent | **pour une tente** poor ewn tahñt |
| for a caravan | **pour une caravane** poor ewn ka-ra-van |

# Self-catering

You can find a variety of self-catering accommodation on **www.gites-de-france.fr**, the website of the national Gîtes de France federation.

| | |
|---|---|
| Who do we contact if there are problems? | **Qui devons-nous contacter en cas de problème?**<br>kee duh-voñ noo koñ-tak-tay ahñ ka duh prob-lehm? |
| How does the heating work? | **Comment marche le chauffage?**<br>ko-mahñ marsh luh shoh-fazh? |
| Is there always hot water? | **Est-ce qu'il y a de l'eau chaude en permanence?**<br>es keel ya duh loh shohd ahñ pe-rma-nahñs? |
| Where is the nearest supermarket? | **Où est le supermarché le plus proche?**<br>oo ay luh sew-pehr-mar-shay luh plew prosh? |
| Where do we leave the rubbish? | **Où est-ce qu'il faut mettre les ordures?**<br>oo es keel foh metr lay zor-dewr? |



> **Sightseeing and tourist office** (p 69)

# Shopping

## Shopping phrases

French shop opening hours are approximately 9 am to 7 pm, but many shops close for lunch (between 12 and 2 pm) and most are closed on Sundays and Mondays.



**FACE TO FACE**

**A** **Qu'est-ce que vous désirez?**
kes kuh voo day-zee-ray?
What would you like?

**B** **Est-ce que vous avez...?**
es kuh voo za-vay...?
Do you have...?

**A** **Oui, bien sûr. Voilà. Et avec ceci?**
wee, byañ sewr. vwa-la. ay a-vek suh-see?
Yes, certainly. Here you are. Anything else?

| | |
|---|---|
| Where is...? | **Où est...?**<br>oo ay...? |
| I'm looking for a present for... | **Je cherche un cadeau pour...**<br>zhuh shehrsh uñ ka-doh poor... |
| my mother | **ma mère**<br>ma mehr |
| a child | **un enfant**<br>uñ nahñ-fahñ |
| Where can I buy...? | **Où est-ce qu'on peut acheter...?**<br>oo es koñ puh ash-tay...? |
| toys | **des jouets**<br>day zhoo-ay |
| gifts | **des cadeaux**<br>day ka-doh |
| Where is the ... department? | **Où se trouve le rayon...?**<br>oo suh troov luh ray-yoñ...? |
| perfume | **parfumerie**<br>par-few-mree |
| jewellery | **bijouterie**<br>bee-zhoo-tree |
| I'd like something similar to this | **Je voudrais quelque chose dans ce genre-là**<br>zhuh voo-dreh kel-kuh shohz dahñ suh zhahñr la |
| It's too expensive for me | **C'est trop cher pour moi**<br>say troh shehr poor mwa |
| Have you anything else? | **Vous n'avez rien d'autre?**<br>voo na-vay ryañ dohtr? |

# Shops

| | |
|---|---|
| **magasin** ma-ga-zañ | shop |
| **soldes** sold | sale |
| **un acheté, un gratuit** uñ nash-tay, uñ gra-twee | buy one, get one free |
| **le rayon alimentation** luh ray-oñ a-lee-mahñ-ta-syoñ | the food department |

| | | |
|---|---|---|
| baker's | **la boulangerie** | boo-lahñzh-ree |
| bookshop | **la librairie** | lee-breh-ree |
| butcher's | **la boucherie** | boo-shree |
| cake shop | **la pâtisserie** | pa-tee-sree |
| cheese shop | **la fromagerie** | fro-mazh-ree |
| clothes shop | **le magasin de vêtements** | ma-ga-zañ duh vetmahñ |
| dry-cleaner's | **le pressing** | pres-eeng |
| gift shop | **le magasin de cadeaux** | ma-ga-zañ duh ka-doh |
| greengrocer's | **le magasin de fruits et légumes** | ma-ga-zañ duh frwee zay lay-gewm |
| grocer's | **l'épicerie** | ay-pees-ree |
| hairdresser's | **chez le coiffeur/ la coiffeuse** | shay luh kwa-fur/ la kwa-fuz |
| hypermarket | **l'hypermarché** | ee-pehr-mar-shay |

| | | |
|---|---|---|
| jeweller's | **la bijouterie** | bee-zhoot-ree |
| market | **le marché** | mar-shay |
| pharmacy/ chemist's | **la pharmacie** | far-ma-see |
| self-service | **le libre-service** | leebr-sehr-vees |
| shoe shop | **le magasin de chaussures** | ma-ga-zañ duh shoh-sewr |
| supermarket | **le supermarché** | sew-pehr-mar-shay |
| tobacconist's | **le tabac** | ta-ba |

# Food (general)

| | | |
|---|---|---|
| bread | **le pain** | pañ |
| bread stick (large) | **le pain** | pañ |
| bread stick (small) | **la baguette** | ba-get |
| bread roll | **le petit pain** | puh-tee pañ |
| butter | **le beurre** | bur |
| cheese | **le fromage** | fro-mazh |
| chicken | **le poulet** | poo-leh |
| coffee (instant) | **le café (instantané)** | ka-fay (añ-stahñ-ta-nay) |
| cream | **la crème** | krem |
| crisps | **les chips** | sheeps |
| eggs | **les œufs** | uh |

| | | |
|---|---|---|
| fish | **le poisson** | pwa-soñ |
| flour | **la farine** | fa-reen |
| ham (cooked) | **le jambon cuit** | zhahñ-boñ kwee |
| ham (cured) | **le jambon cru** | zhahñ-boñ kru |
| honey | **le miel** | myel |
| jam | **la confiture** | koñ-fee-tewr |
| margarine | **la margarine** | mar-ga-reen |
| marmalade | **la confiture d'orange** | koñ-fee-tewr do-rahñzh |
| milk | **le lait** | leh |
| oil | **l'huile** | weel |
| orange juice | **le jus d'orange** | zhew do-rahñzh |
| pasta | **les pâtes** | pat |
| pepper | **le poivre** | pwavr |
| rice | **le riz** | ree |
| salt | **le sel** | sel |
| sugar | **le sucre** | sewkr |
| tea | **le thé** | tay |
| yoghurt | **le yaourt** | ya-oort |

> **Measurements and quantities** (p 113)

# Food (fruit and veg)



## Fruit

| | | |
|---|---|---|
| fruit | **les fruits** | frwee |
| apples | **les pommes** | pom |
| bananas | **les bananes** | ba-nan |
| cherries | **les cerises** | suh-reez |
| grapefruit | **le pamplemousse** | pahñ-pluh-moos |
| grapes | **le raisin** | reh-zañ |
| lemon | **le citron** | see-troñ |
| melon | **le melon** | muh-loñ |
| nectarines | **les nectarines** | nek-ta-reen |
| oranges | **les oranges** | o-rahññzh |
| peaches | **les pêches** | pesh |
| pears | **les poires** | pwahr |
| pineapple | **l'ananas** | a-na-nas |
| plums | **les prunes** | prewn |
| raspberries | **les framboises** | frahñ-bwaz |
| strawberries | **les fraises** | frez |

## Vegetables

| | | |
|---|---|---|
| vegetables | **les légumes** | lay-gewm |
| carrots | **les carottes** | ka-rot |
| cauliflower | **le chou-fleur** | shoo-flur |
| courgettes | **les courgettes** | koor-zhet |
| French beans | **les haricots verts** | a-ree-koh vehr |

| | | |
|---|---|---|
| garlic | **l'ail** | a-yuh |
| lettuce | **la laitue** | leh-tew |
| mushrooms | **les champignons** | shahñ-pee-nyoñ |
| onions | **les oignons** | o-nyoñ |
| peas | **les petits pois** | puh-tee pwa |
| peppers | **les poivrons** | pwa-vroñ |
| potatoes | **les pommes de terre** | pom duh tehr |
| spinach | **les épinards** | ay-pee-nar |
| tomatoes | **les tomates** | to-mat |

## Clothes

Size for clothes is **la taille** (ta-yuh); for shoes it is **la pointure** (pwañ-tewr).

**FACE TO FACE**

**A** **Est-ce que je peux l'essayer?**
es kuh zhuh puh leh-say-yay?
May I try this on?

**B** **Certainement, par ici, s'il vous plaît**
sehr-ten-mahñ, par ee-see seel voo pleh
Certainly, please come this way


> **Paying** (p 90) > **Numbers** (p 115)

**A** **L'avez-vous en plus grand/en plus petit?**
la-vay voo ahñ plew grahñ/ahñ plew puh-tee?
Do you have it in a bigger size/in a smaller size?

**B** **Désolé(e), je n'ai que cette taille dans ce colori**
day-zo-lay, zhuh nay kuh set ta-yuh dahñ suh ko-lo-ree
Sorry, we only have this size in this colour

| | |
|---|---|
| Do you have this in any other colours? | **Est-ce que vous l'avez dans d'autres coloris?**<br>es kuh voo la-vay dahñ dohtr ko-lo-ree? |
| That's a shame! | **C'est dommage!**<br>say do-mazh! |
| It's too... | **C'est trop...**<br>say troh... |
| short | **court**<br>koor |
| long | **long**<br>loñ |
| I'm just looking | **Je regarde seulement**<br>zhuh ruh-gard suhl-mahñ |
| I'll take it | **Je le prends**<br>zhuh luh prahñ |

| YOU MAY HEAR... | |
|---|---|
| **Quelle pointure faites-vous?** kel pwañ-tewr feht voo? | What shoe size do you take? |
| **Quelle est votre taille?** kel eh votr ta-yuh? | What size (clothes) are you? |

# Clothes (articles)

| | |
|---|---|
| **le coton** luh ko-toñ | cotton |
| **la soie** la swa | silk |
| **la dentelle** la dahñ-tel | lace |
| **la laine** la lehn | wool |

| | | |
|---|---|---|
| blouse | **le chemisier** | shuh-mee-zyay |
| bra | **le soutien-gorge** | soo-tyañ gorzh |
| coat | **le manteau** | mahñ-toh |
| dress | **la robe** | rob |
| gloves | **les gants** | gahñ |
| hat | **le chapeau** | sha-poh |
| jacket | **la veste** | vest |
| knickers | **le slip** | sleep |
| nightdress | **la chemise de nuit** | shuh-meez duh nwee |
| pyjamas | **le pyjama** | pee-zha-ma |

| | | |
|---|---|---|
| raincoat | **l'imperméable** | añ-pehr-may-abl |
| sandals | **les sandales** | sahñ-dal |
| scarf (silk) | **le foulard** | foo-lar |
| scarf (woollen) | **l'écharpe** | ay-sharp |
| shirt | **la chemise** | shuh-meez |
| shoes | **les chaussures** | shoh-sewr |
| shorts | **le short** | short |
| skirt | **la jupe** | zhewp |
| socks | **les chaussettes** | shoh-set |
| suit (woman's) | **le tailleur** | ta-yur |
| suit (man's) | **le costume** | kos-tewm |
| swimsuit | **le maillot de bain** | ma-yoh duh bañ |
| tights | **les collants** | ko-lahñ |
| t-shirt | **le t-shirt** | tee-shurt |
| tracksuit | **le survêtement** | sewr-vet-mahñ |
| trainers | **les baskets** | bas-ket |
| trousers | **le pantalon** | pahñ-ta-loñ |



# Maps and guides

Do you have...? **Avez-vous...?**
a-vay vooz...?

a map of the town **un plan de la ville**
uñ plahñ duh la veel

a map of the region **une carte de la région**
ewn kart duh la ray-zhyoñ

> **Paying** (p 90)

| | | |
|---|---|---|
| Can you show me where ... is on the map? | **Pouvez-vous me montrer où est ... sur la carte?** | poo-vay voo muh moñ-tray oo eh ... sewr la kart? |
| Do you have a detailed map of the area? | **Vous avez une carte détaillée de la région?** | voo za-vay ewn kart day-ta-yay duh la ray-zhyoñ? |
| Do you have a guide book/ leaflet in English? | **Vous avez un guide/une brochure en anglais?** | voo za-vay uñ geed/ewn bro-shewr ahñ nahñ-gleh? |
| Where can I/we buy an English newspaper? | **Où est-ce qu'on peut acheter des journaux anglais?** | oo es koñ puh ash-tay day zhoor-noh ahñ-gleh? |
| Do you have any English newspapers/any English novels? | **Vous avez des journaux anglais/des romans anglais?** | voo za-vay day zhoor-noh ahñ-gleh/ day ro-mahñ ahñ-gleh? |

# Post office

Smaller post offices generally shut for lunch (12 to 2 pm).

| | | |
|---|---|---|
| **la poste** | la post | post office |
| **timbres** | tañbr | stamps |



> **Sightseeing** (p 69)

| | |
|---|---|
| Is there a post office near here? | **Il y a un bureau de poste près d'ici?**<br>eel ya uñ bewr-oh duh post preh dee-see? |
| When is it open? | **Il ouvre quand?**<br>eel oovr kahñ? |
| Which counter is it...? | **C'est quel guichet...?**<br>say kel gee-shay...? |
| for stamps | **pour les timbres**<br>poor lay tañbr |
| for parcels | **pour les colis**<br>poor lay ko-lee |
| Three stamps for postcards to Great Britain | **Trois timbres pour cartes postales pour la Grande-Bretagne**<br>trwa tañbr poor kart pos-tal poor la grahñd bruh-ta-nyuh |
| How much is it to send this parcel? | **C'est combien pour envoyer ce colis?**<br>say koñ-byañ poor ahñ-vwa-yay suh ko-lee? |

**YOU MAY HEAR...**

| | |
|---|---|
| **Vous pouvez acheter des timbres au tabac**<br>voo poo-vay ash-tay day tañbr oh ta-ba | You can buy stamps at the tobacconist's |

> **Money** (p 89) > **Paying** (p 90)

# Photos

Tapes and memory cards for cameras, video cameras and camcorders can be bought in supermarkets and photo and hi-fi shops (**magasin hi-fi**).

| | |
|---|---|
| A video tape for this camcorder, please | **Une cassette vidéo pour ce caméscope, s'il vous plaît**<br>ewn ka-set vee-day-oh poor suh ka-may-skop, seel voo pleh |
| Do you have batteries for...? | **Avez-vous des piles pour...?**<br>a-vay voo day peel poor...? |
| this camera/ this camcorder | **cet appareil/ce caméscope**<br>set a-pa-ray/suh ka-may-skop |
| Do you have a memory card for...? | **Avez-vous une carte mémoire pour...?**<br>a-vay voo ewn kart may-mwar poor...? |
| this digital camera | **cet appareil numérique**<br>set a-pa-ray new-may-reek |

# Leisure

## Sightseeing and tourist office

The tourist office is sometimes called **le syndicat d'initiative**, but usually **l'office de/du tourisme**. If you are looking for somewhere to stay, a tourist office will have details of hotels, campsites, etc. Most museums are closed on Tuesdays.

| | |
|---|---|
| Where is the tourist office? | **Où est l'office de tourisme?**<br>oo eh lo-fees duh too-reesm? |
| What is there to visit in the area? | **Qu'est-ce qu'il y a à voir dans la région?**<br>kes keel ya a vwar dahñ la ray-zhyoñ? |
| in ... hours | **en ... heures**<br>ahñ ... ur |
| Do you have any leaflets? | **Avez-vous de la documentation?**<br>a-vay voo duh la do-kew-mahñ-ta-syoñ? |

| | |
|---|---|
| Are there any excursions? | **Est-ce qu'il y a des excursions?** es keel ya day zek-skewr-syoñ? |
| We'd like to go to... | **On voudrait aller à...** oñ voo-dreh a-lay a... |
| How much does it cost to get in? | **C'est combien l'entrée?** say koñ-byañ lahñ-tray? |
| Are there any reductions for...? | **Est-ce que vous faites des réductions pour...?** es kuh voo feht day ray-dewk-syoñ poor...? |
| children | **les enfants** lay zahñ-fahñ |
| students | **les étudiants** lay zay-tew-dyahñ |
| the unemployed | **les chômeurs** lay shoh-mur |
| senior citizens | **les retraités** lay ruh-treh-tay |





> **Maps and guides** (p 65)

# Entertainment

Check at the local tourist office for information about local events. You can also find listings on **www.franceguide.com**.

| | |
|---|---|
| What is there to do in the evenings? | **Qu'est-ce qu'on peut faire le soir?**<br>kes koñ puh fehr luh swar? |
| Do you have a list of events for this month? | **Vous avez une liste des festivités pour ce mois-ci?**<br>Voo za-vay ewn leest day fes-tee-vee-tay poor suh mwa-see? |
| Is there anything for children to do? | **Est-ce qu'il y a des choses à faire pour les enfants?**<br>es keel ya day shohz a fehr poor lay zahñ-fahñ? |



# Leisure/interests

| | |
|---|---|
| Where can I/we...? | **Où est-ce qu'on peut...?**<br>oo es koñ puh...? |
| go fishing | **pêcher**<br>peh-shay |

| | |
|---|---|
| go riding | **faire du cheval**<br>fehr dew shuh-val |
| Are there any good (sandy) beaches near here? | **Est-ce qu'il y a de bonnes plages (de sable) près d'ici?**<br>es keel ya duh bon plazh duh sabl preh dee-see? |
| Is there a swimming pool? | **Est-ce qu'il y a une piscine?**<br>es keel ya ewn pee-seen? |

## Music

| | |
|---|---|
| Are there any good concerts on? | **Il y a de bons concerts en ce moment?**<br>eel ya duh boñ koñ-sehr ahñ suh mo-mahñ? |
| Where can I get tickets for the concert? | **Où est-ce qu'on peut avoir des billets pour le concert?**<br>oo es koñ puh av-war day bee-yeh poor luh koñ-sehr? |
| Where can we hear some classical music/ some jazz? | **Où est-ce qu'on peut aller écouter de la musique classique/du jazz?**<br>oo es koñ puh a-lay ay-koo-tay duh la mew-zeek kla-seek/dew jaz? |





> **Making friends** (p 21)

# Cinema

| | |
|---|---|
| **sous-titré** soo-tee-tray | subtitled |
| **la séance** la sayahñs | performance |
| **VO (version originale)** vehr-syoñ o-ree-zhee-nal | in the original language (i.e. not dubbed) |

What's on at the cinema? **Qu'est-ce qui passe au cinéma?** kes kee pas oh see-nay-ma?

When does the film start/finish? **Le film commence/finit à quelle heure?** luh feelm ko-mahñs/fee-nee a kel ur?

How much are the tickets? **C'est combien les billets?** say koñ-byañ lay bee-yeh?

I'd like two seats at ... euros **Je voudrais deux places à ... euros** zhuh voo-dreh duh plas a ... uh-roh

# Theatre/opera

| | |
|---|---|
| **la pièce** la pyes | play |
| **la représentation** la ruh-pray-zahñ-ta-syoñ | performance |

| | |
|---|---|
| **à l'orchestre** a lor-kestr | in the stalls |
| **au balcon** oh bal-koñ | in the circle |
| **le fauteuil** luh foh-tuh-yuh | seat |
| **le vestiaire** luh ves-tyehr | cloakroom |
| **l'entracte** lahñ-trakt | interval |

| | |
|---|---|
| What is on at the theatre/at the opera? | **Qu'est-ce qu'on joue au théâtre/à l'opéra?** kes koñ zhoo oh tay-atr/ a lo-pay-ra? |
| What prices are the tickets? | **Les billets sont à combien?** lay bee-yeh soñ ta koñ-byañ? |
| I'd like two tickets... | **Je voudrais deux billets...** zhuh voo-dreh duh bee-yeh... |
| for tonight | **pour ce soir** poor suh swar |
| for tomorrow night | **pour demain soir** poor duh-mañ swar |
| for 5th August | **pour le cinq août** poor luh sañk oo(t) |
| When does the performance begin/end? | **Quand est-ce que la représentation commence/finit?** kahñ tes kuh la ruh-pray-zahñ-ta-syoñ ko-mahñs/fee-nee? |

# Television

| | |
|---|---|
| **la télécommande**<br>tay-lay-ko-mahñd | remote control |
| **le feuilleton**<br>luh fuh-yuh-toñ | soap |
| **les informations**<br>lay zañ-for-ma-syoñ | news |
| **mettre en marche**<br>metr ahñ marsh | to switch on |
| **éteindre** ay-tañdr | to switch off |
| **les dessins animés**<br>lay deh-sañ a-nee-may | cartoons |

| | |
|---|---|
| Where is the television? | **Où est la télévision?**<br>oo ay la tay-lay-vee-zyoñ? |
| How do you switch it on? | **Comment la met-on en marche?**<br>ko-mahñ la meh toñ ahñ marsh? |
| What is on television? | **Qu'est-ce qu'il y a à la télé?**<br>kes keel ya a la tay-lay? |
| When is the news? | **Les informations sont à quelle heure?**<br>lay zañ-for-ma-syoñ soñ ta kel ur? |
| Do you have any English-language channels? | **Est-ce qu'il y a des chaînes en anglais?**<br>es keel ya day shen ahñ nahñ-gleh? |

| | |
|---|---|
| Do you have any English videos? | **Avez-vous des vidéos en anglais?** a-vay voo day vee-day-o ahñ nahñ-gleh? |

## Sport

| | |
|---|---|
| Where can I/we...? | **Où est-ce qu'on peut...?** oo es koñ puh...? |
| play tennis | **jouer au tennis** zhoo-ay oh teh-nees |
| play golf | **jouer au golf** zhoo-ay oh golf |
| go swimming | **faire de la natation** fehr duh la na-ta-syoñ |
| go jogging | **faire du jogging** fehr dew jo-geeng |
| How much is it per hour? | **C'est combien l'heure?** say koñ-byañ lur? |
| Do you have to be a member? | **Est-ce qu'il faut être membre?** es keel foh (t)etr mahñbr? |
| Can we hire...? | **Est-ce qu'on peut louer...?** es koñ puh loo-ay...? |
| rackets | **des raquettes** day ra-ket |

| | |
|---|---|
| golf clubs | **des clubs de golf**<br>day club duh golf |
| We'd like to go to see (name of team) play | **Nous voudrions aller voir jouer l'équipe de...**<br>noo voo-dryoñ a-lay vwar zhoo-ay lay-keep duh... |
| Where can I/we get tickets? | **Où est-ce qu'on peut avoir des billets?**<br>oo es koñ puh a-vwar day bee-yeh? |
| What sports do you play? | **Qu'est-ce que vous faites comme sports?**<br>kes kuh voo fet kom spor? |

**YOU MAY HEAR...**

| | |
|---|---|
| **Il n'y a plus de billets pour le match**<br>eel nya plew duh bee-yeh poor luh match | There are no tickets left for the game |

# Skiing

| | |
|---|---|
| **débutant** day-bew-tahñ | beginner (male) |
| **débutante** day-bew-tahñt | beginner (female) |
| **intermédiaire** añ-tehr-may-dyehr | intermediate |
| **avancé(e)** a-vahñ-say | advanced |
| **le ski de fond** luh skee duh foñ | cross-country skiing |
| **le ski de piste** luh skee duh peest | downhill skiing |

I would like to hire skis — **Je voudrais louer des skis** zhuh voo-dreh loo-ay day skee

Are poles included in the price? — **Est-ce que les bâtons sont compris dans le prix?** es kuh lay ba-toñ soñ koñ-pree dahñ luh pree?

Can you adjust my bindings, please? — **Pourriez-vous régler mes fixations, s'il vous plaît?** poo-ree-ay voo ray-glay may feek-sa-syoñ, seel voo pleh?

How much is a pass for...? — **C'est combien le forfait pour...?** say koñ-byañ luh for-feh poor...?

a day — **une journée** ewn zhoor-nay

| | |
|---|---|
| a week | **une semaine**<br>ewn suh-men |
| When does the last chair-lift go up? | **À quelle heure part la dernière benne?**<br>a kel ur par la dehr-nyehr ben? |

**YOU MAY HEAR...**

| | |
|---|---|
| **Vous avez déjà fait du ski?**<br>voo za-vay day-zha feh dew skee? | Have you ever skied before? |
| **Quelle pointure faites-vous?**<br>kel pwañ-tewr fet voo? | What is your shoe size? |
| **Quelle longueur de skis voulez-vous?**<br>kel loñ gur duh skee voo-lay voo? | What length skis do you want? |

# Walking

| | |
|---|---|
| Are there any guided walks? | **Y a-t-il des promenades guidées?**<br>ee ya-teel day prom-nad gee-day? |
| Do you have a guide to local walks? | **Avez-vous un guide des promenades dans la région?**<br>a-vay vooz uñ geed day prom-nad dahñ la ray-zhyoñ? |
| Do you know any good walks? | **Vous connaissez de bonnes promenades?**<br>voo ko-neh-say duh bon prom-nad? |
| How many kilometres is the walk? | **La promenade fait combien de kilomètres?**<br>la prom-nad feh koñ-byañ duh kee-lo-metr? |
| How long will it take? | **Ça prendra combien de temps?**<br>sa prahñ-dra koñ-byañ duh tahñ? |
| Is it very steep? | **Est-ce que ça monte dur?**<br>es kuh sa moñt dewr? |
| We'd like to go climbing | **Nous aimerions faire de l'escalade**<br>noo zeh-muh-ryoñ fehr duh les-ka-lad |





> **Maps and guides** (p 65)

# Communications

## Telephone and mobile

The international code for France is **00 33** plus the French number you require, without the first **0** of the area code. Other international codes are: Belgium – **00 32**, Luxembourg – **00 352**, Switzerland – **00 41**. To phone the UK from France, dial **00 44** plus the UK area code without the first **0**. Always dial the area code before the number in France, even for local calls.

| | |
|---|---|
| I'd like to make a phone call | **Je voudrais téléphoner**<br>zhuh voo-dreh tay-lay-fo-nay |
| Is there a pay phone? | **Il y a un téléphone public?**<br>eel ya uñ tay-lay-fon pew-bleek? |
| A phonecard, please | **Une télécarte, s'il vous plaît**<br>ewn tay-lay-kart, seel voo pleh |
| for ... euros | **de ... euros**<br>duh ... uh-roh |
| Do you have a mobile? | **Vous avez un portable?**<br>voo za-vay uñ por-tabl? |

| | |
|---|---|
| What's your mobile number? | **Quel est le numéro de votre portable?**<br>kel eh luh new-may-ro duh votr por-tabl? |
| Can I use your mobile? | **Je peux emprunter votre portable?**<br>zhuh puh ahñ-pruñ-tay votr por-tabl? |
| My mobile number is... | **Le numéro de mon portable est...**<br>luh new-may-ro duh moñ por-tabl ay luh... |
| Monsieur Brun, please | **Monsieur Brun, s'il vous plaît**<br>muh-syuh bruñ, seel voo pleh |
| Extension... | **le poste...**<br>luh post... |

**FACE TO FACE**

**A** **Âllo?**
alo?
Hello

**B** **Bonjour. Je voudrais parler à..., s'il vous plaît**
boñ-zhoor, zhuh voo-dreh par-lay a..., seel voo pleh
Hello, I'd like to speak to..., please

**A** **C'est de la part de qui?**
say duh la par duh kee?
Who's calling?

**B** **De la part de...**
duh la par duh...
This is...

**A** **Un instant, s'il vous plaît...**
uñ nañ-stahñ seel voo pleh...
Just a moment...

| | |
|---|---|
| Can I speak to...? | **Pourrais-je parler à...?**<br>poo-rezh par-lay a ...? |
| It's (your name) | **... à l'appareil**<br>... a la-pa-ray |
| How do I get an outside line? | **Comment on fait pour avoir une ligne extérieure?**<br>ko-mahñ oñ feh poor a-vwar ewn leen-yuh ek-stay-ree-ur? |
| I'll call back... | **Je vous rappellerai...**<br>zhuh voo ra-pel-ray... |
| later | **plus tard**<br>plew tar |
| tomorrow | **demain**<br>duh-mañ |

| YOU MAY HEAR... | |
|---|---|
| **Je vous le/la passe**<br>zhuh voo luh/la pas | I'm putting you through |
| **C'est occupé**<br>say to-kew-pay | It's engaged |
| **Pouvez-vous rappeler plus tard?**<br>poo-vay voo ra-play plew tar? | Please try later? |
| **Voulez-vous laisser un message?**<br>voo-lay voo leh-say uñ meh-sazh? | Do you want to leave a message? |
| **Veuillez laisser votre message après le bip sonore**<br>vuh-yay lay-say votr meh-sazh a-preh luh beep so-nor | Please leave a message after the tone |
| **S'il vous plaît, éteignez votre portable**<br>seel voo pleh, ay-ten-yay votr por-tabl | Please turn your mobile off |

# Text messaging

| | |
|---|---|
| I will text you | **Je t'enverrai un message**<br>zhuh tahñ-veh-ray uñ meh-sazh |
| Can you text me? | **Tu peux m'envoyer un message?**<br>tew puh mahñ-vwa-yay uñ meh-sazh? |

# E-mail

An informal way of starting an e-mail is **Salut...** (Hi...) and ending it **À bientôt** (Speak to you soon). In more formal e-mails to people you know well, begin either **Cher...** (for a man) or **Chère...** (for a woman) and end with **Amicalement**. In formal and business e-mails, begin **Bonjour...** and end **Cordialement**.

| | |
|---|---|
| New message: | **Nouveau message:** |
| To: | **A:** |
| From: | **De:** |
| Subject: | **Objet:** |
| CC: | **CC:** |
| Attachment: | **Pièce jointe:** |
| Send: | **Envoyer:** |

| | |
|---|---|
| Do you have an e-mail address? | **Vous avez une adresse e-mail?**<br>voo za-vay ewn a-dres ee-mehl? |
| What's your e-mail address? | **Quelle est votre adresse e-mail?**<br>kel ay votr a-dres ee-mehl? |
| How do you spell it? | **Comment ça s'écrit?**<br>ko-mahñ sa say-kree? |
| All one word | **En un seul mot**<br>ahñ uñ suhl moh |
| All lower case | **Tout en minuscules**<br>too tahñ mee-new-skewl |
| My e-mail address is... | **Mon adresse e-mail est...**<br>moñ nad-res ee-mehl ay... |
| caroline.smith@ (company name) .co.uk | **caroline point smith arobase ... point CO point UK**<br>ka-roh-leen pwañ smeet a-roh-baz ... pwañ say oh pwañ ew ka |
| Can I send an e-mail? | **Je peux envoyer un e-mail?**<br>zhuh puh ahñ-vwa-yay uñ nee-mehl? |
| Did you get my e-mail? | **Est-ce que vous avez reçu mon e-mail?**<br>es-kuh voo za-vay ruh-sew moñ nee-mehl? |

# Internet

| | |
|---|---|
| **accueil** a-kuh-yuh | home |
| **nom d'utilisateur** noñ dew-tee-lee-za-tur | username |
| **moteur de recherche** mo-tur duh ruh-shehrsh | search engine |
| **mot de passe** moh duh pas | password |
| **contactez-nous** koñ-tak-tay-noo | contact us |
| **retour vers le sommaire** ruh-toor vehr luh som-mehr | back to menu |

Are there any internet cafés here? — **Est-ce qu'il y a des cyber-cafés par ici?**
es keel ya day see-behr-ka-fay par ee-see?

How much is it to log on for an hour? — **Combien coûte une heure de connection?**
koñ-byañ koot ewn ur duh ko-nek-syoñ?

I can't log on — **Je n'arrive pas à me connecter**
zhuh na-reev pa a muh ko-nek-tay

# Fax

## Addressing a fax

| | |
|---|---|
| **À/De** | To/From |
| **Objet :** | Re: |
| **Nombre de pages** | Number of pages |
| **Veuillez trouver ci-joint...** | Please find attached... |

| | |
|---|---|
| Do you have a fax? | **Avez-vous un fax?**<br>a-vay voo uñ fax? |
| I want to send a fax | **Je voudrais envoyer un fax**<br>zhuh voo-dreh ahñ-vwa-yay uñ fax |
| What is your fax number? | **Quel est votre numéro de fax?**<br>kel ay votr new-may-roh duh fax? |
| My fax number is... | **Mon numéro de fax est le...**<br>moñ new-may-roh duh fax ay luh... |

# Practicalities

## Money

Banks are generally open from 9 am to 4.30 pm Monday to Friday, but as closing times vary you are best advised to go in the morning.

| | |
|---|---|
| **distributeur**<br>dees-tree-bew-tur | cash dispenser |
| **retrait espèces**<br>ruh-treh es-pes | cash withdrawal |

Where can I change some money? — **Où est-ce que je peux changer de l'argent?**
oo es kuh zhuh puh shahñ-zhay duh lar-zhahñ?

I want to change these traveller's cheques — **Je voudrais changer ces chèques de voyage**
zhuh voo-dreh shahñ-zhay say shek duh vwa-yazh

When does the bank open? — **La banque ouvre quand?**
la bahñk oovr kahñ?

| | |
|---|---|
| When does the bank close? | **La banque ferme quand?**<br>la bahñk fehrm kahñ? |
| Can I pay with pounds/euros? | **Je peux payer en livres sterling/en euros?**<br>zhuh puh pay-yay ahñ leevr stehr-leeng/ahñ nuh-roh? |
| Can I use my credit card with this cash dispenser? | **Je peux utiliser ma carte (de crédit) dans ce distributeur?**<br>zhuh puh ew-tee-lee-zay ma kart (duh kray-dee) dahñ suh dee-stree-bew-tur? |
| Do you have any change? | **Vous avez de la monnaie?**<br>voo za-vay duh la mo-neh? |

# Paying

| | |
|---|---|
| **l'addition** la-dee-syoñ | bill (restaurant) |
| **la note** la not | bill (hotel) |
| **la facture** la fak-tewr | invoice |
| **la caisse** la kes | cash desk |

| | |
|---|---|
| How much is it? | **C'est combien?/Ça fait combien?**<br>say koñ-byañ/sa feh koñ-byañ? |
| How much will it be? | **Ça fera combien?**<br>sa fuh-ra koñ-byañ? |

| | |
|---|---|
| Can I pay...? | **Je peux payer...?**<br>zhuh puh pay-yay...? |
| by credit card | **par carte de crédit**<br>par kart duh kray-dee |
| by cheque | **par chèque**<br>par shek |
| Put it on my bill (hotel) | **Mettez-le sur ma note**<br>meh-tay luh sewr ma not |
| The bill, please (restaurant) | **L'addition, s'il vous plaît**<br>la-dee-syoñ seel voo pleh |
| Where do I pay? | **Où doit-on payer?**<br>oo dwa-toñ pay-yay? |
| Do you take credit cards? | **Vous acceptez les cartes de crédit?**<br>voo zak-sep-tay lay kart duh? kray-dee? |
| Is service included? | **Le service est compris?**<br>luh sehr-vees ay koñ-pree? |
| Could you give me a receipt, please? | **Pourriez-vous me donner un reçu, s'il vous plaît?**<br>poo-ree-ay voo muh do-nay uñ ruh-sew, seel voo pleh? |
| Do I pay in advance? | **Est-ce qu'il faut payer à l'avance?**<br>es keel foh pay-yay a la-vahñs? |
| I'm sorry | **Je suis désolé(e)**<br>zhuh swee day-zo-lay |
| I've nothing smaller (no change) | **Je n'ai pas de monnaie**<br>zhuh nay pa duh mo-neh |

# Luggage

| | |
|---|---|
| **le retrait de bagages**<br>luh ruh-treh duh ba-gazh | baggage reclaim |
| **la consigne**<br>la koñ-see-nyuh | left luggage |
| **le chariot à bagages**<br>luh sha-ryoh a ba-gazh | luggage trolley |

My luggage hasn't arrived yet — **Mes bagages ne sont pas encore arrivés**
may ba-gazh nuh soñ pa ahñ-kor a-ree-vay

My suitcase has been damaged on the flight — **Ma valise a été abîmée pendant le vol**
ma va-leez a ay-tay a-bee-may pahñ-dahñ luh vol

Practicalities


> **Train** (p 32) > **Air travel** (p 38)

# Repairs

| | |
|---|---|
| **le cordonnier**<br>luh kor-don-yay | shoe repairer |
| **réparations minute**<br>ray-pa-ra-syoñ mee-newt | repairs while you wait |

This is broken — **C'est cassé**
say ka-say

Where can I get this repaired? — **Où est-ce que je peux le faire réparer?**
oo es kuh zhuh puh luh fehr ray-pa-ray?

Can you repair...? — **Pouvez-vous réparer...?**
poo-vay voo ray-pa-ray...?

these shoes — **ces chaussures**
say shoh-sewr

my watch — **ma montre**
ma moñtr



> **Breakdown** (p 45)

# Laundry

| | |
|---|---|
| **le pressing**<br>luh preh-seeng | dry-cleaner's |
| **la laverie automatique**<br>la lav-ree oh-to-ma-teek | launderette |
| **la lessive en poudre**<br>la leh-seev ahñ poodr | washing powder |

| | |
|---|---|
| Where can I do some washing? | **Où est-ce que je peux faire un peu de lessive?**<br>oo es kuh zhuh puh fehr uñ puh duh leh-seev? |
| Is there ... near here? | **Il y a ... près d'ici?**<br>eel ya ... preh dee-see? |
| a launderette | **une laverie automatique**<br>ewn lav-ree oh-toh-ma-teek |
| a dry-cleaner's | **un pressing**<br>uñ preh-seeng |

# Complaints

| | |
|---|---|
| This doesn't work | **Ça ne marche pas**<br>sa nuh marsh pa |
| It's dirty | **C'est sale**<br>say sal |
| The ... doesn't work | **Le/La ... ne marche pas**<br>luh/la ... nuh marsh pa |
| The ... don't work | **Les ... ne marchent pas**<br>lay ... nuh marsh pa |
| light | **la lumière**<br>la lew-myehr |
| lock | **la serrure**<br>la seh-rewr |
| heating | **le chauffage**<br>luh shoh-fazh |
| air conditioning | **la climatisation**<br>la klee-ma-tee-za-syoñ |
| It's broken | **C'est cassé**<br>say ka-say |
| I want a refund | **Je veux être remboursé(e)**<br>zhuh vuh etr rahñ-boor-say |



> **Hotel desk** (p 53)

# Problems

| | |
|---|---|
| Can you help me? | **Pouvez-vous m'aider?**<br>poo-vay voo meh-day? |
| I speak very little French | **Je parle très peu le français**<br>zhuh parl treh puh luh frahñ-seh |
| Does anyone here speak English? | **Est-ce qu'il y a quelqu'un qui parle anglais ici?**<br>es keel ya kel-kuñ kee parl ahñ-gleh ee-see? |
| I would like to speak to whoever is in charge | **Je voudrais parler au responsable**<br>zhuh voo-dreh par-lay oh reh-spoñ-sabl |
| I'm lost | **Je me suis perdu(e)**<br>zhuh muh swee pehr-dew |
| How do I get to...? | **pour aller à/au...?**<br>poor a-lay a/oh...? |
| I missed... | **J'ai raté...**<br>zhay ra-tay... |
| my train | **mon train**<br>moñ trañ |
| my plane | **mon avion**<br>moñ na-vyoñ |
| my connection | **ma correspondance**<br>ma ko-res-poñ-dahñs |

Practicalities

| | |
|---|---|
| I've missed my flight because there was a strike | **J'ai raté mon avion à cause d'une grève**<br>zhay ra-tay moñ na-vyoñ a kohz dewn grev |
| The coach has left without me | **Le car est parti sans moi**<br>luh kar ay par-tee sahñ mwa |
| Can you show me how this works? | **Pouvez-vous me montrer comment ça marche?**<br>poo-vay voo muh moñ-tray ko-mahñ sa marsh? |
| I have lost my purse | **J'ai perdu mon porte-monnaie**<br>zhay pehr-dew moñ port-mo-neh |
| I need to get to... | **Je dois aller à/au (etc.)...**<br>zhuh dwa a-lay a/oh... |
| Leave me alone! | **Laissez-moi tranquil(le)!**<br>leh-say mwa trahñ-keel! |
| Go away! | **Allez-vous en!**<br>a-lay voo zahñ! |

# Emergencies

| | |
|---|---|
| **police** po-lees | police |
| **ambulance** ahñ-bew-lahñs | ambulance |
| **pompiers** poñ-pyay | fire brigade |
| **commissariat** ko-mee-sar-ya | police station (in large towns) |
| **gendarmerie** zhahñ-darm-ree | police station (in villages and small towns) |
| **urgences** ewr-zhahñs | accident and emergency department |

| | |
|---|---|
| Help! | **Au secours!**<br>oh skoor! |
| Fire! | **Au feu!**<br>oh fuh! |
| Can you help me? | **Pouvez-vous m'aider?**<br>poo-vay voo meh-day? |
| There has been an accident | **Il y a eu un accident**<br>eel ya ew uñ nak-see-dahñ |
| Someone has been injured | **Il y a un blessé**<br>eel ya uñ bleh-say |
| He/she has been knocked down by a car | **Il/elle a été renversé(e) par une voiture**<br>eel/el a ay-tay rahñ-vehr-say par ewn vwa-tewr |
| Please call... | **S'il vous plaît, appelez...**<br>seel voo pleh, a-puh-lay... |

| | |
|---|---|
| the police | **la police**<br>la po-lees |
| an ambulance | **une ambulance**<br>ewn ahñ-bew-lahñs |
| Where is the police station? | **Où est le commissariat?**<br>oo eh luh ko-mee-sar-ya? |
| I want to report a theft | **Je veux signaler un vol**<br>zhuh vuh seen-ya-lay uñ vol |
| I've been robbed/ attacked | **On m'a volé/attaqué(e)**<br>oñ ma vo-lay/a-ta-kay |
| I've been raped | **On m'a violée**<br>oñ ma vee-o-lay |
| I want to speak to a policewoman | **Je veux parler à une femme agent de police**<br>zhuh vuh par-lay a ewn fam a-zhahñ duh po-lees |
| Someone has stolen... | **On m'a volé...**<br>oñ ma vo-lay... |
| my handbag | **mon sac à main**<br>moñ sak a mañ |
| my money | **mon argent**<br>moñ nar-zhahñ |
| My car has been broken into | **On a forcé ma voiture**<br>oñ na for-say ma vwa-tewr |
| My car has been stolen | **On m'a volé ma voiture**<br>oñ ma vo-lay ma vwa-tewr |
| I need to make a telephone call | **Il faut que je passe un coup de téléphone**<br>eel foh kuh zhuh pas uñ koo duh tay-lay-fon |

| | |
|---|---|
| I need a report for my insurance | **Il me faut un constat pour mon assurance**<br>eel muh foh uñ kon-sta poor moñ na-sew-rahñs |
| I didn't know the speed limit | **Je ne savais pas quelle était la limite de vitesse**<br>zhuh nuh sa-veh pa kel ay-teh la lee-meet duh vee-tes |
| How much is the fine? | **C'est une amende de combien?**<br>say tewn a-mahñd duh koñ-byañ? |
| Where do I pay it? | **Où dois-je la payer?**<br>oo dwa-zhuh la pay-yay? |
| Do I have to pay it straight away? | **Est-ce qu'il faut la payer immédiatement?**<br>es keel foh la pay-yay ee-may-dyat-mahñ? |
| I'm very sorry, officer | **Je suis vraiment désolé(e), monsieur l'agent**<br>zhuh swee vray-mahñ day-zo-lay, muh-syuh la-zhahñ |

**YOU MAY HEAR...**

| | |
|---|---|
| **Vous avez brûlé un feu rouge**<br>voo za-vay brew-lay uñ fuh roozh | You went through a red light |
| **Vous n'avez pas cédé la priorité**<br>voo na-vay pa say-day la pree-o-ree-tay | You didn't give way |

# Health

## Pharmacy

| | |
|---|---|
| **la pharmacie**<br>la far-ma-see | pharmacy/chemist's |
| **la pharmacie de garde**<br>la far-ma-see duh gard | duty chemist's |

Can you give me something for...? — **Avez-vous quelque chose pour le/la (etc.)...?** a-vay voo kel-kuh shohz poor luh/la...?

a headache — **le mal de tête** luh mal duh tet

car sickness — **le mal des transports** luh mal day trahñ-spor

flu — **la grippe** la greep

diarrhoea — **la diarrhée** la dya-ray

sunburn — **les coups de soleil** lay koo duh so-leh-yuh

| | |
|---|---|
| Is it safe for children? | **C'est sans danger pour les enfants?**<br>say sahñ dahñ-zhay poor lay zahñ-fahñ? |
| How much should I give him/her? | **Combien je dois lui en donner?**<br>koñ-byañ zhuh dwa lwee ahñ do-nay? |

| YOU MAY HEAR... | |
|---|---|
| **Prenez-en trois fois par jour avant/pendant/ après le repas**<br>pruh-nay zahñ trwa fwa par zhoor avahñ/pahñ-dahñ/ a-preh luh ruh-pa | Take it three times a day before/with/ after meals |

# Doctor

In French the possessive (my, his, her, etc.) is generally not used with parts of the body, e.g.

| | |
|---|---|
| I've broken my leg | **Je me suis cassé(e) la jambe** |
| He has hurt his ankle | **Il s'est fait mal à la cheville** |

Health

| | |
|---|---|
| **hôpital** o-pee-tal | hospital |
| **urgences** ewr-zhahñs | accident and emergency department |
| **consultations** koñ-sewl-ta-syoñ | surgery hours |

**FACE TO FACE**

**A** **Je me sens mal**
zhuh muh sahñ mal
I feel ill

**B** **Vous avez de la fièvre?**
voo za-vay duh la fyehvr?
Do you have a temperature?

**A** **Non, J'ai mal ici**
noñ, zhay mal ee-see
No, I have a pain here

| | |
|---|---|
| I need a doctor | **J'ai besoin d'un médecin** zhay buh-zwañ duñ may-dsañ |
| My son/My daughter is ill | **Mon fils/Ma fille est malade** moñ fees/ma fee ay ma-lad |
| I'm diabetic | **Je suis diabétique** zhuh swee dya-bay-teek |
| I'm pregnant | **Je suis enceinte** zhuh swee ahñ-sañt |

| | |
|---|---|
| I'm on the pill | **Je prends la pilule**<br>zhuh prahñ la pee-lewl |
| I'm allergic to penicillin | **Je suis allergique à la pénicilline**<br>zhuh swee za-lehr-zheek a la pay-nee-see-leen |
| Will she/he have to go to hospital? | **Faut-il la/le transporter à l'hôpital?**<br>foh-teel la/luh trahñ-spor-tay a lo-pee-tal? |
| Will I have to pay? | **Est-ce que je dois payer?**<br>es kuh zhuh dwa pay-yay? |
| How much will it cost? | **Combien ça va coûter?**<br>koñ-byañ sa va koo-tay? |
| I need a receipt for the insurance | **Il me faut un reçu pour l'assurance**<br>eel muh foh uñ ruh-sew poor la-sew-rahñs |

| YOU MAY HEAR... | |
|---|---|
| **Il faut que vous alliez à l'hôpital**<br>eel foh kuh voo zal-yay a lo-pee-tal | You will have to go to hospital |
| **Ce n'est pas très grave**<br>suh nay pa treh grav | It's not serious |

Health



> **Emergencies** (p 98)

# Dentist

| | |
|---|---|
| I need to see a dentist | **J'ai besoin de voir un dentiste**<br>zhay buh-zwañ duh vwar uñ dahñ-teest |
| He/She has toothache | **Il/Elle a mal aux dents**<br>eel/el a mal oh dahñ |
| Can you do a temporary filling? | **Pouvez-vous me faire un plombage momentané?**<br>poo-vay voo muh fehr uñ ploñ-bazh mo-mahñ-ta-nay? |
| Can you give me something for the pain? | **Pouvez-vous me donner quelque chose contre la douleur?**<br>poo-vay voo muh do-nay kel-kuh shohz koñtr la doo-lur? |
| It hurts | **Ça me fait mal**<br>sa muh feh mal |
| Can you repair my dentures? | **Pouvez-vous me réparer mon dentier?**<br>poo-vay voo muh ray-pa-ray moñ dahñt-yay? |
| Do I have to pay? | **Je dois payer?**<br>zhuh dwa pay-yay? |
| How much will it be? | **Combien ça va coûter?**<br>koñ-byañ sa va koo-tay? |

I need a receipt for my insurance **Il me faut un reçu pour mon assurance**
eel muh foh uñ ruh-sew poor moñ na-sew-rahñs

| YOU MAY HEAR... | |
|---|---|
| **Il faut l'arracher** eel foh la-ra-shay | It has to come out |
| **Il faut faire un plombage** eel foh fehr uñ ploñ-bazh | You need a filling |

# Different types of travellers

## Disabled travellers

| | |
|---|---|
| What facilities do you have for disabled people? | **Qu'est-ce que vous avez comme aménagements pour les handicapés?**<br>kes kuh voo za-vay kom a-may-nazh-mahñ poor lay zahñ-dee-ka-pay? |
| Are there any toilets for the disabled? | **Est-ce qu'il y a des toilettes pour handicapés?**<br>es keel ya day twa-let poor ahñ-dee-ka-pay? |
| Do you have any bedrooms on the ground floor? | **Avez-vous des chambres au rez-de-chaussée?**<br>a-vay voo day shahñbr oh ray duh shoh-say? |
| Is there a lift? | **Est-ce qu'il y a un ascenseur?**<br>es keel ya uñ na-sahñ-sur? |
| Where is the lift? | **Où est l'ascenseur?**<br>oo eh la-sahñ-sur? |

| | |
|---|---|
| Do you have wheelchairs? | **Est-ce qu'il y a des fauteuils roulants?**<br>es keel ya day foh-tuh-yuh roo-lahñ? |
| Can you visit ... in a wheelchair? | **On peut visiter ... en fauteuil roulant?**<br>oñ puh vee-zee-tay ... ahñ foh-tuh-yuh roo-lahñ? |
| Do you have an induction loop? | **Est-ce que vous avez une boucle pour mal-entendants?**<br>es kuh voo za-vay ewñ bookl poor mal-ahñ-tahñ-dahñ? |
| Is there a reduction for disabled people? | **Est-ce qu'il y a une réduction pour les handicapés?**<br>es keel ya ewn ray-dewk-syoñ poor lay zahñ-dee-ka-pay? |
| Is there somewhere I can sit down? | **Est-ce qu'il y a un endroit où on peut s'asseoir?**<br>es keel ya uñ nahñ-drwa oo oñ puh sa-swar? |





> **Hotel** (p 50)

# With kids

Public transport is free for children under four. Children between four and twelve pay half price.

| | |
|---|---|
| A child's ticket | **Un billet tarif enfant**<br>un bee-yeh ta-reef ahñ-fahñ |
| He/She is ... years old | **Il/Elle a ... ans**<br>eel/el a ... ahñ |
| Is there a reduction for children? | **Est-ce qu'il y a une réduction pour les enfants?**<br>es keel ya ewn ray-dewk-syoñ poor lay zahñ-fahñ? |
| Do you have a children's menu? | **Est-ce que vous avez un menu enfant?**<br>es kuh voo za-vay uñ muh-new poor ahñ-fahñ? |
| Is it OK to take children? | **On peut y aller avec des enfants?**<br>on puh ee a-lay a-vek day zahñ-fahñ? |
| Do you have...? | **Avez-vous...?**<br>a-vay voo...? |
| a high chair | **une chaise de bébé**<br>ewn shez duh bay-bay |
| a cot | **un lit d'enfant**<br>uñ lee dahñ-fahñ |

| | |
|---|---|
| I have two children | **J'ai deux enfants**<br>zhay duh zahñ-fahñ |
| He/She is 10 years old | **Il/Elle a dix ans**<br>eel/el a dee zahñ |
| Do you have any children? | **Est-ce que vous avez des enfants?**<br>es kuh voo za-vay day zahñ-fahñ? |





> **Pharmacy** (p 101) > **Doctor** (p 102)

# Reference

## Alphabet

The French alphabet is the same as the English alphabet. Below are the words used for clarification when spelling something out.

| | |
|---|---|
| **Comment ça s'écrit?**<br>ko-mahñ sa say-kree? | How do you spell it? |
| **A comme Anatole,<br>B comme Berthe**<br>a kom a-na-tol,<br>bay kom behrt | A for Anatole,<br>B for Berthe |

| | | | |
|---|---|---|---|
| **A** | a | **Anatole** | a-na-tol |
| **B** | bay | **Berthe** | behrt |
| **C** | say | **Célestin** | say-les-tañ |
| **D** | day | **Désiré** | day-zee-ray |
| **E** | uh | **Eugène** | uh-zhen |
| **F** | ef | **François** | frahñ-swa |
| **G** | zhay | **Gaston** | gas-toñ |
| **H** | ash | **Henri** | ahñ-ree |
| **I** | ee | **Irma** | eer-ma |

| | | | |
|---|---|---|---|
| **J** | zhee | **Joseph** | zho-zef |
| **K** | ka | **Kléber** | klay-behr |
| **L** | el | **Louis** | loo-wee |
| **M** | em | **Marcel** | mar-sel |
| **N** | en | **Nicolas** | nee-koh-la |
| **O** | oh | **Oscar** | os-kar |
| **P** | pay | **Pierre** | pyehr |
| **Q** | kew | **Quintal** | kañ-tal |
| **R** | ehr | **Raoul** | ra-ool |
| **S** | es | **Suzanne** | sew-zan |
| **T** | tay | **Thérèse** | tay-rez |
| **U** | ew | **Ursule** | ewr-sewl |
| **V** | vay | **Victor** | veek-tor |
| **W** | doo-bluh-vay | **William** | weel-yam |
| **X** | eex | **Xavier** | za-vyay |
| **Y** | ee-grek | **Yvonne** | ee-von |
| **Z** | zed | **Zoé** | zoh-ay |

# Measurements and quantities

1 lb = approx. 0.5 kilo   1 pint = approx. 0.5 litre

## Liquids

| | |
|---|---|
| 1/2 litre of... | **un demi-litre de...**<br>uñ duh-mee leetr duh... |
| a litre of... | **un litre de...**<br>uñ leetr duh... |
| 1/2 bottle of... | **une demi-bouteille de...**<br>ewn duh-mee-boo-tay-yuh duh... |
| a bottle of... | **une bouteille de...**<br>ewn boo-tay-yuh duh... |
| a glass of... | **un verre de...**<br>uñ vehr duh... |

## Weights

| | |
|---|---|
| 100 grams of... | **cent grammes de...**<br>sahñ gram duh... |
| 1/2 kilo of... | **un demi-kilo de...**<br>uñ duh-mee kee-loh duh... |
| a kilo of... | **un kilo de...**<br>uñ kee-loh duh... |

## Food

| | |
|---|---|
| a slice of... | **une tranche de...**<br>ewn trahñsh duh... |
| a portion of... | **une portion de...**<br>ewn por-syoñ de... |
| a dozen... | **une douzaine de...**<br>ewn doo-zen duh... |
| a box of... | **une boîte de...**<br>ewn bwat duh... |
| a packet of... | **un paquet de...**<br>uñ pa-keh duh... |
| a tin of... | **une boîte de...**<br>ewn bwat duh... |
| a carton of... | **une brique de...**<br>ewn breek duh... |
| a jar of... | **un pot de...**<br>uñ poh duh... |

## Miscellaneous

| | |
|---|---|
| 500 euros of... | **500 euros de...**<br>sañk uh-roh duh... |
| a quarter | **un quart**<br>uñ kar |
| ten per cent | **dix pour cent**<br>dee poor sahñ |
| more... | **plus de...**<br>plew duh... |

| | |
|---|---|
| less... | **moins de...** mwañ duh... |
| enough of... | **assez de...** a-say duh... |
| double | **le double** luh doobl |
| twice | **deux fois** duh fwa |

# Numbers

| | |
|---|---|
| 0 | **zéro** zay-roh |
| 1 | **un** uñ |
| 2 | **deux** duh |
| 3 | **trois** trwa |
| 4 | **quatre** katr |
| 5 | **cinq** sañk |
| 6 | **six** sees |
| 7 | **sept** set |
| 8 | **huit** weet |
| 9 | **neuf** nuhf |
| 10 | **dix** dees |
| 11 | **onze** oñz |
| 12 | **douze** dooz |
| 13 | **treize** trez |
| 14 | **quatorze** ka-torz |
| 15 | **quinze** kañz |

| | |
|---|---|
| 16 | **seize** sez |
| 17 | **dix-sept** dees-set |
| 18 | **dix-huit** deez-weet |
| 19 | **dix-neuf** deez-nuhf |
| 20 | **vingt** vañ |
| 21 | **vingt et un** vañ tay uñ |
| 22 | **vingt-deux** vañt-duh |
| 23 | **vingt-trois** vañt-trwa |
| 30 | **trente** trahñt |
| 40 | **quarante** ka-rahñt |
| 50 | **cinquante** sañk-ahñt |
| 60 | **soixante** swa-sahñt |
| 70 | **soixante-dix** swa-sahñt-dees |
| 71 | **soixante et onze** swa-sahñt-ay-oñz |
| 72 | **soixante-douze** swa-sahñt-dooz |
| 80 | **quatre-vingts** katr-vañ |
| 81 | **quatre-vingt-un** katr-vañ-un |
| 82 | **quatre-vingt-deux** katr-vañ-duh |
| 90 | **quatre-vingt-dix** katr-vañ-dees |
| 91 | **quatre-vingt-onze** katr-vañ-oñz |
| 100 | **cent** sahñ |
| 110 | **cent dix** sahñ dees |
| 200 | **deux cents** duh sahñ |
| 250 | **deux cent cinquante** duh sahñ sañk-ahñt |
| 1,000 | **mille** meel |
| 1 million | **un million** uñ mee-lyoñ |

# Days and months

| | | |
|---|---|---|
| 1st | **premier/première/ 1er/1ère** | pruh-myay/ pruh-myehr |
| 2nd | **deuxième/2e** | duh-zyem |
| 3rd | **troisième/3e** | trwa-zyem |
| 4th | **quatrième/4e** | kat-ree-yem |
| 5th | **cinquième/5e** | sañk-yem |
| 6th | **sixième/6e** | see-zyem |
| 7th | **septième/7e** | set-yem |
| 8th | **huitième/8e** | wee-tyem |
| 9th | **neuvième/9e** | nuh-vyem |
| 10th | **dixième/10e** | dee-zyem |

## Days

| | | |
|---|---|---|
| Monday | **lundi** | luñ-dee |
| Tuesday | **mardi** | mar-dee |
| Wednesday | **mercredi** | mehr-kruh-dee |
| Thursday | **jeudi** | zhuh-dee |
| Friday | **vendredi** | vahñ-druh-dee |
| Saturday | **samedi** | sam-dee |
| Sunday | **dimanche** | dee-mahñsh |

## Months

| | | |
|---|---|---|
| January | **janvier** | zhahñ-vyay |
| February | **février** | fay-vree-yay |
| March | **mars** | mars |
| April | **avril** | av-reel |
| May | **mai** | meh |
| June | **juin** | zhwañ |
| July | **juillet** | zhwee-yeh |
| August | **août** | oo(t) |
| September | **septembre** | sep-tahñbr |
| October | **octobre** | ok-tobr |
| November | **novembre** | no-vahñbr |
| December | **décembre** | day-sahñbr |

## Seasons

| | | |
|---|---|---|
| spring | **printemps** | prañ-tahñ |
| summer | **été** | ay-tay |
| autumn | **automne** | oh-ton |
| winter | **hiver** | ee-vehr |

What is today's date? **Quelle est la date aujourd'hui?**
kel eh la dat oh-zhoor-dwee?

It's the fifth of March **Nous sommes le cinq mars**
noo som luh sañk mars

| | |
|---|---|
| It's 8th May 2007 | **C'est le huit mai deux mille sept**<br>say luh wee may duh meel set |
| 1st January | **Le premier janvier**<br>luh pruhm-yay zhahñ-vyay |
| on Saturday | **samedi**<br>sam-dee |
| on Saturdays | **le samedi**<br>luh sam-dee |
| every Saturday | **tous les samedis**<br>too lay sam-dee |
| this Saturday | **samedi qui vient**<br>sam-dee kee vyañ |
| next Saturday | **samedi prochain**<br>sam-dee pro-shañ |
| last Saturday in June | **samedi dernier en juin**<br>sam-dee dehr-nyay ahñ zhwañ |
| at the beginning of June | **début juin**<br>day-bew zhwañ |
| at the end of June | **fin juin**<br>fañ zhwañ |
| before the summer | **avant l'été**<br>a-vahñ lay-tay |
| during the summer | **pendant l'été**<br>pahñ-dahñ lay-tay |
| after the summer | **après l'été**<br>a-preh lay-tay |

# Time

The 24-hour clock is used a lot more in Europe than in Britain. After 1200 (midday), it continues: 13.00 (**treize heures** - one o'clock in the afternoon), 14.00 (**quatorze heures** - two o'clock), 15.00 (**quinze heures** - three o'clock), etc. until 24.00 (**vingt-quatre heures** - midnight). With the 24-hour clock, the words **quart** (quarter) and **demie** (half) aren't used:

| | |
|---|---|
| 13.15 (1.15 pm) | **treize heures quinze** |
| 19.30 (7.30 pm) | **dix-neuf heures trente** |
| 22.45 (10.45 pm) | **vingt-deux heures quarante-cinq** |

| | |
|---|---|
| What time is it? | **Il est quelle heure?/ Quelle heure est-il?**<br>eel ay kel ur?/kel ur ay-teel? |
| It's... | **Il est...**<br>eel ay... |
| two o'clock | **deux heures**<br>duh zur |
| three o'clock | **trois heures**<br>trwa zur |
| six o'clock (etc.) | **six heures**<br>see zur |

Reference

| | |
|---|---|
| It's one o'clock | **Il est une heure**<br>eel ay (t)ewn ur |
| It's midday | **Il est midi**<br>eel ay mee-dee |
| It's midnight | **Il est minuit**<br>eel ay mee-nwee |
| 9 | **neuf heures**<br>nuh vur |
| 9.10 | **neuf heures dix**<br>nuh vur dees |
| quarter past 9 | **neuf heures et quart**<br>nuh vur ay kar |
| 9.20 | **neuf heures vingt**<br>nuh vur vañ |
| 9.30 | **neuf heures et demie/ neuf heures trente**<br>nuh vur ay duh-mee/ nuh vur trahññt |
| 9.35 | **dix heures moins vingt-cinq**<br>dee zur mwañ vañt-sañk |
| quarter to 10 | **dix heures moins le quart**<br>dee zur mwañ luh kar |
| 10 to 10 | **dix heures moins dix**<br>dee zur mwañ dees |

# Time phrases

| | |
|---|---|
| When does it...? | **Il ... à quelle heure?**<br>eel ... a kel ur? |
| open/close/ begin/finish | **ouvre/ferme/commence/ finit**<br>oovr/fehrm/ko-mahñs/fee-nee |
| at three o'clock | **à trois heures**<br>a trwa zur |
| before three o'clock | **avant trois heures**<br>a-vahñ trwa zur |
| after three o'clock | **après trois heures**<br>a-preh trwa zur |
| today | **aujourd'hui**<br>oh-zhoor-dwee |
| tonight | **ce soir**<br>suh swar |
| tomorrow | **demain**<br>duh-mañ |
| yesterday | **hier**<br>ee-yehr |

# Eating out

## Eating places

**Salon de thé** Generally attached to a cake shop, **pâtisserie**, where you can sit down and sample some of the cakes. Can be quite expensive.

**Crêperie** Specialising in sweet and savoury pancakes (**galettes**). Good for light inexpensive meals.

**Libre-service** Self-service.

**Bistro** Usually cheaper and smaller than **Brasserie**.

**Glacier** Ice-cream parlour.

**Restaurant** Generally open 11.30 am to 2.30 pm and 7.30 to 10.30 pm. The menu is posted outside.

**Table d'hôte** Home cooking using local produce.

**Brasserie** All-day food place often attached to a **bar-café**.

**Frites 500m** Signals a road-side café 500 metres away. Mediocre food (mostly chips).

**Gaufres** Waffles.

# In a bar/café

If you just ask for **un café** you will be served a small, strong, black coffee. If this is not your cup of tea, you should specify the type of coffee you want:

| | |
|---|---|
| **un (café) crème**<br>uñ (ka-fay) krem | white creamy coffee |
| **un grand crème**<br>uñ grahñ krem | large white creamy coffee |
| **un café au lait**<br>uñ ka-fay oh leh | coffee with hot milk |

| | |
|---|---|
| a coffee | **un café**<br>uñ ka-fay |
| an orangeade | **une orangeade**<br>ewn o-rahñ-zhad |

**FACE TO FACE**

**A** **Qu'est-ce que vous prenez?**
kes kuh voo pruh-nay?
What will you have?

**B** **Un thé au lait, s'il vous plaît**
uñ tay oh leh, seel voo pleh
A tea with milk, please

| | |
|---|---|
| with lemon | **au citron**<br>oh see-troñ |
| no sugar | **sans sucre**<br>sahñ sewkr |
| for two | **pour deux personnes**<br>poor duh pehr-son |
| for me | **pour moi**<br>poor mwa |
| for him/her | **pour lui/elle**<br>poor lwee/el |
| for us | **pour nous**<br>poor noo |
| with ice, please | **avec des glaçons, s'il vous plaît**<br>a-vek day gla-soñ, seel voo pleh |
| Some ... mineral water | **De l'eau minérale...**<br>duh loh mee-nay-ral... |
| sparkling | **gazeuse**<br>ga-zuhz |
| still | **plate**<br>plat |

In a bar/café

### Other drinks to try

**un chocolat (chaud)** hot chocolate
**un citron pressé** freshly-squeezed lemon (add water and sugar)
**un diabolo** lemonade and cordial
**une tisane** herb tea

## Reading the menu

Restaurants display their menus outside. Often there is a choice of two or three menus at different prices as well as **à la carte** dishes. French families often go to a restaurant for Sunday lunch, so it is advisable to book.

**Boisson non comprise** Drink not included.

**Plat du jour à 7 € 50 – poisson ou viande ou vollaille garnis** Dish of the day 7 € 50 - fish or meat or poultry with veg and French fries.

**menu du midi – entrée + plat + café** lunchtime menu – starter + main course + coffee.

| | |
|---|---|
| **carte** | menu |
| **entrées** | starters |
| **potages** | soups |
| **assiette de charcuterie** | assorted cold meats |
| **assiette de crudités** | assorted raw veg & dip |
| **viandes** | meat |
| **gibier et volaile** | game & poultry |
| **poissons** | fish |
| **fruit de mer** | seafood |
| **légumes** | vegetables |
| **fromages** | cheese |
| **desserts** | desserts |
| **boissons** | drinks |

# In a restaurant

**FACE TO FACE**

A **Je voudrais réserver une table pour ... personnes**
zhuh voo-dreh ray-zehr-vay ewn tabl poor ... pehr-son
I'd like to book a table for ... people

B **Oui, pour quand?**
wee, poor kahñ?
Yes, when for?

A **Pour ce soir/pour demain soir/pour dix-neuf heures trente**
poor suh swar/poor duh-mañ swar/poor deez-nuh vur trahñt
For tonight/for tomorrow night/for 7.30

| | |
|---|---|
| The menu, please | **Le menu, s'il vous plaît**<br>luh muh-new, seel voo pleh |
| What is the dish of the day? | **Quel est le plat du jour?**<br>kel eh luh pla dew zhoor? |
| I'll have the menu at ... euros, please | **Je prends le menu à ... euros, s'il vous plaît**<br>zhuh prahñ luh muh-new a ... uh-roh, seel voo pleh |
| Can you recommend a local dish? | **Pouvez-vous nous recommander un plat régional?**<br>poo-vay voo noo ruh-ko-mahñ-day uñ pla ray-zhyo-nal? |

| | |
|---|---|
| What is in this? | **Qu'est-ce qu'il y a dedans?**<br>kes keel ya duh-dahñ? |
| I'll have this | **Je prends ça**<br>zhuh prahñ sa |
| More bread... | **Encore du pain...**<br>ahñ-kor dew pañ... |
| More water... | **Encore de l'eau...**<br>ahñ-kor duh loh... |
| please | **s'il vous plaît**<br>seel voo pleh |
| The bill, please | **L'addition, s'il vous plaît**<br>la-dee-syoñ, seel voo pleh |
| Is service included? | **Est-ce que le service est compris?**<br>es kuh luh sehr-vees ay koñ-pree? |

| YOU MAY HEAR... | |
|---|---|
| **Une table pour deux?**<br>ewn tabl poor duh? | A table for two? |

# Vegetarian

Don't expect great things if you're a vegetarian (let alone a vegan) – the French love meat!

| | |
|---|---|
| Are there any vegetarian restaurants here? | **Est-ce qu'il y a des restaurants végétariens ici?**<br>es keel ya day res-toh-rahñ vay-zhay-ta-ryañ ee-see? |
| Do you have any vegetarian dishes? | **Vous avez des plats végétariens?**<br>voo za-vay day pla vay-zhay-ta-ryañ? |
| Which dishes have no meat/fish? | **Quels sont les plats sans viande/poisson?**<br>kel soñ lay plah sahñ vyahñd/pwasoñ? |
| I'd like pasta as a main course | **Je voudrais des pâtes comme plat principal**<br>zhuh voo-dreh day pat kom pla prañ-see-pal |
| I don't like meat | **Je n'aime pas la viande**<br>zhuh nehm pa la vyahñd |
| Is it made with vegetable stock? | **Est-ce que c'est fait avec du bouillon de légumes?**<br>es kuh say feh a-vek dew boo-yoñ duh lay-gewm? |

Eating out

## Possible dishes

**salade verte** green salad
**salade niçoise** salad with tomatoes, olives, tuna and eggs
**artichauts à la sauce fromage** artichokes in cheese sauce
**soupe à l'oignon** French onion soup
**tarte à l'oignon** onion tart
**ratatouille** courgettes, tomatoes, peppers, onions and aubergines

# Wines and spirits

| | |
|---|---|
| The wine list, please | **La carte des vins, s'il vous plaît**<br>la kart day vañ, seel voo pleh |
| white wine/ red wine | **du vin blanc/du vin rouge**<br>dew vañ blahñ/dew vañ roozh |
| Can you recommend a good wine? | **Pouvez-vous nous recommander un bon vin?**<br>poo-vay voo noo ruh-ko-mahñ-day uñ boñ vañ? |
| A bottle... | **Une bouteille...**<br>ewn boo-tay-yuh... |
| A carafe... | **Un pichet...**<br>uñ pee-sheh... |
| of the house wine | **de la cuvée du patron**<br>duh la kew-vay dew pa-troñ |

## Wines

**Barsac** sweet white wine
**Beaujolais** light, fruity wines (Burgundy)
**Bergerac** red and white wines (Dordogne)
**Blanc de blancs** any white wine made from white grapes only
**Blanquette de Limoux** dry sparkling white wine (southwest)
**Bordeaux** region producing red (claret), rosé and dry and sweet white wines
**Bourgueuil** light, fruity red wine to be drunk very young (Loire)
**Brouilly** among the finest Beaujolais: fruity, supple, full of flavour
**Cabernet sauvignon** red wine with a slight blackcurrant aroma
**Cahors** dark, long-lived, powerful red wine from the southwest
**Chablis** very dry, full-bodied white wine (Burgundy)
**Chambertin** one of the finest red Burgundies (Burgundy)
**Champagne** sparkling white/rosé (Champagne)
**Chardonnay** a white grape variety widely used in sparkling wines
**Châteauneuf-du-Pape** good, full-bodied red wine (Rhône)
**Côtes de Beaune** full-bodied red (Burgundy)
**Côtes du Rhône** full-bodied red (Rhône)

**Côtes du Roussillon** good ordinary red (Languedoc-Roussillon)
**Entre-deux-mers** medium-dry white wine from Bordeaux
**Gewürztraminer** fruity, spicy white wine (Alsace)
**Mâcon** good ordinary red and white wines (Burgundy)
**Médoc** principal wine-producing area of Bordeaux
**Mersault** high-class dry white wine (Burgundy)
**Monbazillac** sweet white wine (Dordogne)
**Muscadet** very dry white wine (Loire)
**Pouilly-fuissé** light dry white wine (Burgundy)
**Pouilly-fumé** spicy dry white wine (Loire)
**Rosé d'Anjou** light, fruity rosé (Loire)
**Saint-Emilion** good full-bodied red wine (Bordeaux)
**Sancerre** dry white wine (Loire)
**Sauternes** high-class sweet white wine (Bordeaux)
**Sylvaner** dry white wine (Alsace)
**Vouvray** dry, sweet and sparkling white wines (Loire)

**Demi-sec** medium dry (wine)
**Cuvée** vintage
**Mousseux** sparkling (wine)
**Premier cru** first-class wine

## Spirits and liqueurs

What liqueurs do you have? **Qu'est-ce que vous avez comme digestifs?**
kes kuh voo za-vay kom dee-zheh-steef?

**Armagnac** fine grape brandy from southwest France
**Calvados** apple brandy made from cider (Normandy)
**Cassis** blackcurrant liqueur: ***kir*** white wine and cassis apéritif
**Chartreuse** aromatic herb liqueur made by Carthusian monks
**Cognac** high-quality white grape brandy
**Cointreau** orange-flavoured liqueur
**Crème de menthe** peppermint-flavoured liqueur
**Eau de vie** very strong brandy (often made from plum, pear, etc.)
**Grand Marnier** tawny-coloured, orange-flavoured liqueur
**Kirsch** cherry-flavoured spirit from Alsace
**Marc** white grape spirit
**Mirabelle** plum spirit from Alsace
**Pastis** aniseed-based apéritif (e.g. Pernod) to which water is added

# Menu reader

**à la/à l'/au/aux...** in the style of.../with...
**abats** offal, giblets
**abricot** apricot
**agneau** lamb
**ail** garlic
**aile** wing
**aïoli** rich garlic mayonnaise served on the side and giving its name to the dish it accompanies: cold steamed fish and vegetables
**airelles** bilberries, cranberries
**allumettes** very thin chips
**amande** almond
**amuse-bouche** nibbles
**armoricaine, à l'** cooked with brandy, wine, tomatoes and onions
**ananas** pineapple
**anchoïade** anchovy paste usually served on grilled French bread
**anchois** anchovies
**andouille** (eaten cold), **andouillette** (eaten hot) spicy tripe sausage
**anguille** eel
**anis** aniseed

**arachide** peanut (uncooked)
**araignée de mer** spider crab
**artichaut** artichoke
**asperge** asparagus
**aspic de volaille** chicken in aspic
**assiette** dish, platter
**assiette anglaise** plate of assorted cold meats
**assiette de charcuterie** plate of assorted pâtés and salami
**assiette de crudités** selection of raw vegetables
**assiette du pêcheur** assorted fish or seafood
**aubergine** aubergine
**avocat** avocado

**babas au rhum** rum baba
**Badoit** mineral water, very slightly sparkling
**baekenofe** hotpot of pork, mutton and beef baked in white wine with potato layers (from Alsace)
**bar** sea-bass
**barbue** brill
**barquette** small boat-shaped flan
**basilic** basil
**bavarois** moulded cream and custard pudding, usually served with fruit
**Béarnaise, à la** sauce similar to mayonnaise but flavoured with tarragon and white wine – traditionally served with steak
**bécasse** woodcock
**beignets** fritters, doughnuts

**betterave** beetroot
**beurre** butter
**beurre blanc, au** sauce of white wine and shallots with butter
**bien cuit** well done
**bière** beer
**(bière) pression** draught beer
**bière blonde** lager
**bière brune** bitter
**bifteck** steak
**bigorneau** periwinkle
**bio(logique)** organic
**bis** wholemeal (of bread or flour)
**biscuit de Savoie** sponge cake
**bisque** smooth, rich seafood soup
**blanquette** white meat stew served with a creamy white sauce
**blanquette de veau** veal stew in white sauce
**blanquette de volaille** chicken stew in white sauce
**blé** wheat
**blette** Swiss chard
**bleu** very rare
**bœuf** beef
**bœuf bourguignon** beef in burgundy, onions and mushrooms
**bœuf en daube** rich beef stew with wine, olives, tomatoes and herbs
**bombe** moulded ice cream dessert
**bonite** bonito, small tuna fish

**bouchée** vol-au-vent
**bouchée à la reine** vol-au-vent filled with chicken or veal and mushrooms in a white sauce
**boudin** pudding made with offal and blood
**bouillabaisse** rich seafood dish flavoured with saffron originally from Marseilles
**bouilli** boiled
**bouillon** stock
**boulettes** meatballs
**brandade de morue** dried salt cod puréed with potatoes and olive oil
**brème** bream
**brioche** sweet bun
**brioche aux fruits** sweet bun with glacé fruit
**brochet** pike
**brochette** kebab
**brochette, en** cooked like a kebab (on a skewer)
**brugnon** nectarine
**bugnes** doughnuts from the Lyons area
**bulot** whelk

**cabillaud** fresh cod
**cacahuète** peanut
**café** coffee
**café au lait** coffee with hot milk
**caille** quail
**cajou, noix de** cashew nut
**calisson** almond dessert
**calmar/calamar** squid

**canard** duck
**canard périgourdin** roast duck with prunes, **pâté de foie gras** and truffles
**caneton** duckling
**cannelle** cinnamon
**câpres** capers
**carbonnade de bœuf** braised beef
**cardon** cardoon
**cari** curry
**carottes Vichy** carrots cooked in butter and sugar
**carpe farcie** carp stuffed with mushrooms or **foie gras**
**carrelet** plaice
**carte des vins** wine list
**cassoulet** bean stew with pork or mutton, confit and sausages (there are many regional variations)
**caviar blanc** mullet roe
**caviar niçois** a paste made with anchovies and olive oil
**céleri rémoulade** celeriac in a mustard and herb dressing
**céleri-rave** celeriac
**cèpes** boletus mushrooms, wild mushrooms
**cerfeuil** chervil
**cerise** cherry
**cervelas** smoked pork sausages, saveloy
**cervelle** brains (usually lamb or calf)
**cervelle de Canut** savoury dish of fromage frais, goat's cheese, herbs and white wine

**champignon** mushroom

**champignons à la grecque** mushrooms cooked in wine, olive oil, herbs and tomato

**champignons de Paris** button mushrooms

**chantilly** whipped cream

**charlotte** custard and fruit in lining of almond fingers

**chasseur** literally hunter-style, cooked with white wine, shallots, mushrooms and herbs

**châtaigne** chestnut

**châteaubriand** thick fillet steak

**chaud(e)** hot

**chauffé(e)** heated

**chausson** pasty filled with meat or seafood

**chausson aux pommes** apple turnover

**chèvre** goat

**chevreuil** venison

**chichi** doughnut shaped as a stick

**chicorée** chicory, endive

**chocolat chaud** hot chocolate

**chou** cabbage

**choucroute** sauerkraut

**choucroute garnie** sauerkraut with various types of sausages

**chou-fleur** cauliflower

**choux brocolis** broccoli

**choux de Bruxelles** Brussels sprouts

**ciboule/cive** spring onions

**ciboulette** chives

**cidre** cider, sparkling (**bouché**) or still, quite strong

**citron** lemon
**citron pressé** freshly squeezed lemon juice with water and sugar
**citron vert** lime
**citrouille** pumpkin
**civet** thick stew
**civet de langouste** crayfish in wine sauce
**civet de lièvre** hare stewed in wine, onions and mushrooms
**clafoutis** cherry pudding
**clou de girofle** clove
**cochon** pig
**coco** coconut
**cœur** heart
**cœurs d'artichauts** artichoke hearts
**cœurs de palmier** palm hearts
**coing** quince
**colin** hake
**compote de fruits** mixed stewed fruit
**concombre** cucumber
**condé** rich rice pudding with fruits
**confit** pieces of meat preserved in fat
**confit de canard/d'oie** duck/goose meat preserved in its own fat
**confiture** jam
**confiture d'oranges** marmalade
**congre** conger eel
**consommé** clear soup, generally made from meat or fish stock

**contre-filet** sirloin fillet (beef)
**coq au vin** chicken and mushrooms cooked in red wine
**coquelet** cockerel
**coques** cockles
**coquillages** shellfish
**coquilles Saint-Jacques** scallops
**coquillettes** pasta shells
**cornichon** gherkin
**côtelettes d'agneau** lamb cutlets
**côtes de porc** pork chops
**cotriade** fish stew (Brittany)
**cou** neck
**coulibiac** salmon cooked in puff pastry
**coulis** puréed fruit sauce
**coupe** goblet with ice cream
**courge** marrow
**crabe** crab
**craquelots** smoked herring
**crémant** sparkling wine
**crème** cream
  **crème anglaise** fresh custard
  **crème au beurre** butter cream with egg yolks and sugar
  **crème chantilly** slightly sweetened whipped cream
  **crème pâtissière** thick fresh custard used in tarts and desserts
  **crème renversée** (or **crème caramel**) custard with a caramelised top
**crème de** cream of... (soup)

**crème d'Argenteuil** white asparagus soup
**crème de cresson** watercress soup
**crème de marrons** chestnut purée
**crêpes** sweet and savoury pancakes
**crêpes fourrées** filled pancakes
**crêpes Suzette** pancakes with a Cointreau or Grand Marnier sauce usually flambéed
**crevette** prawn
**crevette grise** shrimp
**crevette rose** large prawn
**croque-madame** grilled cheese and bacon, sausage, chicken or egg sandwich
**croque-monsieur** grilled gruyère cheese and ham sandwich
**croûte, en** in pastry
**croûtes/croûtons, aux** served with croutons (cubes of toasted or fried bread)
**cru(e)** raw
**crudités** assortment of raw vegetables (grated carrots, sliced tomatoes, etc.) served as a starter
**crustacés** shellfish
**cuisses de grenouille** frogs' legs
**cuit** cooked
**culotte** rump steak

**darne** fish steak
**datte** date
**daube** casserole with wine, herbs, garlic, tomatoes and olives

**dauphinoise, à la** baked in milk
**daurade** sea bream
**diabolo menthe** mint cordial and lemonade
**dinde** turkey

**eau** water
**eau de Seltz** soda water
**eau-de-vie** brandy (often made from plum, pear, etc)
**eau minérale** mineral water
**eau du robinet** tap water
**échalote** shallot
**échine** loin of pork
**écrevisse** freshwater crayfish
**églefin** haddock
**encornet** squid
**endive** chicory
**entrecôte** rib steak
**entrées** starters
**entremets** desserts
**épaule** shoulder
**éperlan** whitebait
**épice** spice
**épinards** spinach
**escargots** snails (generally cooked with strong seasonings)
**espadon** swordfish
**estouffade de boeuf** beef stew cooked in red wine, herbs, onions, mushrooms and diced bacon
**estragon** tarragon
**esturgeon** sturgeon

**faisan** pheasant
**farci(e)** stuffed
**faux-filet** sirloin steak
**fenouil** fennel
**feu de bois, au** cooked over a wood fire
**feuille** leaf
**feuilleté(e)** in puff pastry
**fèves** broad beans
**figue** fig
**filet** fillet steak
**filet de bœuf en croûte** steak in pastry
**filet de bœuf** tenderloin
**filet mignon** small pork fillet steak
**fine de claire** high-quality oyster
**fines herbes** mixed, chopped herbs
**flageolet** type of small green haricot bean
**flétan** halibut
**flocons d'avoine** oat flakes
**florentine** with spinach, usually served with mornay sauce
**foie** liver (usually calf's)
**foie de volailles** chicken livers
**foie gras** goose liver
**fond d'artichaut** artichoke heart
**fondue (au fromage)** melted cheeses with white wine into which chunks of bread are dipped
**fondue bourguignonne** small chunks of beef dipped into boiling oil and eaten with different sauces

**fougasse** type of bread with various fillings (olives, anchovies)
**four, au** baked
**fourré(e)** stuffed
**frais (fraîche)** fresh
**fraise** strawberry
**fraises des bois** wild strawberries
**framboise** raspberry
**frappé** iced
**fricassée** a stew, usually chicken or veal, and vegetables
**frisée** curly endive
**frit(e)** fried
**friture** fried food, usually small fish
**froid(e)** cold
**fromage** cheese
**fromage blanc** soft white cheese
**fromage frais** creamy fresh cheese
**froment** wheat
**fruit de la passion** passion fruit
**fruits de mer** shellfish, seafood
**fumé(e)** smoked
**fumet** fish stock

**galantine** meat in aspic
**galette** savoury buckwheat pancake
**gambas** large prawn
**ganache** chocolate cream filling
**garni(e)** garnished i.e. served with something, usually vegetables

**garnitures** side dishes
**gâteau** cake, gateau
**gâteau Saint-Honoré** choux pastry cake filled with custard
**gaufres** waffles (often cream-filled)
**gazeuse** sparkling
**gelée** jelly, aspic
**genièvre** juniper berry
**génoise** sponge cake
**germes de soja** bean sprouts
**gésier** gizzard
**gibier** game
**gigot d'agneau** leg of lamb
**gigot de mer** large fish baked whole
**gingembre** ginger
**glace** ice cream
**gougères** choux pastry with cheese
**goyave** guava
**gratin, au** topped with cheese and breadcrumb and grilled
**gratin dauphinois** potatoes cooked in cream, garlic and Swiss cheese
**grecque, à la** cooked in olive oil, garlic, tomatoes and herbs, can be served hot or cold
**grenade** pomegranate
**grenouilles** frogs' legs
**grenouilles meunière** frogs' legs cooked in butter and parsley
**grillade** grilled meat

**groseille** redcurrant
**groseille à maquereau** gooseberry

**hachis** mince
**hareng** herring
**haricots** beans
**haricots beurre** butter beans
**haricots blancs** haricot beans
**haricots rouges** red kidney beans
**haricots verts** green beans, French beans
**herbes (fines herbes)** herbs
**hollandaise, sauce** sauce made of butter, egg yolks and lemon juice, served warm
**homard** lobster
**homard à l'armoricaine** lobster cooked with onions, tomatoes and wine
**hors d'œuvre variés** selection of appetizers
**huile** oil
**huile d'arachide** groundnut oil
**huile de tournesol** sunflower oil
**huître** oyster

**îles flottantes** soft meringues floating on fresh custard

**jambon** ham
**jambon de Bayonne** cured raw ham from the Basque country
**jambon de Paris** boiled ham

**julienne** with vegetables cut into fine strips
**jus** juice, meat-based glaze or sauce

**lait** milk
**lait (demi)-écrémé** (semi)-skimmed milk
**lait entier** full-cream milk
**laitue** lettuce
**lamproie à la bordelaise** lamprey in red wine
**langouste** crayfish (saltwater)
**langoustines** scampi (large)
**langue** tongue (veal, beef)
**lapin** rabbit
**lard** fat, streaky bacon
**lardon** strip of fat, diced bacon
**laurier** bayleaf
**légumes** vegetables
**levure** yeast
**lièvre** hare
**limande** lemon sole
**lotte** monkfish
**loup de mer** sea-bass

**macaron** macaroon
**macédoine (de fruits)** fresh fruit salad
**macédoine de légumes** mixed cooked vegetables
**madeleine** small sponge cake
**magret de canard** duck breast
**maïs/maïs doux** maize, sweetcorn
**mangue** mango

**maquereau** mackerel
**marcassin** young wild boar
**marinière, à la** in a sauce of white wine, onions and herbs (mussels or clams)
**marjolaine** marjoram
**marron** chestnut
  **marrons glacés** candied chestnuts
  **marrons Mont Blanc** chestnut purée and cream
**matelote** fresh-fish stew
**médaillon** thick, medal-sized slice of meat
**menthe** mint
**merguez** spicy red sausage
**merlan** whiting
**merluche** hake
**mérou** grouper
**merveilles** fritters flavoured with brandy
**mignonnette** small fillet of lamb
**mijoté(e)** stewed
**mille-feuille** thin layers of pastry filled with custard
**mirabelle** small yellow plum; plum brandy from Alsace
**mont-blanc** pudding made with chestnuts and cream
**Mornay, sauce** béchamel and cheese sauce
**morue** dried salt cod
**moules** mussels
  **moules marinière** mussels cooked in white wine
  **moules poulette** mussels in wine, cream and mushroom sauce
**mousseline** mashed potatoes with cream and eggs

**moutarde** mustard
**mouton** mutton or sheep
**mûre** blackberry
**muscade** nutmeg
**myrtille** bilberry

**navet** turnip
**noisette** hazelnut
**noisettes d'agneau** small round pieces of lamb
**noix** walnut; general term for a nut
**nouilles** noodles
**œuf** egg
**œufs à la coque** soft-boiled eggs
**œufs au plat** fried eggs
**œufs brouillés** scrambled eggs
**œufs durs** hard-boiled eggs
**œufs en cocotte** eggs baked in individual containers with wine
**œufs frits** fried eggs and bacon
**oie** goose
**oignon** onion
**omelette nature** plain omelette
**omelette norvégienne** baked Alaska
**onglet** cut of beef (steak)
**orge** barley
**os** bone
**oseille** sorrel
**oursin** sea urchin

**pain** bread, loaf of bread
**pain au chocolat** croissant with chocolate filling
**pain bagnat** bread roll with egg, olives, salad, tuna, anchovies and olive oil
**pain bis** brown bread
**pain complet** wholemeal bread
**pain d'épices** ginger cake
**pain de mie** white sliced loaf
**pain de seigle** rye bread
**pain grillé** toast
**palmier** caramelized puff pastry
**palombe** wood pigeon
**palourde** clam
**pamplemousse** grapefruit
**panais** parsnip
**pané(e)** with breadcrumbs
**panisse** thick chickpea flour pancake
**papillote, en** in filo pastry
**parfait** rich home-made ice cream
**Paris Brest** ring-shaped cake filled with praline-flavoured cream
**parisienne, à la** sautéed in butter with white wine, sauce and shallots
**parmentier** with potatoes
**pastèque** watermelon
**patate douce** sweet potato
**pâté de foie de volailles** chicken liver pâté
**pâté en croûte** pâté encased in pastry

**pâtes** pasta
**paupiettes** meat slices stuffed and rolled
**pavé** thick slice
**pêche** peach
**perche** perch (fish)
**perdreau/perdrix** partridge, grouse
**Périgueux, sauce** with truffles
**persil** parsley
**persillé(e)** with parsley
**pétillant(e)** fizzy
**petit-beurre** butter biscuit
**petits farcis** stuffed tomatoes, aubergines, courgettes and peppers
**petits fours** bite-sized cakes and pastries
**petit pain** roll
**petits pois** small peas
**petit-suisse** thick fromage frais
**pieds et paquets** mutton or pork tripe and trotters
**pignons** pine nuts
**pilon** drumstick (chicken)
**piment** chilli
  **piment doux** sweet pepper
  **piment fort** chilli
**pimenté(e)** peppery, hot
**pintade/pintadeau** guinea fowl
**pipérade** tomato, pepper and onion omelette
**piquant(e)** spicy
**pissaladière** a kind of pizza made mainly in the Nice region, filled with onions, anchovies and black olives

**pistache** pistachio
**pistou** garlic, basil and olive oil sauce from Provence – similar to **pesto**
**plat** dish
**plat (principal)** main course
**plat(e)** still (e.g. water)
**plie** plaice
**poché(e)** poached
**poêlé(e)** pan-fried
**pimenté(e)** peppery, hot
**point, à** medium rare
**poires belle Hélène** poached pears with vanilla ice cream and chocolate sauce
**poireau** leek
**pois** peas
**pois cassés** split peas
**pois-chiches** chickpeas
**poisson** fish
**poitrine** breast (lamb or veal)
**poivre** pepper
**poivron** sweet pepper
**poivron rouge** red pepper
**poivron vert** green pepper
**pomme** apple
**pomme (de terre)** potato
**pommes à l'anglaise** boiled potatoes
**pommes à la vapeur** steamed potatoes
**pommes allumettes** match-stick chips
**pommes dauphine** potato croquettes

**pommes duchesse** potato mashed then baked in the oven
**pommes frites** fried potatoes
**pommes Lyonnaise** potatoes fried with onions
**pommes mousseline** potatoes mashed with cream
**pommes rissolées** small deep-fried potatoes
**porc** pork
**pot au feu** beef and vegetable stew
**potage** soup, generally creamed or thickened
**potée auvergnate** cabbage and meat soup
**potiron** type of pumpkin
**poularde** fattened chicken
**poulet** chicken
**poulet basquaise** chicken stew with tomatoes, mushrooms and peppers
**poulet célestine** chicken cooked in white wine with mushrooms and onion
**poulpe à la niçoise** octopus in tomato sauce
**pousses de soja** bean sprouts
**poussin** baby chicken
**poutargue** mullet roe paste
**praire** clam
**praliné** hazelnut-flavoured
**primeurs** spring vegetables
**provençale, à la** cooked with tomatoes, peppers, garlic and white wine
**pruneau** prune, damson
**purée** mashed potatoes; purée

**quatre-quarts** cake made with equal parts of butter, flour, sugar and eggs
**quenelles** poached balls of fish or meat mousse served in a sauce
**quenelles de brochet** pike mousse in cream sauce
**queue de bœuf** oxtail

**râble** saddle
**radis** radishes
**ragoût** stew, casserole
**raie** skate
**raifort** horseradish
**raisin** grape
**raisin sec** sultana, raisin
**raïto** red wine, olive, caper, garlic and shallot sauce
**ramier** wood pigeon
**râpé(e)** grated
**rascasse** scorpion fish
**ratatouille** tomatoes, aubergines, courgettes and garlic cooked in olive oil
**rave** turnip
**reine-claude** greengage
**rillettes** coarse pork pâté
**rillettes de canard** coarse duck pâté
**ris de veau** calf sweetbread
**riz** rice
**rognon** kidney
**rognons blancs** testicles
**romaine** cos lettuce

**romarin** rosemary
**rond de gigot** lamb leg steak
**rosbif** roast beef
**rôti(e)** roast
**rouget** red mullet
**rouille** spicy version of garlic mayonnaise (**aïoli**) served with fish stew or soup
**roulade** meat or fish, stuffed and rolled
**roulé** sweet or savoury roll
**rutabaga** swede

**sabayon** dessert made with egg yolks, sugar and Marsala wine
**sablé** shortbread
**safran** saffron
**saignant** rare
**Saint-Hubert** game consommé flavoured with wine
**salade** lettuce; salad
**salade de fruits** fruit salad
**salade de saison** mixed salad and/or greens in season
**salade lyonnaise** vegetable salad (cooked), dressed with eggs, bacon and croutons
**salade niçoise** many variations on a famous theme: the basic ingredients are green beans, anchovies, black olives and green peppers
**salade russe** mixed cooked vegetables in mayonnaise
**salade verte** green salad
**salé(e)** salted/spicy

**salsifis** salsify, oyster plant (root vegetable resembling asparagus and palm hearts)
**sanglier** wild boar
**sarrasin** buckwheat
**sarriette** savoury (herb)
**sauce piquante** gherkins, vinegar and shallots
**saucisse/saucisson** sausage
**saumon** salmon
  **saumon fumé** smoked salmon
  **saumon poché** poached salmon
**sauté(e)** sautéed
**sauté d'agneau** lamb stew
**savarin** a filled ring-shaped cake
**savoyarde, à la** with gruyère cheese
**sec** dry, dried
**seiche** cuttlefish
**sel** salt
**selle d'agneau** saddle of lamb
**semoule** semolina
**sole cardinal** sole cooked in wine, served with lobster sauce
  **sole Normande** sole cooked in a cream, cider and shrimp sauce
  **sole Saint Germain** grilled sole with butter and tarragon sauce
**sole-limande** lemon sole
**soufflé au Grand Marnier** soufflé flavoured with Grand Marnier liqueur
  **soufflé au jambon** ham soufflé

**soupe** hearty and chunky soup
**soupe à l'oignon** onion soup usually served with a crisp chunk of French bread in the dish with grated cheese piled on top
**soupe au pistou** vegetable soup with garlic and basil
**soupe aux choux** cabbage soup with pork
**steak** steak
**stea(c)k au poivre** steak with peppercorns
**stea(c)k tartare** minced raw steak mixed with raw egg, chopped onion, tartare or worcester sauce, parsley and capers
**sucre** sugar
**sucré(e)** sweet
**suprême de volaille** breast of chicken in cream sauce
**tapenade** olive paste
**tarte** open tart, generally sweet
**tarte flambée** thin pizza-like pastry topped with onion, cream and bacon (Alsace)
**tarte Normande** apple tart
**tarte tatin** upside down tart with caramelized apples or pears
**tarte tropézienne** sponge cake filled with custard cream and topped with almonds
**tartine** open sandwich
**terrine** terrine, pâté
**terrine de campagne** pork and liver terrine
**terrine de porc et gibier** pork and game terrine
**tête de veau** calf's head

**thé** tea
**thé au citron** tea with lemon
**thé au lait** tea with milk
**thé sans sucre** tea without sugar
**thermidor** lobster grilled in its shell with cream sauce
**thon** tuna fish
**tilleul** lime tea
**timbale** round dish in which a mixture of meat or fish is cooked – often lined with pastry and served with a rich sauce
**timbale d'écrevisses** crayfish in a cream, wine and brandy sauce
**timbale de fruits** pastry base covered with fruits
**tomate** tomato
**tomates à la provençale** grilled tomatoes steeped in garlic
**tomme** type of cheese
**tournedos** thick fillet steak
**tourte à la viande** meat pie usually made with veal and pork
**tripes à la mode de Caen** tripe cooked with vegetables, herbs, cider and calvados
**tripoux** mutton tripe
**truffe** truffle
**truite aux amandes** trout covered with almonds

**vacherin** large meringue filled with cream, ice cream and fruit

**vapeur, à la** steamed
**veau** calf, veal
**veau sauté Marengo** veal cooked in a casserole with white wine, garlic, tomatoes and mushrooms
**velouté** thick creamy white sauce made with fish, veal or chicken stock – also used in soups
**venaison** venison
**verdure, en** garnished with green vegetables
**verjus** juice of unripe grapes
**verveine** herbal tea made with verbena
**viande** meat
**viande séchée** thin slices of cured beef
**vichyssoise** leek and potato soup, served cold
**vin** wine
**vin blanc** white wine
**vin de pays** local regional wine
**vin de table** table wine
**vin rosé** rosé wine
**vin rouge** red wine
**vinaigre** vinegar
**violet** sea squirt
**volaille** poultry

**yaourt** yoghurt

# Grammar

## Nouns

Unlike English nouns, French nouns have a gender: they are either masculine (**le**) or feminine (**la**). Therefore words for *the* and *a(n)* must agree with the noun they accompany. Like English nouns, they can be singular or plural, but the plural words for *the* (**les**) and some (**des**) are the same in both masculine and feminine:

| | masculine | feminine | plural |
|---|---|---|---|
| the | **le chat** | **la rue** | **les chats/ rues** |
| a, an | **un chat** | **une rue** | **des chats/ rues** |

If the noun begins with a vowel (*a*, *e*, *i*, *o* or *u*) or, sometimes, an *h*, **le** and **la** shorten to **l'**, e.g. **l'avion** *(m)*, **l'école** *(f)*, **l'hôtel** *(m)*. The letter *h* is never sounded in French and, unfortunately, there is no rule for distinguishing which words beginning with *h* take **l'** and which **le**/**la**.

Note: **le** and **les** used after the prepositions **à** (to, at) and **de** (any, some, of) contract as follows:

**à + le** = **au** (**au cinéma** but **à la gare**)
**à + les** = **aux** (**aux magasins** – applies to both *m* and *f*)
**de + le** = **du** (**du pain** but **de la confiture**)
**de + les** = **des** (**des pommes** – applies to both *m* and *f*)

# Plurals

The general rule is to add an **s** to the singular:

**le chat → les chats**

Exceptions occur with the following noun endings: **-eau**, **-eu**, **-al**

**le bateau → les bateaux**
**le neveu → les neveux**
**le cheval → les chevaux**

Nouns ending in **s**, **x**, or **z** do not change in the plural.

**le dos → les dos**
**le prix → les prix**
**le nez → les nez**

# Adjectives

Adjectives normally follow the noun they describe in French, e.g:

**la pomme verte** → (the green apple)

French adjectives have to reflect the gender of the noun they describe. To make an adjective feminine, an **e** is added to the masculine form (where this does not already end in an **e**, e.g. **jeune**). A final consonant, which is usually silent in the masculine form, is pronounced in the feminine:

| masc. | fem. |
|---|---|
| **le livre vert**<br>(the green book)<br>luh leevr vehr | **la pomme verte**<br>(the green apple)<br>la pom vehrt |

To make an adjective plural, an **s** is added to the singular form: masculine plural – **verts** (remember the ending is still silent: vehr) or feminine plural – **vertes** (because of the **s**, the **t** is sounded: vehrt).

# My, your, his, her, their...

These words also depend on the gender and number of the noun they accompany and not on the sex of the 'owner'.

| | with masc. sing. noun | with fem. sing. noun | with plural noun |
|---|---|---|---|
| my | **mon** | **ma** | **mes** |
| your (familiar sing.) | **ton** | **ta** | **tes** |
| his/her | **son** | **sa** | **ses** |
| our | **notre** | **notre** | **nos** |
| your (polite/pl.) | **votre** | **votre** | **vos** |
| their | **leur** | **leur** | **leurs** |

e.g. **la clé** (key) — **sa clé** (his/her key)
**le passeport** (passport) — **son passeport** (his/her passport)
**les billets** (tickets) — **ses billets** (his/her tickets)

Grammar

# Pronouns

| subject | | object | |
|---|---|---|---|
| I | **je, j'** | me | **me, m'** |
| you (familiar sing.) | **tu** | you | **te, t'** |
| you (polite/pl.) | **vous** | you | **vous** |
| he/it | **il** | him/it | **la, l'** |
| she/it | **elle** | her/it | **la, l'** |
| we | **nous** | us | **nous** |
| they (masc.) | **ils** | them | **les** |
| they (fem.) | **elles** | them | **les** |

In French there are two words for *you* – **tu** and **vous**. **Tu** is the familiar form, which is used with people you know well (friends and family), children and animals. **Vous**, as well as being the plural form of *you*, is also the polite way of addressing someone. You should take care to use this form until the other person invites you to use the more familiar **tu**.

Object pronouns are placed before the verb, e.g.

| | |
|---|---|
| **il vous aime** | (he loves you) |
| **nous la connaissons** | (we know her) |

However, in commands or requests, object pronouns follow the verb, e.g.

**écoutez-le** (listen to him)
**aidez-moi** (help me)

This does not apply to negative commands or requests, e.g.

**ne le faites pas** (don't do it)

# Verbs

There are three main patterns of endings for verbs in French – those ending -**er**, -**ir** and -**re** in the dictionary.

| | |
|---|---|
| **donner** | **to give** |
| **je donne** | I give |
| **tu donnes** | you give |
| **il/elle donne** | he/she gives |
| **nous donnons** | we give |
| **vous donnez** | you give |
| **ils/elles donnent** | they give |

| | |
|---|---|
| **finir** | **to finish** |
| **je finis** | I finish |
| **tu finis** | you finish |
| **il/elle finit** | he/she finishes |
| **nous finissons** | we finish |
| **vous finissez** | you finish |
| **ils/elles finissent** | they finish |

| | |
|---|---|
| **répondre** | **to reply** |
| **je réponds** | I reply |
| **tu réponds** | you reply |
| **il/elle répond** | he/she replies |
| **nous répondons** | we reply |
| **vous répondez** | you reply |
| **ils/elles répondent** | they reply |

# Irregular verbs

Among the most important irregular verbs are the following:

| | |
|---|---|
| **être** | **to be** |
| **je suis** | I am |
| **tu es** | you are |
| **il/elle est** | he/she is |
| **nous sommes** | we are |
| **vous êtes** | you are |
| **ils/elles sont** | they are |

| | |
|---|---|
| **avoir** | **to have** |
| **j'ai** | I have |
| **tu as** | you have |
| **il/elle a** | he/she has |
| **nous avons** | we have |
| **vous avez** | you have |
| **ils/elles ont** | they have |

| | |
|---|---|
| **aller** | **to go** |
| **je vais** | I go |
| **tu vas** | you go |
| **il/elle va** | he/she goes |
| **nous allons** | we go |
| **vous allez** | you go |
| **ils/elles vont** | they go |

| | |
|---|---|
| **pouvoir** | **to be able** |
| **je peux** | I can |
| **tu peux** | you can |
| **il/elle peut** | he/she can |
| **nous pouvons** | we can |
| **vous pouvez** | you can |
| **ils/elles peuvent** | they can |

# Past tense

To form the simple past tense of most verbs, e.g. *I finished/I have finished*, combine the present tense of the verb **avoir** (to have) with the past participle of the verb (**donné**, **fini**, **répondu**), e.g.

| | |
|---|---|
| **j'ai donné** | I gave/I have given |
| **j'ai fini** | I finished/I have finished |
| **j'ai répondu** | I replied/I have replied |

Not all verbs take **avoir** as their auxiliary verb; some verbs take **être** (**je suis...**, **il est...**, etc.). These are intransitive verbs (which have no object), e.g.

| | |
|---|---|
| **je suis allé** | I went |
| **je suis né** | I was born |

When the auxiliary verb **être** is used, the past participle (**allé**, **né**, etc.) becomes adjectival and agrees with the subject of the verb, e.g.

| | |
|---|---|
| **nous sommes allés** | we went *(plural)* |
| **je suis née** | I was born *(female)* |

# Public holidays

In France public holidays are taken on the day on which they fall. Many of the larger shops now open on public holidays, but it is always best to check before you go.

When a public holiday falls on a Tuesday or Thursday, it is common for people to take the Monday or the Friday off as well. This is known as **faire le pont** (making a bridge).

| | |
|---|---|
| January 1st | **Le Jour de l'An** New Year's Day |
| March or April | **Le Lundi de Pâques** Easter Monday |
| May 1st | **La Fête du Travail** Labour Day/May Day |
| May 8th | **Le huit mai** Victory Day |
| April or May (40 days after Easter) | **L'Ascension** Ascension |
| May or June (49 days after Easter) | **Le Lundi de Pentecôte** Whit Monday (no longer an official holiday, but many employees are still given the day off) |
| July 14th | **La Fête Nationale** Bastille Day |
| August 15th | **L'Assomption** Assumption |
| November 1st | **La Toussaint** All Saints' Day |
| November 11th | **L'Armistice 1918** Armistice Day |
| December 25th | **Noël** Christmas Day |

# English - French



## A

| | | |
|---|---|---|
| **a(n)** | un *m*/une *f* | uñ/ewn |
| **able:** | | |
| ***to be able to*** | pouvoir | poo-vwar |
| **about** (approximately) | vers; environ | vehr; ahñ-vee-roñ |
| (concerning) | au sujet de | oh sew-zheh duh |
| **above** | au-dessus (de) | oh duh-sew (duh) |
| **abroad** | à l'étranger | a lay-trahñ-zhay |
| **to accept** | accepter | ak-sep-tay |
| **access** | l'accès *m* | ak-seh |
| **accident** | l'accident *m* | ak-see-dahñ |
| **accident & emergency department** | les urgences | ewr-zhahñs |
| **accommodation** | le logement | lozh-mahñ |
| **address** | l'adresse *f* | a-dres |
| ***what is the address?*** | quelle est l'adresse? | kel ay la-dres? |
| **admission charge** | l'entrée *f* | ahñ-tray |
| **adult** | l'adulte *m/f* | a-dewlt |
| **aeroplane** | l'avion *m* | a-vyoñ |
| **after** | après | apreh |
| **afternoon** | l'après-midi *m* | a-preh mee-dee |
| ***in the afternoon*** | dans l'après-midi | dahñ la-preh mee-dee |
| ***this afternoon*** | cet après-midi | set a-preh mee-dee |
| **again** | encore | ahñkor |
| **against** | contre | koñtr |
| **age** | l'âge *m* | azh |
| **ago: *a week ago*** | il y a une semaine | eel ya ewn suh-men |
| **air-conditioning** | la climatisation | klee-ma-tee-za-syoñ |
| **airplane** | l'avion *m* | a-vyoñ |
| **airport** | l'aéroport *m* | a-ay-ro-por |
| **airport bus** | la navette pour l'aéroport | navet poor la-ay-ro-por |
| **alarm** | l'alarme *f* | a-larm |
| **alarm clock** | le réveil | ray-vay |

| | | |
|---|---|---|
| **alcohol-free** | sans alcool | sahñ zal-kol |
| **all** | tout(e)/tous/ toutes | too(t)/toos/toot |
| **allergic** | allergique | a-lehr-zheek |
| ***I'm allergic to...*** | je suis allergique à... | zhuh swee za-lehr-zheek a... |
| **allergy** | l'allergie *f* | a-lehr-zhee |
| **all right** (agreed) | d'accord | dakor |
| ***are you all right?*** | ça va? | sa va? |
| **almost** | presque | presk |
| **already** | déjà | day-zha |
| **also** | aussi | oh-see |
| **always** | toujours | too-zhoor |
| **a.m.** | du matin | dew ma-tañ |
| **ambulance** | l'ambulance *f* | ahñ-bew-lahñs |
| **America** | l'Amérique *f* | a-may-reek |
| **American** | américain(e) | a-may-ree-kañ/ ken |
| **and** | et | ay |
| **another** | un(e) autre | uñ/ewn ohtr |
| **antibiotic** | l'antibiotique *m* | ahñ-tee-bee-o-teek |
| **antihistamine** | l'antihista-minique *m* | ahñ-tee-ee-sta-mee-neek |
| **any** | de (du/de la/des) | duh (dew/duh la/day) |
| **anything** | quelque chose | kel-kuh shoz |
| **apartment** | l'appartement *m* | a-par-tuh-mahñ |
| **apple** | la pomme | pom |
| **appointment** | le rendez-vous | rahñ-day-voo |
| **approximately** | environ | ahñ-vee-roñ |
| **April** | avril | av-reel |
| **arm** | le bras | bra |
| **to arrange** | arranger | a-rahñ-zhay |
| **arrival** | l'arrivée *f* | a-ree-vay |
| **to arrive** | arriver | a-ree-vay |
| **to ask** | demander | duh-mahñ-day |
| **aspirin** | l'aspirine *f* | as-pee-reen |
| **asthma** | l'asthme *m* | as-muh |
| ***I have asthma*** | je suis asthmatique | zhuh swee zas-ma-teek |

| | | |
|---|---|---|
| **at** | à | a |
| ***at my/your home*** | chez moi/vous | shay mwa/voo |
| ***at 8 o'clock*** | à huit heures | a weet ur |
| ***at night*** | la nuit | la nwee |
| **August** | août | oo(t) |
| **Australia** | l'Australie *f* | oh-stra-lee |
| **Australian** | australien(ne) | oh-stra-lyañ/lee-en |
| **autumn** | l'automne *m* | oh-ton |
| **available** | disponible | dees-poh-neebl |

## B

| | | |
|---|---|---|
| **baby** | le bébé | bay-bay |
| **baby milk** (formula) | le lait maternisé | leh ma-tehr-nee-zay |
| **baby's bottle** | le biberon | bee-broñ |
| **back** (of body) | le dos | doh |
| **backpack** | le sac à dos | sak a doh |
| **bad** (food, weather) | mauvais(e) | moh-veh/vez |
| **bag** | le sac | sak |
| **baggage** | les bagages | ba-gazh |
| **bank** (money) | la banque | bahñk |
| (river) | la rive; le bord | reev; bor |
| **banknote** | le billet de banque | bee-yeh duh bahñk |
| **bar** | le bar | bar |
| **bath** | le bain | bañ |
| **bathroom** | la salle de bains | sal duh bañ |
| **battery** (for radio, camera, etc.) | la pile | peel |
| **B&B** | la chambre d'hôte | shahñbr doht |
| **to be** | être | etr |
| **beach** | la plage | plazh |
| **beautiful** | beau (belle) | boh (bel) |
| **because** | parce que | pars kuh |
| **bed** | le lit | lee |
| ***double bed*** | le grand lit; le lit de deux personnes | grahñ lee; lee duh duh pehr-son |

| | | |
|---|---|---|
| ***single bed*** | le lit d'une personne | lee dewn pehr-son |
| ***twin beds*** | les lits jumeaux | lee zhew-moh |
| **bedroom** | la chambre (à coucher) | shahñbr (a koo-shay) |
| **beer** | la bière | byehr |
| **before** | avant | a-vahñ |
| **to begin** | commencer | koh-mahñ-say |
| **behind** | derrière | deh-ree-yehr |
| **to belong to** | appartenir à | a-par-tuh-neer a |
| **below** | sous | soo |
| **beside** (next to) | à côté de | a koh-tay duh |
| **better (than)** | meilleur(e) (que) | meh-yur (kuh) |
| **between** | entre | ahñtr |
| **bicycle** | le vélo | vay-loh |
| **big** | grand(e); gros(se) | grahñ(d); groh(s) |
| **bigger (than)** | plus grand(e) (que); plus gros(se) (que) | plew grahñ(d) (kuh); plew groh(s) (kuh) |
| **bill** (restaurant) | l'addition *f* | a-dee-syoñ |
| (hotel) | la note | not |
| (for work done) | la facture | fak-tewr |
| **bin** (dustbin) | la poubelle | poo-bel |
| **bit: *a bit (of)*** | un peu (de) | uñ puh (duh) |
| **bite** (animal) | la morsure | mor-sewr |
| (insect) | la piqûre | pee-kewr |
| **black** | noir(e) | nwar |
| **blanket** | la couverture | koo-vehr-tewr |
| **blind** (person) | aveugle | a-vuh-gluh |
| **blocked** | bouché(e) | boo-shay |
| **blood** | le sang | sahñ |
| **blue** | bleu(e) | bluh |
| **to board** (plane, train, etc.) | embarquer | ahñ-bar-kay |
| **boarding card** | la carte d'embarquement | kart dahñ-bar-kuh mahñ |
| **boat** | le bateau | ba-toh |
| (rowing) | la barque | bark |
| **book** | le livre | leevr |
| **to book** (reserve) | réserver | ray-sehr-vay |

# English - French

| | | |
|---|---|---|
| **booking** | la reservation | ray-sehr-va-syoñ |
| **booking office** | le bureau de location | bew-roh duh lo-ka-syoñ |
| **bookshop** | la librairie | lee-breh-ree |
| **to borrow** | emprunter | ahñ-pruñ-tay |
| **bottle** | la bouteille | boo-tay-yuh |
| **boy** | le garçon | gar-soñ |
| **boyfriend** | le copain | ko-pañ |
| **bread** | le pain | pañ |
| **bread roll** | le petit pain | puh-tee pañ |
| **breakdown** (car) | la panne | pan |
| **breakfast** | le petit déjeuner | puh-tee day-zhuh-nay |
| **bridge** | le pont | poñ |
| **briefcase** | la serviette | sehr-vyet |
| **Britain** | la Grande-Bretagne | grahñd-bruh-tan-yuh |
| **British** | britannique | bree-ta-neek |
| **broken** | cassé(e) | ka-say |
| ***my leg is broken*** | je me suis cassé(e) la jambe | zhuh muh swee ka-say la zhahñb |
| **broken down** (car, etc.) | en panne | ahñ pan |
| **brother** | le frère | frehr |
| **brown** | marron | ma-roñ |
| **building** | l'immeuble *m* | ee-muh-bluh |
| **burger** | le hamburger | añ-bewr-gehr |
| **bus** | le bus | bews |
| (coach) | le car | kar |
| ***bus station*** | la gare routière | gar roo-tyehr |
| ***bus stop*** | l'arrêt de bus *m* | a-reh duh bews |
| ***bus ticket*** | le ticket de bus | tee-keh duh bews |
| **busy** | occupé(e) | o-kew-pay |
| **but** | mais | meh |
| **to buy** | acheter | a-shtay |
| **by** (via) | par | par |
| (beside) | à côté de | a koh-tay duh |
| ***by bus*** | en bus | ahñ bews |
| ***by car*** | en voiture | ahñ vwa-tewr |
| ***by ship*** | en bateau | ahñ ba-toh |
| ***by train*** | en train | ahñ trañ |

## C

| English | French | Pronunciation |
|---|---|---|
| **cab** (taxi) | le taxi | tak-see |
| **café** | le café | ka-fay |
| ***internet café*** | le cybercafé | see-behr-ka-fay |
| **cake** (large) | le gâteau | ga-toh |
| (small) | la pâtisserie; le petit gateau | pa-tee-sree; puh-tee ga-toh |
| **call** (telephone) | l'appel *m* | a-pel |
| **to call** (speak, phone) | appeler | a-puh-lay |
| **camera** | l'appareil photo *m* | a-pa-ray foh-toh |
| **camping gas** | le butane | bew-tan |
| **campsite** | le camping | kahñ-peeng |
| **can** (to be able to) | pouvoir | poo-vwar |
| (to know how to) | savoir | sa-vwar |
| ***I can*** | je peux/sais | zhuh puh/seh |
| ***we can*** | nous pouvons/ savons | noo poo-voñ/ sa-voñ |
| **can** | la boîte | bwat |
| **Canada** | le Canada | ka-na-da |
| **Canadian** | canadien(ne) | ka-na-dyañ/dyen |
| **to cancel** | annuler | a-new-lay |
| **car** | la voiture | vwa-tewr |
| **car hire** | la location de voitures | lo-ka-syoñ duh vwa-tewr |
| **car insurance** | l'assurance automobile *f* | a-sew-rahñs oh-toh-mo-beel |
| **car keys** | les clés de voiture | klay duh vwa-tewr |
| **car park** | le parking | par-keeng |
| **card** | la carte | kart |
| **careful:** | | |
| ***to be careful*** | faire attention | fehr a-tahñ-syoñ |
| ***be careful!*** | attention! | a-tahñ-syoñ! |
| **carpet** (rug) | le tapis | ta-pee |
| (fitted) | la moquette | mo-ket |
| **carriage** (railway) | la voiture | vwa-tewr |
| **case** (suitcase) | la valise | va-leez |
| **cash** | l'argent liquide *m* | ar-zhahñ lee-keed |

| | | |
| --- | --- | --- |
| **cash dispenser** (ATM) | le distributeur automatique (de billets) | dee-stree-bew-tur oh-toh-ma-teek (duh bee-yeh) |
| **castle** | le château | sha-toh |
| **catch** (bus, train) | prendre | prahñdr |
| **cathedral** | la cathédrale | ka-tay-dral |
| **Catholic** | catholique | ka-toh-leek |
| **cellphone** | le (téléphone) portable | (tay-lay-fon) por-tabl |
| **cent** (euro) | un centime | uñ sahñ-teem |
| **central** | central(e) | sahñ-tral |
| **central heating** | le chauffage central | shoh-fazh sahñ-tral |
| **centre** | le centre | sahñtr |
| **cereal** | la céréale | say-ray-al |
| **chair** | la chaise | shez |
| **change** (coins) | la monnaie | mo-neh |
| ***to change*** | changer | shahñ-zhay |
| ***to change money*** | changer de l'argent | shahñ-zhay duh ar-zhahñ |
| ***to change clothes*** | se changer | suh shahñ-zhay |
| ***to change trains*** | changer de train | shahñ-zhay duh trañ |
| **Channel** (English) | la Manche | mahñsh |
| **charge** (fee) | le prix | pree |
| **to charge a phone** | recharger un téléphone | ruh-shar-zhay uñ tay-lay-fon |
| **cheap** | bon marché | boñ mar-shay |
| **cheaper** | moins cher | mwañ shehr |
| **to check** | vérifier | vay-ree-fyay |
| **to check in** | enregistrer | ahñ-ruh-zhee-stray |
| **check-in (desk)** | l'enregistrement | ahñ-ruh-zhees-truh-mahñ |
| (at hotel) | la réception | ray-sep-syoñ |
| **cheers!** | santé! | sahñ-tay! |
| **chemist's** | la pharmacie | far-ma-see |
| **cheque** | le chèque | shek |
| **child** | l'enfant *m* | ahñ-fahñ |
| **children** | les enfants | ahñ-fahñ |

| | | |
|---|---|---|
| ***for children*** | pour enfants | poor ahñ-fahñ |
| **chilli** (fruit) | le piment | pee-mahñ |
| (dish) | le chili con carne | shee-lee kon kar-nay |
| **chips** | les frites | freet |
| **chocolate** | le chocolat | sho-ko-la |
| ***drinking-chocolate*** | le chocolat en poudre | sho-ko-la ahñ poodr |
| ***hot chocolate*** | le chocolat chaud | sho-ko-la shoh |
| **chocolates** | les chocolats | sho-ko-la |
| **to choose** | choisir | shwa-zeer |
| **Christmas** | Noël *m* | noh-el |
| **church** | l'église *f* | ay-gleez |
| **cigarette** | la cigarette | see-ga-ret |
| **cigarette lighter** | le briquet | bree-keh |
| **cinema** | le cinéma | see-nay-ma |
| **city** | la ville | veel |
| **city centre** | le centre-ville | sahñtr-veel |
| **clean** | propre | propr |
| **to clean** | nettoyer | neh-twa-yay |
| **clock** | l'horloge *f* | or-lozh |
| **close by** | proche | prosh |
| **closed** (shop, etc.) | fermé(e) | fehr-may |
| **clothes** | les vêtements | vet-mahñ |
| **coach** (bus) | le car; l'autocar *m* | kar; loh-toh-kar |
| **coast** | la côte | koht |
| **coat** | le manteau | mahñ-toh |
| **coffee** | le café | ka-fay |
| ***white coffee*** | le café au lait | ka-fay oh leh |
| ***black coffee*** | le café noir | ka-fay nwar |
| ***cappuccino*** | le cappuccino | ka-pew-chee-noh |
| ***decaffeinated coffee*** | le café décaféiné/ déca | ka-fay day-ka-fay-ee-nay/ day-ka |
| **coin** | la pièce de monnaie | pyes duh mo-neh |
| **Coke®** | le Coca® | ko-ka |
| **cold** | froid(e) | frwa(d) |
| ***I'm cold*** | j'ai froid | zhay frwa |

| English | French | |
|---|---|---|
| ***it's cold*** | il fait froid | eel feh frwa |
| **cold** (illness) | le rhume | rewm |
| **I have a cold** | j'ai un rhume | zhay uñ rewm |
| **to come** | venir | vuh-neer |
| (to arrive) | arriver | a-ree-vay |
| ***to come back*** | revenir | ruh-vuh-neer |
| ***to come in*** | entrer | ahñ-tray |
| ***come in!*** | entrez! | ahñ-tray! |
| **comfortable** | confortable | coñ-for-tabl |
| **company** (firm) | la compagnie; la société | koñ-pa-nyee; so-syay-tay |
| **to complain** | faire une réclamation | fehr ewn ray-kla-ma-syoñ |
| **complaint** | la plainte | plañt |
| **compulsory** | obligatoire | ob-lee-ga-twar |
| **computer** | l'ordinateur *m* | or-dee-na-tur |
| **concert** | le concert | koñ-sehr |
| **concession** | la réduction | ray-dewk-syoñ |
| **conference** | la conférence | koñ-fay-rahñs |
| **to confirm** | confirmer | koñ-feer-may |
| **confirmation** | la confirmation | koñ-feer-ma-syoñ |
| **consulate** | le consulat | koñ-sew-la |
| **contact lenses** | les verres de contact | vehr duh koñ-takt |
| **convenient:** | | |
| ***it's not convenient*** | ça ne m'arrange pas | nuh ma-rahñzh pa |
| **to cook** (be cooking) | cuisiner | kwee-zee-nay |
| ***to cook a meal*** | préparer un repas | pray-pa-ray uñ ruh-pa |
| **cooker** | la cuisinière | kwee-zee-nyehr |
| **to copy** | copier | ko-pyay |
| **corner** | le coin | kwañ |
| **corridor** | le couloir | koo-lwar |
| **cosmetics** | les produits de beauté | pro-dwee duh boh-tay |
| **cost** | le coût | koo |
| **to cost** | coûter | koo-tay |
| ***how much does it cost?*** | ça coûte combien? | sa koot koñ-byañ |

| | | |
|---|---|---|
| **costume** (swimming) | le maillot (de bain) | ma-yoh (duh bañ) |
| **cough** | la toux | too |
| **cough mixture** | le sirop pour la toux | see-roh poor la too |
| **counter** (shop, etc.) | le comptoir | koñ-twar |
| **country** (not town) | la campagne | kahñ-pa-nyuh |
| (nation) | le pays | pay-ee |
| **couple** (two people) | le couple | koop-luh |
| ***a couple of...*** | deux... | duh... |
| **course** (syllabus) | le cours | koor |
| (of meal) | le plat | pla |
| **cover charge** (restaurant) | le couvert | koo-vehr |
| **crash** (car) | l'accident *m*; la collision | lak-see-dahñ; ko-lee-zyoñ |
| **cream** (food, lotion) | la crème | krem |
| **credit** (on mobile phone) | les unités *(fpl)* | ew-nee-tay |
| **credit card** | la carte de crédit | kart duh kray-dee |
| **crisps** | les chips | sheep |
| **to cross** | traverser | tra-vehr-say |
| **crossing** (by sea) | la traversée | tra-vehr-say |
| **crossroads** | le carrefour; le croisement | kar-foor; krwaz-mahñ |
| **cup** | la tasse | tas |
| **customer** | le/la client(e) | klee-ahñ(t) |
| **customs** | la douane | dwan |
| (duty) | les droits de douane | drwa duh dwan |
| **to cut** | couper | koo-pay |
| **to cycle** | faire du vélo | fehr dew vay-loh |

## D

| | | |
|---|---|---|
| **dairy produce** | les produits laitiers | pro-dwee leh-tyay |
| **dangerous** | dangereux (-euse) | dahñ-zhuh-ruh(z) |
| **date** | la date | dat |
| ***date of birth*** | la date de naissance | dat duh neh-sahñs |

| English | French | |
|---|---|---|
| **daughter** | la fille | fee |
| **day** | le jour | zhoor |
| ***per day*** | par jour | par zhoor |
| ***every day*** | tous les jours | too lay zhoor |
| **deaf** | sourd(e) | soor(d) |
| **dear** (expensive; in letter) | cher (chère) | shehr |
| **debit card** | la carte de paiement | kart duh pay-mahñ |
| **decaffeinated coffee** | le café décaféiné; le déca | ka-fay day-ka-fay-ee-nay; day-ka |
| **December** | décembre | day-sahñbr |
| **to declare** | déclarer | day-kla-ray |
| ***nothing to declare*** | rien à déclarer | ryañ na day-kla-ray |
| **delayed** | retardé(e) | ruh-tar-day |
| **delicatessen** | l'épicerie fine *f* | ay-pees-ree feen |
| **delicious** | délicieux(-euse) | day-lee-syuh(z) |
| **deodorant** | le déodorant | day-oh-doh-rahñ |
| **to depart** | partir | par-teer |
| **department store** | le grand magasin | grahñ ma-ga-zañ |
| **departure** | le départ | day-par |
| **departure lounge** | la salle d'embarquement | sal dahñ-bar-kuh-mahñ |
| **desk** (furniture) | le bureau | bew-roh |
| (information) | l'accueil *m* | a-key |
| **dessert** | le dessert | deh-sehr |
| **to develop** (photos) | faire développer | fehr day-vloh-pay |
| **diabetic** | diabétique | dee-a-bay-teek |
| ***I'm diabetic*** | je suis diabétique | zhuh swee dee-a-bay-teek |
| **to dial** (a number) | composer | koñ-poh-say |
| **dialling code** | l'indicatif *m* | añ-dee-ka-teef |
| **diesel** | le diesel; le gasoil | dee-ay-zel; ga-zwal |
| **diet** | le régime | ray-zheem |
| ***I'm on a diet*** | je suis au régime | zhuh swee zoh ray-zheem |
| **different** | différent(e) | dee-fay-rahñ(t) |

**difficult** difficile dee-fee-seel
**dining room** la salle à manger sal a mahñ-zhay
**dinner** (evening meal) le dîner dee-nay
***to have dinner*** dîner dee-nay
**direct** (train, etc.) direct(e) dee-rekt
**directions** les indications añ-dee-ka-syoñ
***to ask for directions*** demander le chemin duh-mahñ-day luh shuh-mañ
**dirty** sale sal
**disabled** (person) handicapé(e) ahñ-dee-ka-pay
**discount** le rabais ra-beh
**to disturb** déranger day-rahñ-zhay
**to dive** plonger ploñ-zhay
**divorced** divorcé(e) dee-vor-say
**dizzy** pris(e) de vertige pree(z) duh vehr-teezh
**to do** faire fehr
**doctor** le médecin may-dsañ
**documents** les papiers pa-pyay
**dollar** le dollar do-lar
**door** la porte port
**double bed** le grand lit grahñ lee
**double room** la chambre pour deux personnes shahñbr poor duh pehr-son
**down:**
***to go down*** descendre deh-sahñdr
**downstairs** en bas ahñ ba
**dress** la robe rob
**drink** la boisson bwa-soñ
**to drink** boire bwar
**drinking water** l'eau potable *f* oh po-tabl
**to drive** conduire koñ-dweer
**driver** (of car) le conducteur; la conductrice koñ-dewk-tur; koñ-dewk-trees
**driving licence** le permis de conduire pehr-mee duh koñ-dweer
**dry** sec (sèche) sek/sesh
**to dry** sécher say-shay
**dry-cleaner's** le pressing preh-seeng
**during** pendant pahñ-dahñ
**duty-free** hors taxe or tax

## E

| | | |
|---|---|---|
| **each** | chacun/ chacune | sha-kuñ/ sha-kewn |
| **earlier** | plus tôt | plew-toh |
| **early** | tôt | toh |
| **east** | l'est *m* | est |
| **Easter** | Pâques | pak |
| **easy** | facile | fa-seel |
| **to eat** | manger | mahñ-zhay |
| **either ... or** | soit ... soit | swa ... swa |
| **Elastoplast®** | le sparadrap | spa-ra-dra |
| **electric** | électrique | ay-lek-treek |
| **electricity** | l'électricité *f* | ay-lek-tree-see-tay |
| **electronic** | électronique | ay-lek-tro-neek |
| **elevator** | l'ascenseur *m* | a-sahñ-sur |
| **e-mail** | l'e-mail *m* | ee-mehl |
| **to e-mail** | envoyer un e-mail | ahñ-vwa-yay uñ nee-mehl |
| **e-mail address** (on forms) | l'adresse électronique; le mél | a-dres ay-lek-tro-neek; mayl |
| **embassy** | l'ambassade *f* | ahñ-ba-sad |
| **emergency** | l'urgence *f* | ewr-zhahñs |
| **emergency exit** | la sortie de secours | sor-tee duh skoor |
| **end** | la fin | fañ |
| **engaged** (to be married) | fiancé(e) | fee-ahñ-say |
| (phone, toilet, etc.) | occupé(e) | o-kew-pay |
| **engine** | le moteur | moh-tur |
| **England** | l'Angleterre *f* | ahñ-gluh-tehr |
| **English** | anglais(e) | ahñ-gleh(z) |
| (language) | l'anglais *m* | ahñ-gleh |
| **to enjoy** | aimer | ay-may |
| ***I enjoyed the trip*** | le voyage m'a plu | vwa-yazh ma plew |
| **enough** | assez | a-say |
| ***that's enough*** | ça suffit | sa sew-fee |
| **enquiry desk** | les renseignements | rahñ-seh-nyuh-mahñ |
| **to enter** | entrer | ahñ-tray |
| **entrance** | l'entrée *f* | ahñ-tray |

| | | |
|---|---|---|
| **entrance fee** | le prix d'entrée | pree dahñ-tray |
| **equal** | égal | ay-gal |
| **error** | l'erreur *f* | eh-rur |
| **essential** | indispensable | añ-dee-spahñ-sabl |
| **euro** (unit of currency) | l'euro *m* | uh-roh |
| **Europe** | l'Europe *f* | ur-op |
| **European** | européen(ne) | ur-o-pay-añ/en |
| **evening** | le soir | swar |
| ***this evening*** | ce soir | suh swar |
| ***in the evening*** | le soir | swar |
| **every** | chaque | shak |
| **everyone** | tout le monde | too luh moñd |
| **everything** | tout | too |
| **everywhere** | partout | pa-rtoo |
| **example:** | | |
| ***for example*** | par exemple | par eg-zahñpl |
| **excellent** | excellent(e) | ek-seh-lahñ(t) |
| **exchange** | l'échange *m* | ay-shahñzh |
| **exchange rate** | le taux de change | toh duh shahñzh |
| **to exchange** | échanger | ay-shahñ-zhay |
| **to excuse:** | | |
| ***excuse me!*** | excusez-moi! | ek-skew-zay-mwa! |
| (to get by) | pardon! | par-doñ! |
| **exhibition** | l'exposition *f* | ek-spoh-zee-syoñ |
| **exit** | la sortie | sor-tee |
| **expensive** | cher (chère) | shehr |
| **to expire** (ticket, passport, etc.) | expirer | ek-spee-ray |
| **to explain** | expliquer | ek-splee-kay |
| **extra** (additional) | supplémentaire | sew-play-mahñ-tehr |
| (more) | de plus | duh plews |
| **eye** | l'œil *m* | uhy |
| **eyes** | les yeux | yuh |

## F

| | | |
|---|---|---|
| **face** | le visage | vee-zazh |
| **facilities** | les installations | añ-sta-la-syoñ |

| | | |
|---|---|---|
| **to fall** | tomber | toñ-bay |
| ***he has fallen*** | il est tombé | eel eh toñ-bay |
| **family** | la famille | fa-mee |
| **far** | loin | lwañ |
| ***is it far?*** | c'est loin? | say lwañ? |
| **fare** (bus, etc.) | le prix du billet | pree dew bee-yeh |
| **farm** | la ferme | fehrm |
| **fast** | rapide | ra-peed |
| ***too fast*** | trop vite | troh veet |
| **father** | le père | pehr |
| **fault** (defect) | un défaut | uñ day-foh |
| ***it's not my fault*** | ce n'est pas de ma faute | suh nay pa duh ma foht |
| **fax** | le fax | fax |
| ***by fax*** | par fax | par fax |
| ***fax number*** | le numéro de fax | new-may-roh duh fax |
| **to fax** (document) | faxer | fak-say |
| (person) | envoyer un fax à | ahñ-vwa-yay uñ fax a |
| **February** | février | fay-vryay |
| **to feel** | sentir | sahñ-teer |
| ***I feel sick*** | j'ai la nausée | zhay la noh-say |
| ***I don't feel well*** | je ne me sens pas bien | zhuh nuh muh sahñ pa byañ |
| **feet** | les pieds | lay pyay |
| **fever** | la fièvre | fyevr |
| **few** | peu de | puh duh |
| ***a few*** | quelques-un(e)s | kel-kuh-zuñ/zewn |
| **fiancé(e)** | le fiancé; la fiancée | fee-yahñ-say |
| **to fill in** (form) | remplir | rahñ-pleer |
| **film** (movie) | le film | feelm |
| (for camera) | la pellicule | peh-lee-kewl |
| **to find** | trouver | troo-vay |
| **fine** (penalty) | la contravention | koñ-tra-vahñ-syoñ |
| **finger** | le doigt | dwa |
| **to finish** | finir | fee-neer |
| **finished** | fini(e) | fee-nee |
| **fire** | le feu; l'incendie *m* | fuh; añ-sahñ-dee |

| English | French | Pronunciation |
|---|---|---|
| **fire alarm** | l'alarme d'incendie *f* | a-larm dañ-sahñ-dee |
| **fire escape** (staircase) | l'échelle de secours *f* | ay-shel duh skoor |
| **first** | premier(-ière) | pruh-myay/myehr |
| **first aid** | les premiers secours | pruh-myay skoor |
| **first-class** | de première classe | duh pruh-myehr klas |
| **first name** | le prénom | pray-noñ |
| **fish** | le poisson | pwa-soñ |
| **fishing** | la pêche | pesh |
| ***to go fishing*** | aller à la pêche | a-lay a la pesh |
| **fit** (medical) | l'attaque *f* | a-tak |
| **to fit:** | | |
| ***it doesn't fit me*** | ça ne me va pas | sa nuh muh va pa |
| **to fix** (repair) | réparer | ray-pa-ray |
| ***can you fix it?*** | vous pouvez le réparer? | voo poo-vay luh ray-pa-ray? |
| **flash** (for camera) | le flash | flash |
| **flat** (apartment) | l'appartement *m* | a-par-tuh-mahñ |
| **flavour** | le goût | goo |
| (of ice cream, etc.) | le parfum | par-fuñ |
| **flight** | le vol | vol |
| **floor** (of room) | le sol | sol |
| (storey) | l'étage | ay-tazh |
| ***(on the) ground floor*** | (au) rez-de-chaussée | (oh) ray-duh-shoh-say |
| ***(on the) first floor*** | (au) premier étage | (oh) pruh-myayr ay-tazh |
| **flour** | la farine | fa-reen |
| **flower** | la fleur | flur |
| **flu** | la grippe | greep |
| **to fly** (person) | aller en avion | a-lay ahñ na-vyoñ |
| (bird) | voler | vo-lay |
| **food** | la nourriture | noo-ree-tewr |
| **food poisoning** | l'intoxication alimentaire *f* | añ-tok-see-ka-syoñ a-lee-mahñ-tehr |
| **foot** | le pied | pyay |
| ***to go on foot*** | aller à pied | a-lay a pyay |
| **for** | pour | poor |

| | | |
|---|---|---|
| ***for me/you/us*** | pour moi/vous/ nous | poor mwa/voo/ noo |
| ***for him/her/ them*** | pour lui/elle/ eux | poor lwee/el/ uh |
| **forbidden** | interdit(e) | añ-tehr-dee(t) |
| **foreign** | étranger(-ère) | ay-trahñ-zhay/ zhehr |
| **fork** (for eating) | la fourchette | foor-shet |
| **form** (document) | le formulaire | for-mew-lehr |
| (shape, style) | la forme | form |
| **fortnight** | la quinzaine | kañ-zen |
| **fountain** | la fontaine | foñ-ten |
| **fragile** | fragile | fra-zheel |
| **France** | la France | frahñs |
| ***in/to France*** | en France | ahñ frahñs |
| **free** (not occupied) | libre | leebr |
| (costing nothing) | gratuit(e) | gra-twee(t) |
| **freezer** | le congélateur | koñ-zhayla-tur |
| **French** | français(e) | frahñ-seh(z) |
| (language) | le français | frahñ-seh |
| ***French fries*** | les frites | freet |
| **fresh** | frais (fraîche) | freh/fresh |
| **Friday** | vendredi | vahñ-druh-dee |
| **fried** | frit(e) | free(t) |
| **friend** *m/f* | l'ami(e) | a-mee |
| **from** | de | duh |
| ***I'm from England*** | je suis anglais(e) | zhuh swee zahñ-gleh(z) |
| ***I'm from Scotland*** | je suis écossais(e) | zhuh swee zay-ko-seh(z) |
| **front** | le devant | duh-vahñ |
| ***in front of...*** | devant... | duh-vahñ... |
| **frozen** | gelé(e) | zhuh-lay |
| **fruit** | le fruit | frwee |
| ***fruit juice*** | le jus de fruit | jew duh frwee |
| **full** (container) | plein(e) | plañ/plen |
| (e.g. hall) | complet(-ète) | koñ-pleh(t) |
| ***full board*** | la pension complète | pahñ-syoñ koñ-plet |
| **furnished** | meublé(e) | muh-blay |

## G

| | | |
|---|---|---|
| **gallery** | la galerie | gal-ree |
| **game** | le jeu | zhuh |
| **garage** (for petrol) | la station-service | sta-syoñ-sehr-vees |
| (for parking, repair) | le garage | ga-razh |
| **garden** | le jardin | zhar-dañ |
| **garlic** | l'ail *m* | a-yuh |
| **gate** | la porte | port |
| **gents'** (toilet) | les toilettes pour hommes | twa-let poor om |
| **German** | allemand(e) | al-mahñ(d) |
| (language) | l'allemand *m* | al-mahñ |
| **Germany** | l'Allemagne *f* | a-luh-ma-nyuh |
| **to get** (obtain) | obtenir | ob-tuh-neer |
| (to fetch) | aller chercher | a-lay shehr-shay |
| **to get in** (vehicle) | monter | moñ-tay |
| **to get off** (bus, etc.) | descendre | deh-sahñdr |
| **gift** | le cadeau | ka-doh |
| **gift shop** | la boutique de souvenirs | boo-teek duh soo-vneer |
| **girl** | la fille | fee |
| **girlfriend** | la copine | ko-peen |
| **to give** | donner | do-nay |
| **to give back** | rendre | rahñdr |
| **glass** | le verre | vehr |
| ***a glass of water*** | un verre d'eau | uñ vehr doh |
| **glasses** (spectacles) | les lunettes | lew-net |
| **gluten** | le gluten | glew-ten |
| **to go** | aller | a-lay |
| ***I'm going to...*** (I will go to) | je vais à... | zhuh veh a... |
| ***I'm going to...*** (I intend to) | je vais... | zhuh veh... |
| ***we're going to hire a car*** | nous allons louer une voiture | noo za-loñ loo-ay ewn vwa-tewr |
| ***to go back*** | retourner | ruh-toor-nay |
| ***to go in*** | entrer | ahñ-tray |

| | | |
|---|---|---|
| ***to go out*** (leave) | sortir | sor-teer |
| **good** | bon (bonne) | boñ (bon) |
| ***(that's) good!*** | (c'est) bien! | (say) byañ! |
| ***good afternoon*** | bonjour | boñ-zhoor |
| ***goodbye*** | au revoir | oh ruh-vwar |
| ***good night*** | bonne nuit | bon nwee |
| **grandchildren** | les petits-enfants | puh-tee zahñ-fahñ |
| **grandparents** | les grands-parents | grahñ-pa-rahñ |
| **grape** | le raisin | reh-zañ |
| **great** (big) | grand(e) | grahñ(d) |
| (wonderful) | formidable | for-mee-dabl |
| **Great Britain** | la Grande-Bretagne | grahñd-bruh-ta-nyuh |
| **green** | vert(e) | vehr(t) |
| **greengrocer's** | le magasin de fruits et légumes | ma-ga-zañ duh frwee zay lay-gewm |
| **grilled** | grillé(e) | gree-yay |
| **grocer's** | l'épicerie *f* | ay-pee-sree |
| **ground floor** | le rez-de-chaussée | ray-duh-shoh-say |
| ***on the ground floor*** | au rez-de-chaussée | oh ray-duh-shoh-say |
| **group** | le groupe | groop |
| **guest** (in house) | l'invité(e) | añ-vee-tay |
| (in hotel) | le/la client(e) | klee-ahñ(t) |
| **guesthouse** | la pension | pahñ-syoñ |
| **guide** (tourist) | le/la guide | geed |
| **guidebook** | le guide | geed |
| **guided tour** | la visite guidée | vee-zeet gee-day |

## H

| | | |
|---|---|---|
| **hair** | les cheveux | shuh-vuh |
| **hairdryer** | le sèche-cheveux | sesh-shuh-vuh |
| **half** | la moitié | mwa-tyay |
| ***half an hour*** | une demi-heure | ewn duh-mee-ur |
| ***half board*** | la demi-pension | duh-mee-pahñ-syoñ |
| **ham** (cooked) | le jambon | zhahñ-boñ |
| (cured) | le jambon cru | zhahñ-boñ krew |

**hamburger** le hamburger ahñ-bur-ger
**hand** la main mañ
**handbag** le sac à main sak a mañ
**handicapped** handicapé(e) ahñ-dee-ka-pay
**to happen** arriver; se passer suh pa-say
***what happened?*** qu'est-ce qui s'est passé? kes kee say pa-say?
**happy** heureux(-euse) uh-ruh(z)
**hard** (not soft) dur(e) dewr
(not easy) difficile dee-fee-seel
**to have** avoir av-war
**to have to** devoir duh-vwar
**hay fever** le rhume des foins rewm day fwañ
**he** il eel
**head** la tête tet
**headache** le mal de tête mal duh tet
***I have a headache*** j'ai mal à la tête zhay mal a la tet
**health** la santé sahñ-tay
**to hear** entendre ahñ-tahñdr
**heart** le cœur kur
**heartburn** les brûlures d'estomac brew-lewr d'es-toh-ma
**heating** le chauffage shoh-fazh
**heavy** lourd(e) loor(d)
**hello** bonjour boñ-zhoor
(on telephone) allô? a-loh?
**help!** au secours! oh skoor!
***can you help me?*** vous pouvez m'aider? voo poo-vay meh-day?
**her** son/sa/ses soñ/sa/say
***her passport*** son passeport soñ pas-por
***her suitcases*** ses valises say va-leez
**herbal tea** la tisane tee-zan
**here** ici ee-see
***here is...*** voici... vwa-see...
**hi!** salut! sa-lew!
**high** haut(e) oh(t)
**him** lui lwee
**to hire** louer loo-ay

| | | |
|---|---|---|
| **hired car** | la voiture de location | la vwa-tewr duh lo-ka-syoñ |
| **his** | son/sa/ses | soñ/sa/say |
| ***his passport*** | son passeport | soñ pas-por |
| ***his suitcases*** | ses valises | say va-leez |
| **holiday** | les vacances | va-kahñs |
| ***on holiday*** | en vacances | ahñ va-kahñs |
| **home** | la maison | meh-zoñ |
| ***at my/your/ our home*** | chez moi/vous/ nous | shay mwa/voo/ noo |
| **honey** | le miel | myel |
| ***I hope so/not*** | j'espère que oui/non | zheh-spehr kuh wee/noñ |
| **hospital** | l'hôpital *m* | o-pee-tal |
| **hostel** (youth hostel) | l'auberge de jeunesse *f* | oh-behrzh duh zhuh-nes |
| **hot** | chaud(e) | shoh(d) |
| ***I'm hot*** | j'ai chaud | zhay shoh |
| ***it's hot*** (weather) | il fait chaud | eel feh shoh |
| **hotel** | l'hôtel *m* | oh-tel |
| **hour** | l'heure *f* | ur |
| ***half an hour*** | une demi-heure | ewn duh-mee ur |
| **house** | la maison | meh-soñ |
| ***house wine*** | le vin en pichet | vañ ahñ pee-sheh |
| **how** | comment | ko-mahñ |
| ***how much/ many?*** | combien? | koñ-byañ? |
| ***how are you?*** | comment allez-vous? | ko-mahñ ta-lay voo? |
| **hungry:** | | |
| ***to be hungry*** | avoir faim | avwar fañ |
| ***I'm hungry*** | j'ai faim | zhay fañ |
| **hurry:** | | |
| ***I'm in a hurry*** | je suis pressé(e) | zhuh swee preh-say |
| **to hurt:** | | |
| ***to hurt somebody*** | faire du mal à quelqu'un | fehr dew mal a kel-kuñ |
| ***that hurts*** | ça fait mal | sa feh mal |
| **husband** | le mari | ma-ree |

## I

| English | French | Pronunciation |
|---|---|---|
| **I** | je | zhuh |
| **ice** | la glace | glas |
| (cube) | le glaçon | gla-soñ |
| ***with/without ice*** | avec/sans glaçons | a-vek/sahñ gla-soñ |
| **ice cream** | la glace | glas |
| **identity card** | la carte d'identité | kart dee-dahñ-tee-tay |
| **if** | si | see |
| **ill** | malade | ma-lad |
| **illness** | la maladie | ma-la-dee |
| **important** | important(e) | añ-por-tahñ(t) |
| **impossible** | impossible | añ-po-seebl |
| **in** | dans | dahñ |
| ***in two hours' time*** | dans deux heures | dahñ duh zur |
| ***in front of*** | devant | duh-vahñ |
| **included** | compris(e) | koñ-pree(z) |
| **indigestion** | l'indigestion *f* | añ-dee-zhes-tyoñ |
| **information** | les renseignements | rahñ-seh-nyuh-mahñ |
| **injured** | blessé(e) | bleh-say |
| **inside** | à l'intérieur | a lañ-tay-ryur |
| **instead of** | au lieu de | oh lyuh duh |
| **insurance** | l'assurance *f* | a-sew-rahñs |
| **insurance certificate** | l'attestation d'assurance *f* | a-tes-ta-syoñ da-sew-rahñs |
| **insured** | assuré(e) | a-sew-ray |
| **interesting** | intéressant(e) | añ-tay-reh-sahñ(t) |
| **international** | international(e) | añ-tehr-na-syo-nal |
| **into** | dans; en | dahñ; ahñ |
| ***into town*** | en ville | ahñ veel |
| **Ireland** | l'Irlande *f* | eer-lahñd |
| **Irish** | irlandais(e) | eer-lahñ-deh(z) |
| **iron** (for clothes) | le fer à repasser | fehr a ruh-pa-say |
| **is** | est | ay |
| **island** | l'île *f* | leel |

| | | |
|---|---|---|
| **it** | il/elle | eel/el |
| **Italian** | italien(ne) | ee-ta-lyañ/lyen |
| **Italy** | l'Italie *f* | ee-ta-lee |
| **to itch** | démanger | day-mañ-zhay |
| ***it itches*** | ça me démange | sa muh day-mahñzh |

## J

| | | |
|---|---|---|
| **January** | janvier | jahñ-vyay |
| **jeweller's** | la bijouterie | bee-zhoo-tree |
| **jewellery** | les bijoux | bee-zhoo |
| **job** | le travail; l'emploi | tra-va-yuh; ahñ-plwa |
| **journey** | le voyage | vwa-yazh |
| **juice** | le jus | jew |
| ***fruit juice*** | le jus de fruit | jew duh fwree |
| ***orange juice*** | le jus d'orange | jew do-rahñzh |
| **July** | juillet | zhwee-yeh |
| **June** | juin | zhwañ |

## K

| | | |
|---|---|---|
| **to keep** (retain) | garder | gar-day |
| ***keep the change*** | gardez la monnaie | gar-day la mo-neh |
| **key** | la clé/clef | klay |
| ***car key*** | la clé/clef de la voiture | klay duh vwa-tewr |
| **kilo(gram)** | le kilo | kee-loh |
| **kilometre** | le kilomètre | kee-loh-metr |
| **kiosk** (newsstand) | le kiosque | kee-yosk |
| (phone box) | la cabine | ka-been |
| **kitchen** | la cuisine | kwee-zeen |
| **knee** | le genou | zhuh-noo |
| **knife** | le couteau | koo-toh |
| **to know** (how to do, to be aware of) | savoir | sa-vwar |
| (person, place) | connaître | ko-nehtr |
| ***I don't know*** | je ne sais pas | zhuh nuh seh pa |
| ***I don't know Paris*** | je ne connais pas Paris | zhuh nuh ko-neh pa pa-ree |

## L

| | | |
|---|---|---|
| **ladies'** (toilet) | les toilettes pour dames | twa-let poor dam |
| **lamb** | l'agneau *m* | a-nyoh |
| **to land** | atterrir | a-teh-reer |
| **language** | la langue | lahñg |
| **large** | grand(e) | grahñ(d) |
| **last** | dernier(-ière) | dehr-nyay/nyehr |
| ***last month*** | le mois dernier | mwa dehr-nyay |
| ***last night*** (evening) | hier soir | ee-yehr swar |
| (night-time) | la nuit dernière | nwee dehr-nyehr |
| ***last week*** | la semaine dernière | suh-men dehr-nyehr |
| **late** | tard | tar |
| **later** | plus tard | plew tar |
| **lavatory** | les toilettes | twa-let |
| **to leave** (depart for) | partir | par-teer |
| (depart from) | quitter | kee-tay |
| (to leave behind) | laisser | leh-say |
| ***to leave for Paris*** | partir pour Paris | par-teer poor pa-ree |
| ***to leave London*** | quitter Londres | kee-tay loñdr |
| **left:** | | |
| ***on/to the left*** | à gauche | a gohsh |
| **left-luggage** (office) | la consigne | koñ-see-nyuh |
| **leg** | la jambe | zhahñb |
| **lemon** | le citron | see-troñ |
| **lemonade** | la limonade | lee-mo-nad |
| **lens** (contact lens) | la lentille | lahñ-tee |
| **less** | moins | mo-añ |
| ***less than*** | moins de | mwañ duh |
| **letter** | la lettre | letr |
| **lift** (elevator) | l'ascenseur *m* | a-sahñ-sur |
| **light** (not heavy) | léger(-ère) | lay-zhay/zhehr |
| **light** | la lumière | lewm-yehr |
| ***have you got a light?*** | avez-vous du feu? | a-vay-voo dew fuh? |
| **like** (preposition) | comme | kom |

| | | |
|---|---|---|
| ***like this*** | comme ça | kom sa |
| **to like** | aimer | eh-may |
| ***I like coffee*** | j'aime le café | zhem luh ka-fay |
| ***I don't like coffee*** | je n'aime pas le café | zhuh nem pa luh ka-fay |
| ***I'd like...*** | je voudrais... | zhuh voo-dreh... |
| ***we'd like...*** | nous voudrions... | noo voo-dryoñ... |
| **line** (queue) | la file | feel |
| (telephone) | la ligne | lee-nyuh |
| **to listen to** | écouter | ay-koo-tay |
| **litre** | le litre | leetr |
| **little** | petit(e) | puh-tee(t) |
| ***a little...*** | un peu de... | uñ puh duh... |
| **to live** (in a place) | vivre; habiter | veevr; a-bee-tay |
| ***I live in London*** | j'habite à Londres | zha-beet a lahñdr |
| **to lock** | fermer à clé/clef | fe-rmay a klay |
| **London** | Londres | loñdr |
| ***to/in London*** | à Londres | a loñdr |
| **long** | long(ue) | loñ(g) |
| ***for a long time*** | longtemps | loñ-tahñ |
| **to look after** | garder | gar-day |
| **to look at** | regarder | ruh-gar-day |
| **to look for** | chercher | shehr-shay |
| **to lose** | perdre | pehrdr |
| **lost** (object) | perdu(e) | pehr-dew |
| ***I've lost...*** | j'ai perdu... | zhay pehr-dew... |
| ***I'm lost*** | je suis perdu(e) | zhuh swee pehr-dew |
| **lost property office** | le bureau des objets trouvés | bew-roh day zob-zheh troo-vay |
| **lot: *a lot of*** | beaucoup de | boh-koo duh |
| **loud** | fort(e) | for(t) |
| **lounge** (in hotel, airport) | le salon | sa-loñ |
| **love** | l'amour | a-moor |
| **to love** (person) | aimer | eh-may |
| ***I love you*** | je t'aime | zhuh tem |
| (food, activity, etc.) | adorer | a-do-ray |
| ***I love swimming*** | j'adore nager | zha-dor na-zhay |
| **lovely** | beau (belle) | boh (bel) |

| | | |
|---|---|---|
| **low** | bas (basse) | ba(s) |
| **luck** | la chance | shahñs |
| **lucky** | chanceux(-euse) | shahñ-suh(z) |
| **luggage** | les bagages | ba-gazh |
| **luggage trolley** | le chariot | sha-ryoh |
| **lunch** | le déjeuner | day-zhuh-nay |
| **luxury** | le luxe | lewx |

## M

| | | |
|---|---|---|
| **machine** | la machine | ma-sheen |
| **magazine** | la revue; le magazine | ruh-vew; ma-ga-zeen |
| **mail** | le courrier | koo-ryay |
| ***by mail*** | par la poste | par la post |
| **main** | principal(e) | prañ-see-pal |
| **to make** | faire | fehr |
| **make-up** | le maquillage | ma-kee-yazh |
| **male** (person) | masculin | mas-kew-lañ |
| **man** | l'homme *m* | om |
| **manager** | le/la directeur (-trice) | dee-rek-tur/ dee-rek-trees |
| **many** | beaucoup de | boh-koo duh |
| **map** | la carte | kart |
| ***road map*** | la carte routière | kart roo-tyehr |
| ***street map*** | le plan de la ville | plahñ duh la veel |
| **March** | mars | mars |
| **market** | le marché | mar-shay |
| **married** | marié(e) | ma-ryay |
| ***I'm married*** | je suis marié(e) | zhuh swee ma-ryay |
| **mass** (in church) | la messe | mes |
| **match** (sport) | le match | match |
| **matches** | les allumettes | alew-met |
| **to matter:** | | |
| ***it doesn't matter*** | ça ne fait rien | sa nuh feh ryañ |
| ***what's the matter?*** | qu'est-ce qu'il y a? | kes keel ya? |
| **May** | mai | meh |
| **me** | moi | mwa |
| **meal** | le repas | ruh-pa |
| **to mean** | vouloir dire | voo-lwar deer |
| ***what does this mean?*** | qu'est-ce que ça veut dire? | kes kuh sa vuh deer? |

| | | |
|---|---|---|
| **meat** | la viande | vyahñd |
| **medicine** | le médicament | may-dee-ka-mahñ |
| **Mediterranean Sea** | la Méditerranée | may-dee-tay-ra-nay |
| **to meet** | rencontrer | rahñ-koñ-tray |
| **meeting** | la réunion | ray-ew-nyoñ |
| **men** | les hommes | om |
| **to mend** | réparer | ray-pa-ray |
| **menu** (set meal) | le menu | muh-new |
| (card) | la carte | kart |
| **message** | le message | meh-sazh |
| **meter** | le compteur | koñ-tur |
| **metre** | le mètre | metr |
| **metro** | le métro | may-troh |
| **metro station** | la station de métro | sta-syoñ duh may-troh |
| **midday** | midi | mee-dee |
| ***at midday*** | à midi | a mee-dee |
| **middle** | le milieu | mee-lyuh |
| **midnight** | minuit | mee-nwee |
| ***at midnight*** | à minuit | a mee-nwee |
| **mild** (weather, cheese) | doux (douce) | doo(s) |
| (curry) | peu épicé(e) | puh ay-pee-say |
| (tobacco) | léger(-ère) | lay-zhay/zhehr |
| **milk** | le lait | leh |
| ***baby milk*** (formula) | le lait maternisé | leh ma-tehr-nee-zay |
| ***fresh milk*** | le lait frais | leh freh |
| ***soya milk*** | le lait de soja | leh duh so-zha |
| ***with/without milk*** | avec/sans lait | a-vek/sahñ leh |
| **to mind:** | | |
| ***do you mind if I...?*** | ça vous gêne si je...? | sa voo zhen see zhuh...? |
| ***I don't mind*** | ça m'est égal | sa may tay-gal |
| ***do you mind?*** | vous permettez? | voo pehr-meh-tay? |
| **mineral water** | l'eau minérale *f* | oh mee-nay-ral |
| **minute** | la minute | mee-newt |
| **to miss** (train, flight, etc.) | rater | ra-tay |
| **Miss** | Mademoiselle | ma-dmwa-zel |

**missing** (disappeared) disparu(e) dee-spa-rew
**mistake** l'erreur *f* eh-rur
**mobile** (phone) le mobile; le portable mo-beel; por-tabl
**mobile number** le numéro de mobile/portable new-may-roh duh mo-beel/por-tabl
**moment:**
***at the moment*** en ce moment ahñ suh mo-mahñ
**Monday** lundi luñ-dee
**money** l'argent *m* ar-zhahñ
***I have no money*** je n'ai pas d'argent zhuh nay pa dar-zhahñ
**month** le mois mwa
***this month*** ce mois-ci suh mwa-see
***next month*** le mois prochain mwa pro-shañ
**more** encore ahñ-kor
***more wine*** plus de vin plews duh vañ
***more than*** plus de plews duh
**morning** le matin ma-tañ
***in the morning*** le matin luh ma-tañ
***tomorrow morning*** demain matin duh-mañ ma-tañ
**mother** la mère mehr
**motorbike** la moto moh-toh
**motorway** l'autoroute *f* oh-toh-root
**mountain** la montagne moñ-ta-nyuh
**mouth** la bouche boosh
**to move** bouger boo-zhay
**movie** le film feelm
**Mr** Monsieur muh-syuh
**Mrs** Madame ma-dam
**Ms** Madame ma-dam
**much:** ***too much*** trop troh
**museum** le musée mew-zay
**music** la musique mew-zeek
**must** devoir duh-vwar
**my** mon/ma/mes moñ/ma/may

## N

**name** le nom luh noñ

| English | French | Pronunciation |
|---|---|---|
| ***my name is...*** | je m'appelle... | zhuh ma-pel... |
| ***what is your name?*** | comment vous appelez-vous? | ko-mahñ voo za-play voo? |
| **nationality** | la nationalité | na-syo-na-lee-tay |
| **near** | près de | preh duh |
| ***is it near?*** | c'est près d'ici? | say preh dee-see? |
| **to need (to)** | avoir besoin de | a-vwar buh-zwañ duh |
| ***I need...*** | j'ai besoin | zhay buh-zwañ |
| **new** | nouveau(-elle) | noo-voh/vel |
| **news** (TV, etc.) | les informations | añ-for-ma-syoñ |
| **newspaper** | le journal | zhoor-nal |
| **New Zealand** | la Nouvelle-Zélande | noo-vel zay-lahñd |
| **next** | prochain(e) | pro-shañ |
| (after) | ensuite | ahñ-sweet |
| ***next Monday*** | lundi prochain | luñ-dee pro-shañ |
| ***the next train*** | le prochain train | pro-shañ trañ |
| ***next week*** | la semaine prochaine | suh-men pro-shen |
| **next to** | à côté de | a ko-tay duh |
| **nice** | beau (belle) | boh (bel) |
| (enjoyable) | bon (bonne) | boñ (bon) |
| (person) | sympathique | sañ-pa-teek |
| **night** (night-time) | la nuit | nwee |
| (evening) | le soir | swar |
| ***last night*** | hier soir | ee-yeehr swar |
| ***tomorrow night*** (evening) | demain soir | duh-mañ swar |
| ***tonight*** | ce soir | suh swar |
| **nightclub** | la boîte de nuit | bwat duh nwee |
| **no** | non | noñ |
| (without) | sans | sahñ |
| ***no thanks*** | non merci | noñ mehr-see |
| **noisy:** ***it's very noisy*** | il y a beaucoup de bruit | eel ya boh-koo duh brwee |
| **non-smoking** (seat, compartment) | non fumeurs | noñ few-mur |
| **north** | le nord | nor |
| **Northern Ireland** | l'Irlande du Nord *f* | eer-lahñd dew nor |
| **nose** | le nez | nay |

**not** ne ... pas nuh ... pa
***I am not...*** je ne suis pas... zhuh nuh swee pa...
**note** (banknote) le billet bee-yeh
**nothing** rien ryañ
**November** novembre no-vahñbr
**now** maintenant mañ-tuh-nahñ
**number** (quantity) le nombre noñbr
(of room, house) le numéro new-may-roh
**phone number** le numéro de téléphone new-may-roh duh tay-lay-fon

## O

**October** octobre ok-tobr
**of** de duh
***a glass of...*** un verre de... uñ vehr duh...
***made of...*** en... ahñ...
**office** le bureau bew-roh
**often** souvent soo-vahñ
**oil** (for car, food) l'huile *f* weel
**OK** (agreed) d'accord da-kor
(good) bon (bonne) boñ (bon)
**old** vieux (vieille) vyuh (vyeh-yuh)
***how old are you?*** quel âge avez-vous? kel azh a-vay voo?
***I'm ... years old*** j'ai ... ans zhay ... ahñ
**on** (light) allumé(e) a-lew-may
(machine, etc) en marche ahñ marsh
***on the table*** sur la table sewr la tabl
***on time*** à l'heure a lur
**once** une fois ewn fwa
**onion** l'oignon *m* loh-nyoñ
**open** ouvert(e) oo-vehr
**opposite** en face de ahñ fas duh
**or** ou oo
**orange** (fruit) l'orange o-rahñzh
(colour) orange o-rahñzh
**orange juice** le jus d'orange jew do-rahñzh
**order: *out of order*** en panne ahñ pan
**to order** commander ko-mahñ-day
**other** autre ohtr

| | | |
| --- | --- | --- |
| ***have you any others?*** | vous en avez d'autres? | voo zahñ na-vay dohtr? |
| **our** (singular) | notre | notr |
| (plural) | nos | noh |
| ***our room*** | notre chambre | notr shahñbr |
| ***our baggage*** | nos bagages | noh ba-gazh |
| **outside** | dehors | duh-or |

## P

| | | |
| --- | --- | --- |
| **to pack** (luggage) | faire les bagages | fehr lay ba-gazh |
| **package** | le paquet | pa-kay |
| **page** | la page | pazh |
| **paid** | payé(e) | pay-yay |
| ***I've paid*** | j'ai payé | zhay pay-yay |
| **pain** | la douleur | doo-lur |
| **painful** | douloureux (-euse) | doo-loo-ruh(z) |
| **painkiller** | l'analgésique *m* | a-nal-zhay-zeek |
| **pants** (underwear) (trousers) | le slip; le pantalon | sleep; pahñ-ta-loñ |
| **paper** | le papier | pa-pyay |
| **pardon?** | comment? | ko-mahñ? |
| **parents** | les parents | pa-rahñ |
| **park** | le parc | park |
| **to park** | garer (la voiture) | ga-ray (la vwa-tewr) |
| **party** (group) | le groupe | groop |
| (celebration) | la fête; la soirée | fet; swa-ray |
| **pass** (bus, train) | la carte | kart |
| **passenger** | le passager; la passagère | pa-sa-zhay; pa-sa-zhehr |
| **passport** | le passeport | pas-por |
| **pasta** | les pâtes | pat |
| **pastry** | la pâte | pat |
| (cake) | la pâtisserie | pa-tee-sree |
| **to pay** | payer | pay-yay |
| ***I'd like to pay*** | je voudrais payer | zhuh voo-dreh pay-yay |
| ***where do I pay?*** | où est-ce qu'il faut payer? | oo es keel foh pay-yay? |
| **peanut** | la cacahuète | ka-ka-wet |
| **peanut allergy** | l'allergie aux cacahuètes | a-lehr-zhee oh ka-ka-wet |

| | | |
|---|---|---|
| **peas** | les petits pois | puh-tee pwa |
| **pen** | le stylo | stee-loh |
| **pensioner** | le/la retraité(e) | ruh-treh-tay |
| **people** | les gens | zhahñ |
| **pepper** (spice) | le poivre | pwavr |
| (vegetable) | le poivron | pwa-vroñ |
| **per:** ***per day*** | par jour | par zhoor |
| ***per hour*** | à l'heure | a lur |
| ***per person*** | par personne | par pehr-son |
| ***per week*** | par semaine | par suh-men |
| **performance** | le spectacle | spek-takl |
| **person** | la personne | pehr-son |
| **petrol** | l'essence *f* | eh-sahñs |
| ***unleaded petrol*** | l'essence sans plomb | eh-sahñs sahñ ploñ |
| **petrol station** | la station-service | sta-syoñ ser-vees |
| **pharmacy** | la pharmacie | far-ma-see |
| **to photocopy** | photocopier | foh-toh-ko-pyay |
| **photograph** | la photo | foh-toh |
| ***to take a photograph*** | prendre une photo | prahñdr ewn foh-toh |
| **piece** | le morceau | mor-soh |
| **pink** | rose | roz |
| **place of birth** | le lieu de naissance | lyuh duh neh-sahñs |
| **plan** (map) | le plan | plahñ |
| **plate** | l'assiette *f* | a-syet |
| **platform** (railway) | le quai | keh |
| ***which platform?*** | quel quai? | kel keh? |
| **play** (at theatre) | la pièce | pyes |
| **please** | s'il vous plaît | seel voo pleh |
| **pleased to meet you** | enchanté(e) | ahñ-shahñ-tay |
| **poisonous** | vénéneux | vay-nay-nuh |
| **police** (force) | la police | po-lees |
| **police station** | le commissariat; la gendarmerie | ko-mee-sa-rya; zhahñ-dar-mree |
| **pork** | le porc | por |
| **port** (seaport) | le port | por |
| **porter** (for luggage) | le porteur | por-tur |

| | | |
|---|---|---|
| **possible** | possible | po-seebl |
| **post** (letters) | le courrier | koo-ryay |
| ***by post*** | par courrier | par koo-ryay |
| **to post** | poster | po-stay |
| **postbox** | la boîte aux lettres | bwat oh letr |
| **postcard** | la carte postale | kart po-stal |
| **post office** | la poste | post |
| **potato** | la pomme de terre | pom duh tehr |
| **pound** (weight, money) | la livre | leevr |
| **to prefer** | préférer | pray-fa-yray |
| **pregnant** | enceinte | ahñ-sañt |
| **present** (gift) | le cadeau | ka-doh |
| **pretty** | joli(e) | zho-lee |
| **price** | le prix | pree |
| **price list** | le tarif | ta-reef |
| **problem** | le problème | pro-blem |
| **prohibited** | interdit(e) | añ-tehr-dee |
| **public** | public(-ique) | pew-bleek |
| **pudding** | le dessert | deh-sehr |
| **to pull** | tirer | tee-ray |
| **purse** | le porte-monnaie | port-mo-neh |
| **to push** | pousser | poo-say |

## Q

| | | |
|---|---|---|
| **quarter** | le quart | kar |
| **question** | la question | ke-styoñ |
| **quick** | rapide | ra-peed |
| **quickly** | vite | veet |
| **quiet** (place) | tranquille | trahñ-keel |
| **quite** (rather) | assez | a-say |
| (completely) | complètement | koñ-plet-mahñ |
| ***quite good*** | pas mal | pa mal |

## R

| | | |
|---|---|---|
| **railway** | le chemin de fer | shuh-mañ duh fehr |
| **railway station** | la gare | gar |
| **to rain:** | | |
| ***it's raining*** | il pleut | eel pluh |

| | | |
|---|---|---|
| **rare** (steak) | saignant(e) | say-nyahñ(t) |
| **rate of exchange** | le taux de change | toh duh shahñzh |
| **raw** | cru(e) | crew |
| **razor** | le rasoir | ra-zwar |
| **razor blades** | les lames de rasoir | lam duh ra-zwar |
| **ready** | prêt(e) | preh/pret |
| **receipt** | le reçu | ruh-sew |
| **reception** (desk) | la réception | ray-sep-syoñ |
| **to recommend** | recommander | ruh-ko-mahñ-day |
| **red** | rouge | roozh |
| **reduction** | la réduction | ray-dewk-syoñ |
| **remember** | se rappeler | suh ra-play |
| ***I don't remember*** | je ne m'en rappelle pas | zhuh nuh mahñ ra-pel pa |
| **to repair** | réparer | ray-pa-ray |
| **to repeat** | répéter | ray-pay-tay |
| **to report** (theft, etc.) | déclarer | day-kla-ray |
| **reservation** | la réservation | ray-zehr-va-syoñ |
| **to reserve** | réserver | ray-zehr-vay |
| **reserved** | réservé(e) | ray-zehr-vay |
| **rest** (relaxation) | le repos | ruh-poh |
| (remainder) | le reste | rest |
| **restaurant** | le restaurant | reh-stoh-rahñ |
| **retired** | retraité(e) | ruh-treh-tay |
| **to return** (to a place) | retourner | ruh-toor-nay |
| **return ticket** | le billet aller-retour | bee-yeh a-lay-ruh-toor |
| **rice** | le riz | ree |
| **right** (correct) | exact(e) | eg-zakt |
| **right** (not left) | la droite | drwat |
| ***on/to the right*** | à droite | a drwat |
| **river** | la rivière | ree-vyehr |
| **Riviera** (French) | la Côte d'Azur | koht da-zewr |
| **road** | la route | root |
| **road map** | la carte routière | kart roo-tyehr |
| **road sign** | le panneau | pa-noh |
| **roll** (bread) | le petit pain | puh-tee pañ |

| | | |
|---|---|---|
| **room** (in house) | la pièce | pyes |
| (in hotel) | la chambre | shahñbr |
| ***double room*** | la chambre pour deux personnes | shahñbr poor duh pehr-son |
| ***family room*** | la chambre pour une famille | shahñbr poor ewn fa-mee |
| ***single room*** | la chambre pour une personne | shahñbr poor ewn pehr-son |
| **room number** | le numéro de chambre | new-may-roh duh shahñbr |
| **room service** | le service des chambres | sehr-vees day shahñbr |

## S

| | | |
|---|---|---|
| **safe** (for valuables) | le coffre-fort | kofr-for |
| ***is it safe?*** | ce n'est pas dangereux? | suh nay pa dahñ-zhuh-ruh? |
| **salad** | la salade | sa-lad |
| ***salad dressing*** | la vinaigrette | vee-neh-gret |
| **salesman/woman** | le vendeur; la vendeuse | vahñ-dur; vahñ-duhz |
| **salt** | le sel | sel |
| **sandwich** | le sandwich | sahñ-dweetsh |
| ***toasted sandwich*** | le croque-monsieur | krok-muh-syuh |
| **Saturday** | samedi | sam-dee |
| **sauce** | la sauce | sohs |
| **sausage** | la saucisse | so-sees |
| **to say** | dire | deer |
| **scarf** (silk) | le foulard | foo-lar |
| (woollen) | l'écharpe *f* | ay-sharp |
| **school** | l'école *f* | ay-kol |
| **Scotland** | l'Écosse *f* | ay-kos |
| **Scottish** | écossais(e) | ay-ko-say |
| **scuba diving** | la plongée sous-marine | ploñ-zhay soo-ma-reen |
| **sea** | la mer | mehr |
| **seafood** | les fruits de mer | frwee duh mehr |
| **season** (of year) | la saison | seh-zoñ |
| **seat** (chair) | le siège | syezh |
| (in train) | la place | plas |
| (cinema, theatre) | le fauteuil | foh-tuh-yuh |

| | | |
|---|---|---|
| **second** | deuxième; second(e) | duh-zyem; suh-koñ(d) |
| **second class** | seconde classe | suh-koñd klas |
| **to see** | voir | vwar |
| **to sell** | vendre | vahñdr |
| ***do you sell...?*** | vous vendez...? | voo vahñ-day...? |
| **to send** | envoyer | ahñ-vwa-yay |
| **September** | septembre | sep-tahñbr |
| **service** | le service | sehr-vees |
| ***is service included?*** | le service est compris? | sehr-vess ay koñ-pree? |
| **shampoo** | le shampooing | shahñ-pwañ |
| **shaver** | le rasoir électrique | ra-zwar ay-lek-treek |
| **she** | elle | el |
| **sheet** (for bed) | le drap | dra |
| **shirt** | la chemise | shuh-meez |
| **shoe** | la chaussure | shoh-sewr |
| **shop** | le magasin | ma-ga-zañ |
| **to shop** | faire du shopping | fehr dew sho-peeng |
| **shop assistant** | le vendeur; la vendeuse | vahñ-dur; vahñ-duhz |
| **shopping centre** | le centre commercial | sahñtr ko-mehr-syal |
| **short** | court(e) | koor(t) |
| **shorts** | le short | short |
| **shoulder** | l'épaule *f* | ay-pohl |
| **show** | le spectacle | spek-takl |
| **shower** (wash) | la douche | doosh |
| ***to have/take a shower*** | prendre une douche | prahñdr ewn doosh |
| **shower gel** | le gel douche | zhel doosh |
| **sick** (ill) | malade | ma-lad |
| ***I feel sick*** | j'ai envie de vomir | zhay ahñ-vee duh vo-meer |
| **sign** (notice) | le panneau | pa-noh |
| **silk** | la soie | swa |
| **silver** | l'argent *m* | ar-zhahñ |
| **similar (to)** | semblable (à) | sahñ-blabl (a) |
| **since** | depuis | duh-pwee |

| English | French | Pronunciation |
|---|---|---|
| **single** (unmarried) | célibataire | say-lee-ba-tehr |
| (bed, room) | pour une personne | poor ewn pehr-son |
| **single ticket** | l'aller simple *m* | a-lay sañpl |
| **sir** | Monsieur | muh-syuh |
| **sister** | la sœur | sur |
| **size** (clothes) | la taille | ta-yuh |
| (shoe) | la pointure | pwañ-tewr |
| **ski** | le ski | skee |
| ***ski lift*** | le remonte-pente | ruh-moñt pahñt |
| ***ski pass*** | le forfait | for-feh |
| **to ski** | faire du ski | fehr dew skee |
| **skin** | la peau | poh |
| **skirt** | la jupe | zhewp |
| **to sleep** | dormir | dor-meer |
| **slice** (bread, salami, etc.) | la tranche | trahñsh |
| (cake, tart, etc.) | la part | par |
| **slow** | lent(e) | lahñ(t) |
| **slowly** | lentement | lahñ-tuh-mahñ |
| **small** | petit(e) | puh-tee(t) |
| **to smoke** | fumer | few-may |
| ***I don't smoke*** | je ne fume pas | zhuh nuh fewm pa |
| ***can I smoke?*** | on peut fumer? | oñ puh few-may? |
| **smoked** | fumé(e) | few-may |
| **snack** | le casse-croûte | kas-kroot |
| **snail** | l'escargot *m* | es-kar-goh |
| **snow** | la neige | nezh |
| **soap** | le savon | sa-voñ |
| **socks** | les chaussettes | shoh-set |
| **soft drink** | le soda | so-da |
| **some** | du/de la/des | dew/duh la/day |
| **someone** | quelqu'un | kel-kuñ |
| **something** | quelque chose | kel-kuh shohz |
| **sometimes** | quelquefois | kel-kuh fwa |
| **son** | le fils | fees |
| **soon** | bientôt | byañ-toh |
| ***as soon as possible*** | dès que possible | deh kuh po-seebl |
| **sore:** ***to have a sore throat*** | avoir mal à la gorge | a-vwar mal a la gorzh |

| | | |
|---|---|---|
| **sorry:** ***I'm sorry*** | excusez-moi | ek-skew-say-mwa |
| **soup** | le potage; la soupe | po-tazh; soop |
| **south** | le sud | sewd |
| **Spain** | l'Espagne *f* | es-pa-nyuh |
| **Spanish** | espagnol(e) | es-pa-nyol |
| **sparkling** (wine) | mousseux(-euse) | moo-suh(z) |
| (water) | gazeux(-euse) | ga-zuh(z) |
| **to speak** | parler | par-lay |
| ***do you speak English?*** | vous parlez anglais? | voo par-lay ahñgleh? |
| **speciality** | la spécialité | spay-sya-lee-tay |
| **speed limit** | la limitation de vitesse | lee-mee-ta-syoñ duh vee-tes |
| **to spend** (money) | dépenser | day-pahñ-say |
| (time) | passer | pa-say |
| **spoon** | la cuiller | kwee-yehr |
| **sport** | le sport | spor |
| **spring** (season) | le printemps | prañ-tahñ |
| **square** (in town) | la place | plas |
| **squid** | le calmar | calmar |
| **stamp** | le timbre | tañbr |
| **to start** | commencer | ko-mahñ-say |
| **station** | la gare | gar |
| **stay** | le séjour | say-zhoor |
| ***enjoy your stay*** | bon séjour | boñ say-zhoor |
| **to stay** (remain) | rester | res-tay |
| (reside for while) | loger | lo-zhay |
| ***I'm staying at...*** | je loge à... | zhuh lozh a... |
| **steak** | le bifteck | beef-tek |
| **sterling** | la livre sterling | leevr stehr-leeng |
| **still:** ***still water*** | l'eau plate *f* | oh plat |
| **stolen** | volé(e) | vo-lay |
| **stomach** | l'estomac *m* | es-to-ma |
| ***to have a stomach ache*** | avoir mal au ventre | a-vwar mal oh vahñtr |
| **to stop** | arrêter | a-reh-tay |
| **store** (shop) | le magasin | ma-ga-zañ |
| **storey** | l'étage *m* | ay-tazh |
| **straight on** | tout droit | too drwa |
| **strawberries** | les fraises | frez |
| **street** | la rue | rew |

| | | |
|---|---|---|
| **street map** | le plan des rues | plahñ day rew |
| **strong** | fort(e) | for(t) |
| **student** | l'étudiant(e) | ay-tew-dyahñ(t) |
| **student discount** | le tarif étudiant | ta-reef ay-tew-dyahñ |
| **stung** | piqué(e) | pee-kay |
| **suede** | le daim | dañ |
| **sugar** | le sucre | sewkr |
| **sugar-free** | sans sucre | sahñ sewkr |
| **suit** (man's) | le costume | kos-tewm |
| (woman's) | le tailleur | ta-yur |
| **suitcase** | la valise | va-leez |
| **summer** | l'été *m* | ay-tay |
| **sun** | le soleil | so-leh-yuh |
| **to sunbathe** | prendre un bain de soleil | prahñdr uñ bañ duh so-leh-yuh |
| **sunburn** | le coup de soleil | koo duh so-leh-yuh |
| **suncream** | la crème solaire | krem so-lehr |
| **Sunday** | le dimanche | dee-mahñsh |
| **sunglasses** | les lunettes de soleil | lew-net duh so-leh-yuh |
| **sunny:** ***it's sunny*** | il fait beau | eel feh boh |
| **supermarket** | le supermarché | sew-pehr-mar-shay |
| **supper** (dinner) | le souper | soo-pay |
| **supplement** | le supplément | sew-play-mahñ |
| **surname** | le nom de famille | noñ duh fa-mee |
| **sweetener** | l'édulcorant *m* | ay-dewl-ko-rahñ |
| **sweets** | les bonbons | boñ-boñ |
| **to swim** | nager | na-zhay |
| **swimming pool** | la piscine | pee-seen |
| **swimsuit** | le maillot de bain | ma-yoh duhbañ |
| **Swiss** | suisse | swees |
| **to switch off** | éteindre | ay-tañdr |
| **to switch on** | allumer | a-lew-may |
| **Switzerland** | la Suisse | swees |
| **swollen** | enflé(e) | ahñ-flay |

## T

| | | |
|---|---|---|
| **table** | la table | tabl |

| | | |
|---|---|---|
| **table tennis** | le tennis de table | teh-nees duh tabl |
| **table wine** | le vin de table | vañ duh tabl |
| **tablet** | le comprimé | koñ-pree-may |
| **to take** | prendre | prahñdr |
| **to talk (to)** | parler (à) | par-lay (a) |
| **tall** | grand(e) | grahñ(d) |
| **tart** | la tarte | tart |
| **to taste** | goûter | goo-tay |
| ***can I taste it*** | je peux goûter? | zhuh puh goo-tay? |
| **tax** | l'impôt *m* | añ-poh |
| **taxi** | le taxi | tak-see |
| **tea** | le thé | tay |
| ***herbal tea*** | la tisane | tee-zan |
| **teacher** | le professeur | pro-feh-sur |
| **telephone** | le téléphone | tay-lay-fon |
| ***telephone box*** | la cabine téléphonique | ka-been tay-lay-fo-neek |
| ***telephone call*** | le coup de téléphone | koo duh tay-lay-fon |
| ***telephone card*** | la télécarte | tay-lay-kart |
| ***telephone number*** | le numéro de téléphone | new-may-roh duh tay-lay-fon |
| **to telephone** | téléphoner | tay-lay-fo-nay |
| **television** | la télévision | tay-lay-vee-zyoñ |
| **temperature** | la température | tahñ-pay-ra-tewr |
| ***to have a temperature*** | avoir de la fièvre | a-vwar duh la fyevr |
| **tennis** | le tennis | the-nees |
| **tent** | la tente | tahñt |
| **to text** | envoyer un SMS à | ahñ-vwa-yay uñ nes-em-es a |
| ***I'll text you*** | je t'enverrai un SMS | zhuh tahñ-veh-ray uñ nes-em-es |
| **than** | que | kuh |
| **to thank** | remercier | ruh-mehr-syay |
| ***thank you*** | merci | mehr-see |
| ***thank you very much*** | merci beaucoup | mehr-see boh-koo |
| **that** | cela/ça | suh-la/sa |
| ***that one*** | celui-là/celle-là | suh-lwee-la/sel-la |
| **the** | le/la/l'/les | luh/la/l'/lay |

| | | |
|---|---|---|
| **theatre** | le théâtre | tay-atr |
| **their** | leur(s) | lur |
| **them** | eux | uh |
| **there** | là | la |
| ***there is/are...*** | il y a... | eel ya... |
| **these** | ces | say |
| ***these (ones)*** | ceux-ci/celles-ci | suh-see/sel-see |
| **they** | ils/elles | eel/el |
| **thing** | la chose | shohz |
| ***my things*** | mes affaires | may za-fehr |
| **to think** | penser | pahñ-say |
| **thirsty:** | | |
| ***I'm thirsty*** | j'ai soif | zhay swaf |
| **this** | ce/ceci | suh/suh-see |
| ***this one*** | celui-ci/ celle-ci | suh-lwee-see/ sel-see |
| **those** | ces | say |
| ***those (ones)*** | ceux-là/celles-là | suh-la/sel-la |
| **throat** | la gorge | gorzh |
| **through** | à travers | a tra-vehr |
| **Thursday** | jeudi | zhuh-dee |

| | | |
|---|---|---|
| **ticket** | le billet; le ticket | bee-yeh; tee-keh |
| ***a single ticket*** | un aller simple | uñ na-lay sañpl |
| ***a return ticket*** | un aller-retour | uñ na-lay ruh-toor |
| **ticket office** | le guichet | gee-shet |
| **tie** | la cravate | kra-vat |
| **tight** (fitting) | serré(e) | seh-ray |
| **tights** | le collant | ko-lahñ |
| **till** (cash desk) | la caisse | kes |
| **till** (until) | jusqu'à | zhews-ka |
| ***till 2 o'clock*** | jusqu'à deux heures | zhews-ka duh zur |
| **time** | le temps | tahñ |
| (of day) | l'heure *f* | ur |
| ***this time*** | cette fois | set fwa |
| ***what time is it?*** | quelle heure est-il? | kel ur ay-teel? |
| **timetable** | l'horaire *m* | o-rehr |
| **tip** (to waiter, etc.) | le pourboire | poor-bwar |
| **to tip** (waiter, etc.) | donner un pourboire à | do-nay uñ poor-bwar a |

| | | |
|---|---|---|
| **tired** | fatigué(e) | fa-tee-gay |
| **to** | à | a |
| (with name of country) | en/au | ahñ/oh |
| ***to London*** | à Londres | a loñdr |
| ***to the airport*** | à l'aéroport | a la-ay-roh-por |
| ***to France*** | en France | ahñ frahñs |
| ***to Canada*** | au Canada | oh ka-na-da |
| **toast** (to eat) | le pain grillé; le toast | pañ gree-yay; tost |
| **today** | aujourd'hui | oh-zhoor-dwee |
| **toilet** | les toilettes | twa-let |
| **toll** (motorway) | le péage | pay-azh |
| **tomato** | la tomate | to-mat |
| **tomorrow** | demain | duh-mañ |
| ***tomorrow morning*** | demain matin | duh-mañ ma-tañ |
| **tonight** | ce soir | se swar |
| **too** (also) | aussi | oh-see |
| ***it's too big*** | c'est trop grand | say troh grahñ |
| ***it's too hot*** | il fait trop chaud | eel feh troh shoh |
| ***it's too noisy*** | il y a trop de bruit | eel ya troh duh brwee |
| **tooth** | la dent | dahñ |
| ***I have toothache*** | j'ai mal aux dents | zhay mal oh dahñ |
| **toothbrush** | la brosse à dents | bros a dahñ |
| **toothpaste** | le dentifrice | dahñ-tee-frees |
| **top:** | | |
| ***the top floor*** | le dernier étage | dehr-nyay ay-tazh |
| **top** (of pyjamas, bikini, etc.) | le haut | oh |
| (of hill, mountain) | le sommet | so-meh |
| ***on top of*** | sur | sewr |
| **total** (amount) | le total | to-tal |
| **tour** | l'excursion *f* | ek-skewr-syoñ |
| **tourist** | le/la touriste | too-reest |
| **tourist (information) office** | le syndicat d'initiative; l'office de/du tourisme | sañ-dee-ka dee-nee-sya-teev' o-fees duh/dew too-reesm |
| **towel** | la serviette | sehr-vyet |

| | | |
|---|---|---|
| **town** | la ville | veel |
| **town centre** | le centre-ville | sahñtr-veel |
| **town hall** | la mairie | meh-ree |
| **town plan** | le plan de la ville | plahñ duh la veel |
| **traffic** | la circulation | seer-kewla-syoñ |
| **traffic jam** | l'embouteillage *m* | ahñ-boo-tay-yazh |
| **traffic lights** | les feux | fuh |
| **train** | le train | trañ |
| ***by train*** | par le train | par luh trañ |
| ***the next train*** | le prochain train | pro-shañ trañ |
| **tram** | le tramway | tram-way |
| **to translate** | traduire | tra-dweer |
| **to travel** | voyager | vwa-ya-zhay |
| **travel agent's** | l'agence de voyages *f* | a-zhahñs duh vwa-yazh |
| **tree** | l'arbre *m* | arbr |
| **trip** | l'excursion *f* | ek-skewr-syoñ |
| **trolley** | le chariot | sha-ryoh |
| **to try; to try on** (clothes, shoes) | essayer | eh-say-yay |
| **Tuesday** | mardi | mar-dee |
| **tunnel** | le tunnel | tew-nel |
| **to turn off** (light, etc.) | éteindre | ay-tañdr |
| (engine) | couper | koo-pay |
| **to turn on** (light, etc.) | allumer | a-lew-may |
| (engine) | mettre en marche | metr ahñ marsh |
| **twin-bedded room** | la chambre à deux lits | shahñbr a duh lee |
| **tyre** | le pneu | pnuh |

## U

| | | |
|---|---|---|
| **umbrella** | le parapluie | pa-ra-plwee |
| **uncle** | l'oncle *m* | oñkl |
| **uncomfortable** | inconfortable | añ-koñ-for-tabl |
| **under** | sous | soo |

| | | |
|---|---|---|
| **underground** (train) | le métro | may-troh |
| **to understand** | comprendre | koñ-prahñdr |
| ***I don't understand*** | je ne comprends pas | zhuh nuh koñ-prahñ pa |
| ***do you understand?*** | vous comprenez? | voo koñ-pruh-nay? |
| **unemployed** | au chômage | oh shoh-mazh |
| **United Kingdom** | le Royaume-Uni | rwa-yohm ew-nee |
| **United States** | les États-Unis | ay-ta-zew-nee |
| **university** | l'université *f* | ew-nee-vehr-see-tay |
| **unleaded petrol** | l'essence sans plomb *f* | eh-sahñs sahñ ploñ |
| **upstairs** | en haut | ahñ oh |
| **urgent** | urgent(e) | ewr-zhahñ(t) |
| **us** | nous | noo |
| **useful** | utile | ew-teel |
| **usual** | habituel(-elle) | a-bee-tew-el |

## V

| | | |
|---|---|---|
| **vacant** | libre | leebr |
| **vacation** | les vacances | va-kahñs |
| **valid** (ticket, driving licence, etc.) | valable | va-labl |
| **valuables** | les objets de valeur | ob-zheh duh va-lur |
| **VAT** | la TVA | tay-vay-a |
| **vegan** | végétalien(ne) | vay-zhay-ta-lyañ/lyen |
| **vegetables** | les légumes | lay lay-gewm |
| **vegetarian** | végétarien(ne) | vay-zhay-ta-ryañ/ryen |
| **very** | très | treh |
| **video camera** | la caméscope | ka-may-skop |
| **village** | le village | vee-lazh |
| **vinegar** | le vinaigre | vee-negr |
| **virus** | le virus | vee-rews |
| **visa** | le visa | vee-za |
| **visit** | le séjour | say-zhoor |
| **to visit** | visiter | vee-zee-tay |

| English | French | Pronunciation |
|---|---|---|
| **visitor** | le/la visiteur (-euse) | vee-zee-tur/ tuhz |
| **voicemail** | la messagerie vocale | meh-sa-zhree vo-kal |

## W

| English | French | Pronunciation |
|---|---|---|
| **to wait for** | attendre | a-tahñdr |
| **waiter/ waitress** | le/la serveur (-euse) | sehr-vur/ sehr-vuhz |
| **waiting room** | la salle d'attente | sal da-tahñt |
| **to wake up** | se réveiller | suh ray-vay-yay |
| **Wales** | le pays de Galles | pay-yee duh gal |
| **walk:** ***to go for a walk*** | faire une promenade | fehr ewn prom-nad |
| **to walk** | aller à pied; marcher | a-lay a pyay; mar-shay |
| **wall** | le mur | mewr |
| **wallet** | le portefeuille | port-fuh-yuh |
| **to want** | vouloir | voo-lwar |
| ***I want...*** | je veux... | zhuh vuh... |
| ***we want...*** | nous voulons... | noo voo-loñ... |
| **warm** | chaud(e) | shoh(d) |
| ***it's warm*** (weather) | il fait bon | eel feh boñ |
| ***it's too warm*** | il fait trop chaud | eel feh troh shoh |
| **washing machine** | la machine à laver | ma-sheen a la-vay |
| **washing powder** | la lessive | leh-seev |
| **washing-up liquid** | le produit pour la vaisselle | pro-dwee poor la vay-sel |
| **watch** | la montre | moñtr |
| **to watch** (look at) | regarder | ruh-gar-day |
| **water** | l'eau *f* | oh |
| ***drinking water*** | l'eau potable | oh po-tabl |
| ***sparkling mineral water*** | l'eau minérale gazeuse | oh mee-nay-ral ga-zuhz |
| ***still mineral water*** | l'eau minérale plate | oh mee-nay-ral plat |
| **watermelon** | la pastèque | pas-tek |
| **way** (manner) | la manière | ma-nyehr |
| (route) | le chemin | shuh-mañ |

| | | |
|---|---|---|
| **way in** (entrance) | l'entrée *f* | lahñ-tray |
| **way out** (exit) | la sortie | sor-tee |
| **we** | nous | noo |
| **to wear** | porter | por-tay |
| **weather** | le temps | tahñ |
| **weather forecast** | la météo | ma-ytay-oh |
| **Wednesday** | mercredi | mehr-kruh-dee |
| **week** | la semaine | suh-men |
| ***last week*** | la semaine dernière | suh-men dehr-nyehr |
| ***next week*** | la semaine prochaine | suh-men pro-shen |
| ***per week*** | par semaine | par suh-men |
| ***this week*** | cette semaine | set suh-men |
| **weekend** | le week-end | wee-kend |
| **well** (healthy) | en bonne santé | ahñ bon sahñ-tay |
| ***he's not well*** | il est souffrant | eel ay soo-frahñ |
| ***I'm very well*** | je vais très bien | zhuh veh treh byañ |
| **well done** (steak) | bien cuit(e) | byañ kwee(t) |
| **Welsh** | gallois(e) | ga-lwa(z) |
| **west** | l'ouest *m* | oo-est |
| **wet** | mouillé(e) | moo-yay |
| **what** | que; quel/quelle; quoi | kuh; kel; kwa |
| ***what is it?*** | qu'est-ce que c'est? | kes kuh say? |
| **wheelchair** | le fauteuil roulant | foh-tuh-yuh roo-lahñ |
| **when** | quand | kahñ |
| (at what time?) | à quelle heure? | a kel ur |
| ***when is it?*** | c'est quand?; c'est à quelle heure? | say kahñ?; say ta kel ur? |
| **where** | où | oo |
| ***where is it?*** | c'est où? | say oo? |
| ***where is the hotel?*** | où est l'hôtel? | oo ay loh-tel? |
| **which** | quel/quelle | kel |
| ***which (one)?*** | lequel/laquelle? | luh-kel/la-kel? |

| | | |
|---|---|---|
| ***which (ones)?*** | lesquels/ lesquelles? | lay-kel? |
| **white** | blanc (blanche) | blahñ(sh) |
| **who** | qui | kee |
| ***who is it?*** | qui c'est? | kee say? |
| **whose:** | | |
| ***whose is it?*** | c'est à qui? | say ta kee? |
| **why** | pourquoi | poor-kwa |
| **wife** | la femme | fam |
| **window** | la fenêtre | fuh-netr |
| (shop) | la vitrine | vee-treen |
| **wine** | le vin | vañ |
| ***wine list*** | la carte des vins | kart day vañ |
| **winter** | l'hiver *m* | ee-vehr |
| **with** | avec | a-vek |
| ***with ice*** | avec des glaçons | a-vek day gla-soñ |
| ***with milk/ sugar*** | avec du lait/ sucre | a-vek dew leh/ sewkr |
| **without** | sans | soñ |
| ***without ice*** | sans glaçons | sahñ gla-soñ |
| ***without milk/ sugar*** | sans lait/ sucre | sahñ leh/ sewkr |
| **woman** | la femme | fam |
| **wool** | la laine | len |
| **word** | le mot | moh |
| **work** | le travail | tra-va-yuh |
| **to work** (person) | travailler | tra-va-yay |
| (machine, car) | fonctionner; marcher | foñ-ksyo-nay; mar-shay |
| ***it doesn't work*** | ça ne marche pas | sa nuh marsh pa |
| **to write** | écrire | ay-kreer |
| ***please write it down*** | vous me l'écrivez, s'il vous plaît? | voo muh lay-kree-vay seel voo pleh? |
| **wrong** | faux (fausse) | foh(s) |

## X

| | | |
|---|---|---|
| **X-ray** | la radio(graphie) | ra-dyoh (gra-fee) |
| **to X-ray** | faire une radio (graphie) | fehr ewn ra-dyoh (gra-fee) |

## Y

| | | |
|---|---|---|
| **year** | l'an *m*; l'année *f* | ahñ; la-nay |
| ***this year*** | cette année | set a-nay |
| ***next year*** | l'année prochaine | a-nay pro-shen |
| ***last year*** | l'année dernière | a-nay dehr-nyehr |
| **yellow** | jaune | zhohn |
| **Yellow Pages** | les pages jaunes | pazh zhohn |
| **yes** | oui | wee |
| ***yes please*** | oui, merci | wee, mehr-see |
| **yesterday** | hier | ee-yeehr |
| **yet:** ***not yet*** | pas encore | pa (z)ahñ-kor |
| **yoghurt** | le yaourt | ya-oort |
| ***plain yoghurt*** | le yaourt nature | ya-oort na-tewr |
| **you** (familiar) | tu | tew |
| (polite) | vous | voo |
| **young** | jeune | zhuhn |
| **your** (familiar singular) | ton/ta | toñ/ta |
| (familiar plural) | tes | tay |
| (polite singular) | votre | votr |
| (polite plural) | vos | voh |
| **youth hostel** | l'auberge de jeunesse *f* | oh-behrzh duh zhuh-nes |

## Z

| | | |
|---|---|---|
| **zero** | le zéro | zay-roh |
| **zip** | la fermeture éclair | fehr-muh-tewr ay-klehr |
| **zoo** | le zoo | zoh |

# French - English

## A

**à** to; at
**accès interdit** no entry
**accident** *m* accident
**accueil** *m* reception; information
**acheter** to buy
**addition** *f* bill
**adresse** *f* address
***adressez-vous à*** enquire at *(office)*
**aérogare** *f* terminal
**aéroport** *m* airport
**affaires** *fpl* business; belongings
***bonne affaire*** bargain
**affiche** *f* poster; notice
**âge** *m* age
***du troisième âge*** senior citizen
**âgé(e)** elderly
***âgé de ... ans*** aged ... years
**agence** *f* agency; branch
***agence de voyages*** travel agency
***agence immobilière*** estate agent's
**agent de police** police officer
**aider** to help
**aimer** to enjoy; to love *(person)*
**aire:** ***aire de jeux*** play area
***aire de repos*** rest area
***aire de service*** service area
***aire de stationnement*** layby
**alcool** *m* alcohol; fruit brandy
**algues** *fpl* seaweed
**allégé(e)** low-fat
**Allemagne** *f* Germany
**allemand(e)** German
**aller** to go
**aller (simple)** *m* single ticket
**aller-retour** *m* return ticket
**allumé(e)** on *(light)*
***allumez vos phares*** switch on headlights
**alpinisme** *m* mountaineering
**alsacien(ne)** Alsatian
**ambassade** *f* embassy
**ambulance** *f* ambulance
**américain(e)** American
**Amérique** *f* America
**ami(e)** *m/f* friend
***petit(e) ami(e)*** boyfriend/ girlfriend
**amour** *m* love
**ampoule** *f* blister; light bulb
**an** *m* year
***Nouvel An*** *m* New Year

**analgésique** *m* painkiller
**ancien(ne)** old; former
**angine** *f* tonsillitis
**Anglais** *m* Englishman
**anglais** *m* English *(language)*
**anglais(e)** English
**Angleterre** *f* England
**animal** *m* animal
***animal domestique*** pet
**année** *f* year; vintage
**anniversaire** *m* anniversary; birthday
**annonce** *f* advertisement
**annulation** *f* cancellation
**anti-insecte** *m* insect repellent
**antibiotique** *m* antibiotic
**antihistamine** *m* antihistamine
**antimoustique** *m* mosquito repellent
**août** August
**appareil** *m* appliance; camera
***appareil acoustique*** hearing aid
***appareil photo*** camera
**appeler** to call *(speak, phone)*
***appeler en PVC*** to reverse the charges
**appuyer** to press
**après** after
**après-midi** *m* afternoon
**arbre** *m* tree
**argent** *m* money; silver
***argent liquide*** cash
**arrêt** *m* stop
***arrêt d'autobus*** bus stop
**arrêter** to arrest; to stop
***arrêter le moteur*** to turn off the engine
**arrêtez!** stop!
**arrivées** *fpl* arrivals
**arriver** to arrive; to happen
**arrondissement** *m* district
**article** *m* item; article
***articles de toilette*** toiletries
**ascenseur** *m* lift
**assez** enough; quite *(rather)*
**assiette** *f* plate
**assurance** *f* insurance
**assuré(e)** insured
**assurer** to assure; to insure
**asthme** *m* asthma
**atelier** *m* workshop; artist's studio
**attacher** to fasten *(seatbelt)*

# French – English

| | |
|---|---|
| **attendre** | to wait (for) |
| **attention!** | look out! |
| ***faire attention*** | to be careful |
| **au lieu de** | instead of |
| **au revoir** | goodbye |
| **auberge** *f* | inn |
| ***auberge de jeunesse*** | youth hostel |
| **aujourd'hui** | today |
| **aussi** | also |
| **autobus** *m* | bus |
| **automne** *m* | autumn |
| **autoroute** *f* | motorway |
| **autre** | other |
| ***autres directions*** | other routes |
| **avance:** | |
| ***à l'avance*** | in advance |
| **avant** | before |
| **avec** | with |
| **avion** *m* | aeroplane |
| **avis** *m* | notice; warning |
| **avoir** | to have |
| **avril** | April |

## B

| | |
|---|---|
| **bagages** *mpl* | luggage |
| ***bagages à main*** | hand luggage |
| **baie** *f* | bay *(along coast)* |
| **baignade interdite** | no bathing/ swimming |
| **bain** *m* | bath *(act of bathing)* |
| **bal** *m* | ball; dance |
| **balade** *f* | walk; drive; trek |
| **balcon** *m* | circle *(theatre)*; balcony |
| **ball-trap** *m* | clay pigeon shooting |
| **balle** *f* | ball *(small, e.g. golf, tennis)* |
| **ballon** *m* | balloon; ball *(large)*; brandy or large wine glass |
| **banane** *f* | banana; bumbag |
| **banc** *m* | seat; bench |
| **banlieue** *f* | suburbs |
| **banque** *f* | bank |
| **bar** *m* | bar |
| **barbe à papa** | candy floss |
| **barque** *f* | rowing boat |
| **barrage routier** | road block |
| **route barrée** | road closed |
| **bas** *m* | bottom *(of page, etc.)*; stocking |
| **en bas** | below; downstairs |
| **bas(se)** | low |
| **bateau** *m* | boat; ship |
| **bâtiment** *m* | building |
| **bâton (de ski)** *m* | ski pole |

**beau (belle)** lovely; handsome; beautiful; nice *(enjoyable)*
**beaucoup (de)** much/many; a lot of
**bébé** *m* baby
**belge** Belgian
**Belgique** *f* Belgium
**besoin:** ***avoir besoin de*** to need
**bibliothèque** *f* library
**bien** well; right; good
***bien cuit(e)*** well done *(steak, etc.)*
**bientôt** soon; shortly
**bienvenu(e)** welcome!
**bière** *f* beer
***bière (à la) pression*** draught beer
***bière blonde*** lager
***bière brune*** bitter
**bijouterie** *f* jeweller's; jewellery
**billet** *m* note; ticket
***billet aller-retour*** return ticket
***billet d'avion*** plane ticket
***billet de banque*** banknote
***billet simple*** one-way ticket
**biologique** organic
**blanc (blanche)** white; blank
**blessé(e)** injured
**bleu** *m* bruise
**bleu(e)** blue; very rare *(steak, etc.)*
**boire** to drink
**bois** *m* wood
**boisson** *f* drink
***boisson non alcoolisée*** soft drink
**boîte** *f* can; box
***boîte à lettres*** post box
***boîte de nuit*** night club
**bol** *m* bowl *(for soup, etc.)*
**bon** *m* token; voucher
**bon (bonne)** good; right; nice
***bon marché*** inexpensive
**bonbon** *m* sweet
**bonsoir** good evening
**bord** *m* border; edge; verge
***à bord*** on board
***au bord de la mer*** at the seaside
**bouche** *f* mouth
**boucherie** *f* butcher's shop
**bouée de sauvetage** *f* life belt
**boulangerie** *f* bakery

# French - English

**boules** *fpl* game similar to bowls
**Bourgogne** Burgundy
**bout** *m* end
**bouteille** *f* bottle
**bouton** *m* button; switch; spot
***bouton de fièvre*** cold sore
**bras** *m* arm
**brasserie** *f* café; brewery
**Bretagne** *f* Brittany
**breton(ne)** from Brittany
**britannique** British
**brocante** *f* second-hand goods; flea market
**brouillard** *m* fog
**brûlé(e)** burnt
**brûlures d'estomac** *fpl* heartburn
**brun(e)** brown; dark
**bureau** *m* desk; office
***bureau de change*** foreign exchange office
***bureau de poste*** post office
***bureau de renseignements*** information office
***bureau des objets trouvés*** lost-property
**bus** *m* bus
**butane** *m* camping gas

## C

**ça** that
***ça va*** it's OK; I'm OK
***ça va?*** are you OK?
**cabine** *f* beach hut; cubicle
***cabine d'essayage*** changing room
**cadeau** *m* gift
**café** *m* coffee; café
***café au lait*** white coffee
***café crème*** creamy coffee
***café noir*** black coffee
**caisse** *f* cash desk; case
**calmant** *m* sedative
**camping** *m* camping; campsite
**Canada** *m* Canada
**canadien(ne)** Canadian
**canapé** *m* sofa; open sandwich
***canapé-lit*** sofa bed
**canne à pêche** fishing rod
**canot de sauvetage** lifeboat
**car** *m* coach
**carrefour** *m* crossroads

**carte** *f* map; card; menu; pass *(bus, train)*
***carte bleue*** credit card
***carte d'abonnement*** season ticket
***carte d'embarquement*** boarding card/pass
***carte d'identité*** identity card
***carte de crédit*** credit card
***carte des vins*** wine list
***carte postale*** postcard
***carte routière*** road map
***carte vermeille*** senior citizen's rail pass
**casque** *m* helmet
***casque (à écouteurs)*** headphones
**cassé(e)** broken
**casse-croûte** *m* snacks
**cause** *f* cause
**caution** *f* security *(for loan)*; deposit
***caution à verser*** deposit required
**cave** *f* cellar
**ceci** this
**cédez le passage** give way
**ceinture de sécurité** seatbelt
**cela** that
**célèbre** famous
**cent** *m* hundred
**centre** centre
***centre commercial*** shopping centre
***centre de loisirs*** leisure centre
***centre équestre*** riding school
***centre-ville*** city centre
**cercle** *m* circle; ring
**céréales** *fpl* cereal
**cette** this; that
**CFF** *mpl* Swiss Railways
**chacun(e)** each
**chaîne** *f* chain; channel; *(mountain)* range
**chaise** *f* chair
***chaise de bébé*** high chair
**chambre** *f* bedroom; room
***chambre d'hôte*** bed and breakfast
***chambres*** rooms to let *(on sign)*
**champ** *m* field
***champ de courses*** racecourse
**champignon vénéneux** toadstool
**chance** *f* luck
**chantier** *m* building site; roadworks

# French – English

**chaque** each; every
**charbon de bois** charcoal
**charcuterie** *f* pork butcher's; delicatessen; cooked meat
**chariot** *m* trolley
**chasse** *f* hunting; shooting
***chasse gardée*** private hunting
**château** *m* castle; mansion
**chaud(e)** hot
**chauffage** *m* heating
**chaussée déformée** uneven road surface
**chaussée rétrécie** road narrows
**chaussée verglacée** icy road
**chaussette** *f* sock
**chaussure** *f* shoe; boot
**chef de train** train guard
**chemin** *m* path; lane; track; way
***chemin de fer*** railway
**chemise** *f* shirt
**chemisier** *m* blouse
**chèque de voyage** traveller's cheque
**cher (chère)** dear; expensive
**cheval** *m* horse
***faire du cheval*** to ride
**cheveux** *mpl* hair
**chez** at the house of
***chez moi*** at my home
**choix** *m* range; choice; selection
**chose** *f* thing
**cimetière** *m* cemetery; graveyard
**circuit** *m* round trip; circuit
**circulation** *f* traffic
**cirque** *m* circus
**cité** *f* city; housing estate
**clair(e)** clear; light
**classe** *f* grade; class
**clé** *f* key; spanner
**clef** *f* key
**client(e)** *m/f* client; customer
**climatisation** *f* air-conditioning
**climatisé(e)** air-conditioned
**cocher** to 'tick' *(on form – in fact, you must cross)*
**code postal** postcode
**code secret** pin number
**cœur** *m* heart
**coffre-fort** *m* safe
**coiffeur** *m* hairdresser; barber
**coiffeuse** *f* hairdresser
**coin** *m* corner

**col** *m* collar; pass *(in mountains)*
**combien** how much/many
**combinaison de plongée** *f* wetsuit
**comme** like
***comme ça*** like this; like that
**commencer** to begin
**comment** how
***comment?*** pardon?
**commissariat (de police)** *m* police station
**communication** *f* communication; call *(on telephone)*
**compartiment** *m* compartment *(train)*
**complet(-ète)** full (up)
**composer** to dial *(a number)*
**composter votre billet** validate your ticket
**comprenant** including
**comprimé** *m* tablet
**compris(e)** included
***non compris*** not included
**comptant** *m* cash
**compte** *m* number; account
***compte en banque*** bank account
**comptoir** *m* counter *(in shop, bar, etc.)*
**concierge** *m/f* caretaker; janitor
**concours** *m* contest; aid
**conduire** to drive
**confirmer** to confirm
**congélateur** *m* freezer
**conserver** to keep; to retain *(ticket, etc.)*
**consigne** *f* deposit; left luggage
**consommation** *f* drink
**contenu** *m* contents
**continuer** to continue
**contraceptif** *m* contraceptive
**contrat** *m* contract
***contrat de location*** lease
**contravention** *f* fine *(penalty)*
**contre** against; versus
**contrôle** *m* check
***contrôle des passeports*** passport control
***contrôle radar*** speed check
**contrôleur (-euse)** *m/f* ticket inspector
**cordonnerie** *f* shoe repairer's

# French - English

**corps** *m* body
**correspondance** *f* connection (*transport*)
**Corse** *f* Corsica
**costume** *m* suit (*man's*)
**côte** *f* coast; hill; rib
***Côte d'Azur*** French Riviera
**côté** *m* side
***à côté de*** beside; next to
**coton** *m* cotton
**couche (de bébé)** *f* nappy
**couette** *f* continental quilt; duvet
**couleur** *f* colour
**couloir** *m* corridor; aisle
**coup de soleil** sunburn
**coup de téléphone** phone call
**cour** *f* court; courtyard
**courant** *m* power; current
**courrier** *m* mail; post
***courrier électronique*** e-mail
**cours** *m* lesson; course; rate
**course** *f* race (*sport*); errand
***course hippique*** horse race
**court(e)** short
**coût** *m* cost
**couteau** *m* knife
**couvert** *m* cover charge; place setting
**couvert(e)** covered
**couverture** *f* blanket; cover
**crémerie** *f* dairy
**crêperie** *f* pancake shop/restaurant
**crise cardiaque** heart attack
**croisement** *m* junction (*road*)
**croisière** *f* cruise
**croix** *f* cross
**cru(e)** raw
**cuiller/cuillère** *f* spoon
***cuiller/cuillère à café*** teaspoon
**cuir** *m* leather
**cuisine** *f* cooking; cuisine; kitchen
***cuisine familiale*** home cooking
**cuisinière** *f* cook; cooker
**cuit(e)** cooked
***bien cuit(e)*** well done (*steak, etc.*)
**cyclisme** *m* cycling

## D

**dame** *f* lady
***dames*** ladies; ladies' (toilet)

**danger** *m* danger
**dangereux (-euse)** dangerous
**dans** into; in; on
**date** *f* date *(day)*
***date de naissance*** date of birth
**de** from; of; some
**débutant(e)** *m/f* beginner
**décaféiné(e)** decaffeinated
**décembre** December
**déclaration de douane** customs declaration
**décollage** *m* take-off *(plane)*
**décoller** to take off *(plane)*
**décrocher** to lift the receiver
**dedans** inside
**défectueux (-euse)** faulty
**défense de...** no.../ ... forbidden
***défense de fumer*** no smoking
***défense de stationner*** no parking
**dégustation de vins** wine tasting
**dehors** outside; outdoors
**déjeuner** *m* lunch
**délicieux (-euse)** delicious
**délit** *m* offence
**deltaplane** *m* hang-glider
**demain** tomorrow
**demande** *f* application; request
**demander** to ask (for)
**démarqué(e)** reduced *(goods)*
**demi(e)** half
**demi-pension** *f* half board
**demi-tarif** *m* half fare
**demi-tour** *m* U-turn
**dent** *f* tooth
**dentifrice** *m* toothpaste
**départ** *m* departure
**département** *m* county
**dépasser** to exceed; to overtake
**déranger** to disturb
**dernier(-ère)** last; latest
**derrière** at the back; behind
**dès: *dès votre arrivée*** as soon as you arrive
**désolé(e)** sorry
**dessous: *en dessous de*** underneath
**dessus: *au dessus de*** on top (of)

# French – English

**destination:**
***à destination de*** bound for
**détourner** to divert
**deux** two
***deux fois*** twice
***les deux*** both
**deuxième** second
**devant** *m* front; in front (of)
**déviation** *f* diversion
**diabète** *m* diabetes
**diarrhée** *f* diarrhoea
**diététique:**
***produits diététiques*** health foods
**difficile** difficult
**dimanche** *m* Sunday
**dîner** *m* dinner
***dîner spectacle*** cabaret dinner
**dire** to say; to tell
**direct:**
***train direct*** through train
**directeur** *m* manager; headmaster
**disparu(e)** missing *(disappeared)*
**disponible** available
**distributeur automatique** vending machine; cash machine
**divertissements** *mpl* entertainment
**docteur** *m* doctor
**domicile** *m* home; address
**dormir** to sleep
**douane** *f* customs
**douche** *f* shower
**douleur** *f* pain
**douloureux (-euse)** painful
**doux (douce)** mild; gentle; soft; sweet
**douzaine** *f* dozen
**drogue** *f* drug
**droit(e)** right *(not left)*; straight
***à droite*** on/to the right
***tenez votre droite*** keep to right
***tout droit*** straight on
**dur(e)** hard; hard-boiled; tough

## E

**eau** *f* water
***eau de Javel*** bleach
***eau minérale*** mineral water
***eau potable*** drinking water
**échelle de secours** fire escape
**écluse** *f* lock *(in canal)*

| | |
|---|---|
| **école** *f* | school |
| **écossais(e)** | Scottish |
| **Écosse** *f* | Scotland |
| **écouter** | to listen to |
| **écran solaire** | sunscreen lotion |
| **écran total** | sunblock |
| **écrire** | to write |
| **édulcorant** *m* | sweetener |
| **embarquement** *m* | boarding |
| **emporter:** | |
| ***à emporter*** | take-away |
| **en** | some; any; in; to; made of |
| ***en cas de*** | in case of |
| ***en face de*** | opposite |
| ***en gros*** | in bulk; wholesale |
| ***en panne*** | out of order |
| ***en retard*** | late |
| ***en train*** | by train |
| **enceinte** | pregnant |
| **encore** | still; yet; again |
| **enfant** *m/f* | child |
| **enregistrement** *m* | check-in desk |
| **enregistrer** | to record; to check in; to video |
| **ensemble** | together |
| **entracte** *m* | interval |
| **entre** | between |
| **entrée** *f* | entrance; admission; starter *(food)* |
| ***entrée gratuite*** | admission free |
| ***entrée interdite*** | no entry |
| **entrez!** | come in! |
| **environs** *mpl* | surroundings |
| **épicerie** *f* | grocer's shop |
| ***épicerie fine*** | delicatessen |
| **épuisé(e)** | sold out; used up |
| **équipage** *m* | crew |
| **équitation** *f* | horse-riding |
| **erreur** *f* | mistake |
| **escalade** *f* | climbing |
| **escalator** *m* | escalator |
| **escalier** *m* | stairs |
| ***escalier de secours*** | fire escape |
| **Espagne** *f* | Spain |
| **espagnol** *m* | Spanish *(language)* |
| **espagnol(e)** | Spanish |
| **essayer** | to try; to try on |
| **essence** *f* | petrol |
| ***essence sans plomb*** | unleaded petrol |
| **estomac** *m* | stomach |
| **et** | and |
| **étage** *m* | storey |
| **États-Unis** | United States |
| **été** *m* | summer |
| **éteindre** | to turn off |

# French – English

**éteint(e)** out *(light)*
**étiquette** *f* label; tag
**étranger(-ère)** *m/f* foreigner
**être** to be
**étroit(e)** narrow; tight
**étudiant(e)** *m/f* student
**européen(ne)** European
**éviter** to avoid
**exact(e)** right *(correct)*
**excédent de bagages** *m* excess baggage
**excès de vitesse** *m* speeding
**exclu(e)** excluded
**excursion** *f* trip; outing; excursion
**excusez-moi!** excuse me!
**exemplaire** *m* copy
**exposition** *f* exhibition
**extérieur(e)** outside
**extra** top-quality; first-rate

## F

**fabriqué en...** made in...
**face:**
***en face (de)*** opposite
**facile** easy
**facture** *f* invoice
**faire** to make; to do
**fait main** handmade
**falaise** *f* cliff
**famille** *f* family
**farine** *f* flour
**fatigué(e)** tired
**fauteuil** *m* armchair; seat
***fauteuil roulant*** wheelchair
**faxer** to fax
**femme** *f* woman; wife
***femme de chambre*** chambermaid
***femme de ménage*** cleaner
**fenêtre** *f* window
**fente** *f* crack; slot
**fer** *m* iron *(for clothes)*
***fer à repasser***
**férié(e):**
***jour férié*** public holiday
**ferme** *f* farmhouse; farm
**fermé(e)** closed
**fermer** to close/shut; to turn off
***fermer à clé*** to lock
**ferry** *m* car ferry
**fête** *f* holiday; fête; party
***fête foraine*** funfair
**feu** *m* fire; traffic lights
**février** February
**fièvre: *avoir de la fièvre*** to have a temperature

| | |
|---|---|
| **file** *f* | lane; row |
| **filet** *m* | net; fillet *(of meat, fish)* |
| **fille** *f* | daughter; girl |
| **fils** *m* | son |
| **fin** *f* | end |
| **fin(e)** | thin *(material)*; fine *(delicate)* |
| **fini(e)** | finished |
| **finir** | to end; to finish |
| **fleur** *f* | flower |
| **fleuriste** *m/f* | florist |
| **fleuve** *m* | river |
| **foire** *f* | fair |
| **fois** *f* | time (*occasion*) |
| ***cette fois*** | this time |
| ***une fois*** | once |
| **foncé(e)** | dark *(colour)* |
| **fonctionner** | to work *(machine)* |
| **fond** *m* | back *(of hall, room)*; bottom |
| **forêt** *f* | forest |
| **forfait** *m* | fixed price; ski pass |
| **forme** *f* | shape; style |
| **formulaire** *m* | form *(document)* |
| **four** *m* | oven |
| **frais, fraîche** | fresh; cool; wet *(paint)* |
| **français** *m* | French *(language)* |
| **français(e)** | French |
| **frère** *m* | brother |
| **frigo** *m* | fridge |
| **froid(e)** | cold |
| **frontière** *f* | border; boundary |
| **fruit** *m* | fruit |
| **fumer** | to smoke |
| **fumeurs** | smokers |

## G

| | |
|---|---|
| **gagner** | to earn; to win |
| **galerie** *f* | art gallery; arcade; roof-rack |
| **gallois(e)** | Welsh |
| **garage** *m* | garage |
| **garantie** *f* | guarantee |
| **garçon** *m* | boy; waiter |
| **gare** *f* | railway station |
| ***gare routière*** | bus terminal |
| **garer** | to park |
| **gasoil; gaz-oil** *m* | diesel fuel |
| **gauche** | left |
| ***à gauche*** | to/on the left |
| **gazeux(-euse)** | fizzy |
| **gelé(e)** | frozen |
| **gendarme** *m* | policeman *(in rural areas)* |
| **gendarmerie** *f* | police station |
| **gilet** *m* | waistcoat |

# French - English

**_gilet de sauvetage_** life jacket
**gîte** *m* self-catering house/flat
**glace** *f* ice; ice cream; mirror
**glacière** *f* cool-box *(for picnic)*
**glissant(e)** slippery
**gorge** *f* throat; gorge
**goût** *m* flavour; taste
**grand(e)** great; high *(speed, number)*; big; tall
**grand-mère** *f* grandmother
**grand-père** *m* grandfather
**Grande-Bretagne** *f* Great Britain
**gras(se)** fat; greasy
**gratis, gratuit(e)** free (of charge)
**grave** serious
**grippe** *f* flu
**gris(e)** grey
**gros(se)** big; large; fat
**grotte** *f* cave
**guerre** *f* war
**guichet** *m* ticket office; counter
**guide** *m* guide; guidebook
**_guide de conversation_** phrase book

## H

**habiter** to live (in)
**halles** *fpl* covered food market
**handicapé(e)** disabled *(person)*
**haut** *m* top *(of ladder, bikini)*
**_en haut_** upstairs
**haut(e)** high; tall
**hauteur** *f* height
**hébergement** *m* lodging
**herbe** *f* grass
**heure** *f* hour; time of day
**_heure de pointe_** rush hour
**hier** yesterday
**hippisme** *m* horse riding
**hippodrome** *m* racecourse
**hiver** *m* winter
**hollandais(e)** Dutch
**homme** *m* man
**honoraires** *mpl* fee
**hôpital** *m* hospital
**horaire** *m* timetable; schedule
**hors:** ***hors de*** out of
**_hors-saison_** off-season
**_hors service_** out of order

***hors-taxe*** duty-free
**hôte** *m* host; guest
**hôtel** *m* hotel
***hôtel de ville*** town hall
**hôtesse** *f* stewardess
**huile** *f* oil
**hypermarché** *m* hypermarket

## I

**ici** here
**il y a...** there is/are...; ago
***il y a un défaut*** there's a fault
***il y a une semaine*** a week ago
**île** *f* island
**immeuble** *m* building *(offices, flats)*
**impasse** *f* dead end
**imperméable** waterproof
**incendie** *m* fire
**inclus(e)** included; inclusive
**indicatif** *m* dialling code
**indigestion** *f* indigestion
**infirmerie** *f* infirmary
**infirmier(-ière)** *m/f* nurse
**informations** *fpl* news; information
**inondation** *f* flood
**instant** *m* moment
***un instant!*** just a minute!
**institut de beauté** beauty salon
**interdit** forbidden
**intéressant(e)** interesting
**intérieur:**
***à l'intérieur*** indoors
**introduire** to introduce; to insert
**invité(e)** *m/f* guest
**irlandais(e)** Irish
**Irlande** *f* Ireland
**Irlande du Nord** *f* Northern Ireland
**issue de secours** *f* emergency exit
**itinéraire** *m* route
***itinéraire touristique*** scenic route

## J

**jamais** never
**jambe** *f* leg
**janvier** January
**Japon** *m* Japan
**jardin** *m* garden
**jaune** yellow
**jeton** *m* token
**jeu** *m* game; set *(of tools, etc)*; gambling

# French - English

**jeudi** *m* Thursday
**jeune** young
**joli(e)** pretty
**jouer** to play *(games)*
**jouet** *m* toy
**jour** *m* day
***jour férié*** public holiday
**journal** *m* newspaper
**journée** *f* day *(length of time)*
**juif (juive)** Jewish
**juillet** July
**juin** June
**jumelles** *fpl* twins; binoculars
**jus** *m* juice
***jus d'orange*** orange juice
***jus de fruit*** fruit juice
**jusqu'à/au/aux** until; till

## K

**kas(c)her** kosher
**kilométrage illimité** unlimited mileage
**kilomètre** *m* kilometre
**kiosque** *m* kiosk; newsstand
**klaxonner** to sound one's horn

## L

**là** there
**lac** *m* lake
**laine** *f* wool
**laissez en blanc** leave blank
**lait** *m* milk
***lait cru*** unpasteurised milk
***lait démaquillant*** make-up remover
***lait demi-écrémé*** semi-skimmed milk
***lait écrémé*** skim(med) milk
***lait entier*** full-cream milk
***lait longue conservation*** long-life milk
***lait maternisé*** baby milk; formula
***lait solaire*** suntan lotion
**lames de rasoir** razor blades
**langue** *f* tongue; language
**lavable** washable
**lavage** *m* washing
**lave-linge** *m* washing machine
**laver** to wash
***se laver*** to wash (oneself)
**laverie automatique** *f* launderette

| | |
|---|---|
| **leçon** *f* | lesson |
| ***leçons particulières*** | private lessons |
| **légume** *m* | vegetable |
| **lent(e)** | slow |
| **lentement** | slowly |
| **lentille** *f* | lentil; lens *(of glasses)* |
| ***lentille de contact*** | contact lens |
| **lessive** *f* | soap powder; washing |
| **lettre** *f* | letter |
| **leur(s)** | their |
| **lèvre** *f* | lip |
| **librairie** *f* | bookshop |
| **libre** | free; vacant |
| **libre-service** | self-service |
| **lieu** *m* | place *(location)* |
| **ligne** *f* | line; service; route |
| **limitation de vitesse** *f* | speed limit |
| **lin** *m* | linen *(cloth)* |
| **linge** *m* | linen *(bed, table)*; laundry |
| **lingettes** *fpl* | baby wipes |
| **liste** *f* | list |
| **lit** *m* | bed |
| **livre** *f* | pound |
| **livre** *m* | book |
| **location** *f* | hiring (out); letting |
| **logement** *m* | accommodation |
| **loi** *f* | law |
| **loin** | far |
| **Londres** | London |
| **long(ue)** | long |
| ***le long de*** | along |
| **longtemps** | for a long time |
| **louer** | to let; to hire; to rent |
| ***à louer*** | for hire/to rent |
| **lourd(e)** | heavy |
| **lumière** *f* | light |
| **lundi** *m* | Monday |
| **lune de miel** | honeymoon |
| **lunettes** *fpl* | glasses |
| ***lunettes de soleil*** | sunglasses |
| ***lunettes protectrices/de protection*** | goggles |

## M

| | |
|---|---|
| **M** | sign for the Paris metro |
| **machine à laver** | washing machine |
| **magasin** *m* | shop |
| ***grand magasin*** | department store |
| **mai** | May |

# French – English

**maillot de bain** swimsuit
**main** *f* hand
**maintenant** now
**mairie** *f* town hall
**maison** *f* house; home
***maison de campagne*** villa
**mal** badly
**mal** *m* harm; pain
***mal de dents*** toothache
***mal de mer*** seasickness
***mal de tête*** headache
***faire du mal à quelqu'un*** to harm someone
**malade** ill; sick
**malade** *m/f* sick person; patient
**maladie** *f* disease
**Manche** *f* the Channel
**manger** to eat
**marchand** *m* dealer; merchant
**marché** *m* market
***marché aux puces*** flea market
**marcher** to walk; to work *(machine, car)*
***en marche*** on *(machine)*
**mardi** *m* Tuesday
***mardi gras*** Shrove Tuesday
**marée** *f* tide
***marée basse*** low tide
***marée haute*** high tide
**mari** *m* husband
**marié(e)** married
**marionnette** *f* puppet
**marron** brown
**mars** March
**matelas** *m* mattress
**matériel** *m* equipment; kit
**matin** *m* morning
**mécanicien** *m* mechanic
**médecin** *m* doctor
**médicament** *m* medicine; drug; medication
**Méditerranée** *f* Mediterranean Sea
**meilleur(e)** best; better
**mél** *m* e-mail
**membre** *m* member *(of club, etc.)*
**même** same
**méningite** *f* meningitis
**menu** *m* set menu
**mer** *f* sea
**merci** thank you
**mercredi** *m* Wednesday
**mère** *f* mother
**message** *m* message
**messe** *f* mass *(church)*

**messieurs** *mpl* men; gentlemen; gents' (toilet)
**mesure** *f* measurement
**météo** *f* weather forecast
**métier** *m* trade; occupation
**métro** *m* underground
**mettre en marche** to turn on
**meublé(e)** furnished
**meubles** *mpl* furniture
**midi** *m* midday; noon
**Midi** *m* the south of France
**mieux** better; best
**mille** *m* thousand
**millimètre** *m* millimetre
**mineur(e)** under age; minor
**minuit** *m* midnight
**minute** *f* minute
**miroir** *m* mirror
**mistral** *m* strong cold dry wind *(South of France)*
**mixte** mixed
**mode d'emploi** instructions for use
**moins** less; minus
***moins (de)*** less (than)
***moins cher*** cheaper
**mois** *m* month
**moitié** *f* half
***à moitié prix*** half-price
**mon/ma/mes** my
**monde** *m* world
**moniteur** *m* instructor; coach
**monitrice** *f* instructress; coach
**monnaie** *f* currency; change
**monsieur** *m* gentleman
**Monsieur** *m* Mr; Sir
**montagne** *f* mountain
**monter à cheval** to horse-ride
**morceau** *m* piece; bit; cut *(of meat)*
**morsure** *f* bite
**mot** *m* word; note *(letter)*
***mot de passe*** password
**moteur** *m* engine; motor
**moto** *f* motorbike
**mouchoir** *m* handkerchief
**moustique** *m* mosquito
**moyen(ne)** average
**mur** *m* wall
**mûr(e)** mature; ripe
**musée** *m* museum
***musée d'art*** art gallery
**Musulman(e)** Muslim

## N

**natation** *f* swimming
**nature** *f* wildlife
**naturel(le)** natural
**navette** *f* shuttle *(bus service)*
**navigation** *f* sailing
**négatif** *m* negative *(photography)*
**neige** *f* snow
**nettoyage** *m* cleaning
***nettoyage à sec*** dry-cleaning
**neuf (neuve)** new
**névralgie** *f* headache
**nez** *m* nose
**Noël** *m* Christmas
**noir(e)** black
**nom** *m* name; noun
***nom de famille*** family name
***nom de jeune fille*** maiden name
**nombre** *m* number
**nombreux (-euse)** numerous
**non** no; not
**non alcoolisé(e)** non-alcoholic
**non-fumeur** non-smoking
**nord** *m* north
**normal(e)** normal; standard *(size)*
**nos** our
**note** *f* note; bill; memo
**notre** our
**nourriture** *f* food
**nouveau (nouvelle)** new
***de nouveau*** again
**novembre** November
**nuageux(-euse)** cloudy
**nuit** *f* night
***bonne nuit*** good night
**numéro** *m* number; act; issue

## O

**objectif** *m* objective; lens *(of camera)*
**objet** *m* object
***objets de valeur*** valuable items
***objets trouvés*** lost property
**obligatoire** compulsory
**obtenir** to get; to obtain
**occasion** *f* occasion; bargain
**occupé(e)** busy; hired *(taxi)*; engaged
**octobre** October
**office** *m* service *(church)*; office
***office de/du tourisme*** tourist office
**offre** *f* offer

**œil** *m* eye
**or** *m* gold
**orange** orange; amber *(traffic light)*
**orchestre** *m* orchestra; stalls *(in theatre)*
**ordinaire** ordinary
**ordinateur** *m* computer
**ordonnance** *f* prescription
**ordre** *m* order
***à l'ordre de*** payable to
**oreille** *f* ear
**ou** or
**où** where
**oublier** to forget
**ouest** *m* west
**oui** yes
**ouvert(e)** open; on *(tap, gas, etc.)*
**ouvrir** to open

## P

**page** *f* page
**pages jaunes** Yellow Pages
**palais** *m* palace
**panier** *m* basket
**panne** *f* breakdown
**panneau** *m* sign
**pansement** *m* bandage
**papier** *m* paper
***papier cadeau*** gift-wrap
***papier hygiénique*** toilet paper
***papiers*** identity papers; (vehicle) documents
**par exemple** for example
**par jour** per day
**par téléphone** by phone
**parc** *m* park
***parc d'attractions*** funfair
**parce que** because
**parcmètre** *m* parking meter
**pardon!** sorry!; excuse me!
**parent(e)** *m/f* relative
**parfait(e)** perfect
**parfum** *m* perfume; flavour
**parfumerie** *f* perfume shop
**parking** *m* car park
***parking souterrain*** underground car park
***parking surveillé*** attended car park
**parler (à)** to speak (to); to talk (to)
**partie** *f* part; match *(game)*
**partir** to leave; to go
***à partir de*** from
**partout** everywhere
**pas** not

## French - English

| | |
|---|---|
| **passage** *m* | passage |
| ***passage à niveau*** | level crossing |
| ***passage clouté*** | pedestrian crossing |
| ***passage interdit*** | no through way |
| ***passage souterrain*** | underpass |
| **passager (-ère)** *m/f* | passenger |
| **passeport** *m* | passport |
| **passer** | to pass; to spend (*time*) |
| ***se passer*** | to happen |
| **passerelle** *f* | gangway (*bridge*) |
| **passe-temps** *m* | hobby |
| **pastille** *f* | lozenge |
| **patins à glace** | ice skates |
| **patins à roulettes** | roller skates |
| **patinoire** *f* | skating rink |
| **pâtisserie** *f* | cake shop; little cake |
| **payer** | to pay (for) |
| ***payé(e)*** | paid |
| ***payé(e) d'avance*** | prepaid |
| **pays** *m* | land; country |
| ***du pays*** | local |
| **Pays-Bas** *mpl* | Netherlands |
| **Pays de Galles** *m* | Wales |
| **péage** *m* | toll (*motorway, etc.*) |
| **peau** *f* | skin; hide (*leather*) |
| **pêche** *f* | peach; fishing |
| **pêcher** | to fish |
| **pédalo** *m* | pedal boat/ pedalo |
| **pelote** *f* | ball |
| ***pelote basque*** | pelota (*ball game for two players*) |
| **pendant** | during |
| **pendant que** | while |
| **pension** *f* | guesthouse |
| **pension complète** | full board |
| **pente** *f* | slope |
| **perdre** | to lose |
| **perdu(e)** | lost (*object*) |
| **père** *m* | father |
| **périmé(e)** | out of date; expired |
| **périphérique** *m* | ring road |
| **permis** *m* | permit; licence |
| ***permis de chasse*** | hunting permit |
| ***permis de conduire*** | driving licence |
| ***permis de pêche*** | fishing permit |
| **personne** *f* | person |

**pétanque** *f* type of bowls
**petit(e)** small; slight
***petit déjeuner*** breakfast
**peu** little; few
***à peu près*** approximately
***un peu (de)*** a bit (of)
**phare** *m* headlight; lighthouse
**pharmacie** *f* chemist's; pharmacy
**pichet** *m* jug; carafe
**pièce** *f* room *(in house)*; play *(theatre)*; coin
***pièce d'identité*** means of identification
***pièce de rechange*** spare part
**pied** *m* foot
***à pied*** on foot
**piéton** *m* pedestrian

**pile** *f* pile; battery
**pilule** *f* (contraceptive) pill
**piquet** *m* peg *(for tent)*
**piqûre** *f* insect bite; injection; sting
**piscine** *f* swimming pool
**piste** *f* ski-run; runway
***piste de luge*** toboggan run
***piste pour débutants*** nursery slope
**placard** *m* cupboard
**place** *f* square *(in town)*; seat; space *(room)*
**plage** *f* beach
**plainte** *f* complaint
**plaisir** *m* enjoyment; pleasure

**plaît**: ***s'il vous/te plaît*** please
**plan** *m* map *(of town)*
***plan de la ville*** street map
**planche** *f* plank
***planche à repasser*** ironing board
***planche à voile*** sailboard(ing); windsurfer/ing
***planche de surf*** surfboard
**plat** *m* dish; course *(of meal)*; main course
***plat principal*** main course
**plein(e) (de)** full (of)
***le plein!*** fill it up! *(car)*
***plein tarif*** peak rate; full fare
**pleuvoir** to rain
***il pleut*** it's raining
**plonger** to dive

## French – English

**pluie** *f* rain
**plus** more; most
***plus grand(e) (que)*** bigger (than)
***plus tard*** later
**pneu** *m* tyre
***pneu crevé*** burst tyre
***pneu dégonflé*** flat tyre
**poche** *f* pocket
**poêle** *f* frying pan
**poids** *m* weight
***poids lourd*** heavy goods vehicle
**point** *m* place; point; stitch; dot
**pointure** *f* size *(of shoes)*
**poison** *m* poison
**poissonnerie** *f* fishmonger's shop
**police** *f* policy *(insurance)*; police
**pompiers** *mpl* fire brigade
**pont** *m* bridge; deck *(of ship)*
**port** *m* harbour; port
**portable** *m* mobile phone; laptop
**porte** *f* door; gate
**portefeuille** *m* wallet
**porter** to wear; to carry
***porte-clefs*** *m* keyring
***porte-monnaie*** *m* purse
**poste** *f* post; post office
***poste de contrôle*** checkpoint
***poste de secours*** first-aid post
**poster** to post
**potable** drinkable; drinking *(water)*
**poterie** *f* pottery
**poudre** *f* powder
**pour** for
**pourboire** *m* tip
**pourquoi** why
**pousser** to push
**poussette** *f* push chair
**premier(-ière)** first
***premiers secours*** first aid
**prendre** to take; to get; to catch
**prénom** *m* first name
**près de** near (to)
**préservatif** *m* condom
**pressing** *m* dry cleaner's
**prêt(e)** ready
**prêt-à-porter** *m* off-the-peg clothes

**prévision** *f* forecast
**prière de...** please...
**principal(e)** main
**printemps** *m* spring
**priorité** *f* right of way
***priorité à droite*** give way to traffic from right
**privé(e)** private
**prix** *m* price; prize
***à prix réduit*** cut-price
***prix d'entrée*** admission fee
**problème** *m* problem
**prochain(e)** next
**proche** close *(near)*
**produits** *mpl* produce; product
**profond(e)** deep
**promotionnel(le)** on offer
**propriétaire** *m/f* owner
**propriété** *f* property
**provisoire** temporary
**public** *m* audience
**pull(over)** *m* sweater
**PV** *m* parking ticket

## Q

**quai** *m* platform
**quand** when
**quart** *m* quarter
**quartier** *m* neighbourhood; district
**que** that; than; whom; what
***qu'est-ce que c'est?*** what is it?
**quel(le)** which; what
**quelque** some
**quelque chose** something
**queue:** ***faire la queue*** to queue (up)
**qui** who; which

## R

**rabais** *m* reduction
**radiographie** *f* X-ray
**rafraîchissements** *mpl* refreshments
**rage** *f* rabies
**ralentir** to slow down
**randonnée** *f* hike
***randonnée à cheval*** pony-trekking
**rappel** *m* reminder *(on signs)*
**rapide** *m* express train
**raquette** *f* racket; bat; snowshoe
**rasoir** *m* razor
**RATP** *f* Paris transport authority
**RC** ground floor
**récepteur** *m* receiver *(of phone)*

# French - English

**réception** *f* reception; check-in
**recette** *f* recipe
**réchaud de camping** *m* camping stove
**réclamation** *f* complaint
**reçu** *m* receipt
**réduction** *f* reduction; discount; concession
**régime** *m* diet
**région** *f* region
**reine** *f* queen
**relais routier** *m* roadside restaurant
**remède** *m* remedy
**remplir** to fill (up); to fill in/out
**rencontrer** to meet
**rendez-vous** *m* date; appointment
**renseignements** *mpl* information
**réparations** *fpl* repairs
**repas** *m* meal
**repasser** to iron
**répondre (à)** to reply; to answer
**réponse** *f* answer; reply
**représentation** *f* performance
**requis(e)** required
**RER** *m* high-speed Paris commuter train
**réservation** *f* reservation; booking
**réserve naturelle** *f* nature reserve
**réservé(e)** reserved
**restoroute** *m* roadside or motorway restaurant
**retard** *m* delay
**retour** *m* return
**retourner** to go back
**retrait** *m* withdrawal; collection
***retrait d'espèces*** cash withdrawal
**retraité(e)** retired; old-age pensioner
**réveil** *m* alarm clock
**rez-de-chaussée** *m* ground floor
**rhume** *m* cold *(illness)*
***rhume des foins*** hay fever
**rien** nothing
***rien à déclarer*** nothing to declare
**rivière** *f* river
**RN** trunk road
**roi** *m* king
**roman(e)** Romanesque

**rond(e)** round
**rond-point** *m* roundabout
**rose** pink
**rose** *f* rose
**rôtisserie** *f* steakhouse; roast meat counter
**roue** *f* wheel
***roue de secours*** spare wheel
**rouge** red
**rougeur** *f* rash *(skin)*
**route** *f* road; route
***route barrée*** road closed
**Royaume-Uni** *m* United Kingdom
**rue** *f* street
***rue sans issue*** no through road
**ruelle** *f* lane; alley
**russe** Russian

## S

**sable** *m* sand
***sables mouvants*** quicksand
**sac** *m* sack; bag
***sac à dos*** backpack
***sac à main*** handbag
***sac de couchage*** sleeping bag
**saison** *f* season
***basse saison*** low season
***de saison*** in season
***haute saison*** high season
**salle** *f* lounge *(airport)*; hall; ward *(hospital)*
***salle à manger*** dining room
***salle d'attente*** waiting room
***salle de bains*** bathroom
**salon** *m* sitting room; lounge
***salon de beauté*** beauty salon
**samedi** *m* Saturday
**SAMU** *m* emergency services
**sang** *m* blood
**sans** without
***sans alcool*** alcohol-free
***sans issue*** no through road
**santé** *f* health
**sapeurs-pompiers** *mpl* fire brigade
**sauf** except (for)
**savoir** to know *(be aware of)*
***savoir faire quelque chose*** to know how to do sth
**savon** *m* soap
**scène** *f* stage
**sec (sèche)** dry; dried *(fruit, beans, etc.)*

## French - English

**sèche-cheveux** *m* hairdryer
**second(e)** second (*in sequence*)
**seconde** *f* second (*in time*)
**secours** *m* help
***au secours!*** help!
**sécurité** *f* security; safety
**séjour** *m* stay; visit
**sel** *m* salt
**self** *m* self-service restaurant
**semaine** *f* week
**sens** *m* meaning; direction
***sens interdit*** no entry
***sens unique*** one-way street
**septembre** September
**seringue** *f* syringe
**serrure** *f* lock
**servez-vous** help yourself
**service** *m* service; service charge; favour
***service compris*** service included
***service d'urgences*** emergency services
**serviette** *f* towel; briefcase
***serviette hygiénique*** sanitary towel
**seulement** only
**sexe** *m* sex
**shampooing** *m* shampoo
**short** *m* shorts
**si** if; yes (*to negative question*)
**siècle** *m* century
**siège** *m* seat; head office
**signer** to sign
**situé(e)** located
**ski** *m* ski; skiing
***ski de piste*** downhill skiing
***ski de randonnée/fond*** cross-country skiing
***ski nautique*** water-skiing
**SNCB** *f* Belgian Railways
**SNCF** *f* French Railways
**société** *f* company; society
**sœur** *f* sister
**soie** *f* silk
**soif** *f* thirst
***avoir soif*** to be thirsty
**soin** *m* care
***soins du visage*** facial
**soir** *m* evening
**soirée** *f* evening; party
**soldes** *mpl* sales
**soleil** *m* sun; sunshine
**somnifère** *m* sleeping pill
**sorte** *f* kind (*sort, type*)

**sortie** *f* exit
***sortie de secours*** emergency exit
***sortie interdite*** no exit
**sortir** to go out *(leave)*
**souper** *m* supper
**sourd(e)** deaf
**sous** underneath; under
**sous-sol** *m* basement
**sous-titres** *mpl* subtitles
**souterrain(e)** underground
**souvent** often
**sparadrap** *m* sticking plaster
**spectacle** *m* show *(in theatre)*; entertainment
**sport** *m* sport
***sports nautiques*** water-sports
**stade** *m* stadium
**stage** *m* course
**station** *f* station *(metro)*; resort
***station balnéaire*** seaside resort
***station de taxis*** taxi rank
***station-service*** service station
***station thermale*** spa
**stationnement** *m* parking
**sud** *m* south
**suisse** Swiss
**Suisse** *f* Switzerland
**suivre** to follow
**supermarché** *m* supermarket
**supplément** *m* extra charge
**supplémentaire** extra
**sur** on; onto; on top of; upon
***sur place*** on the spot
**sûr** safe; sure
**surf** *m* surfing
***faire du surf*** to surf
***surf des neiges*** snowboarding
**syndicat d'initiative** *m* tourist office

## T

**tabac** *m* tobacco; tobacconist's
**table** *f* table
**tableau** *m* painting; picture; board
**taille** *f* size *(of clothes)*; waist
***taille unique*** one size
***grande taille*** outsize (clothes)
**tard** late
**tarif** *m* price-list; rate; tarif
**tasse** *f* cup; mug
**taux** *m* rate

## French - English

***taux de change*** exchange rate
**taxe** *f* duty; tax *(on goods)*
**taxi** *m* cab *(taxi)*
**télé** *f* TV
**télécabine** *f* gondola lift
**télécarte** *f* phonecard
**téléphérique** *m* cable-car
**téléphone** *m* telephone
***téléphone portable*** mobile phone
**téléphoner (à)** to phone
**télésiège** *m* chair-lift
**télévision** *f* television
**temps** *m* weather; time
**tenir** to hold; to keep
**tension** *f* voltage; blood pressure
**tente** *f* tent
**tenue** *f* clothes; dress
***tenue de soirée*** evening dress
**terrain** *m* ground; land; pitch; course
**terrasse** *f* terrace
**tête** *f* head
**TGV** *m* high-speed train
**thé** *m* tea
***thé au lait*** tea with milk
***thé nature*** black tea
**théâtre** *m* theatre
**ticket** *m* ticket *(bus, cinema, museum)*
***ticket de caisse*** receipt
**timbre** *m* stamp
**tirer** to pull
**tirez** pull
**toilettes** *fpl* toilet(s); washroom
**tonalité** *f* dialling tone
**tôt** early
**total** *m* total *(amount)*
**toucher** to touch
**toujours** always; still; forever
**tour** *f* tower
**tour** *m* trip; walk; ride
**tourisme** *m* sightseeing
**tourner** to turn
**tous** everyone; all
***tous les jours*** daily
**tousser** to cough
**tout** everything
**tout/toute/toutes/tous** all
***tout à l'heure*** in a while
***tout compris*** all inclusive
***tout de suite*** straight away
***tout droit*** straight ahead
***tout le monde*** everyone
***toutes directions*** all routes
**toux** *f* cough

**tradition** *f* custom *(tradition)*
**traduction** *f* translation
**train** *m* train
**tranche** *f* slice
**tranquille** quiet *(place)*
**travail** *m* work
**travailler** to work *(person)*
**travaux** *mpl* road works; alterations *(building)*
**travers:**
***à travers*** through
**traverser** to cross *(road, sea)*
**tremplin de ski** *m* ski jump
**très** very; much
**trop** too; too much
**trottoir** *m* pavement; sidewalk
**trou** *m* hole
**trousse de premiers secours** *f* first aid kit
**TVA** *f* VAT
**typique** typical

## U

**UE** *f* EU
**un(e)** one; a; an
***l'un ou l'autre*** either one
**université** *f* university
**urgence** *f* urgency; emergency
**urgences** accident and emergency department
**usine** *f* factory
**utiliser** to use

## V

**vacances** *fpl* holiday(s)
***en vacances*** on holiday
***grandes vacances*** summer holiday(s)
**vaccin** *m* vaccination
**vache** *f* cow
**valable** valid *(ticket, licence, etc.)*
**valeur** *f* value
**valise** *f* suitcase
**vallée** *f* valley
**valoir** to be worth
***ça vaut...*** it's worth...
**végétal(e)** vegetable
**végétalien(ne)** vegan
**végétarien(ne)** vegetarian
**véhicule** *m* vehicle
***véhicules lents*** slow vehicles
**vélo** *m* bike
**vendre** to sell
***à vendre*** for sale
**vendredi** *m* Friday

**véléneux** poisonous
**venir** to come
**vent** *m* wind
**vente** *f* sale
**verglas** *m* black ice
**verre** *m* glass
***verres de contact*** contact lenses
**vers** toward(s); about
**vestiaire** *m* cloakroom
**vêtements** *mpl* clothes
**vétérinaire** *m/f* vet
**veuillez...** please...
**via** by *(via)*
**viande** *f* meat
**vieux (vieille)** old
**vigne** *f* vine; vineyard
**vignoble** *m* vineyard
**village** *m* village
**ville** *f* town; city
**vin** *m* wine
**virage** *m* bend; corner
**visage** *m* face
**visite** *f* visit; consultation *(of doctor)*
***visite guidée*** guided tour
**visiteur (-euse)** *m/f* visitor
**vite** quickly; fast
**vitesse** *f* gear *(of car)*; speed
***vitesse limitée à...*** speed limit...
**vivre** to live
**voici** here is/are
**voie** *f* lane (of road); line; track
**voilà** there you are
**voile** *f* sail; sailing
**voilier** *m* sailing boat
**voir** to see
**voisin(e)** *m/f* neighbour
**voiture** *f* car; coach *(of train)*
**vol** *m* flight; theft
***vol intérieur*** domestic flight
**volonté:**
***à volonté*** as much as you like
**voyageur (-euse)** *m/f* traveller
**VTT** *m* mountain bike
**vue** *f* view; sight

## W

**w-c** *mpl* toilet(s); washroom
**wagon-couchettes** *m* sleeping car
**wagon-restaurant** *m* dining car

# CONTENTS

# INTRODUCTION

Controlling your carbohydrate intake is the most popular method of weight loss in the 21st century so far. Everyone seems to know someone who has shed several kilos of excess weight on a low-carb diet, and dozens of Hollywood stars claim to follow them when they need to lose weight after giving birth or just stay in shape to face the cameras. The non-fiction bestseller lists are crammed full of carb-control diet and recipe books, and new diet programmes emerge all the time. We'll guide you through four of the most popular on pages 36-51.

The main reason why so many people swear by carb-counting diets is because they work! You *will* lose weight if you follow them and it won't pile back on again a few weeks later if you follow the long-term maintenance guidelines they offer. You don't feel starving when you are following a controlled-carb diet and the food choices are not so restrictive that it becomes impossible to eat out.

It's not necessary to spend hours in the kitchen preparing every single meal. Whereas with calorie-counting diets you need a calculator to tot up your daily intake (which could be anywhere between 1,000 and 2,500 calories), carb-counting uses the kind of arithmetic you can do in your head (with daily totals of just 20 to 80g, depending on the diet you're following).

In many ways, carb-counting systems seem to be the diets we've all been looking for over the past few decades – but there are a few warnings you must heed before you launch into your weight-loss programme (see pages 31-5). Let's start by finding out how they work. To do this, it's necessary to understand a little about the basic food groups and how they are processed in the body.

### Did Nutritionists Get It Wrong?

The food we eat is made up of three major types of nutrients – proteins, carbohydrates and fats – as well as smaller quantities of vitamins and minerals (micronutrients), which are essential for the body to grow, heal and continue to function. The differences between the major diet systems on the market lie in the proportions of each nutrient that they recommend.

In the latter half of the 20th century, doctors and nutritionists tended to advise that we eat a low-fat, high-carbohydrate diet to maintain a healthy heart and digestive system. The Food Pyramid was designed to simplify their recommendations. It advised that an adult's daily diet should consist of the following:

6–11 servings of bread, cereal, rice and pasta
3–5 servings of vegetables
2–4 servings of fruit
2–4 servings of dairy products (milk, yoghurt and cheese)
2–3 servings of protein (meat, poultry, fish, beans, eggs and nuts)
sparing amounts of fats, oils and sweets

This diet was designed to provide sufficient vitamins and minerals for good health, plenty of fibre to keep the digestive system functioning smoothly, a smaller amount of protein than most people in the West were used to (thus limiting their consumption of 'bad' animal fats), and a drastically reduced intake of all fats and oils, which are weight-for-weight much higher in calories than other nutrients.

As early as 1972, Dr Robert C. Atkins was telling them they'd got it all wrong. His first book, *The Diet Revolution*, recommended a diet that virtually turned the Food Pyramid on its head. You could eat unlimited amounts of full-fat proteins but no bread, cereal, pasta, rice or fruit and very small quantities of vegetables. He has since modified his position in subsequent books to allow some whole grains, fruits and more vegetables, but the high-protein, low-carbohydrate basis remains (see pages 36-40 for a fuller explanation of the Atkins principles).

The reaction from the majority of the medical establishment at the time, and over the following three decades, was hostile. Many doctors claimed that his diet could cause heart disease, strokes, kidney disease, malnutrition, and all kinds of life-threatening illnesses. Dr Atkins stood his ground and the battle lines were drawn.

In the 1980s and 90s lots of people tried low-fat, high-carbohydrate diets, in line with the government-approved recommendations, and some did manage to achieve their ideal weight – but many didn't. They found that their weight loss slowed drastically after an initial drop, and the kilos even began to pile back on again. They frequently felt hungry and got cravings for specific foods, and they found it difficult to eat out in restaurants without quizzing waiters at length about how each dish was cooked.

Gradually, more and more experts began to re-evaluate Dr Atkins' approach and agree with some – if not all – of his theories. During the last few years, cardiologists have been developing much more sophisticated tests for measuring the level of fats in the blood, and they no longer rely solely on the basic cholesterol test that had originally convinced them to recommend that we cut down on animal fats. In fact, it seems that for as many as a third of the population, a low-fat diet could do more harm than good – but cardiologists remain adamant that the type of fat eaten is crucial. See pages 18-22 for more on The Big Fat Question.

Let's take a closer look at the chemical conundrums that they are arguing about.

### The Insulin Trap

Carbohydrates are a broad category, covering everything from bread, rice and pasta to vegetables, fruits, grains and pulses. They mostly come from plant-based sources but, if you glance at the listings section of this book, you'll find that all sorts of unexpected sources contain carbohydrates. Sausages may contain bread and 'filler'; sauces often contain flour; and dairy products (milk, butter, cheese and yoghurt) all contain some carbohydrate.

Carbohydrates are broken down in the digestive system to the simple sugars they are composed of (such as glucose and fructose). The pancreas then releases a hormone called insulin to enable them to be transported through the bloodstream to the sites where they are needed to provide energy, to be stored as glycogen in the liver, or in the cells as fat. It is now believed that calories derived from these sugars are more likely to be stored as fat than calories derived from protein sources, or from dietary fat itself.

'Simple' carbohydrates, such as the sugar you stir into a cup of tea or the fructose in fruits, are absorbed more quickly than 'complex' carbohydrates, such as whole grains, beans and vegetables. Refined foods, including white bread, cakes, biscuits and white rice, are all high in simple carbohydrates. Whole foods, like brown rice, pulses and stalky vegetables, all contain fibre, which has to be separated off by the digestive system before they can be broken down into sugars, so it takes longer for their sugars to reach your bloodstream. The fibre then passes through the digestive tract without being absorbed.

If you eat a meal or snack that is composed largely of simple, refined carbohydrates – white toast with jam, a Danish pastry, a chocolate bar or a bowl of pasta – the sugars hit your bloodstream in one great rush, triggering the pancreas to produce lots of insulin to mop them up. This excess of insulin signals to the liver that it should store any excess energy as fat, then signals the body to conserve the fat. You feel good with your sugar rush until your blood sugar level begins to dip again not long afterwards, bringing on a feeling of tiredness and cravings for more carbohydrates to lift your energy levels. Ever struggled not to fall asleep at your desk after a lunch of pizza and garlic bread? Now you know why.

Insulin is nicknamed the 'hunger hormone' because of its influence on our appetites. People who eat a lot of carbohydrates throughout the day will experience peaks and troughs in their blood sugar level, causing cravings and the urge to eat more. Their insulin levels will stay high, and they often produce more than they need. This means the body will store more fat – and it has another side effect as well. As insulin levels begin to drop after a balanced meal, this triggers the release of serotonin, the feel-good brain chemical, to let us know that we are satiated. People with high insulin levels may not experience this cut-off point, so rarely feel satisfied by their food.

Those who control their carbohydrate intake and eat mainly the more slowly absorbed complex carbohydrates will be able to regulate their insulin levels to avoid the highs and the lows, so will feel less hunger and will store less sugar as body fat. That is the basic argument behind carbohydrate-controlled diets although, as you'll see, there are several different theories about how much carbohydrate you can eat – and when.

**Good Carbs versus Bad Carbs**

The simplest way to distinguish between easily absorbed simple carbohydrates and the more slowly absorbed complex ones is by taste. The sweeter a food tastes, the quicker you're going to get a sugar 'hit' – and the subsequent blood sugar dip. Scientists have developed a more accurate system, though, called the Glycaemic Index. Foods with high glycaemic index numbers will increase your blood sugar level more than those with lower glycaemic numbers. All carb-controlled diets and virtually all nutrition experts recommend that you favour foods that are low on the glycaemic index – see page 16 for some listings.

The glycaemic index can be misleading, though, because it doesn't take into account average portion sizes. You would have to eat around 750g of carrots for them to have a noticeable effect on your blood sugar, while a dessertspoonful of jam would give you an almost instant 'peak', yet they have similar glycaemic index numbers. This difference is compounded when you eat fats or high-fibre foods along with your carbohydrate because both substances slow the

## Glycaemic Index

| Food | GI | Food | GI |
|---|---|---|---|
| Apple juice | 40 | Jam | 49 |
| Apples | 38 | Kidney beans, boiled | 28 |
| Asparagus | <15 | Lentils, green, boiled | 29 |
| Bagel, plain | 72 | Mangoes | 56 |
| Baked beans, tinned | 48 | Mars Bar | 64 |
| Bananas | 52 | Milk chocolate bar | 49 |
| Beetroot | 64 | Milk, whole | 27 |
| Broad beans | 79 | Muesli | 56 |
| Broccoli | <15 | Multi-grain bread | 48 |
| Cake, sponge | 46 | Mushrooms | <15 |
| Carrots | 47 | Oranges | 42 |
| Cauliflower | <15 | Peanuts | 15 |
| Chips | 75 | Pearl barley | 25 |
| Couscous | 65 | Peas, green | 48 |
| Crisps | 54 | Peppers | <15 |
| Cucumber | <15 | Pitta bread, white | 57 |
| Digestive biscuits | 58 | Pizza, cheese | 60 |
| Doughnut | 76 | Plums | 39 |
| Gnocchi | 67 | Polenta | 69 |
| Grapefruit | 25 | Porridge | 49 |
| Grapes | 46 | Potato, baked | 85 |
| Green beans | <15 | Rice cakes | 77 |
| Honey | 58 | Rice, brown | 55 |
| Ice-cream | 61 | Rice, white | 58 |

absorption of sugars – and fats and fibre also help you to feel fuller, so you are likely to eat less.

In this guide, total carbohydrate counts per portion size are given, and also the net carbs, which give a better indication of how much the food will affect your blood sugar level. Net carbs are generally total carbs minus the fibre content, so it's an easy calculation to do with any processed foods you buy, which should list both carbohydrate and fibre on the packaging. You'll see that an average portion of grated carrot (weighing 40g) has a net carb count of 2.6g, while a tablespoon of strawberry jam (15g) has a net carb count of 9.6. So the jam would have much more impact on your total daily carb count, and would cause a bigger blood sugar peak when you eat it.

The Dr Atkins diets are the only ones of the four we examine in the book that instruct you to count net carbs, but the rest advise that you choose carbs that are low on the glycaemic index, or complex carbohydrates with high fibre counts, and you can use the net carb column in this book to help you make those judgements.

Note also that the cooking and preparation methods can have a significant impact on net carbs. If you peel the skin from an apple, you will significantly reduce its fibre count, and apple juice has even less fibre again, so the sugars are absorbed more quickly. The more 'whole' a food is, the less its impact on your blood sugar. Multi-grain bread is much more wholesome than white bread that has had the husks and grains stripped away; brown rice is better than easy-cook white rice; raw fruits and vegetables have more fibre, vitamins and minerals than cooked or juiced ones.

**FIBRE:** One of the concerns experts have about low-carb diets is that they may not provide enough fibre to keep the digestive system functioning smoothly. Lack of fibre causes constipation and can lead to more serious digestive complaints in the long-term. Most nutritionists recommend that we consume 25 to 30g of fibre every day, so check the fibre column of the listings section in this book to confirm you are getting enough. In the induction phases of low-carb diets, you might be advised to take a spoonful of psyllium (also sold as Fibogel) to keep your digestive processes working smoothly.

### The Big Fat Question

There are two main categories of dietary fats – saturated and unsaturated. Most saturated fats are solid at room temperature and they tend to come from animal sources – the white fat on meat, or butter, dripping, lard, cream and cheese – but a few, such as coconut oil and palm oil, come from plants. Unsaturated fats are found in vegetable, nut and fish oils and some of them are essential for good health.

Saturated fats got a bad name because they tend to contain high levels of cholesterol, a substance that can clog up your arteries, leading to blockages that can trigger heart attacks and strokes. It's now known that there isn't necessarily a direct correlation between the amount of saturated fat in your diet and the levels in your blood, and they've found that a significant percentage (some surveys say as many as 50 per cent) of those who die of a heart attack had blood cholesterol levels within the normal range.

Advanced analyses of 'lipids' (or fats) in the blood have pointed to several other heart attack warning signs and cardiologists now distinguish between HDL cholesterol (high density), which helps to protect the heart, and LDL cholesterol (low density) – especially small LDL particles, which are extremely dangerous. High levels of other substances, including triglycerides, will also ring loud warning bells for heart specialists. Those people who died of a heart attack while their blood cholesterol looked normal will probably have had several chemical warning signs that sophisticated tests will be able to detect in future.

**FAT SOURCES**

- Monounsaturated fats: olive oil, walnuts, almonds
- Omega 3-containing polyunsaturated fats: oily fishes, like salmon, herring, sardines and mackerel; flaxseed oils, wheatgerm and soya beans.
- Other polyunsaturated fats: vegetable and corn oils.
- Saturated fats: beef, pork, lamb and chicken; whole-fat milk, cheese and yoghurt; butter; cocoa butter, palm and coconut oils.
- Trans fats: vegetable shortening, some margarines, pies, cakes, biscuits, crisps, pastries, crackers, peanut butters and fast foods.

It's now a much more complex science than it was a few decades ago when cardiologists started to recommend that we reduce our intake of fats. In fact, studies in the United States have found that low-fat diets can be dangerous for around a third of the population, causing them to produce the lethal small LDL particles that often precede a heart attack. But this doesn't mean these people should eat more animal fats again – quite the contrary. You would be hard-pressed to find a cardiologist who doesn't recommend that you cut right back on saturated fats in your diet. They don't recommend that you stop using fat altogether but that you opt for 'good' fats and avoid the 'bad' saturated ones as much as possible.

Olive oil is a 'good' fat, and levels of heart disease are much lower in Mediterranean countries where it is used for cooking and salad dressings than in places where animal fats like lard are predominantly used.

Fish oils contain an essential fatty acid called 'Omega 3' which has loads of heart-friendly side effects, prompting nutritionists to recommend that we eat fish, especially the oily fishes like salmon, herring, mackerel and sardines, at least twice a week. Nuts and seeds also contain 'good' fats, as well as protein and a range of essential vitamins and minerals.

One last category of fats that nutritionists are unanimous we should avoid is trans fats. These are hydrogenated, or partially hydrogenated fats often used in processed foods to extend their shelf life and add texture. Check the labels on supermarket-bought cakes, biscuits, breads, spreads and ready-made meals and don't buy them if they mention hydrogenated fats. They can be more dangerous than saturated fats, so give them a wide berth.

Watch out also for products labelled 'low-fat', which may have sugar or other carbohydrates added to make them more palatable. Read the labels carefully.

Authors of low-carb and controlled-carb diet plans take different positions on the fat question, as you'll see on pages 36-54. It's a crucial issue and will affect the way you approach the next dietary nutrient we're going to discuss – proteins.

**CARDIOLOGIST RECOMMENDATIONS ON FAT:**

- Use olive oil for cooking and salad dressings.
- Dip bread into a saucer of olive oil instead of using butter – or choose a monounsaturated spread.
- Avoid products containing trans fats; they could be labelled 'hydrogenated or partially hydrogenated vegetable oils'.
- Choose lean cuts of meat and trim away any visible fat.
- When you're having poultry, choose white meat rather than dark and remove the skin.
- Choose low-fat or fat-free versions of dairy foods, but watch out for those with increased sugar content.
- Eat at least two servings of oily fish a week.

### Choosing Your Protein

Proteins are the building blocks from which the cells of body tissues and fluids are made – bones, muscles, skin, hair, nails, blood, enzymes and hormones. They are broken down in the digestive system into amino acids, which are used to keep the body functioning and growing in a healthy way.

There is a misconception that carbohydrate-controlled diets are high-protein; in fact, some are while others merely recommend that you balance your protein intake against your intake of carbohydrates and fats.

As with carbohydrates and fats, it makes sense to choose 'good' proteins rather than 'bad' (high saturated fat) ones. In this day and age when farmed animals and fish are routinely fed antibiotics, it is advisable to buy organic if you can afford it. Organic produce is strictly regulated and comes from animals that aren't kept in cramped conditions, so don't need drugs to prevent diseases caused by overcrowding.

Some diets recommend that you discard egg yolks and make whites-only omelettes, or use egg substitutes; others claim that egg yolks have a neutral verging on positive effect on blood cholesterol and their vitamin content makes whole eggs an all-round nutritious protein source. Most cardiologists would urge you to restrict your intake of egg yolks, although a recent Harvard study found that most people could eat an egg a day without ill effects (see page 119).

Vegetable proteins are found in tofu, broccoli, beans and pulses, brown rice, bananas and soya. Many experts recommend that we substitute soya protein sources for animal ones at a few meals a week, because of soya's many health benefits, but read the labels – soya is often genetically modified and the jury is still out on this issue in the UK.

How much of your daily diet should be made up of proteins? Nutritionists and government health guidelines say between 15 and 20 per cent. The average adult doesn't need more than 60g of protein a day. Some of the low-carb diets we are about to examine recommend substantially more.

**PROTEINS**

- Animal proteins: beef, pork, lamb, chicken, duck, bacon, ham, sausages, fish and seafood, milk, butter, cheese, eggs.
- Vegetarian proteins: soya, tofu, pasta, broccoli, raisins, sweetcorn, beans, pulses, brown rice, bananas, cherries, and many more foods that we think of as carbohydrates. Check the protein column for each food in the listings section of this book.

### To Supplement or Not to Supplement?

The best diets are the ones that permit the widest range of foods, giving you the best chance of consuming all the vitamins and minerals you need on a daily or at least weekly basis. Most controlled-carb diets have an induction plan, which you follow for two weeks to normalize your blood sugar and insulin levels, and they recommend that you take a daily multivitamin supplement during this period. Some recommend that supplements are taken during the ongoing weight loss and lifelong weight maintenance phases of the diet as well, since mass production of food and modern growing methods can mean that vitamins and minerals are leached from foods before they reach our kitchens.

Check that the diet you plan to follow contains foods with each of the following micronutrients on a daily or at least weekly basis and, if not, consider choosing another programme or taking appropriate supplements to make up the shortfall.

**VITAMINS AND MINERALS**

**Vitamin A** Eggs, butter, fish oils, dark green and yellow fruits and vegetables, liver.
*Essential for:* strong bones, good eyesight, healthy skin, healing.

**Vitamin B1** (*Thiamine*): Plant and animal foods, especially wholegrain products, brown rice, seafood and beans.
*Essential for:* growth, nerve function, conversion of blood sugar into energy.

**Vitamin B2** (*Riboflavin*): Milk and dairy produce, green leafy vegetables, liver, kidneys, yeast.
*Essential for:* cell growth and reproduction, energy production.

**Vitamin B3** (*Niacin*): Meats, fish and poultry, wholegrains, peanuts and avocados.
*Essential for:* digestion, energy, the nervous system.

**Vitamin B5** (*Pantothenic acid*): Organ meats, fish, eggs, chicken, nuts and wholegrain cereals.

*Essential for*: strengthening immunity and fighting infections, healing wounds.

**Vitamin B6** (*Pyridoxine*): Meat, eggs, wholegrains, yeast, cabbage, melon, molasses.
*Essential for*: the production of new cells, a healthy immune system, production of antibodies and white blood cells.

**Vitamin B12** (*Cyanocolbalamin*): Fish, dairy produce, beef, pork, lamb, organ meats, eggs and milk.
*Essential for*: energy and concentration, production of red blood cells, growth in children.

**Vitamin C:** Fresh fruit and vegetables, potatoes, leafy herbs and berries.
*Essential for*: healthy skin, bones, muscles, healing, eyesight and protection from viruses.

**Vitamin D:** Milk and dairy produce, eggs, fatty fish.
*Essential for*: healthy teeth and bones, vital for growth.

**Vitamin E:** Nuts, seeds, eggs, milk, wholegrains, leafy vegetables, avocados and soya.
*Essential for*: absorption of iron and essential fatty acids, slowing the ageing process, increasing fertility.

**Vitamin K:** Green vegetables, milk products, apricots, wholegrains, cod liver oil.
*Essential for*: blood clotting.

**Calcium:** Dairy produce, leafy green vegetables, salmon, nuts, root vegetables, tofu.
*Essential for*: strong bones and teeth, hormones and muscles, blood clotting and the regulation of blood pressure.

**Iron:** Liver, kidney, cocoa powder, dark chocolate, shellfish, pulses, dark green vegetables, egg yolks, red meat, beans, molasses.
*Essential for*: supply of oxygen to the cells and healthy immune system.

**Magnesium**: Brown rice, soya beans, nuts, wholegrains, bitter chocolate, legumes.

*Essential for:* transmission of nerve impulses, development of bones, growth and repair of cells.

**Potassium:** Avocados, leafy green vegetables, bananas, fruit and vegetable juices, potatoes and nuts.

*Essential for:* maintaining water balance, nerve and muscle function.

**Chromium:** Liver, whole grains, meat and cheese, brewer's yeast, mushrooms, egg yolk.

*Essential for:* stimulating insulin. Chromium also governs the 'glucose tolerance factor' which is often not working properly in failed dieters.

**Iodine:** Fish and seafood, pineapple, dairy produce, raisins.

*Essential for:* keeping hair, skin, nails and teeth healthy.

**Folic acid**: Fruit, green leafy vegetables, nuts, pulses, yeast extracts.

*Essential for:* production of new cells (working with vitamin B12) and is especially important during pregnancy to prevent birth defects.

---

**WARNING BOX**

- Never exceed the Recommended Daily Allowance (RDA) for vitamin and mineral supplements except under medical advice. Some of them can be dangerous in high doses.
- Note that vitamin B12 deficiency can be a problem for vegetarians and vegans, so they are advised to take a daily B12 supplement.

---

**SALT**: Too much salt can cause heart problems, so cut back on the amount of salt you add to food and choose low-salt (or low-sodium) products.

---

**Finding your Ideal Body Weight**

We only have partial control over our weight. Height, bone structure, metabolism and the body's tendency to store fat are all influenced by genetic predisposition. Some families seem to stay slim effortlessly while others have to work harder at maintaining a healthy weight.

Everyone is born with a 'natural weight range'. If you consistently eat too much and don't exercise, it is possible to reach a weight well above this natural range. It is much harder to maintain a weight that is below your natural range. Long-term dieters, especially 'crash dieters', can end up confusing their metabolism, so that they gain weight quickly as soon as they stop dieting.

Charts that give ideal weight ranges for your height, such as the one on pages 32-3, are just approximations that reflect cultural averages. Two people of the same height can have completely different weights and yet both be healthy. Muscle weighs more than fat, so someone who exercises regularly might weigh more than someone of the same height who is sedentary. Weight also depends on body frame, so you should calculate whether you are small, medium or large-framed before consulting height and weight charts.

## Determining your Frame Size

Measure around the narrowest part of your wrist then refer to the list below to detemine whether you have a small, medium or large frame.

**WOMEN**

*Height under 1.58m:*

- Small frame = wrist size less than 14cm
- Medium frame = wrist size 14cm to 15cm
- Large frame = wrist size over 15cm

*Height 1.58 to 1.65m:*

- Small frame = wrist size less than 15cm
- Medium frame = wrist size 15cm to 16cm
- Large frame = wrist size over 16cm

*Height over 1.65m:*

- Small frame = wrist size less than 16cm
- Medium frame = wrist size 16 to 17cm
- Large frame = wrist size over 17cm

**MEN**

*Height under 1.65m:*

- Small frame = wrist size less than 16cm
- Medium frame = wrist size 16 to 17cm
- Large frame = wrist size over 17cm

*Height over 1.65m:*

- Small frame = wrist size less than 17cm
- Medium frame = wrist size 17cm to 19cm
- Large frame = wrist size over 19cm

The ideal body weight chart (pages 32-3) gives standard body weights for people of around 30 years of age. You will need to check your frame size (see page 29) before using it.

Remember that your ideal weight is the one at which you feel healthy and most attractive, give or take a few kilos. This might vary naturally during the year – some people put on a little more weight in winter and lose it in summer – and it also tends to change with age. So long as you feel comfortable and are within the average category for your frame and height, then you are a healthy weight.

**Body Mass Index**

Much more commonly used nowadays than height and weight charts, the Body Mass Index uses a height to weight formula to calculate whether people are clinically underweight, overweight or obese. Weight in the average range is considered to be healthy. This formula is a good approximation of total body fat, but may not work for some individuals, such as heavily muscled athletes or pregnant women.

To find your body mass index, divide your weight in kilograms by the square of your height in metres, i.e. weight ÷ height$^2$. Check your total against the

list below to see if you fall into an average range. For example, if you are 1.75m tall and weigh 64kg,
1.75 x 1.75 = 3.06
64 ÷ 3.06 = 20.91

BMI SCALE

| | |
|---|---|
| less than 15 | emaciated |
| 15–19 | underweight |
| 19–25 | average |
| 25–30 | overweight |
| 30–40 | obese |

If your BMI is in the emaciated or obese range in this scale, you should visit your doctor for advice, as you could be seriously endangering your health.

**Deciding Which Diet is for You**

Before you start any kind of weight-loss programme, you should consult a doctor if any of the following apply to you:

- You have a chronic condition, especially coronary heart disease, high blood pressure, diabetes, kidney disease or liver disorders.
- You take any medication.
- You are pregnant.
- You are over 40 years old and have more than a few kilos to lose.
- You are planning to start an exercise programme as well, but have not exercised regularly for a few years.

## Tables for Standard Body Weight

### Men

| Height m (ft) | Small Frame kg (lbs) | Medium Frame kg (lbs) | Large Frame kg (lbs) |
|---|---|---|---|
| 1.55 (5′1″) | 49–59 (107–130) | 51–61 (113–134) | 55–64 (121–140) |
| 1.57 (5′2″) | 50–60 (110–132) | 53–63 (116–138) | 56–65 (124–144) |
| 1.60 (5′3″) | 51–61 (113–134) | 54–64 (119–140) | 58–68 (127–150) |
| 1 63 (5′4″) | 53–61 (116–135) | 55–65 (122–142) | 59–70 (131–154) |
| 1.65 (5′5″) | 54–62 (119–137) | 57–66 (125–146) | 60–72 (133–159) |
| 1.68 (5′6″) | 56–64 (123–140) | 59–68 (129–149) | 62–74 (137–163) |
| 1.70 (5′7″) | 58–65 (127–143) | 60–69 (133–152) | 64–76 (142–167) |
| 1.73 (5′8″) | 60–66 (131–145) | 62–71 (137–155) | 66–78 (146–171) |
| 1.75 (5′9″) | 61–68 (135–149) | 64–72 (141–158) | 68–80 (150–175) |
| 1.78 (5′10″) | 63–69 (139–152) | 66–73 (145–161) | 70–81 (154–179) |
| 1.80 (5′11″) | 65–70 (143–155) | 68–75 (149–165) | 72–83 (159–183) |
| 1.83 (6″) | 67–72 (147–159) | 70–77 (153–169) | 74–85 (163–187) |
| 1.85 (6′1″) | 69–75 (151–165) | 71–80 (157–175) | 76–86 (167–189) |
| 1.88 (6′2′) | 70–76 (155–168) | 73–81 (161–179) | 78–89 (171–197) |
| 1.90 (6′3″) | 72–79 (157–173) | 75–84 (166–185) | 80–92 (176–202) |

| Women | | | |
|---|---|---|---|
| **Height m (ft)** | **Small Frame kg (lbs)** | **Medium Frame kg (lbs)** | **Large Frame kg (lbs)** |
| 1.47 (4′10″) | 41–49 (91–108) | 43–52 (95–115) | 47–54 (103–119) |
| 1.50 (4′11″) | 42–51 (93–112) | 44–55 (98–121) | 48–57 (106–125) |
| 1.52 (5′) | 44–52 (96–115) | 46–57 (101–124) | 49–58 (109–128) |
| 1.55 (5′1″) | 45–54 (99–118) | 47–58 (104–127) | 51–59 (112–131) |
| 1.57 (5′2″) | 46–55 (102–121) | 49–60 (107–132) | 52–61 (115–135) |
| 1.60 (5′3″) | 48–56 (105–124) | 50–62 (110–135) | 54–63 (118–138) |
| 1.63 (5′4″) | 49–58 (108–127) | 51–63 (113–138) | 55–65 (122–142) |
| 1.65 (5′5″) | 50–59 (111–130) | 53–64 (117–141) | 57–66 (126–145) |
| 1.68 (5′6″) | 52–60 (115–133) | 55–66 (121–144) | 59–67 (130–148) |
| 1.70 (5′7″) | 54–62 (119–136) | 57–67 (125–147) | 61–69 (134–151) |
| 1.73 (5′8″) | 56–63 (123–139) | 58–68 (128–150) | 62–71 (137–155) |
| 1.75 (5′9″) | 58–64 (127–142) | 60–69 (133–153) | 64–73 (141–159) |
| 1.78 (5′10″) | 59–66 (131–145) | 62–71 (137–156) | 66–75 (146–165) |
| 1.80 (5′11″) | 61–68 (135–148) | 64–72 (141–159) | 68–77 (150–170) |
| 1.83 (6′) | 63–69 (138–151) | 65–74 (143–163) | 69–79 (153–173) |

All carbohydrate-control diets are particularly effective at targetting excess fat around the waist, so they are good for those with that classic 'beer-belly' shape. People who are heavy round the middle are at higher risk of heart disease than those who carry weight on their hips and thighs. Check your waist to hip ratio. If the circumference of your waist is close in size to or even bigger than your hip circumference, you fall into this category, and you should trim up quickly on a low-carb diet.

Carbohydrate-control diets are also worth trying for anyone who has started other diet systems and found they couldn't stick to them. Maybe they got too hungry, or found the meal preparation too laborious, or that the weight wasn't dropping off as consistently as they had hoped.

On the following pages, we are going to examine four of the most popular carbohydrate-control diets and at the end of each, you will find a list of pros and cons. On pages 214-23 you'll find some sample low-carb menus, so think about the ones that would fit most easily into your lifestyle and suit your food preferences.

Once you've chosen your diet, read the book or books that explain the diet system thoroughly (see Further

Reading, pages 236-8) and make sure you understand the rules and principles. You will then be able to slip your *Gem Carb Counter* into a bag or pocket and take it with you when you go to the supermarket, restaurant or café to work out the carb counts of individual meals and snacks.

Low-carb diets are hard for vegetarians and vegans to stick to, as they would have to substitute soya for animal proteins at most meals. If you want to try this, *Zone Diet* author Barry Sears has written a version of his diet for vegans, entitled *The Soy Zone*.

### THE IMPORTANCE OF EXERCISE

If you combine any weight-loss diet with a consistent exercise programme, you will see results much more quickly. Most carb-controlled diets recommend a certain amount of exercise, but note that medical experts think we should be getting aerobic exercise (the kind that raises your heart rate) for 30 minutes a day to keep our hearts healthy. Here are some other reasons to exercise:

- Muscles burn up energy, even when you are not using them, so the more muscle you have, the faster you will shed fat.
- Exercising causes the release of endorphins, which make you feel good and can relieve stress and depression.
- Regular load-bearing exercise, such as walking or running, can help to prevent osteoporosis in later life.
- If you keep your joints flexible, you will have a better chance of remaining fit and active when you are older.

### Dr Atkins' *New Diet Revolution* and *Atkins for Life*

The pioneering Dr Atkins died in 2003 but his diet industry lives on and his books still top the bestseller lists in the UK and US. His *New Diet Revolution* is a high-protein diet on which sugar and refined carbohydrates are never permitted. In fact, there is almost no carbohydrate at all in his initial start-up plan – just 3 cups of green salad per day, or 2 cups of salad and 1 cup of non-starchy green vegetables. The aim of this two-week plan is to induce a state known as 'ketosis', in which the body begins to burn fat for fuel and weight loss is rapid (between 1 and 5kg in the first week).

When fat is broken down, it is converted into ketone particles which are mostly treated as waste by the body and are excreted in the urine or on the breath. It is essential that you drink at least eight large glasses of water a day to help your body excrete the ketones or you could risk dehydration and kidney problems.

For the subsequent phases of the diet, you can check that you are still in ketosis by buying a urine-testing kit from a chemist, or simply by weighing yourself frequently and cutting back on carbs when weight loss begins to slow.

During the Atkins induction phase, you eat protein and good fats, and just 20g of net carbs a day. In the second phase, known as Ongoing Weight Loss (OWL), you add another 5g of net carbs a day in weekly increments – i.e. in week 3 you'd eat 25g of net carbs a day and in week 4, 30g. The carbs you add should be nuts, seeds, vegetables, cheese and berries.

Keep adding 5g a week until your weight loss ceases and you will have found the level at which your carbohydrate balance is in equilibrium – normally between 40 and 60g per day. When you get within 2 to 4 kg of your target weight, you can slightly increase the level again and by the time you reach it, you will know the amount of daily net carbs you can afford to eat to maintain that weight.

Dr Atkins recommends that you exercise while following his diets and take certain supplements, including calcium. When you have achieved your goal weight, you should follow his *Atkins for Life* recommendations and recipes to stay there. See an abbreviated list of the permitted food choices on page 39.

HOW HEALTHY IS IT?

The state of ketosis that Atkins diets induce could be dangerous for anyone with kidney problems – but they shouldn't be doing these diets in the first place. There have been news reports of ketosis causing life-threatening imbalances of minerals, such as calcium and potassium, in the bloodstream, but Atkins experts claim that this should not be the case if the diet is followed accurately. They state that no one under the age of eighteen should follow their diet and that you should get a full medical check-up before you start.

Don't ever be tempted to follow the induction phase for longer than two weeks, because it is not designed as a long-term health diet.

The main problem that many in the medical profession have with the diets is that Atkins believes there is no need to avoid saturated fats when you are controlling your carbohydrates. He claims that fat adds flavour to food and helps us to feel full, so we don't eat so much. He also claims that blood tests on people following his diet have shown that it can reduce blood pressure and improve the balance of those undesirable lipids in the blood. To learn more about the Atkins case on this issue, see the website www.atkinscenter.com.

As we've seen earlier, cardiologists still believe we should drastically reduce saturated fat intake – so the argument rages on. If you have any kind of chronic

**Carbohydrates that you can eat on an Atkins Ongoing Maintenance Programme**

| Eat regularly | Eat in moderation | Eat sparingly |
|---|---|---|
| Green vegetables | Carrots | Sweetcorn |
| Butter beans | Green peas | Potatoes |
| Aubergine, onions | Squash | Sweet potato |
| Peppers, tomatoes | Tomato juice | White bread |
| Cheese | Muesli (no sugar) | Cornflakes |
| Most nuts | Milk | Couscous |
| Pumpkin seeds | Peanuts | Icecream with sugar |
| Sesame seeds | Soya beans, roasted | Chestnuts |
| Pine nuts | Black-eyed beans | Pasta, pizza |
| Chickpeas | Multi-grain bread | White rice |
| Kidney beans | Rye bread | Shredded wheat |
| Barley, oatmeal | Buckwheat | Baked beans |
| Wheat bran | Brown rice | Fruit juices |
| Lentils | Popcorn | Banana |
| Tofu | Apricots | Prunes |
| Unsweetened soya | Fresh pineapple | Raisins |
| milk | Grapes | |
| Apple | Kiwi fruit | |
| Berries (all kinds) | Mango | |
| Cherries | Melon | |
| Grapefruit | Nectarine | |
| Oranges | Papaya | |
| Peaches | | |
| Pears, plums | | |

medical condition or are worried about your heart (perhaps because there is a family history of coronary heart disease) then ask your doctor's advice before starting an Atkins diet.

You may well become constipated due to the lack of fibre in the induction phase, and your breath will smell. There are health concerns about some of the sugar-free sweeteners that Atkins recommends – seek medical advice if you want to use them.

**PROS**

- You will see results faster than on most other diets, losing from 1 to 5kg in the first week and from 1 to 2kg per week thereafter.
- Counting net carbs is easy and the principles of the system are pretty straightforward.

**CONS**

- Bad breath and constipation (plus other health concerns – see above).
- Lack of sufficient fibre long-term could cause digestive problems.
- It would be very difficult to follow this diet if you are vegetarian or vegan, because of the emphasis on animal proteins.
- Everyone should visit their doctor for a check-up before starting this diet and no one under the age of 18 should try it.

### *The Carbohydrate Addict's Diet*

Drs Rachael and Richard F. Heller explain that a high percentage of overweight people have an imbalance in their blood chemistry causing them to release too much insulin and store more sugars as fat. They invite you to take a short quiz to find out whether or not you are a 'carbohydrate addict' and, if you are, this diet will help you to regulate your blood sugar and insulin levels.

The Hellers argue that it is not just the amount of carbohydrate you eat that causes peaks and troughs, but the number of times you eat it in a day. By restricting carbohydrates to one meal a day, you will help to stabilize your blood chemistry, reduce your hunger and encourage the body to shed weight.

Their programme consists of a two-week induction plan, followed by four separate plans (A, B, C and D) from which you can choose, depending on how your weight loss is going. They recommend that you weigh yourself at the same time every day and calculate an average over each week, thus evening out any 'blips'. At the end of each week, you decide how much you want to lose in the following week and choose your eating plan accordingly. The rate of weight loss you should aim at is 1 per cent of your current weight each week.

During the induction phase you are allowed to eat two 'complementary' meals a day, consisting of 75 to 125g of meat, fish or chicken or 2 cups of cheese, along with 2 cups of salad or non-starchy vegetables. You are also encouraged to have two complementary snacks a day, each equivalent to around half of a complementary meal. Then, once a day, at the same time each day, you are allowed a 'reward' meal in which there are no banned foods and quantities are unlimited, although you are encouraged to opt for a good balance of nutrients. You can also drink alcohol with your reward meal, but it must be consumed within one hour – no more, no less.

There's an easy rule of thumb to remember: any food that contains more than 4g of carbohydrate per portion can only be eaten at a reward meal.

The Hellers also advise that you drink at least 6 glasses of water a day and, if you don't follow a daily exercise routine, make sure that you keep active during the day.

HOW HEALTHY IS IT?

*The Carbohydrate Addict's Diet* recommends that you use polyunsaturated or olive oils to sauté foods. They don't stipulate that you must opt for low-fat protein sources but say that it would be easy to do so if your

| The Carbohydrate Addict's Diet | |
|---|---|
| **Allowed at Complementary Meals** | **Banned at Complementary Meals** |
| All meats, except processed ones with added filler | Fruit |
| Fish and shellfish | Fruit juices |
| Butter or margarine | Bread |
| Corn oil, olive oil, peanut oil, vegetable oil | Cereal |
| Mayonnaise and salad dressings | Pasta |
| Up to 50g milk daily | Rice |
| Two eggs daily | Beans and pulses |
| 50g cheese or 100-125g cottage cheese daily | Anything that contains sucrose, fructose, dextrose, corn syrup, starch |
| Green vegetables, except those on the banned list | Artichokes |
| Aubergine | Avocados |
| Mushrooms | Beets |
| Salad vegetables | Broccoli |
| Onions | Carrots |
| Tomatoes (no more than half a medium one) | Chickpeas |
| Gelatin desserts with whipped cream | Corn |
| | Peas |
| | Potatoes |
| | Water chestnuts |

doctor has recommended that you follow a low-fat diet. In fact, they provide a list demonstrating how *The Carbohydrate Addict's Diet* can help you to follow government health recommendations by opting for low-fat products, increasing your fibre intake, reducing salt and sugar in the diet, and including plenty of calcium- and iron-rich foods.

The levels of protein intake are much higher than mainstream nutritionists advise; you could be consuming up to 250g of protein in the complementary meals alone, whereas UK nutrition guidelines are that we only need 60 to 70g a day. There could be vitamin or mineral deficiencies if a dieter didn't choose reward meal foods wisely to ensure they were consuming a wide-enough range of foods.

---

**PROS**

- Ideal for those who can't bear to give up bread and pasta, because the next meal at which they are allowed is never more than 24 hours away.
- Meals can be extremely flexible if you follow the basic rules.

**CONS**

- If dieters over-indulge at reward meals, they could easily gain weight rather than lose it.
- You may find it difficult to fit the one-hour-long reward meal into your schedule at the same time every day.

---

### ***The Zone Diet***

The aim of Barry Sears' *Zone Diet* is to keep your insulin levels within steady limits – in 'the Zone' – by carefully balancing the carbohydrate and protein in each meal and snack. Fibre and fats slow the absorption of carbohydrate sugars into the bloodstream so by balancing the components of your diet correctly, you can avoid any peaks and troughs in blood sugar levels. It's not a high-protein diet, he claims, but an adequate protein one and, unlike Atkins diets, saturated fats are kept to a minimum.

In the *Zone Diet*, foods are divided into blocks. One block of protein contains 7g of low-fat protein – lean meats, skinless poultry, fish, egg whites or soya. Each protein block has to be balanced with a carbohydrate block containing 9g of complex carbohydrate, and he favours vegetables and fruits over breads and starches, because they supply more fibre, vitamins and minerals. Each protein and carbohydrate block must be eaten with a block of 1.5g fat to slow the absorption of the carbs. All meals and snacks are based on exact proportions of 1 block protein/1 block carbohydrate/1 block fat.

The average woman will consume 3 blocks of each nutrient at meals and a man will have 4 blocks of each. You are also encouraged to eat 2 snacks a day to maintain your insulin balance and avoid hunger. Never let five hours go by without a Zone meal or snack.

This may all sound complicated, but Sears claims that once you are familiar with the system, you can balance your plate by eye. At one meal, you should never eat more protein than you can fit in the palm of your hand, and it shouldn't be thicker than your hand. The protein should take up a third of the space on your plate and vegetables should take the other two-thirds, while the fat can be added as salad dressing, for cooking, or in the form of flaked nuts or olives sprinkled on top.

**RECOMMENDED ZONE DIET FOODS**

Chicken, turkey

Lean cuts of beef

Fish

Low-fat cottage cheese

Soya foods

Fruits and vegetables, fresh or frozen

Premium extra virgin olive oil

Oatmeal, whole grain (not quick-cook)

Protein powder, especially soyabean isolate

Nuts, especially macadamia nuts, almonds, cashews, pistachios

Almond butter

Herbs and spices

Natural sweeteners – fructose or stevia

Consistent exercise is recommended, and Sears also suggests several supplements are taken because modern food production methods can destroy the vitamin and mineral content. He is particularly keen on fish oil supplements, which help to control insulin levels, and vitamin E, as well as vitamin C and magnesium.

HOW HEALTHY IS IT?

The *Zone Diet* favours moderate quantities of low-fat protein (around 115g per day for a man and 85g for a woman), and it has enough carbohydrate to avoid the ketosis state that Atkins diets promote. It is also full of vitamin-rich fruit and vegetables, making it a healthy diet to follow long-term.

Portion sizes are restricted, and most daily menus contain between 1,200 and 1,500 calories, which may not be enough for very active people. Once you have reached your target weight, you will probably have to increase the quantities eaten to stop yourself losing any more.

**PROS**

- The recipes are delicious – Sautéd Scallops with Wine-Flavoured Vegetables, Swordfish with Peach and Cucumber Salsa, Chicken and Courgette Italiano, Portuguese Pork with Clams, to name but a few.
- Sears also has a version of the diet for vegans, entitled *The Soy Zone*.

CONS

- The Zone Diet wouldn't suit those who like the all-you-can-eat of permitted foods approach, since all portions are measured.
- If you are following the strict calculation methods, there is a lot of weighing and counting of individual ingredients at each meal.

### *The South Beach Diet*

It's not yet as well-known as the other three controlled-carb diets we've discussed, because *The South Beach Diet* was only published in the UK in 2003, but it originated in Florida in the 1990s as cardiologist Dr A. Agatston struggled to find an eating plan that would help his patients lose weight and improve their heart health. Word of his diet leaked out into the community and it seemed to be so effective that everyone wanted to try it, leading him to write a book. His diet is not about low carbs or low fats, but about eating the right carbs and the right fats. Incredibly, there are no calorie counts, no percentages of fats, carbs and proteins or rules about portion size. So how does it work?

During the first two-week induction phase of the diet, you eat ample protein, good fats and carbohydrates that are low on the glycaemic index. No bread, rice, potatoes, pasta, sweets or alcohol are allowed and fruits and starchy vegetables are off limits. After the two weeks, you will have normalised your insulin levels and any cravings for sugars and starches should have virtually disappeared, so you can begin to slowly add back carbs that are higher on the glycaemic index, such as apples, grapefruit, berries, cantaloupe melon, or bran cereal or porridge eaten with skimmed milk and sugar substitute. You are also allowed low-fat yoghurt and red wine, but should still avoid white flour products, beetroot, carrots, corn, potatoes, bananas and fruit juices. You follow phase two until you have reached your ideal weight, and then you begin phase three, which allows more multi-grain bread and brown rice, and forms a healthy eating plan for life.

**SOME SOUTH BEACH DIET TIPS**

- Instead of mashed potato, try mashed cauliflower.
- Instead of baked potato, have baked sweet potato.
- Roll up a tasty protein inside an iceberg lettuce leaf instead of a floury tortilla wrap.
- Whole foods are better than chopped or sliced, which are better than diced, which are better than mashed or puréed, which are better than juiced.
- Fats, proteins and fibre slow the absorption of carbohydrates, so combinations of nutrients are better than carbohydrates on their own.

Agatston recommends that you don't weigh yourself every day, but keep an eye on how clothes are fitting and how you're feeling, and cut down on carbs if you start to gain weight. He also advises that you exercise for at least 20 minutes a day and take fish oil capsules.

HOW HEALTHY IS IT?

This is an all-round healthy diet that would suit almost everyone and the author claims that it can improve many health conditions, from coronary heart disease to diabetes and polycystic ovary syndrome. However, if you suffer from any chronic condition, always check with your medical specialist before starting a weight-loss programme. Of the four controlled-carb diet systems we have looked at, this is the one that would keep your cardiologist happiest – probably because the author is one himself!

**PROS**

- No weighing, measuring and calorie counting makes it the easiest of the controlled-carb diets to follow, although you may have to work out which carbs are low and high on the glycaemic index (use the net carbs column in this book as a guide).
- A healthy long-term diet with delicious-sounding recipes, some created by gourmet chefs in Florida restaurants.

**CONS**

- It would be possible to overeat permitted foods and gain weight.

| The South Beach Diet | |
|---|---|
| **Phase 1: Foods to enjoy** | **Foods to avoid** |
| Lean cuts of beef | Fatty cuts of beef |
| Skinless white poultry | Chicken legs, duck, goose |
| Fish and shellfish | Full-fat cheeses, brie and edam |
| Fat-free or low-fat cheeses | Carrots, corn, potatoes |
| Pistachios, peanuts, pecans | Fruit and fruit juices |
| Egg whites, tofu | Breads, rice, pasta |
| Most non-starchy vegetables | Yoghurt, milk |
| Olive oil | Alcohol |
| **Phase 2: Foods to reintroduce** | **Foods to avoid (or eat rarely)** |
| Most fruits | White rice |
| Low-fat yoghurt, skimmed milk | Baked potatoes |
| High-fibre cereals, oatmeal | White breads |
| Brown rice | Biscuits |
| Wholewheat pasta | Carrots, corn |
| Popcorn | Bananas, pineapple |
| Red wine | Fruit juices |
| Multigrain bread | Watermelon |
| Barley | Honey/jam |
| **Phase 3** | |
| A healthy diet following the South Beach rules and compensating for any occasional slip-ups! | |

## How to Use This Book

The foods in this book are grouped into categories – Bakery, Biscuits, Condiments and Sauces, etc. – and listed in alphabetical order in the left-hand column of each page, together with portion sizes and cooking methods, where applicable. There are some well-known branded foods, but the emphasis is on whole foods, since these are the mainstay of all the carb-controlled diets.

If you buy ready-made foods, you'll find the nutritional information you need on the packaging. Note that manufacturers' ideas of portion sizes may be vastly different from the ones your diet recommends – they could be larger or smaller.

Remember: to calculate net carbs, you can subtract the fibre content per portion from the carbohydrate content.

The portion sizes given are 'average' ones that you might eat in a single serving, such as one medium apple, or 100g of chicken breast. We have also used cup measurements where they are helpful, because it's easier to visualise a cup of salad than to weigh out a specific weight of lettuce leaves, especially if you are eating in a restaurant. Note: think of a teacup-full rather than a huge mug!

The first column gives the carbohydrate content of the portion in grams; the second lists its fibre content and the third is net carbs; the fourth column from the left gives the calorie count, in kilocalories, and the fifth and sixth give protein and fat counts in grams.

These portion sizes may not accord with the portion sizes your diet recommends or that you wish to eat. To find the values for a 28g piece of chicken breast (a typical *Zone Diet* serving), you would have to divide the figures given by 100 and multiply by 28.

Note that values are given for cooked products rather than raw. Pasta, rice and pulses swell up to approximately three times their weight when cooked, but food packaging often gives the values for their dry weight. Therefore, 100g of boiled white rice has a net carb count of 30.8g while 100g of dry uncooked white rice has a net carb count of 80g.

The way in which you use this book depends on the diet you are following:

- For the Atkins diets, you have to keep a daily net carb total, and you can check these in the third column of the *Carb Counter* listings.

- *The Carbohydrate Addict's Diet* recommends that you don't eat anything with more than 4g of carbohydrate per serving, except at reward meals. Check carbohydrate counts per portion in the first column of the listings.

- *The Zone Diet* asks you to balance blocks of protein, carbohydrate and fat: 7g of protein to 9g of carbohydrate to 1.5g of fat. Check the values of these in the fifth, first and sixth columns of the listings respectively.

- *The South Beach Diet* urges you to avoid or limit foods that are high on the glycaemic index. You'll be able to identify these quickly by looking at their net carb counts in the third column of the listings.

Values for unbranded foods have been obtained from *The Composition of Foods* (5th edition, 1991 and 6th summary edition, 2002) and *Vegetables, Herbs and Spices* (supplement, 1991), and have been reproduced by permission of Controller of Her Majesty's Stationery Office. Asda kindly supplied additional information.

The publishers are grateful to all manufacturers who gave information on their products. If you cannot find a particular food here, you can obtain much fuller listings of nutrient counts in branded foods from *Collins Gem Calorie Counter.*

# CONVERSION CHART

## Metric to imperial

100 grams (g) = 3.53 ounces (oz)
1 kilogram (kg) = 2.2 pounds (lb)
100 millilitres (ml) = 3.38 fluid ounces (fl oz)
1 litre = 1.76 pints

## Imperial to metric

1 ounce (oz) = 28.35 grams (g)
1 pound (lb) = 453.60 grams (g)
1 stone (st) = 6.35 kilograms (kg)
1 fluid ounce (fl oz) = 29.57 millilitres (ml)
1 pint = 0.568 litres (l)

## Abbreviations used in the listings

| | |
|---|---|
| g | gram |
| kcal | kilocalorie |
| ml | millilitre |
| n/a | not available |

## Portion Size Guidelines

It's important to be able to judge portion sizes by eye, because modern life is too complicated to start weighing every ingredient at every meal. Here are a few guidelines that will help:

BAKERY

- A medium-cut slice of bread about twice the height and width of this book will weigh around 30g.
- A 2cm thick slice of French bread is around 33g.
- A bagel the size of a can of tuna weighs around 70g.
- A muffin that fits in a fairy cake wrapper will be around 60g.
- A slice of cake weighing 75g will be roughly 7.5cm wide.

BAKING PRODUCTS

- 3tsp of baking powder, flour or cornflour is 10g.

BEANS AND PULSES

- Half a cup of cooked beans weighs about 115g.
- A small can of beans is around 200g.

BREAKFAST CEREALS

- 30g of flaked or puffed cereal will go halfway up a normal bowl; 40g of All Bran or grapenuts will be about the same volume; and 50g of muesli or granola is half a standard bowl.

CONDIMENTS AND SAUCES

- 15ml is about a tablespoon and 5ml is a teaspoon.

DAIRY

- 15g of butter is the amount that you would spread on one slice of bread for even but not thick coverage.
- A 25g piece of cheese will be around 1 x 1 x 4cm (or the size of your thumb).
- Standard pots of yoghurt contain 125g.

FRUIT

- A medium apple or orange is about the size of a tennis ball, and weighs around 200g.
- A medium banana should fit on the average side plate, and weighs around 150g peeled.
- A half teacup of chopped fruit or berries is around 75g.

JAMS AND SPREADS

- A teaspoon of jam is about 5g and a tablespoon about 15g.
- 2 tablespoons of peanut butter, about the size of a golfball, weighs 30g.

MEAT AND POULTRY

- A 75g piece of meat or chicken would be the size of a pack of tissues; a 100g piece would be more like the size of a pack of cards.

- Burgers range in size from 85g for skinny ones up to 125g for thick ones. A 'quarterpounder' is 120g.

RICE

- 2 tablespoons of dry rice will give around 75g cooked – a mound that's roughly the size of a woman's fist.

SNACKS

- 25g of nuts is roughly the amount a small child could hold in one hand.
- 25g of crisps is a large handful for an adult. The standard size for a bag of crisps is 34.5g.

VEGETABLES

- A teacup of salad greens is around 30g; half a cup of boiled cabbage is around 75g. Vegetable weights vary, but the portion sizes given in the listings relate to half a teacupful, unless otherwise stated.

You will find more tips on portion sizes throughout the listings section.

**Low-carb Cooking**

The way you cook food will affect its carb and fat content and its nutritional values.

- Sugar added during cooking will increase the carbohydrate content. 100g of apples stewed without sugar have just 8.1g carb, while 100g stewed with sugar have more than double the amount, at 19.1g carb.
- Tofu (soya bean curd) is a good alternative to animal protein. Drain the water from it first by placing a few plates on top of a block of tofu and allowing it to sit for an hour or so. Slice it thinly and stir-fry it in a little olive oil with mixed vegetables and spices.
- Shred cabbage or thinly slice courgettes to make your own low-carb 'noodles'.
- When you stir-fry, use a thin film of olive oil and keep stirring to prevent sticking and make sure your food is cooked evenly.
- Meats can be fried, braised, baked or grilled – but don't add any breading or batter.
- If you boil vegetables, vitamins and minerals leach out into the cooking water; steaming, stir-frying or

cooking briefly in a microwave retains more of them. Roasting is also good for bringing out the flavour of vegetables.

- Soups, stews and casseroles preserve more of the nutritional value of foods, as vitamins and minerals will be retained in the broth.

- Remember that fats make you feel fuller, so include enough in each meal to satisfy your appetite.

- In general, the shorter the cooking time, the more nutrients will be retained – and the better chance you have of getting all the nutrition your body needs.

# The Listings

## BAKERY

You won't be using this section of the book during the induction phase of a low-carb diet, but later stages allow wholemeal and multigrain breads, rolls and wholewheat pitta bread. Rye, pumpernickel and sourdough breads are all easier on your blood sugar level than standard white or wheatgerm, but read the labels to make sure they don't contain added white flour or sugar. As you know in your heart of hearts, cakes, pies, tarts and muffins have no place on a weight-loss diet, but we all need occasional treats. Just read the labels to make sure they don't contain trans fats, hydrogenated or partially hydrogenated vegetable oils – see page 18.

**TIP:** The listings opposite give values for a medium-cut slice of bread weighing about 30g. Many packaged loaves will give the nutritional information per slice, but if they give a value 'per serving', this probably means per two slices.

| Food type | Carb (g) | Fibre (g) | Net carb (g) | Cal (kcal) | Pro (g) | Fat (g) |
|---|---|---|---|---|---|---|
| **Bread** | | | | | | |
| Brown, 1 slice | 13.3 | 1.8 | 11.5 | 65 | 2.6 | 0.6 |
| Brown, toasted, 1 slice | 17.0 | 2.1 | 14.9 | 82 | 3.1 | 0.6 |
| Chapattis: | | | | | | |
| *made with fat, each* (50g) | 24.1 | – | 24.1 | 164 | 4 | 6.5 |
| *made without fat, each* (50g) | 21.8 | – | 21.8 | 101 | 3.6 | 0.5 |
| Ciabatta, 1 slice | 15 | 0.7 | 14.3 | 81 | 3.1 | 1.2 |
| Currant loaf, 1 slice | 15.2 | 1.3 | 13.9 | 87 | 2.2 | 1.1 |
| French stick, 1 slice (2cm thick) | 18.4 | 1.7 | 16.7 | 90 | 3.2 | 0.9 |
| Garlic bread, pre-packed, frozen, 1 slice | 13.5 | – | 13.5 | 110 | 2.3 | 5.5 |
| Granary, 1 slice | 13.9 | 1.9 | 12.0 | 70 | 2.8 | 0.8 |
| High-bran, 1 slice | 10.1 | 2.4 | 7.7 | 64 | 3.9 | 0.8 |
| Malt, 1 slice | 17.1 | 2.0 | 15.1 | 80 | 2.5 | 0.7 |
| Naan, plain, half | 35.0 | 2.0 | 33.0 | 209 | 5.5 | 5.2 |
| Oatmeal, 1 slice | 12.4 | 1.1 | 11.3 | 70 | 2.4 | 1.2 |
| Pitta bread, white, medium: | 28.9 | 1.1 | 27.8 | 133 | 4.6 | 0.6 |
| *white with sesame* | 24 | 1.5 | 22.5 | 131 | 4.8 | 1.8 |
| *wholewheat* | 20.5 | 3.1 | 17.4 | 114 | 5.4 | 1.2 |
| Pitta bread, 2 mini (10g each) | 11.4 | 0.7 | 10.7 | 52 | 1.7 | 0.3 |
| Rye, 1 slice | 13.7 | 1.7 | 12 | 66 | 2.4 | 0.5 |
| Sourdough, 1 slice | 14.7 | 0.9 | 13.9 | 78 | 2.5 | 0.9 |
| Stoneground wholemeal, 1 slice | 11.8 | 2.2 | 9.6 | 65 | 2.9 | 0.7 |
| Wheatgerm, 1 slice | 12.5 | 1.5 | 11.0 | 64 | 2.8 | 0.6 |

| Food type | Carb (g) | Fibre (g) | Net carb (g) | Cal (kcal) | Pro (g) | Fat (g) |
|---|---|---|---|---|---|---|
| White, 1 slice | 14.8 | 1.2 | 13.6 | 71 | 2.5 | 0.6 |
| White, fried in oil/lard, 1 slice | 14.5 | 1.2 | 13.3 | 151 | 2.4 | 9.6 |
| White, toasted, 1 slice | 17.1 | 1.4 | 15.7 | 80 | 2.8 | 0.5 |
| Wholemeal, 1 slice | 12.5 | 2.2 | 11.3 | 65 | 2.8 | 0.8 |
| **Rolls** | | | | | | |
| Bagels, each (70g): | 37.2 | 1.5 | 35.7 | 192 | 7.8 | 1.0 |
| *onion bagels* | 37.7 | 1.5 | 36.2 | 192 | 7.8 | 1.1 |
| *sesame bagels* | 36.9 | 1.5 | 35.4 | 190 | 7.9 | 1.3 |
| *cinnamon & raisin* | 39.2 | 1.5 | 37.7 | 197 | 7.4 | 1.3 |
| Baps, white, each (60g) | 26.2 | 1.6 | 24.6 | 141 | 5.9 | 2.6 |
| Brown, crusty, each (60g) | 30.2 | 4.3 | 25.9 | 153 | 6.2 | 1.7 |
| Brown, soft, each (60g) | 31.1 | 3.8 | 27.3 | 161 | 6 | 2.3 |
| Hamburger bun, each (60g) | 29.3 | 0.9 | 28.4 | 158 | 5.5 | 3 |
| White, crusty, each (60g) | 34.6 | 2.6 | 32.0 | 168 | 6.5 | 2.6 |
| White, soft, each (60g) | 31.0 | 2.3 | 28.7 | 161 | 5.5 | 2.5 |
| Wholemeal, each (60g) | 29.0 | 5.3 | 23.7 | 145 | 5.4 | 1.7 |
| Taco shells, each (30g) | 18.2 | – | 18.2 | 146 | 2.2 | 13.8 |
| Tortillas, each (30g): | | | | | | |
| *corn* | 13.2 | – | 13.2 | 95 | 3.0 | 3.3 |
| *flour* | 18.0 | – | 8.0 | 103 | 3.0 | 2.0 |

**TIP:** Bread that is labelled 'brown bread' may just contain white flour coloured brown with caramel or molasses. Look for the labels 'wholegrain' or '100% wholewheat' if you want a healthier option.

| Food type | Carb (g) | Fibre (g) | Net carb (g) | Cal (kcal) | Pro (g) | Fat (g) |
|---|---|---|---|---|---|---|
| **Tea Breads, Buns, Pastries** | | | | | | |
| Brioche, each (60g) | 35.0 | – | 35.0 | 209 | 4.9 | 5.6 |
| Chelsea bun, each (70g) | 39.3 | 1.2 | 38.1 | 256 | 5.4 | 9.8 |
| Croissant, each (70g) | 26.8 | 1.8 | 25 | 252 | 5.8 | 14 |
| Crumpet, each (50g) | 17.9 | – | 17.9 | 89 | 3.6 | 0.4 |
| Currant bun, each (70g) | 36.9 | – | 36.9 | 207 | 5 | 4.6 |
| Danish pastry, each (70g) | 35.9 | 1.1 | 34.8 | 262 | 4 | 12.6 |
| Doughnut, each (70g): | | | | | | |
| *jam* | 34.2 | – | 34.2 | 235 | 3.9 | 10.5 |
| *ring* | 33 | – | 33 | 278 | 4.3 | 15.4 |
| Eccles cake, each (60g) | 35.6 | 1.0 | 34.6 | 285 | 2.3 | 15.6 |
| Fruit loaf, slice (70g) | 42.5 | – | 42.5 | 217 | 5.3 | 2.9 |
| Hot cross bun, each (70g) | 40.9 | 1.2 | 39.7 | 217 | 5.3 | 4.8 |
| Muffin, each (70g): | | | | | | |
| *English* | 32.7 | 1.6 | 31.1 | 167 | 6.3 | 1.2 |
| *blueberry* | 34.9 | 0.8 | 34.1 | 300 | 3 | 0.8 |
| Potato scone, each (60g) | 25.2 | 2.6 | 22.6 | 124 | 2.8 | 1.3 |
| Raisin and cinnamon loaf, slice (70g) | 37 | 2.9 | 36.1 | 193 | 5.2 | 2.7 |
| Scone, each (60g): | | | | | | |
| *fruit* | 31.7 | – | 31.7 | 190 | 4.4 | 5.9 |

**TIP:** In restaurants, avoid temptation by telling the waiter to bring a dish of olives instead of the bread basket. If you decide to give in to a delicious piece of granary bread, dip it in olive oil instead of buttering it.

| Food type | Carb (g) | Fibre (g) | Net carb (g) | Cal (kcal) | Pro (g) | Fat (g) |
|---|---|---|---|---|---|---|
| Scones contd: | | | | | | |
| *plain* | 32.2 | 1.0 | 31.2 | 218 | 4.3 | 8.9 |
| *wholemeal* | 25.9 | 3.1 | 22.8 | 196 | 5.2 | 8.4 |
| Scotch pancake, each (60g) | 26.2 | 0.8 | 25.4 | 175 | 3.5 | 7.2 |
| **Cakes and Cream Cakes** | | | | | | |
| Almond slice (50g bar) | 29.3 | 0.8 | 28.5 | 191 | 3.4 | 6.5 |
| Apple Danish (50g bar) | 21.4 | 0.5 | 20.9 | 120 | 2.1 | 12 |
| Bakewell slice (50g) | 29.7 | 0.5 | 29.2 | 218 | 1.9 | 10 |
| Banana cake, slice (75g) | 41.9 | 0.5 | 41.4 | 260 | 2.4 | 6 |
| Battenburg, slice (75g) | 52.7 | 0.9 | 52.8 | 323 | 5.3 | 6.5 |
| Brownies, chocolate, each (75g) | 36.7 | 1 | 35.7 | 311 | 3.9 | 15.7 |
| Caramel shortcake, piece (50g) | 27.6 | 0.5 | 27.1 | 248 | 2 | 14.5 |
| Carrot cake, slice (75g) | 39.6 | 0.6 | 39 | 283 | 2.6 | 12 |
| Chocolate cake, slice (75g) | 42.3 | 1 | 41.3 | 268 | 4.3 | 10.5 |
| Chocolate mini roll, each (50g) | 26.6 | 0.5 | 26.1 | 210 | 2.7 | 10.5 |
| Chocolate sandwich sponge, slice (50g) | 23.4 | 0.6 | 22.8 | 189 | 2.9 | 9.5 |
| Date and walnut loaf, slice (75g) | 32.4 | 1.1 | 32.3 | 287 | 4.7 | 15.4 |

**TIP:** Nutritional values of cakes will vary from one manufacturer to the next. Check the packaging if you need to be precise.

| Food type | Carb (g) | Fibre (g) | Net carb (g) | Cal (kcal) | Pro (g) | Fat (g) |
|---|---|---|---|---|---|---|
| Chocolate éclair, each (75g) | 19.5 | 0.6 | 18.9 | 297 | 4.2 | 23.2 |
| Fancy cake, iced, each (50g) | 34.4 | – | 34.4 | 204 | 1.9 | 7.5 |
| Flapjack, each (75g) | 45.3 | 2 | 43.3 | 363 | 3.4 | 20.3 |
| Fruit cake, slice (75g): | | | | | | |
| *plain* | 43.4 | – | 43.4 | 265.5 | 3.8 | 9.8 |
| *rich* | 44.9 | 1.1 | 43.8 | 257 | 2.9 | 8.5 |
| *rich, iced* | 47 | 1.3 | 45.7 | 267 | 3 | 8.3 |
| *wholemeal* | 39.6 | 1.8 | 37.8 | 272 | 4.5 | 12 |
| Ginger cake, slice (75g) | 45.1 | 0.9 | 44.2 | 291 | 2.6 | 11.2 |
| Greek pastries (sweet), each (50g) | 20 | – | 20 | 161 | 2.4 | 8.5 |
| Lemon cake, slice (75g) | 41.6 | 0.8 | 40.8 | 289 | 3.4 | 13.5 |
| Marble cake, slice (75g) | 41.5 | 0.9 | 40.6 | 278 | 3.9 | 10..5 |
| Madeira cake, slice (75g) | 43.8 | 0.7 | 43.1 | 295 | 4 | 12.8 |
| Mince pie, each (50g) | 27.9 | 0.7 | 27.2 | 184 | 1.75 | 7 |
| Sponge cake, slice (50g): | | | | | | |
| *plain* | 26.2 | 0.4 | 25.8 | 234 | 3.2 | 13.6 |
| *fat-free* | 26.5 | 0.4 | 26.1 | 147 | 5 | 3 |
| *jam-filled* | 32.1 | 0.9 | 31.2 | 151 | 2.1 | 2.5 |
| *with butter icing* | 26.2 | 0.3 | 25.9 | 245 | 2.3 | 15.5 |
| Swiss roll, original, slice (50g) | 30.2 | 0.6 | 29.6 | 146 | 2.6 | 1.6 |
| Trifle sponge, each (50g) | 33.5 | 0.5 | 33 | 162 | 2.6 | 16 |

**TIP:** Dark chocolate usually has less sugar than milk chocolate. Bear this in mind if you're giving in to a chocoholic urge.

## BAKING PRODUCTS

All of the low-carb diets advise that you reject white flour in favour of the more fibre-rich rye or wholemeal varieties, and some prefer low-carb soya flour (see the Vegetarian section on page 198). The healthiest baking products are more likely to be found in health-food shops than the aisles of your local supermarket. Try to add healthy ingredients into your baking, such as nuts, seeds, dried fruits, even sprouted wheat, and select 'good' fats and natural sweeteners.

**TIP:** Almond flour can be used in a number of low-carb recipes. You can make your own almond flour by processing dry blanched almonds in a food processor or blender until finely ground.

| Food type | Carb (g) | Fibre (g) | Net carb (g) | Cal (kcal) | Pro (g) | Fat (g) |
|---|---|---|---|---|---|---|
| **Baking agents** | | | | | | |
| Baking powder, 10g (3tsp) | 3.8 | – | 3.8 | 16.3 | 0.5 | – |
| Cornflour, 25g | 20.9 | – | 20.9 | 88 | 0.2 | 0.2 |
| Flour, 100g: | | | | | | |
| *rye, whole* | 75.9 | 11.7 | 64.2 | 335 | 8.2 | 20 |
| *wheat, brown* | 68.5 | 6.4 | 62.1 | 323 | 12.6 | 1.8 |
| *wheat, white, breadmaking* | 75.3 | 3.1 | 72.2 | 341 | 11.5 | 1.4 |
| *wheat, white, plain* | 77.7 | 3.1 | 74.6 | 341 | 9.4 | 1.3 |
| *wheat, white, self-raising* | 75.6 | 3.1 | 72.5 | 330 | 8.9 | 1.2 |
| *wheat, wholemeal* | 63.9 | 9 | 54.9 | 310 | 12.7 | 2.2 |
| Ground rice, 100g | 86.8 | 0.5 | 86.3 | 361 | 6.5 | 1 |
| Pastry, 50g: | | | | | | |
| *filo, uncooked* | 31 | 1 | 30 | 156 | 4.5 | 1.5 |
| *flaky, cooked* | 23 | 0.7 | 22.3 | 280 | 2.8 | 20.3 |
| *puff, uncooked* | 15 | 0.8 | 14.2 | 210 | 2.5 | 15.5 |
| *shortcrust, cooked* | 27.1 | 1.1 | 26 | 260 | 3.3 | 16.2 |
| *shortcrust, mix* | 30.4 | 1.1 | 29.3 | 234 | 3.7 | 11.6 |
| *wholemeal, cooked* | 22.3 | 3.1 | 19.2 | 250 | 4.5 | 16.l |
| Sugar, caster, 50g | 50 | – | 50 | 200 | – | – |
| Yeast, bakers' | | | | | | |
| *compressed, 25g* | 0.3 | – | 0.3 | 13 | 2.9 | 0.1 |
| *dried, 15g* | 0.5 | – | 0.5 | 25 | 5.3 | 0.2 |

**TIP:** Choose baking ingredients designed for diabetics. They will always be low in sugar, or sugar-free.

| Food type | Carb (g) | Fibre (g) | Net carb (g) | Cal (kcal) | Pro (g) | Fat (g) |
|---|---|---|---|---|---|---|
| **Fats** | | | | | | |
| Butter, 25g | 0.2 | – | 0.2 | 186 | 0.2 | 21 |
| Cooking fat, 25g | – | – | – | 225 | – | 25 |
| Lard, 1tbsp | – | – | – | 134 | – | 14.8 |
| Margarine, hard (over 80% animal/vegetable fat), 25g | 0.2 | | 0.2 | 180 | 0.1 | 20 |
| Margarine, soft (over 80% polyunsaturated fat), 25g | 0.05 | – | 0.05 | 187 | – | 20.7 |
| Suet, shredded, 1 tbsp | 1.8 | 0.1 | 1.7 | 124 | – | 13 |
| **Mixes** | | | | | | |
| Batter mix, 100g | 77.2 | 3.7 | 73.5 | 338 | 9.3 | 1.2 |
| Cheesecake mix, 100g: | | | | | | |
| *strawberry* | 31.5 | – | 31.5 | 258 | 3 | 12 |
| *toffee* | 37.5 | – | 37.5 | 342 | 3.2 | 19.3 |
| Crumble mix, 100g | 67.6 | 1.5 | 66.1 | 422 | 5.5 | 16.3 |
| Egg custard mix, no bake, 100g | 13.5 | – | 13.5 | 109 | 3.5 | 4.5 |
| Madeira cake mix, 100g | 56 | – | 56 | 339 | 4.9 | 12.4 |
| Pancake mix, 100g | 65.9 | 2.3 | 63.6 | 322 | 13.4 | 2.5 |
| Victoria sponge mix, 100g | 52 | – | 52 | 367 | 6 | 15 |

**TIP:** Almonds are a terrific part of a low-carb diet. Toasted almonds provide a tasty addition to everything from salads and savoury dishes to bread and desserts.

| Food type | Carb (g) | Fibre (g) | Net carb (g) | Cal (kcal) | Pro (g) | Fat (g) |
|---|---|---|---|---|---|---|
| **Sundries** | | | | | | |
| Almonds, flaked/ground, 25g | 1.7 | 0.3 | 1.4 | 153 | 5.3 | 14 |
| Cherries, *glacé*, 25g | 16.6 | 0.2 | 16.4 | 63 | 0.1 | – |
| Cherry pie filling, 100g | 21.5 | 0.4 | 21.1 | 82 | 0.4 | – |
| Currants, dried, 25g | 17 | 0.5 | 16.5 | 67 | 0.6 | 0.1 |
| Ginger, glacé, 25g | 18.5 | – | 18.5 | 76 | – | 0.2 |
| Lemon juice, 50ml | 0.8 | – | 0.8 | 1.8 | – | – |
| Marzipan, 50g | 33.8 | 1 | 32.8 | 202 | 2.7 | 7.2 |
| Mincemeat (sweet), 50g | 31 | 0.7 | 30.3 | 137 | 0.3 | 2.1 |
| Mixed peel, 25g | 14.8 | – | 14.8 | 57.8 | – | 0.2 |
| Raisins, seedless, 25g | 17.3 | 0.5 | 16.8 | 68 | 0.5 | 0.5 |
| Royal icing, 50g | 49 | 0 | 49 | 195 | 0.7 | 0 |
| Sultanas, 25g | 17.3 | 0.5 | 16.8 | 69 | 0.7 | 0.5 |

**TIP:** Note that some cake and crumble mixes need an egg added, while others need milk. You will have to add in the values of the additional ingredients to those of any mix you choose.

## BEANS, PULSES AND CEREALS

It's a good idea to include lots of different beans, chickpeas and lentils in your cooking, but keep the quantities fairly small. They have a high carb count, but a good part of it is offset by their fibre count, and they are good sources of protein, B vitamins, calcium, magnesium, iron and potassium. Shop-bought baked beans often contain sugar or molasses, so should be avoided – or make your own. Barley, buckwheat, whole-wheat couscous and oat bran are also good sources of fibre, vitamins and minerals.

**TIP:** Couscous is delicious served cold in a salad. Add finely chopped crisp vegetables, fresh coriander and a spicy yoghurt dressing.

| Food type | Carb (g) | Fibre (g) | Net carb (g) | Cal (kcal) | Pro (g) | Fat (g) |
|---|---|---|---|---|---|---|
| **Beans and Pulses** | | | | | | |
| Aduki beans, 115g | 26 | 6.3 | 19.7 | 140 | 10.6 | 0.3 |
| Baked beans, small can (200g): | | | | | | |
| *in tomato sauce* | 30.6 | 13.8 | 16.8 | 168 | 10.4 | 1.2 |
| *tomato sauce, no added sugar* | 17.2 | 7.4 | 9.8 | 112 | 9.4 | 0.4 |
| Baked beans with pork sausages, small can (200g) | 22.4 | 5.2 | 17.2 | 178 | 11 | 5 |
| Baked beans with vegetable sausages, small can (200g) | 20.4 | 5.8 | 14.6 | 192 | 11.6 | 7.2 |
| Blackeyed beans, 115g | 23 | 4 | 19 | 133 | 10 | 0.8 |
| Borlotti beans, half can (100g) | 20.5 | 5.5 | 15.0 | 121 | 8.7 | 0.5 |
| Broad beans, small can (200g) | 17 | 8.4 | 8.6 | 128 | 13.4 | 0.6 |
| Butter beans: | | | | | | |
| *small can* (200g) | 26 | 9.2 | 16.8 | 154 | 11.8 | 1 |
| *dried, boiled* (115g) | 21 | 5.9 | 15.1 | 118 | 8.1 | 0.7 |
| Cannellini beans, small can (200g) | 27 | 12 | 15 | 168 | 13.6 | 0.6 |
| Chick peas: | | | | | | |
| *small can* (200g) | 32.2 | 8.2 | 24 | 230 | 14.4 | 5.4 |
| *dried, boiled* (115g) | 20.8 | 4.9 | 15.9 | 138 | 9.6 | 2.4 |

**TIP:** Vitamin B1 (thiamine), found in beans, oats and whole grains, is a great nerve tonic, and can help you feel calmer and more clear-headed in times of stress.

| Food type | Carb (g) | Fibre (g) | Net carb (g) | Cal (kcal) | Pro (g) | Fat (g) |
|---|---|---|---|---|---|---|
| Chilli beans, small can (200g) | 27.6 | 7.4 | 20.2 | 158 | 9.6 | 1 |
| Flageolet beans, half can (100g) | 22.4 | 2.4 | 20.0 | 132 | 9.0 | 0.7 |
| Haricot beans, 115g | | | | | | |
| *dried, boiled* | 19.6 | 7 | 12.6 | 109 | 7.5 | 0.6 |
| Hummus, 2 tbsp | 6.2 | 1.6 | 4.6 | 53 | 1.5 | 2.6 |
| Lentils, 115g: | | | | | | |
| *green/brown, boiled* | 19.3 | 4.3 | 15 | 120 | 10 | 0.8 |
| *red, split, boiled* | 20 | 2.2 | 17.8 | 114 | 8.7 | 0.5 |
| Marrow fat peas: | | | | | | |
| *small can* (200g) | 24.6 | 9.8 | 14.8 | 154 | 11.8 | 1 |
| *quick-soak,* 115g | 47.9 | 16 | 31.9 | 331 | 28.9 | 2.7 |
| Mung beans, 115g | | | | | | |
| *boiled* | 17.4 | 3.4 | 14 | 104 | 9 | 0.5 |
| Pinto beans: | | | | | | |
| *boiled,* 115g | 27.3 | – | 27.3 | 157 | 10.1 | 0.8 |
| *refried,* 2 tbsp | 4.6 | – | 4.6 | 32 | 1.9 | 0.3 |
| Red kidney beans: | | | | | | |
| *small can* (200g) | 35.6 | 17 | 18.6 | 200 | 13.8 | 1.2 |
| *boiled,* 115g | 19.8 | 10.3 | 9.5 | 118 | 9.6 | 0.6 |
| Soya beans, 115g | | | | | | |
| *dried, boiled* | 5.8 | 7 | – | 161 | 16 | 8.3 |
| Split peas, 115g, *boiled* | 25.9 | 3.1 | 22.8 | 144 | 9.5 | 1 |

**TIP:** Add beans, chickpeas or lentils to soups and casseroles as a good source of fibre and to make the meal more filling.

| Food type | Carb (g) | Fibre (g) | Net carb (g) | Cal (kcal) | Pro (g) | Fat (g) |
|---|---|---|---|---|---|---|
| Tofu (soya bean curd), 2 tbsp: | | | | | | |
| *steamed* | 0.9 | – | 0.9 | 94 | 10.4 | 5.4 |
| *fried* | 2.6 | – | 2.6 | 337 | 30 | 22.8 |
| | | | | | | |
| **Cereals** | | | | | | |
| Barley, pearl, 100g | 83.6 | 7.3 | 76.3 | 360 | 7.9 | 1.7 |
| Bran, 100g: | | | | | | |
| *wheat, dry* | 26.8 | 39.6 | – | 206 | 14.1 | 5.5 |
| *soya, cooked* | 15 | 55 | – | 169 | 16 | 5 |
| Bulgur wheat, dry, 100g | 75 | 1.8 | 73.2 | 354 | 11 | 1.5 |
| Couscous, dry, 100g | 72.5 | 2 | 70.5 | 355 | 23.5 | 1.9 |
| Cracked wheat, 100g | 75 | 1.8 | 73.2 | 354 | 11 | 1.5 |
| Polenta, ready-made, 100g | 15.7 | – | 15.7 | 71.9 | 1.6 | 0.3 |
| Wheatgerm, 100g | 44.7 | 15.6 | – | 302 | 26.7 | 9.2 |
| | | | | | | |
| Fresh beans & peas: | | | | | | |
| *see Vegetables* | | | | | | |
| For more soya products: | | | | | | |
| *see Vegetarian* | | | | | | |

**TIP:** Check the packaging on soya beans to see if they are genetically modified, if this is an issue that concerns you.

**TIP:** Rinse canned beans thoroughly before you use them to get rid of toxins.

## BISCUITS, CRACKERS AND CRISPBREADS

Watch out for trans fats – hydrogenated or partially hydrogenated oils – in your biscuits. You may have to go to health food shops to find alternatives without these dangerous fats. Obviously, biscuits are a naughty treat if you're on a carb-controlled diet. They're largely 'empty calories' (i.e. without much nutritional benefit), but they contain loads of sugars to be laid down as fat cells. If you want to have crackers or crispbreads with your cheese, choose the ones with the highest fibre count – rye or wholegrain crispbread, oatcakes or high-fibre Ryvita.

**TIP:** Almost all packets of biscuits have a 'per biscuit' nutrition breakdown on the packet. Check this on whichever ones you choose, as values can vary from one manufacturer to the next. Watch the sugar and salt content in biscuits. Opt for the lowest.

| Food type | Carb (g) | Fibre (g) | Net carb (g) | Cal (kcal) | Pro (g) | Fat (g) |
|---|---|---|---|---|---|---|
| **Sweet biscuits** | | | | | | |
| Abbey crunch, each | 7.3 | 0.3 | 7 | 48 | 0.6 | 1.8 |
| Boasters, each: | | | | | | |
| *chocolate chunk* | 9.3 | 0.3 | 9 | 78 | 0.9 | 4.1 |
| *hazelnut & chocolate chunk* | 8.3 | 0.3 | 8 | 82 | 1 | 5 |
| Bourbon creams, each | 7 | – | 7 | 47 | – | 1.9 |
| Caramel wafers, each | 6.8 | – | 6.8 | 45 | 0.5 | 2 |
| Chocolate chip cookies, diet, | 6.6 | 0.3 | 6.3 | 50 | 0.7 | 2.2 |
| each | 6.6 | 0.1 | 6.5 | 43 | 0.5 | 1.6 |
| Chocolate cream wafers, each | 31.6 | – | 31.6 | 26 | 0.3 | 1.4 |
| Chocolate fingers, each: | | | | | | |
| *milk & plain chocolate* | 6.4 | 0.1 | 6.3 | 53 | 0.7 | 2.7 |
| *white chocolate* | 6.3 | 0.1 | 6.2 | 53 | 0.7 | 2.8 |
| Club biscuits (Jacob's), each: | | | | | | |
| *fruit* | 9.2 | 0.3 | 8.9 | 75 | 0.9 | 3.8 |
| *milk chocolate* | 9.4 | 0.3 | 9.1 | 77 | 0.9 | 3.9 |
| *mint* | 9.4 | 0.3 | 9.1 | 78 | 0.8 | 4 |
| *orange* | 9.3 | 0.3 | 9 | 78 | 0.8 | 4.1 |
| Custard creams, each | 7 | 0.2 | 6.8 | 51 | 0.6 | 2.3 |
| Digestive biscuits, each: | 10.3 | 0.7 | 9.6 | 71 | 0.9 | 3.1 |
| *organic* | 8.1 | 0.8 | 7.3 | 59 | 0.8 | 2.5 |
| *chocolate* (milk & plain) | 10 | 0.5 | 9.5 | 74 | 1 | 3.6 |
| Fig rolls (Fig Newtons), each | 6.8 | 0.4 | 6.4 | 35 | 0.4 | 0.8 |
| Garibaldi (plain), each | 6.7 | 0.3 | 6.4 | 40 | 0.6 | 1.2 |
| Gingernuts, each | 7.9 | 0.1 | 7.8 | 46 | 0.6 | 1.5 |

| Food type | Carb (g) | Fibre (g) | Net carb (g) | Cal (kcal) | Pro (g) | Fat (g) |
|---|---|---|---|---|---|---|
| Gipsy creams, each | 9.9 | 0.4 | 9.5 | 77 | 0.7 | 3.9 |
| Hob Nobs (McVitie's), each | 6.4 | 0.5 | 5.9 | 49 | 0.8 | 2.2 |
| Jaffa cakes, each | 7.4 | 0.1 | 7.3 | 38 | 0.4 | 0.8 |
| Lemon puff, each | 5.8 | 0.2 | 5.6 | 54 | 0.6 | 3.1 |
| Nice biscuits, each | 6.9 | 0.4 | 6.5 | 46 | 0.7 | 1.7 |
| Oat & raisin biscuits, each | 6.3 | 0.4 | 5.9 | 47 | 0.8 | 2.1 |
| Rich tea biscuits, each | 7.7 | 0.2 | 7.5 | 48 | 0.7 | 1.6 |
| Shortbread fingers, each | 12.8 | 0.4 | 12.4 | 100 | 1.2 | 5.2 |
| Shortcake biscuits, each | 6.7 | 0.2 | 6.5 | 48 | 0.6 | 2 |
| Stem ginger cookies, diet, each | 6.5 | 0.1 | 6.4 | 40 | 0.5 | 1.3 |
| Viennese whirls, each | 7.7 | 0.2 | 7.5 | 75 | 0.6 | 4.6 |
| Wafer biscuits, cream-filled, each | 4.6 | N | 4.6 | 37 | 0.3 | 2 |
| **Crackers and Crispbreads** | | | | | | |
| Bath Oliver, each | 6.8 | 0.3 | 5.5 | 43 | 1 | 0.3 |
| Bran crackers, 4 | 12.6 | 0.4 | 12.2 | 91 | 1.9 | 3.6 |
| Cheese crackers (Cheddars), 4 | 8.3 | 0.4 | 7.9 | 81 | 1.5 | 4.7 |
| Cornish wafers, each | 5.4 | 0.2 | 5.2 | 53 | 0.8 | 0.2 |
| Crackerbread, each: | | | | | | |
| *original* | 7.9 | 0.3 | 7.6 | 38 | 1 | 0.3 |
| *cheese-flavoured* | 7.5 | 0.3 | 7.2 | 38 | 1.3 | 0.3 |
| *high-fibre* | 6 | 1.7 | 4.3 | 32 | 1.2 | 0.3 |

**TIP:** If it's chocolate you crave, why not have a couple of squares of rich, dark organic chocolate without the biscuit part attached?

| **Food type** | Carb (g) | Fibre (g) | Net carb (g) | Cal (kcal) | Pro (g) | Fat (g) |
|---|---|---|---|---|---|---|
| Crackers, salted (Ritz), 5: | | | | | | |
| *cheese* | 8.3 | 0.3 | 8 | 74 | 1.6 | 3.8 |
| *original* | 8.3 | 0.3 | 8 | 76 | 1 | 4.3 |
| Cream crackers, each | 0.7 | 0.2 | 0.5 | 44 | 1 | 1.6 |
| Matzo crackers, each | 7.7 | 0.6 | 7.1 | 34 | 1 | – |
| Oatcakes, each: | | | | | | |
| *cheese* | 5.5 | 0.6 | 4.9 | 47 | 1.4 | 2.5 |
| *fine* | 6.6 | 0.9 | 5.7 | 44 | 1 | 1.9 |
| *organic* | 6.5 | 0.8 | 5.7 | 43 | 1 | 0.8 |
| *rough* | 6.5 | 0.6 | 5.9 | 43 | 1 | 0.6 |
| *traditional* | 6.4 | 0.8 | 5.6 | 44 | 1.2 | 1.8 |
| Rye crispbread, each: | | | | | | |
| *dark rye* | 5.6 | 1.7 | 3.9 | 27 | 0.9 | 0.2 |
| *multigrain* | 6.4 | 1.8 | 4.6 | 37 | 1.3 | 0.7 |
| *original* | 5.7 | 1.6 | 4.1 | 27 | 0.8 | 0.2 |
| *sesame* | 5.3 | 1.4 | 4.1 | 31 | 0.9 | 0.6 |
| Water biscuits, 3: | | | | | | |
| *high bake* | 7.6 | 0.3 | 7.3 | 41 | 1 | 0.3 |
| *regular (table)* | 8.2 | 0.3 | 7.9 | 44 | 1 | 0.3 |
| Wholemeal crackers, 4 | 10.8 | 0.6 | 10.2 | 62 | 1.6 | 1.7 |
| *See also Snacks and dips* | | | | | | |

**TIP:** Cereal bars have more fibre and nutrients than a chocolate digestive, but check the label, as some can be very high in sugars as well. See pages 84-5 for the nutritional content of cereal bars.

## BREAKFAST CEREALS AND CEREAL BARS

Many people say that breakfast is the hardest meal for them to adapt for a low-carb diet, but it doesn't have to be bacon and eggs every day (and we strongly recommend that it isn't). All of the controlled-carb diet programmes list loads of delicious breakfast suggestions, from omelettes and soufflés through to yoghurts and fruit 'smoothie' drinks made with unsweetened soya milk. If you're used to having cereal in the morning, you'll have to change your ways at least for the early stages of a low-carb diet. Once you've got your insulin levels under control, though, many diets will let you eat whole-oat porridge, whole-grain cereals and muesli, so long as they don't contain any added sugar.

**TIP:** Most cereal boxes carry a 'per serving' nutrition breakdown. This is approximately three-quarters of an average bowl. Children's individual packs contain 20g.

| Food type | Carb (g) | Fibre (g) | Net carb (g) | Cal (kcal) | Pro (g) | Fat (g) |
|---|---|---|---|---|---|---|
| **Breakfast Cereals** | | | | | | |
| All-bran (Kellogg's), 40g | 18.4 | 10.8 | 7.6 | 112 | 5.6 | 1.8 |
| Bran flakes (Kellogg's), 30g | 20.1 | 4.5 | 15.6 | 99 | 3 | 0.6 |
| Cheerios (Nestlé), 40g: | 30.4 | 2.5 | 27.9 | 148 | 3.2 | 1.5 |
| *honey-nut* | 31.3 | 2.3 | 29 | 149 | 2.8 | 1.5 |
| Cornflakes (Kellogg's), 30g: | 25.3 | 0.7 | 24.6 | 111 | 2.1 | 0.2 |
| *Crunchy nut* | 24.9 | 0.8 | 24.1 | 117 | 1.8 | 1 |
| Frosties (Kellogg's), 30g: | 26.1 | 0.6 | 25.5 | 111 | 1.4 | 0.1 |
| *Chocolate Frosties* | 24.6 | 0.9 | 23.7 | 117 | 1.4 | 1.4 |
| Fruit 'n' Fibre (Kellogg's), 30g | 21 | 2.7 | 18.3 | 105 | 2.4 | 1.5 |
| Grape Nuts (Kraft), 40g | 29 | 3.4 | 25.6 | 138 | 4.2 | 0.8 |
| Malted Wheats (Weetabix), 30g | 23.5 | 1.7 | 21.8 | 108 | 3.2 | 1.5 |
| Multi-grain Start (Kellogg's), 30g | 24.6 | 1.2 | 23.4 | 111 | 2.1 | 0.6 |
| Oat Bran Flakes (Kellogg's), 30g | 20.1 | 0.6 | 19.5 | 99 | 3 | 0.6 |
| Oat Krunchie (Quaker)s, 30g | 18.9 | 3.3 | 15.6 | 108 | 3.1 | 2.1 |
| Puffed Wheat (Quaker), 30g | 18.7 | 1.7 | 17 | 98 | 4.6 | 0.4 |
| Rice Krispies (Kellogg's), 30g: | 26.1 | 0.3 | 25.8 | 114 | 1.8 | 0.3 |
| *chocolate (Coco Pops)* | 25.5 | 0.6 | 24.9 | 114 | 1.4 | 0.8 |
| *frosted (Ricicles)* | 27 | 0.3 | 26.7 | 114 | 1.2 | 0.2 |
| Shredded wheat (Nestlé), 30g: | 19.8 | 3.4 | 16.4 | 99 | 3.4 | 0.6 |
| *bitesize* | 20.3 | 3.5 | 16.8 | 100 | 3.4 | 0.7 |

**TIP:** Try adding some berries – blueberries, raspberries, strawberries or cranberries – to bran flakes and topping with low-fat unsweetened yoghurt.

| Food type | Carb (g) | Fibre (g) | Net carb (g) | Cal (kcal) | Pro (g) | Fat (g) |
|---|---|---|---|---|---|---|
| *frosted* | 21.6 | 2.7 | 19.5 | 105 | 3 | 0.6 |
| *fruit-filled* | 20.7 | 2.7 | 18 | 96 | 2.7 | 0.6 |
| *honey nut* | 20.6 | 3 | 17.6 | 114 | 3.3 | 2 |
| Special K (Kellogg's) , 30g: | 22.2 | 0.9 | 21.3 | 111 | 4.8 | 0.3 |
| *with red berries* | 22.5 | 1.2 | 21.3 | 111 | 4.2 | 0.3 |
| Sultana Bran (Kellogg's), 30g | 20.4 | 3.6 | 16.8 | 96 | 2.4 | 0.6 |
| Weetabix , 30g | 20.3 | 3.2 | 17.1 | 102 | 3.4 | 0.8 |
| **Hot Cereals** | | | | | | |
| Oatbran (Mornflake), 100g | 49.7 | 15.2 | 34.5 | 345 | 14.8 | 9.7 |
| Oatmeal (medium or fine), (Mornflake) 100g | 60.4 | 8.5 | 51.9 | 359 | 11 | 8.1 |
| Oats, 100g: | | | | | | |
| *jumbo (Mornflake)* | 60.4 | 8.5 | 51.9 | 359 | 11 | 8.1 |
| *organic (Mornflake)* | 60.4 | 8.5 | 51.9 | 359 | 11 | 8.1 |
| *Quaker* | 62 | 7 | 55 | 368 | 11 | 8 |
| *Scott's porridge (Quaker)* | 62 | 7 | 55 | 368 | 11 | 8 |
| *Superfast (Mornflake)* | 60.4 | 8.5 | 52.9 | 359 | 11 | 8.1 |
| Porridge (cooked), 100g: | | | | | | |
| *made with water* | 9 | 0.8 | 8.2 | 49 | 1.5 | 1 |
| *made with whole milk* | 13.7 | 0.8 | 12.9 | 116 | 4.8 | 5.1 |

**TIP:** Don't buy 'quick-cook' oats, which are stripped of their husks. Traditional whole oats take much longer to prepare but are high-fibre and full of vitamins and minerals.

| **Food type** | **Carb (g)** | **Fibre (g)** | **Net carb (g)** | **Cal (kcal)** | **Pro (g)** | **Fat (g)** |
|---|---|---|---|---|---|---|
| Oatso Simple (Quaker), 100g: | 62 | 7 | 58 | 372 | 11 | 8.5 |
| *baked apple* | 71 | 5.5 | 65.5 | 374 | 8 | 6 |
| *berry burst* | 71 | 5.5 | 65.5 | 374 | 8 | 6 |
| *golden syrup* | 72 | 5 | 67 | 376 | 7.5 | 6 |
| **Muesli** | | | | | | |
| Muesli, 50g: | | | | | | |
| *Alpen (Weetabix)* | 33 | 3.8 | 29.2 | 182 | 5 | 3.4 |
| *apricot (Holland & Barrett)* | 29.6 | 2.8 | 26.8 | 142 | 3.8 | 1.8 |
| *deluxe (Dorset Cereals)* | 28.1 | 5.8 | 22.3 | 172 | 5.4 | 5 |
| *high fibre (Holland & Barrett)* | 35.4 | 3 | 32.4 | 158 | 5.2 | 3 |
| *natural (Jordans)* | 31.5 | 4.3 | 27.2 | 173 | 4.8 | 3.1 |
| *organic (Jordans)* | 31.2 | 4.6 | 26.6 | 190 | 5 | 5.1 |
| *swiss-style* | 36.5 | 3.2 | 33.3 | 182 | 4.9 | 3 |
| *swiss-style, organic (Jordans)* | 31.4 | 3.7 | 27.7 | 180 | 4.8 | 3.8 |
| *with no added sugar* | 33.5 | 3.9 | 29.6 | 183 | 5.2 | 3.9 |
| Original Crunchy (Jordans), 50g: | | | | | | |
| *maple & pecan* | 30.0 | 3.2 | 26.7 | 224 | 5 | 9.3 |
| *raisin & almond* | 33 | 2.5 | 30.5 | 205 | 4.2 | 6.2 |
| Sultana & Apple Crunch (Mornflake), 50g | 29.6 | 6.2 | 23.4 | 189 | 3.8 | 6.1 |

**TIP:** Hot cereal measurements of 100g include the weight of water or milk added to mix them – but if you've made them with milk, you'll need to count the nutritional value (see page 95) in your totals.

| Food type | Carb (g) | Fibre (g) | Net carb (g) | Cal (kcal) | Pro (g) | Fat (g) |
|---|---|---|---|---|---|---|
| **Cereal Bars** | | | | | | |
| Alpen apple & blackberry, 30g | 21.9 | 0.9 | 21 | 126 | 1.7 | 3.5 |
| Alpen strawberry & yoghurt, 30g | 22.2 | 0.9 | 21.3 | 125 | 1.7 | 3.3 |
| Banana Break (Jordans), each | 27.6 | 2 | 25.6 | 152 | 2.3 | 2 |
| Cornflakes, cereal & milk bar (Kellogg's), 30g | 19.8 | 0.6 | 19.2 | 132 | 2.7 | 4.8 |
| Frosties cereal & milk bar (Kellogg's), 30g | 20.7 | 1.4 | 19.3 | 132 | 2.4 | 4.5 |
| Fruit & Nut Break (Jordans), each | 23.2 | 3 | 20.2 | 137 | 2.6 | 3.8 |
| Frusli bar (Jordans), each: | | | | | | |
| *Absolutely Apricot* | 21.3 | 2.1 | 19.2 | 122 | 1.7 | 3.3 |
| *Raisin & Hazelnut* | 20.4 | 1.3 | 19.1 | 142 | 2.1 | 5.8 |
| Muesli Break (Jordans), each | 30.6 | 2 | 28.6 | 178 | 2.7 | 5 |
| Nutri-grain bar (Kellogg's), 30g: | | | | | | |
| *Apple* | 20.4 | 0.9 | 19.5 | 10.8 | 1.0 | 2.7 |
| *Cappucino* | 19.8 | 0.7 | 19.1 | 111 | 1.4 | 3 |
| *Cherry* | 20.4 | 0.9 | 19.5 | 108 | 1.2 | 2.7 |
| *Chocolate* | 19.8 | 1.0 | 18.8 | 114 | 1.4 | 3.3 |
| *Orange* | 20.4 | 1.2 | 19.2 | 11.1 | 1.5 | 2.7 |
| *Strawberry* | 20.4 | 0.9 | 19.5 | 10.8 | 1.2 | 2.7 |

**TIP:** Don't ever skip breakfast or you'll suffer a blood-sugar dip mid-morning that could cause you to binge.

| Food type | Carb (g) | Fibre (g) | Net carb (g) | Cal (kcal) | Pro (g) | Fat (g) |
|---|---|---|---|---|---|---|
| Rice Krispies cereal & milk bar (Kellogg's), 30g | 20.7 | 0.4 | 19.3 | 135 | 2.1 | 4.8 |
| Rice Krispies cereal & milk bar, (Kellogg's), 30g | 19.8 | 0.3 | 19.5 | 138 | 2.7 | 5.4 |
| Special K cereal & milk bar (Kellogg's), 30g | 22.5 | 0.6 | 21.9 | 117 | 2.1 | 2.1 |
| Tracker (Mars), 30g: | | | | | | |
| *Chocolate chip* | 17.8 | n/a | n/a | 159 | 2.4 | 8.7 |
| *Roasted nut* | 19.3 | n/a | n/a | 147 | 1.9 | 7 |

**TIP:** Many breakfast-type cereal bars on the market are simply sugar-coated, high-carb cereals formed into a bar – often with extra sweeteners or toppings. Although muesli bars can be loaded with sugar (read the labels – there is a huge difference between bars), they are the healthier alternative, especially if they contain dried fruit, nuts and seeds.

## CONDIMENTS, SAUCES AND GRAVY

There are loads of great sauces and seasonings that can be used on low-carb diets and they are highly recommended to add flavour to your food – so long as you avoid sugar and white flour ingredients. Fresh or dried herbs, spices, vinegar, mustard, pepper, chilli powder, soy sauce, garlic, Tabasco and horseradish are all low-carb. Watch out for tomato ketchup and brown sauce, though, as they're usually loaded with sugar or molasses. *The Zone Diet* has recipes for barbecue sauce, brown sauce, mustard sauce and a number of others that will spice up your meals, and most can be frozen in individual portions for use when you need them.

---

**TIP:** In restaurants, ask for the sauce to be served on the side. You'll probably only eat half as much as they give you.

| Food type | Carb (g) | Fibre (g) | Net carb (g) | Cal (kcal) | Pro (g) | Fat (g) |
|---|---|---|---|---|---|---|
| **Table Sauces** | | | | | | |
| Apple sauce (Colman's), 1 tbsp | 3.8 | 0.2 | 3.6 | 16 | – | – |
| Barbecue sauce (Heinz), 1 tbsp | 4.3 | – | 4.3 | 18 | 0.2 | – |
| Beetroot in redcurrant jelly (Baxter's), 1 tbsp | 6.6 | 0.1 | 6.5 | 25 | 0.1 | – |
| Branston fruity sauce (Crosse & Blackwell), 1 tbsp | 3.6 | 0.2 | 3.4 | 17 | 0.1 | – |
| Brown sauce, 1 tbsp | 3.8 | 0.1 | 3.7 | 15 | 0.2 | – |
| Burger sauce (Burgess), 1 tbsp | 1.6 | 0 | 1.6 | 89 | 0.3 | 9 |
| Chilli sauce (HP), 1 tsp | 1.6 | – | 1.6 | 7 | 0.1 | – |
| Cranberry jelly (Baxters), 1 tbsp | 10 | 0 | 10 | 40 | 0 | 0 |
| Cranberry sauce (Baxters), 1 tbsp | 6.8 | 0.1 | 6.7 | 27 | – | 0 |
| Garlic sauce (Lea & Perrins), 1 tsp | 0.9 | – | 0.9 | 17 | 0.1 | 1.5 |
| Ginger sauce (Lea & Perrins), 1 tsp | 1.4 | – | 1.4 | 6 | – | – |
| Horseradish, creamed (Burgess), 2 tsp | 2 | 0.2 | 1.8 | 18 | 0.2 | 1 |
| Horseradish relish (Colman's), 2 tsp | 1 | 0.3 | 0.7 | 11 | 0.2 | 0.6 |
| Horseradish sauce, 2 tsp | 1.8 | 0.3 | 1.5 | 15 | 0.3 | 0.8 |
| HP fruity sauce, 1 tbsp | 4.1 | – | 4.1 | 18 | 0.1 | 0.1 |

**TIP:** Monosodium glutamate, often used in the sauces in Chinese food, is made from beets and is very high in carbs.

| Food type | Carb (g) | Fibre (g) | Net carb (g) | Cal (kcal) | Pro (g) | Fat (g) |
|---|---|---|---|---|---|---|
| Mint jelly (Baxters), 1 tbsp | 9.9 | 0 | 9.9 | 40 | 0 | 0 |
| Mint sauce (Baxters), 1 tbsp | 2 | 0 | 2 | 9 | 0.3 | – |
| Mushroom ketchup (Burgess), 1 tbsp | 0.8 | – | 0.8 | 4 | 0.1 | – |
| Redcurrant jelly (Baxters), 1 tbsp | 9.8 | 0 | 9.8 | 39 | 0 | 0 |
| Soy sauce, (light & dark), 2 tsp | 0.8 | 0 | 0.8 | 4 | 0.8 | – |
| Tabasco, 1 tsp | 0 | 0 | 0 | 0 | 0 | 0 |
| Tartare sauce (Baxters), 1 tbsp | 1.2 | – | 1.2 | 77 | 0.2 | 8 |
| Tomato ketchup, 1 tbsp | 3.7 | 0.1 | 3.6 | 16 | 0.1 | – |
| Wild rowan jelly (Baxters), 2 tsp | 6.7 | 0 | 6.7 | 27 | 0 | 0 |
| Worcestershire sauce (Lea & Perrins), 1 tsp | 1.1 | – | 1.1 | 4 | 0.2 | – |
| **Mustards** | | | | | | |
| Dijon mustard (Colman's), 1 tsp | 0.3 | 0.2 | 0.1 | 6 | 0.3 | 0.5 |
| English mustard (Colman's), 1 tsp | 1 | 0.1 | 0.9 | 9 | 0.4 | 0.5 |
| French mustard (Burgess), 1 tsp | 0.7 | – | 0.7 | 7 | 0.4 | 0.2 |
| Honey mustard (Colman's), 1 tsp | 1.2 | 0.3 | 0.9 | 9 | 0.3 | 0.2 |
| Horseradish mustard (Colman's), 1 tsp | 1.2 | 0.2 | 1 | 8 | 0.3 | 0.2 |
| Peppercorn mustard (Colman's), 1 tsp | 0.8 | 0.3 | 0.5 | 7 | 0.4 | 0.3 |

**TIP:** Add a little mustard powder to your salad dressing mix for a bit of zing!

| **Food type** | **Carb (g)** | **Fibre (g)** | **Net carb (g)** | **Cal (kcal)** | **Pro (g)** | **Fat (g)** |
|---|---|---|---|---|---|---|
| Wholegrain mustard (Colman's), 1tsp: | 0.8 | 0.2 | 0.6 | 7 | 0.4 | 0.2 |
| *hot*, 1 tsp | 0.6 | 0.4 | 0.2 | 7 | 0.4 | 0.2 |
| **Pickles and Chutneys** | | | | | | |
| Apple chutney, 1 tbsp | 7.8 | 0.2 | 7.6 | 30 | 0.1 | – |
| Barbecue relish (Burgess), 1 tbsp | 4.4 | 0.2 | 4.2 | 20 | 0.3 | 0.1 |
| Branston Original (Crosse & Blackwell), 1 tbsp: | 5.1 | 0.2 | 4.9 | 21 | 0.1 | – |
| *small chunk* | – | 0.2 | – | 21 | 0.1 | – |
| *spicy* | 5.1 | 0.2 | 4.9 | 21 | 0.1 | – |
| Lime pickle (Sharwood), 1 tbsp | 2.2 | 0.4 | 1.8 | 23 | 0.3 | 1.4 |
| Mango chutney (Burgess), 1 tbsp | 9.2 | 0.1 | 9.1 | 42 | – | 0.5 |
| Mango with ginger chutney (Baxters), 1 tbsp | 6.9 | 0.1 | 6.8 | 28 | 0.1 | – |
| Mediterranean chutney (Baxters), 1 tbsp | 3.9 | 0.2 | 3.7 | 17.9 | 0.3 | 0.1 |
| Mustard pickle, mild (Heinz), 1 tbsp | 4 | 0.1 | 3.9 | 19 | 0.4 | 0.2 |
| Piccalilli (Heinz), 1 tbsp | 3 | 0.1 | 2.9 | 13 | 0.8 | – |

**TIP:** Read the label on that low-fat salad dressing – you might find it's higher in sugar (and therefore carbs) than the full-fat alternative.

| Food type | Carb (g) | Fibre (g) | Net carb (g) | Cal (kcal) | Pro (g) | Fat (g) |
|---|---|---|---|---|---|---|
| Ploughman's pickle (Heinz), 1 tbsp | 4 | 0.1 | 3.9 | 17 | 0.1 | – |
| Sandwich pickle, tangy (Heinz), 1 tbsp | 4.8 | 0.2 | 4.6 | 20 | 0.1 | – |
| Sauerkraut, 2 tbsp | 0.4 | 0.6 | – | 3 | 0.4 | – |
| Spiced fruit chutney (Baxters), 1 tbsp | 5.2 | 0.1 | 5.1 | 21 | 0.1 | – |
| Spreadable chutney, Green Label (Sharwoods), 1 tbsp | 7.5 | 0.2 | 7.3 | 30 | 0.1 | – |
| Sweet pickle, 1 tbsp | 5.2 | 0.2 | 5 | 20 | 0.1 | – |
| Tomato chutney, 1 tbsp | 6.1 | 0.2 | 5.9 | 24 | 0.2 | – |
| Tomato pickle, tangy (Heinz), 1 tbsp | 3.5 | 0.3 | 3.2 | 25 | 0.3 | – |
| Tomato with red pepper chutney (Baxters), 1 tbsp | 5.7 | 0.2 | 5.5 | 25 | 0.3 | |
| **Salad Dressings** | | | | | | |
| Blue cheese dressing, 2 tbsp | 2.6 | 0 | 2.6 | 137 | 0.6 | 13.9 |
| Blue cheese-flavoured low-fat (Weight Watchers), 2 tbsp | 1.7 | 0 | 1.7 | 18 | 0.5 | 1 |
| Creamy Caesar dressing (Kraft), 2 tbsp | 2.4 | – | 2.4 | 101 | 0.9 | 9.6 |

**TIP:** Use extra-virgin olive oil and balsamic vinegar shaken with fresh herbs and seasonings to make a delicious salad dressing.

| Food type | Carb (g) | Fibre (g) | Net carb (g) | Cal (kcal) | Pro (g) | Fat (g) |
|---|---|---|---|---|---|---|
| Caesar-style low-fat dressing (Weight Watchers), 2 tbsp | 1.7 | 0 | 1.7 | 18 | 0.5 | 1 |
| Creamy low-fat salad dressing, (Crosse & Blackwell), 2 tbsp | 4.3 | – | 4.3 | 36 | 0.3 | 1.9 |
| French dressing, 2 tbsp | 1.4 | 0 | 1.4 | 139 | – | 14.8 |
| Italian dressing (Kraft), 2 tbsp | 1.6 | 0.2 | 1.4 | 35 | – | 3 |
| *fat free* | 1.9 | 0.2 | 1.7 | 9 | – | – |
| Mayonnaise (Hellmann's), 1 tbsp | 0.2 | 0 | 0.2 | 109 | 0.2 | 11.8 |
| *light, reduced calorie*, 1 tbsp | 1 | – | 1 | 45 | 0.1 | 5 |
| Salad cream (Heinz), 1 tbsp | 2.5 | – | 2.5 | 52 | 0.2 | 4.7 |
| *light*, 1 tbsp | 1.9 | 0 | 1.9 | 35 | 0.2 | 3 |
| Seafood sauce (Baxters), 1 tbsp | 14.8 | 0.1 | 14.7 | 80 | 0.2 | 8.1 |
| Thousand Island (Kraft), 1 tbsp | 2.9 | – | 2.9 | 54 | 0.1 | 4.6 |
| *fat free*, 1 tbsp | 2.9 | 0.4 | 2.5 | 12 | 0.1 | – |
| **Vinegars** | | | | | | |
| Balsamic vinegar (Carapelli), 1 tbsp | 3.2 | 0 | 3.2 | 15 | – | 0 |
| Cider vinegar (Dufrais), 1 tbsp | 0.2 | 0.1 | 0.1 | 3 | – | 0 |
| Red wine vinegar (Dufrais), 1 tbsp | 0.1 | 0 | 0.1 | 4 | – | 0 |

**TIP:** Greek yoghurt is lower in carbs than many other yoghurts, and has a richer, creamy taste. Use it as a base for sauces to serve with your food, combined with herbs and spices.

| Food type | Carb (g) | Fibre (g) | Net carb (g) | Cal (kcal) | Pro (g) | Fat (g) |
|---|---|---|---|---|---|---|
| Sherry vinegar (Dufrais), 1 tbsp | 0.3 | 0 | 0.3 | 4 | – | 0 |
| White wine vinegar (Dufrais), 1 tbsp | 0.1 | 0 | 0.1 | 3 | – | 0 |
| **Cooking Sauces** | | | | | | |
| Bread sauce, 100ml: | | | | | | |
| *made with semi-skimmed milk* | 11.1 | 0.6 | 0.5 | 128 | 4.2 | 1 |
| *made with whole milk* | 10.9 | 0.6 | 10.3 | 150 | 4.1 | 10.3 |
| Cheese sauce, 100ml: | | | | | | |
| *made with semi-skimmed milk* | 8.8 | 0.2 | 8.6 | 181 | 8.2 | 12.8 |
| *made with whole milk* | 8.7 | 0.2 | 8.5 | 198 | 8.1 | 14.8 |
| Curry sauce, canned, 100ml | 7.1 | – | 7.1 | 78 | 1.5 | 5 |
| Onion sauce, 100ml: | | | | | | |
| *made with semi-skimmed milk* | 8.4 | 0.4 | 8.0 | 86 | 2.9 | 5 |
| *made with whole milk* | 8.3 | 0.4 | 7.9 | 99 | 2.8 | 6.5 |
| White sauce, 100ml: | | | | | | |
| *made with semi-skimmed milk* | 10.7 | 0.2 | 10.5 | 130 | 4.4 | 8 |
| *made with whole milk* | 10.6 | 0.2 | 10.4 | 151 | 4.2 | 10.3 |
| For pasta sauces, *see under: Pasta and Pizza* | | | | | | |

**TIP:** Shop-bought cook-in sauces can be very high in carbs. If you're carb-counting, buy dry sauce mixes and make them up with skimmed milk, olive oil or just water.

| Food type | Carb (g) | Fibre (g) | Net carb (g) | Cal (kcal) | Pro (g) | Fat (g) |
|---|---|---|---|---|---|---|
| **Stock Cubes** | | | | | | |
| Beef stock cubes (Oxo), each | 4.2 | 0.2 | 4 | 29 | 1.9 | 0.5 |
| Chicken stock cubes (Oxo), each | 4 | 0.2 | 3.8 | 27 | 1.2 | 0.4 |
| Fish stock cubes (Knorr), each | 1.8 | 0.1 | 1.7 | 36 | 2.1 | 2.2 |
| Garlic herb & spice cubes (Oxo), each | 5.3 | 0.4 | 4.9 | 33 | 1.5 | 0.6 |
| Ham stock cubes (Knorr), each | 2.7 | 0 | 2.7 | 34 | 1.3 | 2 |
| Lamb stock cubes (Knorr), each | 4.8 | 0.2 | 4.6 | 32 | 1.7 | 0.6 |
| Marmite stock cubes, each | 2.8 | – | 2.8 | 27 | 2.8 | 0.6 |
| Rice saffron stock cubes (Knorr), each | 1.4 | 0.4 | 1 | 32 | 1.6 | 2.2 |
| Pork stock cubes (Knorr), each | 1.9 | – | 1.9 | 37 | 1.3 | 2.7 |
| Vegetable stock cubes (Oxo), each | 4.6 | 0.2 | 4.4 | 28 | 1.2 | 0.5 |
| **Gravy Granules** | | | | | | |
| Bisto Original, 5g | 2.99 | 0.06 | 2.93 | 12 | 0.1 | 0.01 |
| Gravy instant granules, 5g | 2.0 | – | 2.0 | 23 | 0.2 | 1.6 |
| Marigold Swiss Vegetable Bouillon powder, 4g | 1.1 | – | 1.1 | 11 | 0.4 | 0.5 |
| Vegetable gravy granules, 5g | 2.98 | 0.05 | 2.93 | 16 | 0.4 | 0.25 |

**TIP:** One stock cube makes around 450 to 500ml of stock. With powders and granules, 5g makes around 250ml, but check the packaging for preparation instructions.

## DAIRY

Low-fat versions of some types of dairy products will have higher carb counts than their full-fat equivalents, but you need to balance this against health concerns associated with high saturated fat content. Make sure your daily diet includes some dairy – either skimmed milk, low-fat cheeses or low-fat unsweetened yoghurt – because they are important sources of calcium. Lack of sufficient calcium can cause osteoporosis, particularly in post-menopausal women. Butter is predominantly saturated fat, with 8.1g in a 15g serving, but many margarines contain trans fats. If you are worried about your fat intake, choose an olive oil spread or try Benecol or Flora Pro.active, which contain cholesterol-lowering substances called stanols.

**TIP:** If a spread is labelled 'low-fat', it must have less than 40g fat per 100g; if it's labelled 'very low fat', it should have no more than 20–30g. For other products, 'fat-free' means less than 0.15g of fat per 100g; 'low fat' means less than 3g of fat per 100g; and 'reduced fat' means at least 25% less fat than the full-fat version.

| Food type | Carb (g) | Fibre (g) | Net carb (g) | Cal (kcal) | Pro (g) | Fat (g) |
|---|---|---|---|---|---|---|
| **Milk and Cream** | | | | | | |
| Buttermilk, 250ml | 13.8 | – | 13.8 | 100 | 10.8 | 0.3 |
| Cream: | | | | | | |
| *extra thick,* 2 tbsp | 1.1 | – | 1.1 | 88 | 0.7 | 9 |
| *fresh, clotted,* 2 tbsp | 0.7 | – | 0.8 | 176 | 0.5 | 19 |
| *fresh, double,* 2 tbsp | 0.5 | – | 0.5 | 149 | 0.5 | 16.1 |
| *fresh, single,* 2 tbsp | 0.7 | – | 0.7 | 58 | 1 | 5.7 |
| *fresh, soured,* 2 tbsp | 0.9 | – | 0.9 | 62 | 1.1 | 6.0 |
| *fresh, whipping,* 2 tbsp | 0.8 | – | 0.8 | 114 | 0.6 | 12 |
| *sterilised, canned,* 2 tbsp | 1.1 | – | 1.1 | 76 | 0.6 | 7.2 |
| *UHT, aerosol spray,* 2 tbsp | 2.2 | – | 2.2 | 86 | 0.7 | 7.2 |
| *UHT, double Elmlea,* 2 tbsp | 1.2 | 0.1 | 1.1 | 105 | 0.7 | 10.8 |
| *UHT, single Elmlea,* 2 tbsp | 1.4 | 0.06 | 1.34 | 44 | 0.9 | 3.9 |
| Crème fraiche: | | | | | | |
| *full fat,* 2 tbsp | 19 | – | 19 | 113 | 0.5 | 0.7 |
| *half fat,* 2 tbsp | 4.5 | – | 4.5 | 49 | 0.8 | 1.3 |
| Milk, fresh: | | | | | | |
| *cows', whole,* 250ml | 11.3 | – | 11.3 | 165 | 82.5 | 9.8 |
| *cows', semi-skimmed,* 250ml | 11.8 | – | 11.8 | 115 | 8.5 | 4.25 |
| *cows', skimmed,* 250ml | 11 | – | 11 | 80 | 8.5 | 0.5 |
| *cows', Channel Island,* 250ml | 12.8 | – | 12.8 | 195 | 9 | 12 |

**TIP:** A 120ml glass of red wine and a 30g chunk of cheese is a perfect Zone-balanced snack. Get to know portion sizes by sight: 30g of cheese is about the size of your thumb.

| Food type | Carb (g) | Fibre (g) | Net carb (g) | Cal (kcal) | Pro (g) | Fat (g) |
|---|---|---|---|---|---|---|
| Milk, contd: | | | | | | |
| *goats', pasteurised*, 250ml | 11 | – | 11 | 155 | 7.8 | 9.3 |
| *sheep's*, 250ml | 9.3 | – | 9.3 | 150 | 7.8 | 11 |
| Milk, evaporated (Nestlé): | | | | | | |
| *original*, 100ml | 54.3 | – | 54.3 | 330 | 8.3 | 9.1 |
| *light*, 100ml | 10.3 | – | 10.3 | 107 | 7.8 | 4.1 |
| Milk, dried, skimmed, 250ml | 132.3 | – | 132.5 | 870 | 90.3 | 1.5 |
| Milk, condensed: | | | | | | |
| *whole milk, sweetened*, 100ml | 55.5 | – | 55.5 | 333 | 8.5 | 10.1 |
| *skimmed milk, sweetened*, 100ml | 60 | – | 60 | 267 | 10 | 0.2 |
| Soya milk: | | | | | | |
| *unsweetened*, 250ml | 1.3 | 0.5 | 0.8 | 65 | 6 | 4 |
| *sweetened*, 250ml | 6.3 | – | 6.3 | 108 | 7.8 | 6 |
| Rice drink (Provamel): | | | | | | |
| *calcium enriched*, 250ml | 25 | – | 25 | 125 | 0.3 | 2.8 |
| *vanilla, organic*, 250ml | 25 | – | 25 | 123 | 0.3 | 2.5 |
| **Yoghurt and Fromage Frais** | | | | | | |
| Fromage frais, 1 pot (50g): | | | | | | |
| *fruit* | 6.9 | – | 6.9 | 62 | 2.6 | 2.8 |
| *plain* | 2.8 | – | 2.8 | 56 | 3.4 | 3.5 |
| *virtually fat free, fruit* | 2.8 | 0.2 | 2.6 | 25 | 3.2 | 0.1 |

**TIP:** Soya milk is not a true dairy product. If you are using it as a low-carb alternative to milk, make sure it is fortified with calcium.

| Food type | Carb (g) | Fibre (g) | Net carb (g) | Cal (kcal) | Pro (g) | Fat (g) |
|---|---|---|---|---|---|---|
| *virtually fat free, plain* | 2.3 | – | 2.3 | 25 | 3.8 | 0.05 |
| Fruit Corner (Müller), 125g: | | | | | | |
| *blueberry* | 18.9 | n/a | n/a | 140 | 4.6 | 4.9 |
| *strawberry* | 21.4 | n/a | n/a | 148 | 4.6 | 4.9 |
| Greek-style, cows, fruit, 1 pot (125g) | 14 | – | 14 | 171 | 6 | 10.5 |
| Greek-style, cows, plain, 1 pot (125g) | 6 | – | 6 | 166 | 7.1 | 12.7 |
| Greek-style, sheep, 1 pot (125g) | 6.25 | – | 6.25 | 115 | 6 | 7.5 |
| Low fat, fruit, 1 pot (125g) | 17.1 | 0.25 | 16.85 | 98 | 5.2 | 1.4 |
| Low fat, plain, 1 pot (125g) | 9.25 | – | 9.25 | 70 | 6 | 1.25 |
| Müllerlight (Müller), 125g: | | | | | | |
| *banana yoghurt* | 10.9 | n/a | n/a | 66 | 5.5 | 0.1 |
| *cherry yoghurt* | 9.9 | n/a | n/a | 62 | 5.5 | 0.1 |
| vanilla yoghurt | 10.4 | n/a | n/a | 66 | 5.7 | 0.1 |
| Natural Bio Yoghurt (Holland & Barrett), 125g | 7 | – | 7 | 68 | 5.5 | 1.9 |
| Orange fat-free bio yoghurt (St Ivel Shape), each | 11.3 | 0.1 | 11.2 | 61 | 5.4 | 0.2 |
| Raspberry drinking yoghurt (St Ivel), per bottle | 12.5 | 0.1 | 12.4 | 78 | 2.9 | 1.8 |
| Soya, fruit, 1 pot (125g) | 16.1 | 0.4 | 15.7 | 91 | 2.6 | 2.25 |

**TIP:** Probiotic yoghurts have special bacteria added, which can help to relieve digestive problems, such as irritable bowel syndrome.

| Food type | Carb (g) | Fibre (g) | Net carb (g) | Cal (kcal) | Pro (g) | Fat (g) |
|---|---|---|---|---|---|---|
| Virtually fat free, fruit, 1 pot (125g) | 8.75 | – | 8.75 | 59 | 6 | 0.25 |
| Virtually fat free, plain, 1 pot (125g) | 10.2 | – | 10.2 | 67.5 | 6.8 | 0.25 |
| Vitality Drink (Müller), 125ml: | | | | | | |
| *natural yoghurt* | 8.6 | n/a | n/a | 84 | 6.9 | 2.4 |
| *peach* | 16.2 | n/a | n/a | 94 | 3.2 | 1.8 |
| Whole milk, fruit, 1 pot (125g) | 22.1 | – | 22.1 | 136 | 5 | 3.75 |
| Whole milk, plain, 1 pot (125g) | 9.8 | – | 9.8 | 99 | 7.1 | 3.75 |
| Yoplait (Dairy Crest), 125ml: | | | | | | |
| *black cherry* | 19.8 | n/a | n/a | 138 | 6.1 | 2 |
| *peach & passionfruit* | 17 | n/a | n/a | 105 | 4.8 | 2 |
| **Butter and Margarine** | | | | | | |
| Butter: | | | | | | |
| *lightly salted*, 15g | – | – | – | 108 | – | 12 |
| *spreadable*, 15g | 12.3 | – | 12.3 | 112 | – | 12 |
| *salted*, 15g | 0.1 | – | 0.1 | 112 | 0.1 | 12.3 |
| Margarine, hard | | | | | | |
| *animal & vegetable fat, over 80% fat*, 15g | 0.1 | – | 0.1 | 108 | – | 12 |

**TIP:** The daily requirement for calcium is 700–1000mg; 100ml of semi-skimmed milk contains 122mg, while 30g of Cheddar cheese will have up to 200mg.

| Food type | Carb (g) | Fibre (g) | Net carb (g) | Cal (kcal) | Pro (g) | Fat (g) |
|---|---|---|---|---|---|---|
| Margarine, soft | | | | | | |
| *polyunsaturated, over 80%* | | | | | | |
| *fat*, 15g | 0.03 | – | 0.03 | 112 | – | 12.4 |
| **Spreads** | | | | | | |
| Benecol, 15g | 0 | 0 | 0 | 86 | 0 | 9.6 |
| *light* | 0 | 0 | 0 | 48 | 0 | 5.4 |
| Flora: | | | | | | |
| *buttery*, 15g | 0.07 | – | 0.07 | 95 | 0.06 | 10.5 |
| *light*, 15g | 0.5 | 0.1 | 0.4 | 54 | – | 5.7 |
| *low salt*, 15g | – | – | – | 95 | – | 10.5 |
| *pro.active*, 15g | 0.5 | 0.04 | 0.46 | 49 | – | 5.3 |
| *sunflower spread*, 15g | – | – | – | 95 | – | 10.5 |
| I Can't Believe It's Not Butter, 15g | 0.1 | – | 0.1 | 94 | – | 10.3 |
| Olivio, 15g | 0.1 | – | 0.1 | 80 | – | 8.8 |
| *very low fat* (20-25%) | 0.4 | 0 | 0.4 | 39 | 0.9 | 3.8 |
| Utterly Butterly, 15g | 0.24 | – | 0.24 | 92 | – | 10 |
| Vitalite, 15g | 0.18 | – | 0.18 | 87 | – | 9.5 |
| **Cheeses** | | | | | | |
| Babybel, 25g | – | – | – | 77 | 5.8 | 6 |
| Bavarian smoked, 25g | 0.1 | – | 0.1 | 69 | 4.3 | 5.8 |

**TIP:** Try using low-fat cottage cheese to add texture to a vegetarian lasagne. Just add a layer where the recipe calls for minced beef or lamb.

| Food type | Carb (g) | Fibre (g) | Net carb (g) | Cal (kcal) | Pro (g) | Fat (g) |
|---|---|---|---|---|---|---|
| Boursin: | | | | | | |
| *ail & fines herbs*, 25g | 0.5 | – | 0.5 | 104 | 1.8 | 10.5 |
| *au naturel*, 25g | 0.5 | – | 0.5 | 106 | 1.8 | 10.8 |
| *au poivre*, 25g | 0.5 | – | 0.5 | 104 | 1.8 | 10.5 |
| Brie, 25g | – | – | – | 86 | 5.1 | 7.3 |
| Caerphilly, 25g | – | – | – | 92 | 5.8 | 8 |
| Cambozola, 25g | 0.1 | – | 0.1 | 108 | 3.4 | 10.4 |
| Camembert, 25g | – | – | – | 72 | 5.4 | 5.7 |
| Cheddar: | | | | | | |
| *English*, 25g | – | – | – | 104 | 6.4 | 8.8 |
| *vegetarian*, 25g | – | – | – | 98 | 1.4 | 8 |
| Cheddar-type, half fat, 25g | – | – | – | 68 | 8.2 | 4 |
| Cheshire, 25g | – | – | – | 95 | 6 | 7.9 |
| Cottage cheese: | | | | | | |
| *plain*, 100g | 3.1 | – | 3.1 | 101 | 12.6 | 4.3 |
| *reduced fat*, 100g | 3.3 | – | 3.3 | 79 | 13.3 | 1.5 |
| *with additions*, 100g | 2.6 | – | 2.6 | 95 | 12.8 | 3.8 |
| Cream cheese, full fat, 25g | – | – | – | 110 | 0.8 | 12 |
| Danish Blue, 25g | – | – | – | 86 | 5.1 | 7.2 |
| Dolcelatte, 25g | 0.2 | – | 0.2 | 99 | 4.3 | 9 |
| Double Gloucester, 25g | – | – | – | 101 | 6.1 | 8.5 |
| Edam, 25g | – | – | – | 85 | 6.7 | 6.5 |

**TIP:** Top a whole round brie with some fresh tomatoes, basil and garlic, and grill until piping hot for a delicious low-carb treat.

| Food type | Carb (g) | Fibre (g) | Net carb (g) | Cal (kcal) | Pro (g) | Fat (g) |
|---|---|---|---|---|---|---|
| Emmenthal, 25g | 0.1 | – | 0.1 | 103 | 6.3 | 8.6 |
| Feta, 25g | 0.4 | – | 0.4 | 63 | 3.9 | 5 |
| Goats' milk soft cheese, 25g | 0.3 | – | 0.3 | 80 | 5.3 | 6.5 |
| Gorgonzola, 25g | – | – | – | 78 | 4.8 | 9 |
| Gouda, 25g | – | – | – | 94 | 6.2 | 7.7 |
| Grana Padano, 25g | – | – | – | 96 | 8.3 | 7 |
| Gruyère, 25g | – | – | – | 99 | 6.8 | 8 |
| Jarlsberg, 25g | – | – | – | 90 | 6.8 | 7 |
| Lancashire, 25g | – | – | – | 95 | 5.9 | 8 |
| Mascarpone, 25g | 0.8 | – | 0.8 | 105 | 0.9 | 11.1 |
| Mature cheese, reduced fat (Weight Watchers), 25g | – | – | – | 77 | 6.8 | 5.5 |
| Medium-fat soft cheese, 25g | 0.9 | – | 0.9 | 49.8 | 2.5 | 4 |
| Mild cheese, reduced fat (Weight Watchers), 25g | – | – | – | 77 | 6.8 | 5.5 |
| Mozzarella, 25g | – | – | – | 64 | 4.7 | 5 |
| Parmesan, fresh, 25g | 0.2 | – | 0.2 | 103.8 | 9 | 7.4 |
| Philadelphia soft cheese (Kraft): | | | | | | |
| *full fat*, 25g | 0.8 | – | 0.8 | 63 | 1.5 | 6 |
| *light medium fat*, 25g | 0.9 | – | 0.9 | 48 | 1.9 | 4 |
| *light with chives*, 25g | 0.9 | – | 0.9 | 46 | 1.9 | 3.8 |
| *light with tomato & basil*, 25g | 1.1 | 0.1 | 1 | 45 | 1.9 | 3.5 |

**TIP:** Blue cheese can be melted and mixed with a little crème fraiche to make a tasty topping for fish or chicken.

| Food type | Carb (g) | Fibre (g) | Net carb (g) | Cal (kcal) | Pro (g) | Fat (g) |
|---|---|---|---|---|---|---|
| Quark, 25g | 1 | – | 1 | 15 | 2.8 | – |
| Red Leicester, 25g | – | – | – | 100 | 6 | 8.4 |
| Ricotta, 25g | 0.5 | – | 0.5 | 34 | 2.3 | 2.5 |
| Roquefort, 25g | – | – | – | 89 | 5.8 | 7.3 |
| Sage Derby, 25g | 0.7 | – | 0.7 | 104 | 6.1 | 8.5 |
| Shropshire blue, 25g | – | – | – | 102 | 5.6 | 8.9 |
| Stilton: | | | | | | |
| *blue*, 25g | – | – | – | 103 | 5.9 | 8.8 |
| *white*, 25g | – | – | – | 90 | 5 | 7.8 |
| *white, with apricots*, 25g | 2.6 | – | 2.6 | 88 | 4.2 | 6.8 |
| Wensleydale, 25g | – | – | – | 94 | 5.7 | 7.9 |
| *with cranberries*, 25g | 2.4 | – | 2.4 | 92 | 5.3 | 6.8 |
| **Cheese Spreads and Processed Cheese** | | | | | | |
| Cheese spread: | | | | | | |
| *plain*, 25g | 1.1 | – | 1.1 | 67 | 2.9 | 5.7 |
| *reduced fat*, 25g | 2 | – | 2 | 44 | 3.8 | 2.4 |
| Cheese slices: | | | | | | |
| *singles*, 25g | 1.9 | – | 1.9 | 65 | 3.4 | 3.7 |
| *singles light*, 25g | 1.5 | – | 1.5 | 51 | 5 | 2.8 |

**TIP:** If you don't like milk and yoghurt, make sure that you select semi-soft, aged cheeses such as cheddar, which give the most calcium per serving.

| Food type | Carb (g) | Fibre (g) | Net carb (g) | Cal (kcal) | Pro (g) | Fat (g) |
|---|---|---|---|---|---|---|
| Dairylea cheese portions, 25g | 1.8 | – | 1.8 | 56 | 2.5 | 4.4 |
| Dairylea cheese strip cheese, 25g | 0.5 | – | 0.5 | 90 | 6.1 | 6.9 |
| Primula spread: | | | | | | |
| *original*, 25g | 0.5 | – | 0.5 | 60 | 3.3 | 5 |
| *cheese & chive*, 25g | 0.3 | – | 0.3 | 59 | 3.2 | 5 |
| *cheese & shrimp*, 25g | 0.5 | – | 0.5 | 60 | 3.3 | 5 |
| *cheese & ham*, 25g | 0.4 | – | 0.4 | 59 | 3.2 | 5 |
| *cheese & garlic*, 25g | 1 | – | 1 | 62 | 3.9 | 5 |
| *light*, 25g | 1.7 | – | 1.7 | 43 | 4 | 5 |
| Processed cheese, plain, 25g | 1.3 | – | 1.3 | 74 | 2 | 5 |
| *See* also: *Jams, Marmalades and Spreads* | | | | | | |

**TIP:** Many low-carb diets, such as Atkins, suggest that you limit dairy products in the early weeks of the plan, because they all contain some carbohydrate.

## DESSERTS AND PUDDINGS

This is traditionally dangerous territory for dieters, but all the controlled-carb diets suggest recipes for nutritious low-carb puddings. If you can't resist that trifle or cheesecake, try taking three spoonfuls only and you may find it's enough to satisfy your tastebuds. Check the carb counts on desserts that are labelled 'low-fat' to make sure they're not even higher than full-fat alternatives due to added sugars, and watch out for artificial sweeteners in diet desserts – there are particular health concerns about aspartame.

**TIP:** Strawberries and cream are an easy low-carb dessert. Get the strawberries in season and you won't need any sweeteners.

| Food type | Carb (g) | Fibre (g) | Net carb (g) | Cal (kcal) | Pro (g) | Fat (g) |
|---|---|---|---|---|---|---|
| **Puddings** | | | | | | |
| Bread pudding, 100g | 48 | 1.2 | 46.8 | 289 | 5.9 | 9.5 |
| Christmas pudding, 100g | 56.3 | 1.7 | 54.6 | 329 | 3 | 11.8 |
| Creamed rice (Ambrosia), 100g | 15.2 | – | 15.2 | 90 | 3.1 | 1.9 |
| Meringue, 100g | 95.4 | – | 95.4 | 379 | 5.3 | – |
| Pavlova, with raspberries, 100g | 45 | – | 45 | 297 | 2.5 | 11.9 |
| Profiteroles, 100g | 18.5 | 0.4 | 18.1 | 358 | 6.2 | 29.2 |
| Rice pudding, 100g: | 19.6 | 0.1 | 19.5 | 130 | 4.1 | 4.3 |
| *with sultanas & nutmeg* | 16.6 | 0.1 | 16.5 | 105 | 3.2 | 2.9 |
| Sago pudding, 100g: | | | | | | |
| *made with semi-skimmed milk* | 20.1 | 0.1 | 20 | 93 | 4 | 0.2 |
| *made with whole milk* | 19.6 | 0.1 | 19.5 | 130 | 4.1 | 4.3 |
| Semolina pudding, 100g: | | | | | | |
| *made with semi-skimmed milk* | 20.1 | 0.1 | 20 | 93 | 4 | 0.2 |
| *made with whole milk* | 19.6 | 0.1 | 19.5 | 130 | 4.1 | 4.3 |
| Sponge pudding (Heinz): | | | | | | |
| *with chocolate sauce*, 100g | 48.2 | 1.4 | 46.8 | 285 | 2.7 | 9.1 |
| *lemon*, 100g | 50.1 | 0.6 | 49.5 | 306 | 2.7 | 10.6 |
| *treacle*, 100g | 49.2 | 0.6 | 48.6 | 278 | 2.3 | 8 |
| Spotted Dick (McVitie's), 100g | 51.2 | 2.3 | 48.9 | 357 | 5.7 | 15 |
| Tapioca pudding, 100g: | | | | | | |
| *made with semi-skimmed milk* | 20.1 | 0.1 | 20 | 93 | 4 | 0.2 |

**TIP:** The *South Beach Diet* has several delicious dessert recipes using low-fat ricotta cheese with different flavourings.

| Food type | Carb (g) | Fibre (g) | Net carb (g) | Cal (kcal) | Pro (g) | Fat (g) |
|---|---|---|---|---|---|---|
| Tapioca pudding, 100g, contd: | | | | | | |
| *made with whole milk* | 19.6 | 0.1 | 19.5 | 130 | 4.1 | 4.3 |
| Trifle, 100g | 22.3 | 0.5 | 21.8 | 160 | 3.6 | 6.3 |
| Trifle with fresh cream, 100g | 19.5 | 0.5 | 19 | 166 | 2.4 | 9.2 |
| **Sweet Pies and Flans** | | | | | | |
| Apple & blackcurrant pies (Mr Kipling), each | 52.7 | 1.5 | 51.2 | 331 | 3.4 | 13 |
| Apple pie (McVitie's), 100g | 35.3 | 0.9 | 34.4 | 235 | 2.8 | 9.6 |
| Bakewell tart (Lyons), 100g | 56.7 | 0.9 | 55.8 | 397 | 3.8 | 17 |
| *cherry bakewell (Mr Kipling)* | 58.5 | 1.2 | 57.3 | 412 | 3.9 | 18 |
| Cheesecake, 100g: | 33 | 0.9 | 32.1 | 242 | 5.7 | 10.6 |
| *raspberry (Young's)* | 31.9 | 0.6 | 31.3 | 299 | 4.7 | 17.2 |
| Custard tart, 100g | 32.4 | 1.2 | 31.2 | 277 | 6.3 | 15 |
| Dutch apple tart (McVitie's), 100g | 34.4 | 0.6 | 33.8 | 237 | 3.2 | 9.9 |
| Fruit pie, individual: | 56.7 | – | 56.7 | 369 | 4.3 | 16 |
| *pastry top & bottom*, 100g | 34 | 1.8 | 32.2 | 260 | 3 | 13 |
| *wholemeal one crust*, 100g | 26.6 | 2.7 | 23.9 | 183 | 2.6 | 8.1 |
| Jam tart, 100g | 63.4 | – | 63.4 | 368 | 3.3 | 13 |
| Lemon meringue pie (Sara Lee), 100g | 45.9 | 0.7 | 45.2 | 319 | 4.5 | 14 |

**TIP:** Shop-bought tarts and pies often give a nutritional breakdown per sixth or per eighth of the product.

| Food type | Carb (g) | Fibre (g) | Net carb (g) | Cal (kcal) | Pro (g) | Fat (g) |
|---|---|---|---|---|---|---|
| Mince pies (Mr Kipling), 100g | 56.8 | 1.5 | 55.3 | 372 | 3.8 | 14 |
| *luxury*, 100g | 55.7 | 1.5 | 54.2 | 387 | 3.7 | 14 |
| Treacle tart, 100g | 60.4 | 1.1 | 59.3 | 368 | 3.7 | 1.1 |
| **Chilled and Frozen Desserts** | | | | | | |
| Crème brulée (McVitie's), 100g | 23.5 | 0.2 | 23.3 | 251 | 1.3 | 17 |
| Crème caramel (Nestlé), 100g | 20.6 | – | 20.6 | 109 | 3 | 2.2 |
| Chocolate nut sundae, 100g | 26.2 | 0.2 | 26 | 243 | 2.6 | 14.9 |
| Ice cream, 100g: | | | | | | |
| *Cornish (Lyons Maid)* | 11.3 | n/a | n/a | 92 | 19 | 4.4 |
| *chocolate (Fiesta)* | 20.6 | n/a | n/a | 187 | 3.5 | 10.6 |
| *Neapolitan (Fiesta)* | 20.1 | n/a | n/a | 173 | 3.6 | 9.3 |
| *peach melba (Lyons Maid)* | 13.2 | n/a | n/a | 94 | 1.7 | 3.8 |
| *raspberry ripple (Fiesta)* | 24.3 | n/a | n/a | 192 | 3.2 | 9.8 |
| *strawberry (Lyons Maid)* | 10.5 | n/a | n/a | 84 | 1.7 | 3.8 |
| *tiramisu (Carte d'Or)* | 15.2 | n/a | n/a | 112 | 2.1 | 4.6 |
| *vanilla (Walls)* | 11.4 | n/a | n/a | 90 | 1.5 | 4.5 |
| Ice cream bar, chocolate-covered, 100g | 21.8 | – | 21.8 | 311 | 5 | 23.3 |
| Ice cream dessert, frozen, 100g | 21 | – | 21 | 251 | 3.5 | 17.6 |
| Instant dessert powder, 100g: | | | | | | |
| *made up with whole milk* | 14.8 | 0.2 | 14.6 | 111 | 3.1 | 6.3 |

**TIP:** Gelatin desserts are all low-carb, but remember that some carb-controlled diets limit your consumption of fruit.

| Food type | Carb (g) | Fibre (g) | Net carb (g) | Cal (kcal) | Pro (g) | Fat (g) |
|---|---|---|---|---|---|---|
| Jelly, 100g | | | | | | |
| *all flavours, made with water* | 15.1 | – | 15.1 | 61 | 1.2 | – |
| Mousse, 100g: | | | | | | |
| *chocolate* | 19.9 | – | 19.9 | 139 | 4 | 2.1 |
| *fruit* | 18 | – | 18 | 137 | 4.5 | 5.7 |
| Sorbet, 100g: | | | | | | |
| *fruit* | 24.8 | – | 24.8 | 97 | 0.2 | 0.3 |
| *lemon* | 34.2 | – | 34.2 | 131 | 0.9 | – |
| Tiramisu (McVitie's), 100g | 31.2 | 0.3 | 30.9 | 337 | 3.5 | 22.2 |
| Vanilla Soya Dessert | | | | | | |
| (Provamel), each | 16.4 | 1.3 | 15.1 | 101 | 3.8 | 2.3 |
| For yoghurt, *see under Dairy* | | | | | | |
| | | | | | | |
| **Toppings and Sauces** | | | | | | |
| Brandy flavour sauce mix | | | | | | |
| (Bird's), 50ml | 38.2 | – | 38.2 | 208 | 3.0 | 4.7 |
| Brandy sauce, ready to serve | | | | | | |
| (Bird's), 50ml | 8.2 | – | 8.2 | 48 | 1.4 | 0.8 |
| Chocolate custard mix (Bird's), | | | | | | |
| 50ml: | | | | | | |
| *chocolate flavour* | 39.3 | 0.1 | 39.2 | 208 | 3.0 | 4.4 |
| *low fat* | 39.3 | 0.1 | 39.2 | 202 | 2.2 | 4.1 |

**TIP:** Poach fruits with wine and spices like ginger and cinnamon for a great dinner party dessert.

| Food type | Carb (g) | Fibre (g) | Net carb (g) | Cal (kcal) | Pro (g) | Fat (g) |
|---|---|---|---|---|---|---|
| Custard, 50ml: | | | | | | |
| *made with skimmed milk* | 8.4 | – | 8.4 | 40 | 1.9 | 0.05 |
| *made with whole milk* | 8.3 | – | 8.3 | 59 | 1.8 | 2.2 |
| *canned* | 7.8 | – | 7.8 | 51 | 1.4 | 1.5 |
| Devon Custard (Ambrosia), 50ml | 8.2 | 0.05 | 8.15 | 52 | 1.4 | 1.5 |
| Dream Topping (Bird's), 50ml | 16.2 | 0.25 | 15.95 | 345 | 3.4 | 29.3 |
| *sugar-free* | 15.2 | 0.25 | 14.95 | 348 | 3.6 | 30.2 |
| Maple syrup, organic, 1 tsp | 3.4 | – | 3.4 | 13 | 0 | – |
| Rum sauce (Bird's), 50ml | 7.8 | – | 7.8 | 46 | 1.4 | 0.8 |
| White sauce, sweet, 50ml | | | | | | |
| *made with semi-skimmed milk* | 9.3 | 0.1 | 9.2 | 76 | 2 | 3.7 |
| *made with whole milk* | 9.2 | 0.1 | 9.1 | 86 | 2 | 4.8 |

**TIP:** 50ml is about 3 tablespoons of dessert topping or sauce; 100ml is about 6 tablespoons.

## DRINKS

Most alcohol is full of 'empty calories' and fairly high in carbs, so should be restricted to your 'treats' category. Beer is particularly high on the glycaemic index because of its main ingredient, maltose. White wine is better and red wine is best of all because it contains reservatol, which has some heart-friendly benefits. Fizzy drinks, such as colas, deliver an instant blood sugar peak, and although diet drinks are low carb, they fill you up without providing nutrients. Coffee and tea are fine in moderation; add skimmed milk and natural sweeteners, to taste. Fruit juices do have some nutrients but the high fructose content without enough fibre to slow its absorption means they could lead to fluctuating blood sugar. Don't forget the most important drink of all: carb-controlled diets advise that you drink six to eight large glasses of water a day.

**TIP:** Watch out for sugar or corn syrup on soft drinks labels – some have very high levels. See page 132 for some other names you might find sugar called by.

| Food type | Carb (g) | Fibre (g) | Net carb (g) | Cal (kcal) | Pro (g) | Fat (g) |
|---|---|---|---|---|---|---|
| **Alcoholic** | | | | | | |
| Advocaat, 25ml | 7.1 | – | 7.1 | 68 | 1.2 | 5.3 |
| Beer, bitter, 500ml: | | | | | | |
| *canned* | 11.5 | – | 11.5 | 160 | 1.5 | – |
| *draught* | 11.5 | – | 11.5 | 160 | 1.5 | – |
| *keg* | 11.5 | – | 11.5 | 155 | 1.5 | – |
| Beer, mild draught, 500ml | 8.0 | – | 8.0 | 125 | 1.0 | – |
| Brandy, 25ml | – | – | – | 56 | – | – |
| Brown ale, bottled, 500ml | 15 | – | 15 | 140 | 1.5 | – |
| Cherry brandy, 25ml | 8.2 | – | 8.2 | 63.8 | – | – |
| Cider, 500ml: | | | | | | |
| *dry* | 13 | – | 13 | 180 | – | – |
| *sweet* | 21.5 | – | 21.5 | 210 | – | – |
| *vintage* | 36.5 | – | 36.5 | 505 | – | – |
| Cognac, 25ml | – | – | – | 88 | – | – |
| Cointreau, 25ml | – | – | – | 85 | – | – |
| Curacao, 25ml | 7 | – | 7 | 78 | – | – |
| Gin, 25ml | – | – | – | 56 | – | – |
| Grand Marnier, 25ml | – | – | – | 80 | – | – |
| Irish cream liqueur, 25ml | – | – | – | 80 | – | – |
| Lager, bottled, 500ml | 7.5 | – | 7.5 | 145 | 1.0 | – |

**TIP:** 'Lite' beers are lower in carbs than non-lite, but the best low-carb alcoholic drink is a spritzer made with half sparkling water and half dry white wine.

| Food type | Carb (g) | Fibre (g) | Net carb (g) | Cal (kcal) | Pro (g) | Fat (g) |
|---|---|---|---|---|---|---|
| Pale ale, bottled, 500ml | 10 | – | 10 | 160 | – | – |
| Port, 25ml | 3 | – | 3 | 39 | 0.1 | – |
| Rum, 25ml | – | – | – | 56 | – | – |
| Sherry, 25ml | | | | | | |
| *dry* | 0.4 | – | 0.4 | 29 | 0.1 | – |
| *medium* | 0.8 | – | 0.8 | 30 | – | – |
| *sweet* | 2 | – | 2 | 34 | 0.1 | – |
| Stout, 500ml: | | | | | | |
| *bottled* | 21 | – | 21 | 185 | 1.5 | – |
| *extra* | 10.5 | – | 10.5 | 195 | 1.5 | – |
| Strong ale, 500ml | 30.5 | – | 30.5 | 360 | 3.5 | – |
| Tia Maria, 25ml | – | – | – | 66 | – | – |
| Vermouth, 50ml: | | | | | | |
| *dry* | 2.75 | – | 2.75 | 59 | 0.05 | – |
| *sweet* | 8.0 | – | 8.0 | 76 | – | – |
| *bianco* | – | – | – | 72 | – | – |
| *extra dry* | – | – | – | 48 | – | – |
| *rosso* | – | – | – | 70 | – | – |
| Vodka, 25ml | – | – | – | 56 | – | – |
| Whisky, 25ml | – | – | – | 56 | – | – |
| Wine, per glass (175ml): | | | | | | |
| *red* | 0.5 | – | – | 119 | 0.4 | – |

**TIP:** With spirits, in general the higher the proof, the lower the carbs – but the drunker they'll make you!

| Food type | Carb (g) | Fibre (g) | Net carb (g) | Cal (kcal) | Pro (g) | Fat (g) |
|---|---|---|---|---|---|---|
| *rosé* | 4.4 | – | 4.4 | 124 | 0.2 | – |
| *white, dry* | 1 | – | 1 | 116 | 0.2 | – |
| *white, medium* | 6 | – | 6 | 131 | 0.2 | – |
| *white, sparkling* | 10 | – | 10 | 133 | 0.4 | – |
| *white, sweet* | 10 | – | 10 | 165 | 0.4 | – |
| **Juices and Cordials** | | | | | | |
| Apple juice, unsweetened 250ml | 24.8 | – | 24.8 | 95 | 0.3 | 0.3 |
| Apple & elderflower juice, 250ml | 25.5 | – | 25.5 | 108 | 1 | – |
| Apple & mango juice, 250ml | 25.3 | – | 25.3 | 108 | 1 | – |
| Barley water, 250ml: | | | | | | |
| *lemon, original* | 49 | – | 49 | 220 | 0.8 | – |
| *no added sugar* | 27.5 | – | 27.5 | 28 | 0.5 | – |
| *orange, original* | 52.5 | – | 52.5 | 223 | 0.8 | – |
| Blackcurrant & apple juice, 250ml | 31.3 | – | 31.3 | 125 | – | – |
| Carrot juice, 250ml | 14.3 | – | 14.3 | 60 | 1.3 | 0.3 |
| Cranberry juice, 250ml | 25.2 | – | 25.2 | 110 | – | – |
| Grape juice, unsweetened, 250ml | 29.3 | – | 29.3 | 115 | 0.8 | 0.3 |

**TIP:** When you feel hungry, try drinking a glass of water before reaching for food. What feels like hunger might actually be thirst.

| Food type | Carb (g) | Fibre (g) | Net carb (g) | Cal (kcal) | Pro (g) | Fat (g) |
|---|---|---|---|---|---|---|
| Grapefruit juice, 250ml | 22 | 0.8 | 21.2 | 90 | 0.5 | – |
| Lemon squash, | | | | | | |
| low calorie, 250ml | 1 | – | 1 | 5 | 0.3 | – |
| Lime juice cordial, | | | | | | |
| undiluted 25ml | 6.1 | – | 6.1 | 26 | – | – |
| Orange & mango | | | | | | |
| fruit juice, 250ml | 26 | – | 26 | 115 | 1.5 | – |
| Orange & pineapple | | | | | | |
| fruit juice, 250ml | 27.5 | – | 27.5 | 120 | 1.3 | – |
| Orange juice, | | | | | | |
| unsweetened, 250ml | 22 | 0.3 | 21.7 | 90 | 1.3 | 0.3 |
| Orange squash, | | | | | | |
| low calorie, 250ml | 6 | – | 6 | 25 | 0.3 | – |
| Pineapple juice, | | | | | | |
| unsweetened, 250ml | 26.3 | 0.3 | 26 | 103 | 0.8 | 0.3 |
| Tomato juice, 250ml: | 7.5 | 1.5 | 6 | 35 | 2 | – |
| *cocktail (Britvic)*, 250ml | 8 | – | 8 | 47 | 2.3 | 0.3 |
| **Fizzy Drinks** | | | | | | |
| Apple drink, sparkling, 330ml | 38.3 | – | 38.3 | 155 | – | – |
| Bitter lemon, 355ml | 27 | – | 27 | 112 | – | – |

**TIP:** The standard size for fizzy drinks cans is 330ml. Smaller cans of mixers tend to be 150ml. Watch out for artificial sweeteners in diet drinks – the evidence against them is mounting.

| Food type | Carb (g) | Fibre (g) | Net carb (g) | Cal (kcal) | Pro (g) | Fat (g) |
|---|---|---|---|---|---|---|
| Canada Dry Ginger Ale, 330ml | 30 | – | 30 | 124 | – | – |
| Cherry Coke, 330ml | 37 | – | 37 | 148 | – | – |
| Cherryade, 330ml | – | – | – | 4 | – | – |
| Coca-Cola, 330ml | 35 | – | 35 | 142 | – | – |
| *diet* | – | – | – | 2 | – | – |
| Cream Soda, 330ml | 23.8 | – | 23.8 | 96 | – | – |
| Dandelion & Burdock, 330ml | 17.8 | – | 17.8 | 74 | – | – |
| Ginger Ale, American (Britvic), 330ml | 30.4 | – | 30.4 | 126 | – | – |
| Ginger Ale, dry (Schweppes), 330ml | 12.5 | – | 12.5 | 53 | – | – |
| Ginger beer, 330ml | 28 | – | 28 | 120 | – | – |
| Irn Bru, 330ml | 33.3 | – | 33.3 | 135 | – | – |
| *diet*, 330ml | – | – | – | 2.3 | – | – |
| Lemon drink, sparkling, 330ml | 37.3 | – | 37.3 | 155 | – | – |
| *low calorie* | 0.3 | – | 0.3 | 3 | – | – |

**TIP:** If a fruit juice is labelled 'pure juice', it has no extra sugar added. If it's labelled 'not from concentrate', it is taken from fruit that is squeezed in the country of origin then lightly pasteurised before shipment. 'Freshly squeezed' juice is taken from fruit that is shipped whole then squeezed for immediate use in the country where it is sold; it will have a limited shelf life of around 14 days. In fact, there's nothing wrong with 'concentrates'; recent studies found they contain the same nutrients as fresh (and are cheaper).

| Food type | Carb (g) | Fibre (g) | Net carb (g) | Cal (kcal) | Pro (g) | Fat (g) |
|---|---|---|---|---|---|---|
| Lemonade, 330ml | 18.5 | – | 18.5 | 69 | – | – |
| *low calorie* | – | – | – | 3 | – | – |
| Lucozade, 330ml | 59.1 | – | 59.1 | 241 | – | – |
| Orange drink (Tango), 330ml | 22.1 | – | 22.1 | 95 | – | – |
| *low calorie* | 2.3 | – | 2.3 | 18 | – | – |
| Pepsi, 330ml | – | – | – | 155 | – | – |
| *Diet* | – | – | – | 1 | – | – |
| Ribena, sparkling, 330ml | 43.9 | – | 43.9 | 178 | – | – |
| *low calorie* | 0.3 | – | 0.3 | 7 | – | – |
| Tonic water, 330ml | 16.8 | – | 16.8 | 72 | – | – |
| Water, flavoured, 330ml | 0.7 | – | 0.7 | 3.3 | – | – |
| | | | | | | |
| **Hot and Milky Drinks** | | | | | | |
| Beef instant drink, per mug | 9.75 | – | 9.75 | 452 | 99 | – |
| Cappuccino (Nescafé), per mug: | | | | | | |
| *original* | 10.9 | – | 10.9 | 80 | 3.1 | – |
| *unsweetened* | 7.6 | – | 7.6 | 74 | 2.4 | – |
| Chicken instant drink, per mug | 48.5 | 5.2 | 43.3 | 322 | 24 | 3.5 |
| Cocoa, per mug | | | | | | |
| *made with semi-skimmed milk* | 17.5 | 0.5 | 17.0 | 142 | 8.7 | 4.8 |
| *made with whole milk* | 17.0 | 0.5 | 16.5 | 190 | 8.5 | 10.5 |

**TIP:** Excess caffeine in coffee, tea and colas can stimulate the production of insulin and cause your blood sugar to soar and then drop dramatically, leading to cravings for sweets.

| Food type | Carb (g) | Fibre (g) | Net carb (g) | Cal (kcal) | Pro (g) | Fat (g) |
|---|---|---|---|---|---|---|
| Coffee, black, per mug | – | – | – | – | 0.25 | – |
| Coffee creamer, per tsp | 3.9 | – | 3.9 | 35 | 0.1 | 1.9 |
| *virtually fat free*, per tsp | 5 | – | 5 | 25 | 0.1 | 0.8 |
| Drinking chocolate, per mug | | | | | | |
| *made with semi-skimmed milk* | 27 | – | 27 | 178 | 8.7 | 4.7 |
| *made with whole milk* | 26.5 | – | 26.5 | 225 | 8.5 | 10.2 |
| Espresso (Nescafé), per 100ml | 10 | 1.1 | 8.9 | 104 | 15.2 | 0.4 |
| Ice tea, per mug | 18 | – | 18 | 75 | – | – |
| Malted milk (Ovaltine), per mug | | | | | | |
| *made with semi-skimmed milk* | 32.5 | – | 32.5 | 198 | 9.8 | 6.7 |
| *made with whole milk* | 27.2 | – | 27.2 | 242 | 9.5 | 9.5 |
| Malted milk (Horlicks) light, | | | | | | |
| *made with water, per mug* | 55.8 | 2.2 | 53.6 | 305 | 11 | 3.5 |
| Strawberry milkshake, 250ml | | | | | | |
| *made with semi-skimmed milk* | 62.2 | – | 62.2 | 387 | 17 | 8.5 |
| *made with whole milk* | 47.2 | – | 47.2 | 420 | 17 | 19.5 |
| Tea, black, per cup | – | – | – | – | 0.1 | – |

**TIP:** The average mug contains 250ml; a teacup will only contain around half that volume. On many low-carb diets, coffee and tea should be taken either black or with cream or full-fat milk, because skimmed milk is higher in carbs.

## EGGS

Eggs are an excellent source of protein, vitamins and minerals, and the yolks in particular are a good source of vitamin E, which is a natural antioxidant that can protect against heart disease and cancer. However, egg yolks also contain cholesterol, which is why many nutritionists recommend that you remove the yolks and cook with the whites only – or use one of the egg substitutes on the market. Most of the carb-controlled diets offer different advice on the quantity of eggs you can eat and the ways you should cook them. If you're frying, it makes sense to use olive oil rather than butter or margarine.

**TIP:** Make omelettes with any non-starchy vegetables you have to hand – asparagus, peppers, spinach and mushrooms all work well.

| Food type | Carb (g) | Fibre (g) | Net carb (g) | Cal (kcal) | Pro (g) | Fat (g) |
|---|---|---|---|---|---|---|
| Eggs, chicken, 1 medium: | | | | | | |
| *raw, whole* | 0.6 | 0 | 0.6 | 78 | 6.3 | 5.3 |
| *raw, white only* | 0.3 | 0 | 0.3 | 17 | 3.5 | 0 |
| *raw, yolk only* | 0.3 | 0 | 0.3 | 59 | 2.8 | 5.1 |
| *boiled* | 0.6 | 0 | 0.6 | 76 | 6.3 | 5.3 |
| *fried, in vegetable oil* | 0.6 | 0 | 0.6 | 93 | 7 | 7 |
| *poached* | 0.6 | 0 | 0.6 | 76 | 6.3 | 5.3 |
| Eggs, duck, raw, whole | 0.6 | 0 | 0.6 | 84 | 7.3 | 6 |
| Omelette (2 eggs, 10g butter): | | | | | | |
| *plain* | 1.2 | 0 | 1.2 | 228 | 12.6 | 18.6 |
| *with 25g cheese* | 1.3 | 0 | 1.3 | 475 | 27.8 | 39.5 |
| Scrambled (2 eggs with 15 ml milk, 20g butter) | 1.9 | 0 | 1.9 | 310 | 13 | 27.1 |

**TIP:** Many nutritionists are changing their views on eggs. A recent Harvard study of nearly 120,000 health professionals found that most could eat an egg a day without increased risk of heart disease or stroke. Some of the low-carb diets claim that cholesterol is lowered naturally if you consume high levels of protein, and advise that you eat the whole egg and not just the white.

## FISH AND SEAFOOD

More and more surveys proclaim the benefits of eating oily fish a few times a week to help prevent heart attacks and strokes. If you can't manage this consistently, do take fish oil capsules to make sure you're getting enough essential Omega 3 fatty acids. The best natural sources are cold-water fish, such as salmon, mackerel, sardines and herring. Heart specialists used to advise against eating shellfish such as lobster, oysters, scallops and crab, but it has now been found that they have no effect on your blood lipid levels. They still advise that you go easy on prawns and squid, though, as they are both high in cholesterol. Seafood is rich in minerals, including iron, zinc, calcium, magnesium and iodine, and is a great addition to a healthy diet.

---

**TIP:** In restaurants and supermarkets, choose fish from local waters to get the best chance of freshness. Don't avoid canned fish though – a can of salmon is an excellent source of calcium and Omega 3 oils.

| Food type | Carb (g) | Fibre (g) | Net carb (g) | Cal (kcal) | Pro (g) | Fat (g) |
|---|---|---|---|---|---|---|
| **Fish and Seafood** | | | | | | |
| Anchovies, canned in oil, | | | | | | |
| *drained*, 100g | 0 | 0 | 0 | 280 | 25.2 | 19.9 |
| Cockles, boiled, 100g | – | 0 | – | 48 | 17.2 | 2 |
| Cod: | | | | | | |
| *baked fillets*, 100g | 0 | 0 | 0 | 96 | 21.4 | 1.2 |
| *dried, salted, boiled*, 100g | 0 | 0 | 0 | 138 | 32.5 | 0.9 |
| *in batter, fried*, 100g | 11.7 | 0.5 | 11.2 | 247 | 16.1 | 15.4 |
| *in crumbs, fried*, 100g | 15.2 | 0 | 15.2 | 235 | 12.4 | 14.3 |
| *in parsley sauce, boiled*, 100g | 2.8 | 0 | 2.8 | 84 | 12 | 2.8 |
| *poached fillets*, 100g | 0 | 0 | 0 | 94 | 20.9 | 1.1 |
| *steaks, grilled*, 100g | 0 | 0 | 0 | 95 | 20.8 | 1.3 |
| Cod roe, hard, fried, 100g | 3 | 0.1 | 2.9 | 202 | 20.9 | 11.9 |
| Coley fillets, steamed, 100g | 0 | 0 | 0 | 99 | 23.3 | 0.6 |
| Crab | | | | | | |
| *boiled*, 100g | 0 | 0 | 0 | 127 | 20.1 | 5.2 |
| *canned*, 100g | 0 | 0 | 0 | 81 | 18.1 | 0.9 |
| *dressed (Young's)*, 100g | 0 | 0 | 0 | 105 | 16.9 | 14.2 |
| Eels, jellied, 100g | – | 0 | 0 | 98 | 8.4 | 7.1 |
| Haddock: | | | | | | |
| *in crumbs, fried*, 100g | 12.6 | 0 | 12.6 | 196 | 14.7 | 10 |

**TIP:** Breaded and battered fish provide extra carbs and are often cooked in saturated fats, so opt for grilled, baked, pan-fried or steamed fish without batter if you're weight-watching.

| Food type | Carb (g) | Fibre (g) | Net carb (g) | Cal (kcal) | Pro (g) | Fat (g) |
|---|---|---|---|---|---|---|
| Haddock, contd: | | | | | | |
| *smoked, steamed,* 100g | 0 | 0 | 0 | 101 | 23.3 | 0.9 |
| *steamed,* 100g | 0 | 0 | 0 | 98 | 22.8 | 0.8 |
| Halibut, steamed, 100g | 0 | 0 | 0 | 131 | 23.8 | 4 |
| Herring: | | | | | | |
| *fried,* 100g | 1.5 | – | 1.5 | 234 | 23.1 | 15.1 |
| *grilled,* 100g | 0 | 0 | 0 | 199 | 20.4 | 13 |
| Kippers, grilled, 100g | 0 | 0 | 0 | 205 | 25.5 | 11.4 |
| Lemon sole: | | | | | | |
| *steamed,* 100g | 0 | 0 | 0 | 91 | 20.6 | 0.9 |
| *goujons, baked,* 100g | 14.7 | – | 14.7 | 187 | 16 | 14.6 |
| *goujons, fried,* 100g | 14.3 | – | 14.3 | 374 | 15.5 | 28.7 |
| Lobster, boiled, 100g | 0 | 0 | 0 | 119 | 22.1 | 3.4 |
| Mackerel, fried, 100g | 0 | 0 | 0 | 188 | 21.5 | 11.3 |
| Mussels, boiled, 100g | 0 | 0 | 0 | 87 | 17.2 | 2 |
| Pilchards, | | | | | | |
| *canned in tomato sauce,* 100g | 0.7 | – | 0.7 | 126 | 18.8 | 5.4 |
| Plaice | | | | | | |
| *in batter, fried,* 100g | 12 | 0 | 12 | 257 | 15.2 | 16.8 |
| *in crumbs, fried,* 100g | 8.6 | 0 | 8.6 | 228 | 18 | 13.7 |
| *goujons, baked,* 100g | 27.7 | – | 27.7 | 304 | 8.8 | 18.3 |

**TIP:** Although fish has a delicate flavour, it can be enhanced rather than masked by spicy marinades using ginger, soy sauce, cumin, garlic, lemon or lime juice.

| Food type | Carb (g) | Fibre (g) | Net carb (g) | Cal (kcal) | Pro (g) | Fat (g) |
|---|---|---|---|---|---|---|
| *goujons, fried*, 100g | 27 | 0 | 27 | 426 | 8.5 | 32.3 |
| *steamed*, 100g | 0 | 0 | 0 | 93 | 18.9 | 1.9 |
| Prawns: *boiled*, 100g | 0 | 0 | 0 | 107 | 22.6 | 1.8 |
| *boiled, weighed in shells*, 175g | 0 | 0 | 0 | 72 | 15 | 1.2 |
| *king prawns, freshwater*, 100g | 0 | 0 | 0 | 70 | 16.8 | 0.3 |
| *North Atlantic, peeled*, 100g | 0 | 0 | 0 | 61 | 15.1 | 0.1 |
| *tiger king, cooked*, 100g | 0 | 0 | 0 | 61 | 13.5 | 0.6 |
| Roe: | | | | | | |
| *cod, hard, fried*, 100g | 3 | 0.1 | 2.9 | 202 | 20.9 | 11.9 |
| *herring, soft, fried*, 100g | 4.7 | – | 4.7 | 244 | 21.1 | 15.8 |
| Salmon: | | | | | | |
| *pink, canned in brine, drained*, 100g | 0 | 0 | 0 | 155 | 20.3 | 8.2 |
| *grilled steak*, 100g | 0 | 0 | 0 | 215 | 24.2 | 13.1 |
| *smoked*, 100g | 0 | 0 | 0 | 142 | 25.4 | 4.5 |
| *steamed, flesh only*, 100g | 0 | 0 | 0 | 197 | 20.1 | 13 |
| Sardines: | | | | | | |
| *canned in oil, drained*, 100g | 0 | 0 | 0 | 217 | 23.7 | 13.6 |
| *canned in tomato sauce*, 100g | 0.9 | – | 0.9 | 177 | 17.8 | 11.6 |
| Scampi tails, premium (Lyons), 100g | 26 | – | 26 | 230 | 8.4 | 10.9 |

**TIP:** Make fish kebabs for a summer barbecue using firm-fleshed fish such as halibut, tuna or salmon, along with peppers, onions and cherry tomatoes. Drizzle with olive oil and lime juice.

| Food type | Carb (g) | Fibre (g) | Net carb (g) | Cal (kcal) | Pro (g) | Fat (g) |
|---|---|---|---|---|---|---|
| Shrimps: | | | | | | |
| *canned, drained,* 100g | 0 | 0 | 0 | 94 | 20.8 | 1.2 |
| *frozen, without shells,* 100g | 0 | 0 | 0 | 73 | 16.5 | 0.8 |
| Skate, fried in butter, 100g | 4.9 | 0.2 | 4.7 | 199 | 17.9 | 12.1 |
| Sole: *see* Lemon sole | | | | | | |
| Swordfish, grilled, 100g | 1.4 | 0 | 1.4 | 139 | 17 | 9.9 |
| Trout: | | | | | | |
| *brown, steamed,* 100g | 0 | 0 | 0 | 135 | 23.5 | 4.5 |
| *rainbow, grilled,* 100g | 0 | 0 | 0 | 135 | 21.5 | 5.4 |
| Tuna, fresh, grilled, 100g | 0 | 0 | 0 | 215 | 24.2 | 13.1 |
| *canned in brine,* 100g | 0 | 0 | 0 | 99 | 23.5 | 0.6 |
| *canned in oil,* 100g | 0 | 0 | 0 | 189 | 27.1 | 9 |
| Whelks, boiled, | | | | | | |
| *weighed with shells,* 100g | – | 0 | – | 14 | 2.8 | 0.3 |
| Whitebait, fried, 100g | 5.3 | 0.2 | 5.1 | 525 | 19.5 | 47.5 |
| Whiting: | | | | | | |
| *steamed, flesh only,* 100g | 0 | 0 | 0 | 92 | 20.9 | 0.9 |
| *in crumbs, fried,* 100g | 7 | 0.3 | 6.7 | 191 | 18.1 | 10.3 |
| Winkles, boiled, | | | | | | |
| *weighed with shells,* 100g | – | 0 | – | 14 | 2.9 | 0.3 |

**TIP:** There have been health scares about fish from polluted waters containing high levels of mercury and pesticides. If you want to limit your exposure, avoid the larger fishes, such as swordfish and marlin.

| Food type | Carb (g) | Fibre (g) | Net carb (g) | Cal (kcal) | Pro (g) | Fat (g) |
|---|---|---|---|---|---|---|
| **Breaded, battered or in sauces** | | | | | | |
| Calamari in batter, 100g | 15.8 | 0.7 | 15.1 | 299 | 13.7 | 20.4 |
| Fish cakes (Birds Eye) | | | | | | |
| *fried, each* | 15.1 | – | 15.1 | 188 | 9.1 | 10.5 |
| Fish fingers | | | | | | |
| *fried in oil*, 100g | 17.2 | 0.6 | 16.6 | 233 | 13.5 | 12.7 |
| *grilled*, 100g | 19.3 | 0.7 | 18.6 | 214 | 15.1 | 9 |
| *oven crispy*, 100g | 15.8 | 0.4 | 15.4 | 218 | 10.4 | 12.6 |
| Fish steaks in butter sauce, 100g | 2.9 | 0.1 | 2.8 | 93 | 9.4 | 4.9 |
| Fish steaks in parsley sauce, 100g | 2.9 | 0.1 | 2.8 | 85 | 9.4 | 4.9 |
| Kipper fillets with butter, 100g | 0 | 0 | 0 | 205 | 15 | 16 |
| Prawn Cocktail (Lyons), 100g | 4.5 | – | 4.5 | 429 | 5.7 | 42.9 |
| Seafood sticks, 100g | 14.1 | 0 | 14.1 | 97 | 10.7 | 14.1 |
| Shrimps, potted, 100g | 0 | 0 | 0 | 358 | 16.5 | 32.4 |

**TIP:** Fish and seafood have higher levels of beneficial Omega 3 oils than many other food sources. Here are some comparisons:
fish has 210mg/100g; oysters 150mg/100g; prawns 120mg/100g; turkey 35mg/100g; beef 22mg/100g; lamb 18mg/100g; while pork and veal have no Omega 3.

## FRUIT

Most carb-controlled diets advise that you don't eat fruits during the induction phase while you're bringing your blood sugar levels under control, because they deliver a burst of easily absorbed fruit sugar into your blood stream. Don't restrict fruits for too long, though, as they contain a host of important vitamins and minerals. Bananas are high on the glycaemic index so will be restricted or banned on most low-carb diets, but all kinds of berries, grapefruit, plums, peaches and apples are recommended. Eat the whole fruit (including the skin, where applicable) and make sure your fruit is as fresh as possible. Choose organic produce to avoid pesticide residues. If you can't afford it, wash the fruit carefully before eating. Choose unwaxed fruit, as wax can trap pesticides against the rind or skin.

**TIP:** Canned fruits usually have added sugar or corn syrup, so should be avoided. You can freeze fruits yourself, if you want to enjoy seasonal favourites all year round. Put the fresh fruit on a baking tray in the freezer. Once frozen, place in small, sealed plastic bags to maintain freshness.

| Food type | Carb (g) | Fibre (g) | Net carb (g) | Cal (kcal) | Pro (g) | Fat (g) |
|---|---|---|---|---|---|---|
| Apple, 1 medium | 21 | 3.8 | 17.4 | 82 | 0.2 | 0.6 |
| Apples, stewed | | | | | | |
| *with sugar* (60g) | 11.5 | 0.7 | 10.8 | 44 | 0.2 | 0.06 |
| *without sugar* (60g) | 4.9 | 0.9 | 4 | 19.8 | 0.2 | 0.06 |
| Apricots: 1 fresh | 3.9 | 0.8 | 3.1 | 16 | 0.5 | 0.1 |
| *dried, 8 halves* | 17 | 2.5 | 14.5 | 66 | 1 | 0.2 |
| *canned in juice*, 100g | 8.4 | 0.9 | 7.5 | 34 | 0.5 | 0.1 |
| *canned in syrup*, 100g | 16.1 | 0.9 | 15.2 | 63 | 0.4 | 0.1 |
| Avocado, half medium | 8 | 3.4 | 4.6 | 160 | 1.9 | 16.4 |
| Banana, 1 medium | 23.2 | 3.1 | 20.1 | 95 | 1.2 | 0.3 |
| Blackberries: | | | | | | |
| *fresh*, 75g | 3.8 | 2.3 | 1.5 | 19 | 0.7 | 0.2 |
| *stewed with sugar*, 75g | 10.4 | 1.8 | 8.6 | 42 | 0.5 | 0.05 |
| *stewed without sugar*, 75g | 3.3 | 1.9 | 1.4 | 15 | 0.6 | 0.05 |
| Blackcurrants: | | | | | | |
| *fresh*, 75g | 4.9 | 2.7 | 2.2 | 21 | 0.7 | – |
| *stewed with sugar*, 75g | 11.2 | 2.1 | 9.1 | 44 | 0.5 | – |
| *canned in syrup*, 75g | 13.8 | 2.7 | 11.1 | 54 | 0.5 | – |
| Blueberries, fresh, 75g | 7.6 | 1.6 | 6.0 | 32 | 0.4 | 0.2 |
| Cherries, half cup fresh (90g) | 10.4 | 0.8 | 9.6 | 43 | 0.8 | 0.09 |
| Cherries, cocktail & glacé: | | | | | | |
| *see under Baking products* | | | | | | |

**TIP:** Squirt lemon juice onto cut apples and pears to prevent them turning brown.

| Food type | Carb (g) | Fibre (g) | Net carb (g) | Cal (kcal) | Pro (g) | Fat (g) |
|---|---|---|---|---|---|---|
| Clementines, 1 medium | 6.6 | 0.9 | 5.7 | 28 | 0.7 | 0.1 |
| Coconut: | | | | | | |
| *creamed*, 2 tbsp | 1.4 | N | 1.4 | 134 | 1.2 | 13.7 |
| *desiccated*, 2 tbsp | 1.3 | 2.7 | – | 121 | 1 | 12.4 |
| Cranberries, fresh, 75g | 4 | 4.8 | – | 17 | 0.5 | – |
| Damsons: | | | | | | |
| *fresh*, 75g | 7.2 | 1.4 | 5.8 | 28 | 0.4 | – |
| *stewed with sugar* (2 tbsp) | 5.8 | 0.4 | 5.4 | 22 | 0.1 | – |
| Dates, quarter cup (50g) | 15.6 | 0.9 | 14.7 | 62 | 0.8 | 0.05 |
| Figs: | | | | | | |
| *1 fresh* | 9.6 | 1.7 | 7.9 | 37 | 0.4 | 0.2 |
| *dried, ready to eat, 50g* | 24.3 | 3.5 | 20.8 | 104 | 1.6 | 0.75 |
| *canned in syrup*, 100g | 14 | – | 14 | 59 | 0.5 | – |
| Fruit cocktail, 100g | | | | | | |
| *canned in juice* | 14.8 | 1 | 13.8 | 57 | 0.4 | – |
| *canned in syrup* | 20.1 | 1 | 19.1 | 77 | 0.4 | 1 |
| Gooseberries: | | | | | | |
| *fresh*, 75g | 9.7 | 1.8 | 8.6 | 40 | 0.5 | 0.2 |
| *stewed with sugar* (2 tbsp) | 5.5 | 0.6 | 4.9 | 22 | 0.1 | – |
| Grapefruit, half, fresh | 7.8 | 1.5 | 6.3 | 34 | 0.9 | 0.1 |

**TIP:** Make fruit smoothies by blending skimmed milk, low-fat yoghurt and your choice of fruits, along with some flaked almonds. Experiment with combinations such as raspberry and lime, blueberry and melon, or strawberry and orange.

| Food type | Carb (g) | Fibre (g) | Net carb (g) | Cal (kcal) | Pro (g) | Fat (g) |
|---|---|---|---|---|---|---|
| Grapes, black/white, seedless, | | | | | | |
| *fresh*, 75g | 11.6 | 0.5 | 11.1 | 45 | 0.3 | 0.75 |
| Greengages: | | | | | | |
| *fresh*, 75g | 6.4 | 1.2 | 5.2 | 26 | 0.4 | – |
| *stewed with sugar* (2 tbsp) | 8 | 0.4 | 7.6 | 32 | 0.4 | – |
| Guavas, fresh, 60g | 3 | 2.2 | 0.8 | 16 | 0.5 | 0.3 |
| Honeydew melon: *see* Melon | | | | | | |
| Jackfruit, fresh, 75g | 16 | – | 16 | 66 | 1.0 | 0.2 |
| Kiwi fruit, peeled, each | 10.6 | 1.9 | 8.7 | 49 | 1.1 | 0.5 |
| Lemon, whole | 3.2 | N | 3.2 | 19 | 1 | 0.3 |
| Lychees, fresh, 75g | 10.7 | 0.5 | 10.2 | 44 | 0.7 | 0.07 |
| *canned in syrup*, 100g | 17.7 | 0.5 | 17.2 | 68 | 0.4 | – |
| Mandarin oranges, 100g: | | | | | | |
| *canned in juice* | 7.7 | 0.3 | 7.4 | 32 | 0.7 | – |
| *canned in syrup* | 14.4 | 0.2 | 14.2 | 52 | 0.5 | – |
| Mangos, 1 medium | 16 | 0.2 | 15.8 | 66 | 0.8 | 0.2 |
| Melon, fresh, medium slice: | | | | | | |
| *cantaloupe* | 4.8 | 1.3 | 3.5 | 22 | 0.7 | 0.1 |
| *galia* | 6.4 | 0.5 | 5.9 | 27 | 0.6 | 0.1 |
| *honeydew* | 7.5 | 0.7 | 6.8 | 32 | 0.7 | 0.1 |
| *watermelon* | 8.1 | 0.1 | 8 | 35 | 0.6 | 0.3 |
| Nectarines, 1 medium | 13.5 | 1.8 | 11.7 | 60 | 2.1 | 0.1 |

**TIP:** Half a cup of fresh strawberries has 3.4g net carbs, 40mg of vitamin C and 125mg of potassium.

| Food type | Carb (g) | Fibre (g) | Net carb (g) | Cal (kcal) | Pro (g) | Fat (g) |
|---|---|---|---|---|---|---|
| Oranges, 1 medium | 12.8 | 2.5 | 10.3 | 56 | 1.6 | 0.1 |
| Papaya, half, fresh | 10 | 2.5 | 7.5 | 41 | 0.6 | 0.1 |
| Passionfruit, 75g | | | | | | |
| fresh (flesh & pips only) | 4.4 | 2.5 | 1.9 | 27 | 1.9 | 0.3 |
| Paw-paw, half, fresh | 10 | 2.5 | 7.5 | 41 | 0.6 | 0.1 |
| Peach, 1 medium | 11.4 | 2.2 | 9.2 | 50 | 1.3 | 0.1 |
| *canned in juice*, 100g | 9.7 | 0.8 | 8.9 | 39 | 0.6 | – |
| *canned in syrup*, 100g | 14 | 0.9 | 13.1 | 55 | 0.5 | – |
| Pear, 1 medium | 15 | 3.3 | 11.7 | 60 | 0.4 | 0.1 |
| *canned in juice*, 100g | 8.5 | 1.4 | 7.1 | 33 | 0.3 | – |
| *canned in syrup*, 100g | 13.2 | 1.1 | 12.1 | 50 | 0.2 | – |
| Pineapple, fresh, 60g | 6.0 | 0.3 | 5.7 | 25 | 0.2 | 0.1 |
| *canned in juice*, 100g | 12.2 | 0.5 | 11.7 | 47 | 0.3 | – |
| *canned in syrup*, 100g | 16.5 | 0.7 | 15.8 | 64 | 0.5 | – |
| Plums, 1 medium | 8.8 | 1.6 | 7.2 | 36 | 0.6 | 0.1 |
| Prunes, canned in juice, 100g | 19.7 | 2.4 | 17.3 | 79 | 0.7 | 0.2 |
| *canned in syrup*, 100g | 23 | 2.8 | 20.2 | 90 | 0.6 | 0.2 |
| Prunes, dried: *see under* Snacks | | | | | | |
| Raisins: *see under* Snacks | | | | | | |
| Raspberries, fresh, 60g | 2.8 | 1.5 | 1.3 | 15 | 0.8 | 0.2 |
| Rhubarb, fresh, raw, 60g | 0.5 | 0.8 | 0.3 | 4 | 0.5 | 0.06 |

**TIP:** Fresh pineapple is low in carbs and high in dietary fibre. Try grilling it and serving it with crème fraiche mixed with a little cinnamon for a delicious, low-carb dessert.

| Food type | Carb (g) | Fibre (g) | Net carb (g) | Cal (kcal) | Pro (g) | Fat (g) |
|---|---|---|---|---|---|---|
| Rhubarb: | | | | | | |
| *stewed with sugar* (2 tbsp) | 3.4 | 0.4 | 3 | 14.3 | 0.3 | – |
| *stewed without sugar* (2 tbsp) | 0.2 | 0.4 | – | 2 | 0.3 | – |
| Satsumas, 1 medium | 12.8 | 2 | 10.8 | 54 | 1.4 | 0.1 |
| Strawberries, 70g | 4.2 | 0.8 | 3.4 | 19 | 0.6 | 0.07 |
| Tangerines, fresh, one | 8 | 1.3 | 6.7 | 35 | 0.9 | 0.1 |
| Watermelon, *see under* Melon | | | | | | |

**TIP:** Fruits should be eaten after a meal high in protein, not as an in-between meal snack or for breakfast. This is because fructose can play havoc with your blood sugar levels, depending on your sensitivity. By having it as a 'dessert' you are using the protein of the meal to slow down the absorption of the fructose.

## JAMS, MARMALADES AND SPREADS

On a low-carb diet, you need to watch out for sugar in all its forms, including corn syrup, dextrose, lactose, maltose, molasses, sucrose and honey. When you eat jam or honey, you may as well take a spoonful of sugar, because they will have the same effect on your blood sugar, sending it hurtling upwards. Eating high-sugar foods at breakfast can set up a cycle of blood-sugar peaks and troughs for the day. Why not opt for a savoury instead of a sweet breakfast? Peanut butter has many health benefits, as peanuts are an excellent source of vitamin E, folate, fibre, protein and minerals. Dip celery sticks into nut butters for a snack, or make peanut satay sauces to go with chicken or beef.

**TIP:** Some of the low-carb diets will let you reintroduce bread after the initial weeks. If you find it hard to do without toast in the morning, you could be eating it again after just two weeks on *The South Beach Diet*.

| Food type | Carb (g) | Fibre (g) | Net carb (g) | Cal (kcal) | Pro (g) | Fat (g) |
|---|---|---|---|---|---|---|
| **Jams and Marmalades** | | | | | | |
| Apricot conserve (Baxter's), 1 tsp | 3.2 | – | 3.2 | 13 | – | – |
| Apricot fruit spread, 1 tsp: | | | | | | |
| *Heinz Weight Watchers* | 1.4 | – | 1.4 | 6 | – | – |
| *organic (Meridian)* | 1.8 | 0.1 | 1.7 | 7 | – | – |
| Apricot jam, 1 tsp: | | | | | | |
| *reduced sugar (Baxter's)* | 2.7 | – | 2.7 | 11 | – | – |
| *sucrose free (Dietade)* | 3.2 | – | 3.2 | – | – | – |
| Blackcurrant jam, 1 tsp: | | | | | | |
| *reduced sugar (Baxter's)* | 2.7 | 0.1 | 2.6 | 11 | – | – |
| *sucrose free (Dietade)* | 3.4 | – | 3.4 | 8.5 | – | – |
| Blueberry & blackberry jam, | | – | | | – | – |
| organic (Baxter's), 1 tsp | 3 | 0.1 | 2.9 | 13 | – | – |
| Grapefruit fruit spread (Meridian), 1 tsp | 1.9 | 0.1 | 1.8 | 7 | – | – |
| Honey, 1 tsp: | | | | | | |
| *clear* | 3 | – | 3 | 12 | – | – |
| *honeycomb* | 3.9 | – | 3.9 | 14 | – | – |
| *set* | 3.9 | – | 3.9 | 14 | – | – |
| Lemon curd, 1 tsp | 3 | – | 3 | 14 | – | – |
| Marmalade, 1tsp | 3.5 | – | 3.5 | 13 | – | – |

**TIP:** If you want a healthy spread to go on a piece of wholegrain toast, try tahini, a paste made from sesame seeds.

| Food type | Carb (g) | Fibre (g) | Net carb (g) | Cal (kcal) | Pro (g) | Fat (g) |
|---|---|---|---|---|---|---|
| Marmalade, contd: | | | | | | |
| *orange (Dietade)*, 1 tsp | 3.3 | – | 3.3 | 8 | – | – |
| *organic (Baxter's)*, 1 tsp | 3.2 | – | 3.2 | 13 | – | – |
| *Scotch orange (Baxter's)*, 1 tsp | 2.7 | – | 2.7 | 11 | – | – |
| Morello cherry fruit spread | | | | | | |
| *organic (Meridian)*, 1 tsp | 1.8 | 0.5 | 1.3 | 7 | – | – |
| Pineapple & ginger fruit spread (Meridian), 1 tsp | 1.9 | 0.1 | 1.8 | 7 | – | – |
| Raspberry conserve (Baxter's), 1 tsp | 3.2 | – | 3.2 | 13 | – | – |
| Raspberry fruit spread, 1 tsp: | | | | | | |
| *Heinz WeightWatchers* | 1.4 | – | 1.4 | 6 | – | – |
| *organic (Meridian)* | 7.5 | – | 7.5 | 7 | – | – |
| Raspberry jam, 1 tsp: | 3.5 | 0.1 | 3.4 | 13 | – | – |
| *organic (Baxter's)* | 3.2 | – | 3.2 | 13 | – | – |
| *reduced sugar (Baxter's)* | 2.7 | 0.1 | 2.6 | 11 | – | – |
| *sucrose free (Dietade)* | 3.2 | – | 3.2 | 8 | – | – |
| Rhubarb & ginger jam, | | | | | | |
| *reduced sugar (Baxter's)*, 1 tsp | 2.7 | – | 2.7 | 11 | – | – |
| Seville orange fruit spread, 1 tsp | | | | | | |
| *Heinz WeightWatchers* | 1.4 | – | 1.4 | 6 | – | – |

**TIP:** Before you buy reduced-sugar jams, check the type of sweetener they use in its place. Some people have adverse reactions to aspartame, in particular.

| Food type | Carb (g) | Fibre (g) | Net carb (g) | Cal (kcal) | Pro (g) | Fat (g) |
|---|---|---|---|---|---|---|
| *Meridian organic* | 1.8 | 0.1 | 1.7 | 7 | – | – |
| Strawberry conserve | | | | | | |
| (Baxter's), 1 tsp | 3.2 | – | 3.2 | 13 | – | – |
| Strawberry fruit spread, 1 tsp | 1.4 | – | 1.4 | 6 | – | – |
| *organic (Meridian)* | 1.8 | 0.1 | 1.7 | 7 | – | – |
| Strawberry jam, 1 tsp: | | | | | | |
| *reduced sugar (Baxter's)* | 2.7 | – | 2.7 | 11 | – | – |
| *sucrose free (Dietade)* | 3.2 | – | 3.2 | 8 | – | – |
| Wild blackberry jelly, | | | | | | |
| *reduced sugar (Baxter's)*, 1 tsp | 2.7 | 0.1 | 2.6 | 11 | – | – |
| Wild blueberry fruit spread, | 1.8 | 0.2 | 1.6 | 7 | – | – |
| *organic (Meridian)*, 1 tsp | | – | | | – | – |
| **Nut Butters** | | | | | | |
| Almond butter (Meridian), | | | | | | |
| 1 tsp | 0.3 | – | 0.3 | 31 | 1.3 | 2.8 |
| Cashew butter (Meridian), | | | | | | |
| 1 tsp | 0.9 | – | 0.9 | 31 | 1 | 2.6 |
| Chocolate nut spread, 1 tsp | 3 | – | 3 | 28 | 0.3 | 1.7 |
| Hazelnut butter (Meridian), | | | | | | |
| 1 tsp | 0.2 | – | 0.2 | 34 | 0.8 | 3.3 |

**TIP:** Reservatol, the phytochemical found in red wine and grapes that is thought to prevent deposits of cholesterol in the arteries, is also found in peanuts.

| Food type | Carb (g) | Fibre (g) | Net carb (g) | Cal (kcal) | Pro (g) | Fat (g) |
|---|---|---|---|---|---|---|
| Peanut butter, 1 tsp: | | | | | | |
| *crunchy (Sunpat)* | 0.7 | 0.3 | 0.4 | 30 | 1.4 | 2.4 |
| *smooth (Sunpat)* | 0.7 | 0.4 | 0.3 | 29 | 1.4 | 2.4 |
| *organic (Meridian)* | 0.6 | 0.4 | 0.2 | 30 | 1.6 | 2.4 |
| *stripy chocolate (Sunpat)* | 1.7 | 0.2 | 1.5 | 31 | 0.7 | 2.3 |
| Tahini paste, 1 tsp | – | 0.4 | – | 30 | 0.9 | 2.9 |
| **Savoury Spreads and Pastes** | | | | | | |
| Beef spread (Shippams), 1 tsp | 0.1 | – | 0.1 | 9 | 0.8 | 0.6 |
| Cheese spread, 1 tsp: | 0.2 | – | 0.2 | 13 | 0.6 | 1.1 |
| *reduced fat (Kerrygold)* | 0.4 | – | 0.4 | 9 | 0.8 | 0.5 |
| *very low fat (Primula)* | 0.4 | – | 0.4 | 7 | 0.8 | 0.3 |
| *See also under:* Dairy | | | | | | |
| Chicken spread (Shippams), 1 tsp | 0.1 | – | 0.1 | 8 | 0.8 | 0.5 |
| Crab spread (Shippams), 1 tsp | 0.3 | – | 0.3 | 7 | 0.7 | 0.3 |
| Fish paste, 1 tsp | 0.2 | – | 0.2 | 8 | 0.8 | 0.5 |
| Hummus, 1tsp | 0.6 | 0.1 | 0.5 | 9 | 0.4 | 0.6 |
| Marmite Yeast Extract, half tsp | 0.7 | 0.1 | 0.6 | 12 | 22 | – |
| Meat paste, 1 tsp | 0.2 | – | 0.2 | 4 | 0.8 | 0.6 |
| Salmon spread (Shippams), 1 tsp | 0.2 | – | 0.2 | 9 | 0.7 | 0.5 |

**TIP:** Hummus is rich in B vitamins. Use it as a dip for crudités, a side dish with chicken or fish, or as a spread.

| **Food type** | Carb (g) | Fibre (g) | Net carb (g) | Cal (kcal) | Pro (g) | Fat (g) |
|---|---|---|---|---|---|---|
| Sandwich spread (Heinz), 1 tsp | 1.3 | – | 1.3 | 11 | 0.1 | 0.6 |
| *cucumber*, 1 tsp | 0.9 | – | 0.9 | 9.3 | 0.1 | 0.6 |
| Taramosalata, 1 tsp | 0.4 | 0.1 | 0.3 | 26 | 0.1 | 2.7 |
| Toasty Toppers (Heinz), 1 tsp: | | | | | | |
| *chicken & mushroom* | 0.3 | 0.01 | 0.29 | 2.8 | 0.2 | 0.07 |
| *ham & cheese* | 0.4 | – | 0.4 | 4.8 | 0.4 | 0.2 |
| Vegemite (Kraft), 1 tsp | 1 | – | 1 | 9 | 1.2 | – |

**TIP:** Marmite contains niacin, thiamine, riboflavin, folic acid and vitamin B12, making it an excellent part of a healthy low-carb diet. If carbs are completely off your menu, though, meaning you can't have it on toast or crackers, why not use it to flavour beef or lamb stews or soups?

## MEAT AND POULTRY

Meats and poultry generally don't contain carbohydrates, unless they are added during processing, such as in sausages, luncheon meat and black pudding. Processed meats, including bacon and sausage, may contain preservatives called nitrates and nitrites, which have been implicated as a cause of stomach and colon cancers, so seek out preservative-free varieties. Check cold meats, such as ham, to see if they have added sugars. It makes sense to buy organic meat to avoid the antibiotics and hormones that are routinely fed to cooped-up animals, and follow the low-fat guidelines on page 22 (unless you are on an Atkins diet).

**TIP:** Don't char meats until they are black, as this can create carcinogenic compounds. Stir-fry instead of deep-fat frying, or grill on a grilling rack that allows fats to drip away.

| Food type | Carb (g) | Fibre (g) | Net carb (g) | Cal (kcal) | Pro (g) | Fat (g) |
|---|---|---|---|---|---|---|
| **Cooked Meats** | | | | | | |
| Bacon, 3 rashers, back (50g): | | | | | | |
| *dry fried* | 0 | 0 | 0 | 148 | 12.1 | 11 |
| *grilled* | 0 | 0 | 0 | 144 | 11.6 | 10.8 |
| *microwaved* | 0 | 0 | 0 | 154 | 12.1 | 11.7 |
| Bacon, 3 rashers, middle (50g), *grilled* | 0 | 0 | 0 | 154 | 12.4 | 11.6 |
| Bacon, 3 rashers, streaky (50g): | | | | | | |
| *fried* | 0 | 0 | 0 | 168 | 11.9 | 13.3 |
| *grilled* | 0 | 0 | 0 | 169 | 11.9 | 13.5 |
| Beef, 100g: | | | | | | |
| *roast rib* | – | – | – | 300 | 29.1 | 20.4 |
| *mince, stewed* | – | – | – | 209 | 21.8 | 13.5 |
| *rump steak, lean, grilled* | – | – | – | 177 | 31 | 5.9 |
| *rump steak, lean, fried* | – | – | – | 183 | 30.9 | 6.6 |
| *sausages, see under* Sausages | | | | | | |
| *silverside, lean only, boiled* | – | – | – | 184 | 30.4 | 6.9 |
| *stewing steak, stewed* | – | – | – | 223 | 30.9 | 11 |
| *topside, lean only, roasted* | – | – | – | 202 | 36.2 | 6.3 |
| *topside, lean & fat, roasted* | – | – | – | 244 | 32.8 | 12.5 |
| Beef grillsteaks, grilled, 100g | 0.5 | – | 0.5 | 305 | 22.1 | 23.9 |

**TIP:** Make your own low-carb sausages or burgers using lean minced pork, lamb or beef and herbs, without any fillers.

| Food type | Carb (g) | Fibre (g) | Net carb (g) | Cal (kcal) | Pro (g) | Fat (g) |
|---|---|---|---|---|---|---|
| Burgers, each: | | | | | | |
| *beefburgers* (100g) *fried* | 0.1 | 0 | 0.1 | 329 | 28.5 | 23.9 |
| *beefburgers* (100g) *grilled* | 0.1 | 0 | 0.1 | 326 | 26.5 | 24.4 |
| *quarter-pounder* (120g) | 4 | 0.2 | 3.8 | 220 | 17.5 | 12.7 |
| *chicken burger (Bird's Eye)* | 9.6 | 0.2 | 9.4 | 150 | 7.8 | 8.7 |
| *vegetable burger (Linda McCartney)* | 21 | 1.7 | 19.3 | 179 | 2.3 | 9.5 |
| *vegetable quarter pounder (Bird's Eye)* | 23 | 1.8 | 21.2 | 190 | 4.3 | 9.1 |
| Black pudding, 2 slices, fried | 29 | 0.4 | 28.6 | 519 | 18 | 37.6 |
| Chicken, 100g: | | | | | | |
| *breast, grilled* | – | – | – | 148 | 32 | 2.2 |
| *breast in crumbs, fried* | 14.8 | 0.7 | 14.1 | 242 | 18 | 12.7 |
| *breast, stir fried* | – | – | – | 161 | 29.7 | 4.6 |
| *1 drumstick, roast* | – | – | – | 185 | 25.8 | 9.1 |
| *1 leg quarter, roast (175g)* | – | – | – | 413 | 45.1 | 15.9 |
| *light & dark meat, roasted* | – | – | – | 177 | 27.3 | 7.5 |
| *light meat, roasted* | – | – | – | 153 | 30.2 | 3.6 |
| Duck, 100g: | | | | | | |
| *crispy, Chinese style* | 0.3 | 0 | 0.3 | 331 | 27.9 | 24.2 |

**TIP:** Try an Asian-style marinade for meat: combine the juice of a lime, a dessertspoon of light soy sauce, a dessertspoon of Thai fish sauce and a teaspoon of Muscovado sugar or natural sweetener. You can also use this as a salad dressing.

| Food type | Carb (g) | Fibre (g) | Net carb (g) | Cal (kcal) | Pro (g) | Fat (g) |
|---|---|---|---|---|---|---|
| *meat only, roasted* | – | – | – | 195 | 25.3 | 10.4 |
| *meat, fat & skin, roasted* | – | – | – | 423 | 20 | 38.1 |
| Frankfurters, 2 medium | 2.4 | – | 2.4 | 286 | 10 | 26 |
| Gammon, joint, boiled, 100g | – | – | – | 204 | 23.3 | 12.3 |
| Gammon, rashers, grilled, 100g | – | – | – | 199 | 27.5 | 9.9 |
| Goose, roasted, 100g | – | – | – | 301 | 27.5 | 21.2 |
| Haggis, boiled, 100g | 19.2 | – | 19.2 | 310 | 10.7 | 21.7 |
| Kidney, lamb, fried, 100g | – | – | – | 188 | 23.7 | 10.3 |
| Lamb, 100g: | | | | | | |
| *breast, lean only, roasted* | – | – | – | 273 | 26.7 | 18.5 |
| *breast, lean & fat, roasted* | – | – | – | 359 | 22.4 | 29.9 |
| *cutlets, lean only, grilled* | – | – | – | 238 | 28.5 | 13.8 |
| *cutlets, lean & fat, grilled* | – | – | – | 367 | 24.5 | 29.9 |
| *loin chops, lean only, grilled* | – | – | – | 213 | 29.2 | 10.7 |
| *loin chops, lean & fat, grilled* | – | – | – | 305 | 26.5 | 22.1 |
| *leg, lean only, roasted* | – | – | – | 203 | 29.7 | 9.4 |
| *leg, lean & fat, roasted* | – | – | – | 240 | 28.1 | 14.2 |
| *mince*, stewed | – | – | – | 208 | 24.4 | 12.3 |
| *stewed* | – | – | – | 240 | 26.6 | 14.8 |
| *shoulder, lean only, roasted* | – | – | – | 218 | 27.2 | 12.1 |

**TIP:** Coat a fillet steak in cracked black pepper and cook in a little olive oil. Remove the steak, add some red wine to the cooking juices and boil till it is reduced by half, then spoon the sauce over your steak.

| Food type | Carb (g) | Fibre (g) | Net carb (g) | Cal (kcal) | Pro (g) | Fat (g) |
|---|---|---|---|---|---|---|
| Lamb, 100g, contd: | | | | | | |
| *shoulder, lean & fat, roasted* | – | – | – | 298 | 24.7 | 22.1 |
| Liver, calf, fried, 100g | – | – | – | 176 | 22.3 | 9.6 |
| Liver, chicken, fried, 100g | – | – | – | 169 | 22.1 | 8.9 |
| Liver, lamb, fried, 100g | – | – | – | 237 | 30.1 | 12.9 |
| Oxtail, stewed, 100g | – | – | – | 243 | 30.5 | 13.4 |
| Pheasant, roasted, 100g | – | – | – | 220 | 27.9 | 12 |
| Pork, 100g: | | | | | | |
| *belly rashers, grilled* | – | – | – | 320 | 27.4 | 23.4 |
| *loin chops, lean, grilled* | – | – | – | 184 | 31.6 | 6.4 |
| *leg, lean only, roasted* | – | – | – | 182 | 33 | 5.5 |
| *leg, lean & fat, roasted* | – | – | – | 215 | 30.9 | 10.2 |
| *steaks* | – | – | – | 162 | 18 | 10 |
| Pork sausages: *see* Sausages | | | | | | |
| Rabbit, meat only, stewed, 100g | – | – | – | 114 | 21.2 | 3.2 |
| Sausages: | | | | | | |
| *beef sausages* (2), grilled | 14.7 | 0.8 | 13.9 | 313 | 15 | 21.9 |
| *Cumberland sausages (2)* | 3.6 | 0.4 | 3.2 | 218 | 14.2 | 16.0 |
| *Frankfurters* (2) | 2.3 | – | 2.3 | 377 | 13.5 | 34.9 |
| *Lincolnshire sausages* (2) | 9.8 | 1.6 | 8.2 | 345 | 14 | 27.3 |
| *Pork sausages* (2), fried | 11 | 0.8 | 10.2 | 347 | 15.6 | 26.9 |
| *Saveloy*, 100g | 10.8 | 0.8 | 11 | 296 | 13.8 | 22.3 |

**TIP:** Minced turkey and chicken are much lower in fat than minced lamb or beef.

| Food type | Carb (g) | Fibre (g) | Net carb (g) | Cal (kcal) | Pro (g) | Fat (g) |
|---|---|---|---|---|---|---|
| Tongue, fat & skin removed, *stewed*, 100g | – | – | – | 289 | 18.2 | 24 |
| Tripe, dressed, 100g | – | – | – | 33 | 7.1 | 0.5 |
| Turkey, 100g: | | | | | | |
| *breast fillet, grilled* | – | – | – | 155 | 35 | 1.7 |
| *dark meat, roasted* | – | – | – | 177 | 29.4 | 6.6 |
| *light meat, roasted* | – | – | – | 153 | 33.7 | 2 |
| Veal, escalope, fried, 100g | 4.4 | 0 | 4.4 | 195 | 33.7 | 6.8 |
| Venison, haunch, meat only, *roasted*, 100g | – | – | – | 165 | 35.6 | 2.5 |
| White pudding, 100g | 36.3 | – | 36.3 | 450 | 7 | 31.8 |
| **Cold Meats** | | | | | | |
| Beef, roasted, 50g | | | | | | |
| *silverside* | 1.2 | – | 1.2 | 69 | 9.6 | 2.9 |
| *topside* | 0.2 | 0 | 0.2 | 79 | 12.7 | 3 |
| Chicken, roasted breast meat, 50g | 0 | 0 | 0 | 76 | 15.1 | 1.8 |
| Chorizo, 50g | 2 | 0 | 2 | 19 | 11.5 | 15.5 |
| Corned beef, 50g | 0.5 | – | 0.5 | 102 | 13 | 5.4 |
| Garlic sausage, 50g | 2.9 | 0.3 | 2.6 | 95 | 7.7 | 5.8 |
| Ham & pork, chopped, 50g | 0.7 | 0.2 | 0.5 | 138 | 7.2 | 11.8 |

**TIP:** Stuff chicken breasts with tasty mixtures of black-olive tapenade, green pesto and sun-blushed tomatoes.

| Food type | Carb (g) | Fibre (g) | Net carb (g) | Cal (kcal) | Pro (g) | Fat (g) |
|---|---|---|---|---|---|---|
| Ham, 50g: | | | | | | |
| *canned* | 0 | – | 0 | 60 | 9.2 | 2.6 |
| *honey-roast* | 1.4 | 0.5 | 0.9 | 68 | 10 | 2.2 |
| *mustard* | 0.6 | 0.4 | 0.2 | 70 | 11.3 | 2.5 |
| *on the bone* | 0.4 | 0.3 | 0.1 | 68 | 10.4 | 7.7 |
| *beechwood smoked* | 0.25 | 0 | 0.25 | 75 | 10.3 | 1.3 |
| *parma* | 0.05 | 0 | 0.05 | 60 | 6.4 | 3.8 |
| *Wiltshire* | 0.75 | 0.55 | 0.2 | 100 | 10 | 6.4 |
| *Yorkshire* | 0.6 | 0 | 0.6 | 96 | 7.7 | 7.9 |
| Haslet, 50g | 9.3 | 0.4 | 8.9 | 72 | 6.4 | 1 |
| Kabanos, 50g | 0.5 | 0.25 | 0.25 | 120 | 12.2 | 7.7 |
| Liver pâté, 50g | 0.8 | – | 0.8 | 348 | 12.6 | 32.7 |
| *reduced fat* | 3 | – | 3 | 191 | 18 | 12 |
| Liver sausage, 50g | 3 | 0.4 | 2.6 | 113 | 6.7 | 8.4 |
| Luncheon meat, canned, 50g | 1.8 | 0.1 | 1.7 | 140 | 6.5 | 11.9 |
| Pâté, Brussels, 50g | 0.5 | 0 | 0.5 | 163 | 6.5 | 15 |
| Pepperami, hot, 50g | 1.3 | 0.6 | 0.7 | 277 | 9.5 | 26 |
| Pork salami sausage, 50g | 0.9 | 0.1 | 0.8 | 268 | 11 | 24.5 |
| Polony, 50g | 7.1 | – | 7.1 | 141 | 4.7 | 10.6 |
| Pork, 50g: | | | | | | |
| *luncheon meat* | 1.6 | 0 | 1.6 | 130 | 7 | 10.7 |
| *oven-baked* | 0.7 | 0.4 | 0.3 | 92 | 13 | 0.7 |

**TIP:** Feeling peckish? Try a Zone-balanced snack of four slices low-fat ham, half an apple and a macadamia nut.

| Food type | Carb (g) | Fibre (g) | Net carb (g) | Cal (kcal) | Pro (g) | Fat (g) |
|---|---|---|---|---|---|---|
| Salami, 50g: | | | | | | |
| *Danish* | 0.3 | 0.1 | 0.2 | 219 | 10.5 | 19.6 |
| *German* | 0.5 | 0 | 0.5 | 198 | 9.5 | 17.5 |
| *Milano* | 1.5 | 0 | 1.5 | 214 | 11.5 | 18 |
| Scotch eggs, 100g | 13.1 | – | 13.1 | 241 | 12 | 16 |
| Tongue, lunch, 50g | 0.2 | 0 | 0.2 | 88 | 9.7 | 5.2 |
| Turkey, breast, roasted, 50g | 0.2 | 0.4 | 0.2 | 54 | 11.5 | 0.8 |

**TIP:** 'Reduced fat' meats have at least 25% less fat than the full-fat versions, but they may have higher carb counts if extra filler has been used in their manufacture. Most 'deli-style' meat loaves, hams and sausages have sugar and/or starch filler added.

## OILS AND FATS

For salad dressings, dips or quick stir-frying, the healthiest choice is extra-virgin olive oil (from the first pressing of the olives). Note that it begins to smoke and decompose at relatively low temperatures though, so choose light, refined olive oil for longer periods of cooking. Rapeseed oil is another healthy monounsaturated oil. Safflower, sunflower, corn and soya oils are polyunsaturated; the 'vegetable' oils on sale in a supermarket will probably contain a combination of these, but they do not have the health benefits of olive oil. Remember that coconut and palm oils are saturated fats, as are lard, dripping and ghee.

**TIP:** Store oils in a cool place, away from direct light, and only keep them for about six months or they could go off. Flavour olive oils with herbs, chilli or garlic by adding them to the bottle and leaving them to steep.

| Food type | Carb (g) | Fibre (g) | Net carb (g) | Cal (kcal) | Pro (g) | Fat (g) |
|---|---|---|---|---|---|---|
| Coconut oil, 1 tbsp | 0 | 0 | 0 | 135 | – | 13.8 |
| Cooking fat, 1 tbsp | 0 | 0 | 0 | 135 | 0 | 15 |
| Corn oil, 1 tbsp | 0 | 0 | 0 | 135 | – | 15 |
| Dripping, beef, 1 tbsp | 0 | 0 | 0 | 134 | – | 15 |
| Ghee: | | | | | | |
| *butter*, 1 tbsp | 0 | 0 | 0 | 135 | – | 15 |
| *palm*, 1 tbsp | 0 | 0 | 0 | 135 | – | 15 |
| Lard, 1 tbsp | 0 | 0 | 0 | 134 | – | 15 |
| Olive oil, 1 tbsp | 0 | 0 | 0 | 135 | – | 15 |
| Palm oil, 1 tbsp | 0 | 0 | 0 | 135 | – | 15 |
| Peanut oil, 1 tbsp | 0 | 0 | 0 | 135 | – | 15 |
| Rapeseed oil, 1 tbsp | 0 | 0 | 0 | 135 | – | 15 |
| Safflower oil, 1 tbsp | 0 | 0 | 0 | 135 | – | 15 |
| Sesame oil, 1 tbsp | 0 | 0 | 0 | 135 | – | 15 |
| Soya oil, 1 tbsp | 0 | 0 | 0 | 135 | – | 15 |
| Stir-fry oil, 1 tbsp | 0 | 0 | 0 | 135 | 0 | 15 |
| Suet, shredded, 1 tbsp | 0 | 0 | 0 | 124 | – | 13 |
| Sunflower oil, 1 tbsp | 0 | 0 | 0 | 124 | 0 | 13.8 |
| Vegetable oil, 1 tbsp | 0 | 0 | 0 | 135 | – | 15 |
| Wheatgerm oil, 1 tbsp | 0 | 0 | 0 | 135 | – | 15 |
| For butter and margarine, *see under Dairy* | | | | | | |

**TIP:** Flaxseed and nut oils, such as walnut, almond or macadamia, are great for drizzling on salads, but don't try to heat them.

## PASTA AND PIZZA

It would be a shame to give up these popular Italian dishes altogether, especially since they are such a good way of eating tomatoes, which contain lycopene, a great anti-cancer agent. You won't be allowed pasta and pizza in the early stages of a low-carb diet, but if you are treating yourself later on, minimise the impact on your blood sugar by choosing wholewheat pasta and thin-crust pizza. Choose sauces or toppings with loads of vegetables (for fibre) and olives, Parmesan or mozzarella cheese (for fat) to stop the carbs being absorbed so quickly. Watch out for added sugar in prepared pasta sauces.

**TIP:** Try a raw tomato sauce on pasta. Dice the tomatoes, add plenty of garlic, fresh basil, crushed almonds, a drizzle of olive oil and seasoning, then leave to marinate for at least an hour before serving the cold sauce on hot pasta.

| Food type | Carb (g) | Fibre (g) | Net carb (g) | Cal (kcal) | Pro (g) | Fat (g) |
|---|---|---|---|---|---|---|
| **Pasta** | | | | | | |
| Dried lasagne sheets, cooked weight 100g: | | | | | | |
| *standard* | 18.1 | – | 18.1 | 89 | 3.1 | 0.4 |
| *verdi* | 18.3 | – | 18.3 | 93 | 3.2 | 0.4 |
| Dried pasta shapes, cooked weight 100g: | | | | | | |
| *standard* | 18.1 | – | 18.1 | 89 | 3.1 | 0.4 |
| *verdi* | 18.3 | – | 18.3 | 93 | 3.2 | 0.4 |
| Fresh egg pasta, 100g: | | | | | | |
| *conchiglie, penne, fusilli* | 31 | 1.4 | 29.6 | 170 | 7 | 2 |
| *lasagne sheets* | 29 | 4.6 | 24.4 | 150 | 6 | 1.1 |
| *spaghetti* | 23 | 1.6 | 21.4 | 135 | 6 | 2.1 |
| *tagliatelle* | 25 | 1.5 | 23.5 | 134 | 5 | 1.6 |
| Macaroni, boiled, 100g | 18.5 | 0.9 | 17.6 | 86 | 3 | 0.5 |
| Spaghetti, cooked weight 100g: | | | | | | |
| *dried, egg* | 22.2 | 1.2 | 21 | 104 | 3.6 | 0.7 |
| *wholemeal* | 23.2 | 3.5 | 19.5 | 113 | 4.7 | 0.9 |
| Stuffed fresh pasta, 100g: | | | | | | |
| *four cheese tortellini* | 20.1 | 0.9 | 19.2 | 133 | 5.6 | 3.3 |
| *spinach & ricotta tortellini verdi* | 21 | 2.4 | 18.6 | 149 | 6 | 4.5 |

**TIP:** *The South Beach Diet* has an ingenious recipe for a 'pizza' with a base made of Portobello mushrooms instead of dough. Try it with your own choice of toppings.

| Food type | Carb (g) | Fibre (g) | Net carb (g) | Cal (kcal) | Pro (g) | Fat (g) |
|---|---|---|---|---|---|---|
| Stuffed fresh pasta, contd: | | | | | | |
| *ham & cheese tortellini* | 19.7 | 0.5 | 19.2 | 131 | 6.1 | 3.1 |
| *cheese & porcini ravioli* | 21.6 | 2.8 | 18.8 | 164 | 7.8 | 5.2 |
| **Pasta Sauces** | | | | | | |
| Amatriciana, fresh, low fat, 100ml | 6.3 | 1.2 | 5.1 | 50 | 2.3 | 1.9 |
| Arrabbiata, fresh, low fat, 100ml | 6.3 | 1.1 | 5.2 | 42 | 1.5 | 1.3 |
| Bolognese, 100ml | 2.5 | 0.6 | 1.9 | 161 | 11.8 | 11.6 |
| Carbonara: | | | | | | |
| *fresh*, 100ml | 5.7 | 0.6 | 5.1 | 197 | 5.2 | 17.3 |
| *fresh, low fat*, 100ml | 5.5 | 0.6 | 4.9 | 97 | 4.8 | 6 |
| Pesto: | | | | | | |
| *creamy fresh*, 100ml | 6 | 1.4 | 4.6 | 45 | 2.2 | 1.3 |
| *green pesto, jar*, 100ml | 3.5 | 1.4 | 2.1 | 427 | 4.7 | 43.8 |
| *red pesto, jar*, 100ml | 3.1 | 0.4 | 2.7 | 358 | 4.1 | 36.6 |
| Tomato & basil, fresh, 100ml | 8.8 | 1.3 | 7.5 | 51 | 1.8 | 0.9 |
| **Tinned pasta** | | | | | | |
| Ravioli in tomato sauce (Heinz), 200g can | 26 | 1.2 | 24.8 | 146 | 5.2 | 2.2 |

**TIP:** Lightly crush fresh basil, pine nuts, garlic and Parmesan cheese for a low-carb, easy pesto. Serve it with wholemeal pasta, or with chicken, fish or vegetables.

| Food type | Carb (g) | Fibre (g) | Net carb (g) | Cal (kcal) | Pro (g) | Fat (g) |
|---|---|---|---|---|---|---|
| Spaghetti Bolognese (Heinz), 200g can | 25.6 | 1.4 | 21.2 | 172 | 6.8 | 4.6 |
| Spaghetti Hoops (Heinz), 200g | 23.4 | 1.2 | 22.2 | 112 | 3.8 | 1.2 |
| Spaghetti in tomato sauce, (Heinz), 200g can | 26 | 1 | 25 | 122 | 3.4 | 0.4 |
| *WeightWatchers*, 200g | 20.2 | 1.2 | 19 | 100 | 3.6 | 0.4 |
| Spaghetti with sausages in tomato sauce (Heinz), 200g | 22 | 1 | 21 | 164 | 7.4 | 5.2 |
| Spicy pepperoni pasta (Heinz), 200g can | 18.2 | 1 | 17.2 | 166 | 5.8 | 7.8 |
| Spicy salsa twists (Heinz), 200g | 21.8 | 1.6 | 20.2 | 150 | 5.4 | 4.6 |
| **Pasta Ready Meals** | | | | | | |
| Bolognese shells Italiana (Weight Watchers), per 100g | 9.6 | 0.8 | 8.8 | 71 | 5.2 | 1.3 |
| Canneloni bolognese (Dolmio), per 100g | 11.8 | n/a | n/a | 149 | 6.1 | 8.3 |
| Deep Pasta Bake, chicken & tomato (Findus), per 100g | 13 | 1.3 | 11.7 | 95 | 4.5 | 3 |
| Lasagne (Birds Eye), each | 46 | n/a | n/a | 440 | 24 | 18 |
| *vegetable (Ross)*, per 100g | 12.6 | 0.9 | 11.7 | 110 | 5.3 | 4.7 |

**TIP:** Lightly fry pork, chicken or fish in butter, with chopped olives, sundried tomatoes and fresh basil for an authentic Italian dinner. Add red chillies if you like a little zest!

| Food type | Carb (g) | Fibre (g) | Net carb (g) | Cal (kcal) | Pro (g) | Fat (g) |
|---|---|---|---|---|---|---|
| Pasta Bolognese (Birds Eye), per 100g | 54 | n/a | n/a | 375 | 18 | 9.6 |
| Ravioli Bianche (Dolmio), 100g | 29.7 | n/a | n/a | 200 | 9.6 | 4.7 |
| Risotto, beef (Vesta), per pack | 57.8 | 5.6 | 52.2 | 346 | 15.3 | 5.9 |
| Spaghetti bolognese (Birds Eye), each | 48 | n/a | n/a | 405 | 17 | 16 |
| **Pizza** | | | | | | |
| Cheese & onion deep filled pizza (McVitie's), 100g slice | 30.3 | 1.3 | 29 | 223 | 8.4 | 8.2 |
| Cheese & tomato pizza, 100g slice: | 24.8 | 1.5 | 23.3 | 235 | 9 | 11.8 |
| *deep pan base* | 35.1 | 2.2 | 32.9 | 249 | 12.4 | 7.5 |
| *French bread base* | 31.4 | – | 31.4 | 230 | 10.6 | 7.8 |
| *thin base* | 33.9 | 1.9 | 32 | 277 | 14.4 | 10.3 |
| French bread pizza (Findus), 100g slice | 32.4 | 1.8 | 30.6 | 235 | 9.3 | 7.8 |
| Ham & mushroom pizza (San Marco), 100g slice | 29.5 | 1.1 | 28.4 | 227 | 11.4 | 7.5 |
| Pepperoni & sausage pizza (San Marco) 100g slice | 24.8 | 1.3 | 23.5 | 226 | 10.9 | 9.9 |

**TIP:** To cut down on carbs, use a wholemeal 'wrap' as a base for homemade pizza. Top with fresh tomato sauce, plenty of mozzarella cheese and some fresh mushrooms.

| Food type | Carb (g) | Fibre (g) | Net carb (g) | Cal (kcal) | Pro (g) | Fat (g) |
|---|---|---|---|---|---|---|
| Pepperoni deep crust pizza (McCain), 100g slice | 26.8 | – | 26.8 | 229 | 10.1 | 9 |
| Pizza bases, 20cm diameter: | | | | | | |
| *deep pan* | 73 | – | 73 | 387 | 11 | 5.7 |
| *mini* | 72.8 | – | 72.8 | 387 | 11 | 5.7 |
| *standard* | 72.8 | – | 72.8 | 387 | 11 | 5.7 |
| *stone baked* | 72.8 | – | 72.8 | 356 | 11 | 2.9 |
| Pizza topping (Napolina), 100g: | | | | | | |
| *spicy tomato* | 9 | 1 | 8 | 66 | 1.6 | 2.6 |
| *tomato, cheese, onion & herbs* | 8.1 | 0.9 | 7.2 | 80 | 3 | 4 |
| *tomato, herbs & spices* | 9.4 | 0.8 | 8.6 | 67 | 1.5 | 2.6 |
| For more pizzas, *see under* Fast food | | | | | | |

**TIP:** A study by Instituto di Richerche Farmacologiche in Milan discovered that people who ate pizza had a significantly lower incidence of cancers involving the mouth, throat, oesophagus and colon than those who didn't eat pizza. The reason for this may be the high concentrations of lycopene, a cancer-preventing chemical found in the tomato sauce. Interestingly, the study showed that toppings were irrelevant – pizza is a healthy food!

## PIES AND QUICHES

Pastry is undoubtedly high in carbs, but choosing savoury fillings can help to slow down the transport of sugar in the body. If you do choose a pie on a 'reward day', opt for topless or bottomless pies and eat as little of the base as you can. Wholemeal pies and pastries are a better alternative than those made with refined white flours, which play havoc with blood sugar. Watch out also for those favourite British pies topped with potato, such as cottage pie, shepherd's pie and fish pie.

**TIP:** Why not consider crustless pies? Make your favourite pie filling, place it in a greased ramekin and bake. Top with toasted nuts or cheese to add a little texture.

| Food type | Carb (g) | Fibre (g) | Net carb (g) | Cal (kcal) | Pro (g) | Fat (g) |
|---|---|---|---|---|---|---|
| Beef & kidney pie, canned (Tyne Brand), 100g | 13.3 | – | 13.3 | 154 | 8.7 | 8.1 |
| Chicken & mushroom pie (Fray Bentos), each | 25.6 | 1.1 | 24.5 | 294 | 7.7 | 17.9 |
| Cornish pasty (Tamarfood Cornish Pride), each | 37.3 | 2.0 | 35.3 | 452 | 11.0 | 28.9 |
| Game pie, 100g | 34.7 | 1.3 | 33.4 | 381 | 12.2 | 22.5 |
| Pork pie, each | 23.7 | 0.9 | 22.8 | 363 | 10.8 | 25.7 |
| Quiche Lorraine, 100g: | 19.6 | 0.7 | 18.9 | 358 | 13.7 | 25.5 |
| *cheese & egg*, 100g | 17.1 | 0.6 | 16.5 | 315 | 12.4 | 22.3 |
| Sausage rolls, each: | | | | | | |
| *flaky pastry* | 25.4 | 1 | 24.4 | 383 | 9.9 | 27.6 |
| *short pastry* | 19.4 | 0.8 | 18.6 | 289 | 11.1 | 19.3 |
| Shepherd's pie (Bird's Eye), per pack | 11 | 0.8 | 10.2 | 101 | 4.1 | 4.5 |
| Steak & mushroom pie, canned (Fray Bentos), 100g | 12.9 | – | 12.9 | 157 | 7.5 | 8.3 |
| Steak & kidney pie (Fray Bentos), each | 25.6 | 0.9 | 24.7 | 323 | 9.1 | 21.2 |
| Yorkshire pudding, each (Aunty Betty's) | 5.5 | 0.2 | 5.3 | 47 | 1.5 | 1.8 |

**TIP:** Quiche is a healthy, high-protein option and it's easy to make without a crust – just bake the egg and cheese mixture in a well-greased pan. Add plenty of vegetables and serve with green salad.

## RICE AND NOODLES

When rice is processed to make it easier and faster to cook, the fibre and nutrients are removed, leaving starch and empty calories. Choose brown or wild rice instead of white, and wholegrain noodles instead of egg ones, and make your digestive system do some work! Don't avoid rice altogether though – brown and wild rice are good sources of protein, vitamin B1 and magnesium. (Note: wild rice is actually the seed of a water grass plant and is not actually 'wild' as it's grown in commercial rice paddies – but it's still good for you!)

**TIP:** Two tablespoons of dry rice will make about 75g of cooked rice. Brown rice takes longer to cook than white rice – check the instructions on the packaging.

| Food type | Carb (g) | Fibre (g) | Net carb (g) | Cal (kcal) | Pro (g) | Fat (g) |
|---|---|---|---|---|---|---|
| **Crisps** | | | | | | |
| Cheesy Wotsits, per pack (21g) | 10.6 | 0.2 | 10.4 | 114 | 1.8 | 7.1 |
| Hula Hoops, per pack (24g) | 13.3 | 0.5 | 12.8 | 124 | 0.8 | 7.5 |
| Kettle chips: | | | | | | |
| *lightly salted*, 25g | 12.9 | 1.5 | 11.4 | 116.3 | 1.6 | 6.48 |
| *mature cheddar with chives*, 25g | 13.6 | 0.7 | 12.9 | 120 | 2 | 6.4 |
| *salsa with mesquite*, 25g | 13.5 | 1.4 | 12.1 | 115 | 1.5 | 1.5 |
| *sea salt with balsamic vinegar*, 25g | 15.2 | 1.1 | 14.1 | 117 | 1.5 | 6.1 |
| Potato crisps: | | | | | | |
| *cheese & onion (Walkers), per pack* (34.5g) | 12.3 | 1.2 | 11.1 | 181 | 1.5 | 8.4 |
| *pickled onion (Golden Wonder), per pack* (34.5g) | 16.9 | 1.5 | 15.4 | 181 | 1.9 | 11.7 |
| *prawn cocktail (Golden Wonder), per pack* (34.5g) | 16.9 | 1.5 | 15.4 | 180 | 2 | 11.6 |
| *ready salted (Golden Wonder), per pack* (34.5g) | 17.2 | 1.6 | 15.6 | 186 | 1.9 | 12.2 |
| *roast chicken (Walkers Lites), per pack* (28g) | 17.1 | 1.4 | 15.7 | 130 | 2.1 | 5.9 |

**TIP:** Crisps are better for your blood sugar than baked potatoes, because the fat they are cooked in means their carbs are absorbed into the bloodstream more slowly. They're still not advised on carb-control diets, though!

| Food type | Carb (g) | Fibre (g) | Net carb (g) | Cal (kcal) | Pro (g) | Fat (g) |
|---|---|---|---|---|---|---|
| *salt & vinegar (Golden Wonder), per pack* (34.5g) | 16.7 | 1.5 | 15.2 | 180 | 1.9 | 11.7 |
| *salt & vinegar (Walkers Lites), per pack* (28g) | 17.1 | 1.4 | 15.7 | 130 | 2.1 | 5.9 |
| *smokey bacon (Golden Wonder), per pack* (34.5g) | 16.9 | 1.5 | 15.4 | 181 | 2 | 11.6 |
| Quavers, per pack (20g) | 12.1 | 0.2 | 11.9 | 103 | 0.6 | 5.8 |
| Wheat crunchies: | | | | | | |
| *bacon flavour, per pack* (35g) | 17.3 | 0.8 | 16.5 | 152 | 3.4 | 7.7 |
| *salt & vinegar, per pack* (35g) | 19.1 | 0.9 | 18.2 | 170 | 3.7 | 8.7 |
| *spicy tomato, per pack* (35g) | 17.2 | 0.8 | 16.4 | 151 | 3.3 | 7.7 |
| *Worcester sauce, per pack* (35g) | 16.7 | 1.5 | 15.2 | 180 | 2 | 11.7 |
| **Nibbles** | | | | | | |
| Bombay mix, 50g | 19.2 | 3.1 | 16.1 | 262 | 8.2 | 17 |
| Doritos, per pack (40g) | | | | | | |
| *cool original* | 25 | 1.4 | 23.6 | 204 | 3 | 10.5 |
| *pizza pizza* | 23 | 1.4 | 21.6 | 202 | 3 | 11 |
| *tangy cheese* | 23 | 1.2 | 21.8 | 204 | 3.2 | 11 |
| Japanese rice crackers, 50g | 39.9 | 0.2 | 39.7 | 199 | 4.5 | 2.3 |
| Nachos (Old El Paso kit), 100g | 31 | – | 31 | 230 | 4 | 10 |
| Peanuts & raisins, 50g | 18.8 | 2.2 | 16.6 | 218 | 7.7 | 13 |

**TIP:** Make your own spicy dip by mixing low-fat cottage cheese, horseradish, Tabasco sauce, black pepper and a little skimmed milk.

| Food type | Carb (g) | Fibre (g) | Net carb (g) | Cal (kcal) | Pro (g) | Fat (g) |
|---|---|---|---|---|---|---|
| *yoghurt coated*, 50g | 24.9 | 0.9 | 24 | 245 | 4.9 | 13.8 |
| Popcorn | | | | | | |
| *candied*, 50g | 38.8 | – | 38.8 | 240 | 1 | 10 |
| *plain*, 50g | 24.3 | – | 24.3 | 296 | 3.1 | 21.4 |
| Poppadums, each | 11.2 | 2.6 | 8.6 | 70 | 5.3 | 0.4 |
| *fried in veg oil* | 9.8 | – | 9.8 | 92 | 4.3 | 4.2 |
| *spiced* | 11.4 | 2.6 | 8.8 | 70 | 5.1 | 0.5 |
| Prawn crackers, 25g | 15.5 | 0.3 | 15.2 | 132 | 0.1 | 7.7 |
| Tortilla chips (Old El Paso), 50g | 30 | 2.5 | 27.5 | 230 | 3.8 | 11.3 |
| *chili flavour* | 32 | – | 32 | 248 | 3.5 | 13 |
| *jalapeño cheese flavour* | 30.5 | – | 30.5 | 260 | 3.5 | 13.5 |
| *salsa flavour* | 32.5 | – | 32.5 | 247 | 3.5 | 13 |
| Trail mix, 50g | 18.6 | 2.2 | 16.4 | 216 | 4.6 | 14.3 |
| Twiglets (Jacob's), 50g | 30 | 3.4 | 26.6 | 201 | 5.9 | 6.3 |
| *curry* | 28 | 3 | 25 | 225 | 4 | 10.7 |
| *tangy* | 28 | 2.8 | 25.2 | 227 | 4 | 2.8 |
| | | | | | | |
| **Dried Fruit** | | | | | | |
| Apple rings, 25g | 15 | 2.4 | 12.6 | 60 | 0.5 | 0.1 |
| Apricots, 25g | 15.5 | 2 | 13.5 | 60 | 1 | 0.1 |
| Banana, 25g | 13.4 | 2.5 | 10.9 | 55 | 0.8 | 0.2 |
| Banana chips, 25g | 15 | 0.3 | 14.7 | 128 | 0.3 | 7.9 |

**TIP:** Drying fruits concentrates the sugars, so a small piece may have a carb total that is as high as the whole fruit.

| Food type | Carb (g) | Fibre (g) | Net carb (g) | Cal (kcal) | Pro (g) | Fat (g) |
|---|---|---|---|---|---|---|
| Currants, 25g | 17 | 0.5 | 16.5 | 67 | 0.6 | 0.1 |
| Dates, flesh & skin, 25g | 17 | 1 | 16 | 68 | 0.8 | 0.1 |
| Figs, 25g | 13.2 | 1.9 | 11.3 | 57 | 0.9 | 0.4 |
| Fruit salad, 25g | 20.3 | 2 | 18.3 | 46 | 0.8 | 0.3 |
| Mixed fruit, 25g | 13.2 | 0.6 | 12.6 | 57 | 0.9 | 0.4 |
| Pineapple, diced, 25g | 17 | 2 | 15 | 69 | 0.6 | 0.3 |
| Prunes, 25g | 8.4 | 3.4 | 5 | 34 | 0.5 | – |
| Raisins, seedless, 25g | 17.3 | 0.5 | 16.8 | 68 | 0.5 | 0.1 |
| Sultanas, 25g | 17.3 | 0.5 | 16.8 | 69 | 0.7 | 0.1 |
| **Nuts and Seeds** | | | | | | |
| Almonds: | | | | | | |
| *weighed with shells*, 50g | 1.3 | 2.4 | – | 115 | 3.9 | 5.2 |
| *flaked/ground*, 25g | 1.7 | 3.2 | – | 153 | 5.3 | 14 |
| Brazils: | | | | | | |
| *weighed with shells*, 50g | 0.7 | 1.9 | – | 157 | 3.3 | 15.7 |
| *kernel only*, 25g | 0.8 | 2 | – | 171 | 3.5 | 17 |
| Cashews: | | | | | | |
| *kernel only*, 25g | 5.3 | 2 | 3.3 | 146 | 4.8 | 11.8 |
| *pieces*, 25g | 4.3 | 0.8 | 3.5 | 156 | 6 | 12.7 |
| Chestnuts, kernel only, 25g | 9.2 | 1 | 8.2 | 43 | 0.5 | 0.7 |

**TIP:** Instead of dipping tortilla chips into dips, cut up crudités of raw vegetables – florets of broccoli, celery sticks, sugar-snap peas and strips of peppers and cucumber all work well.

| Food type | Carb (g) | Fibre (g) | Net carb (g) | Cal (kcal) | Pro (g) | Fat (g) |
|---|---|---|---|---|---|---|
| Coconut: *see under* Fruit | | | | | | |
| Hazelnuts: | | | | | | |
| *weighed with shell*, 50g | 1.2 | 1.3 | – | 124 | 1.4 | 6 |
| *kernel only*, 25g | 1.5 | 1.6 | – | 163 | 3.5 | 15.9 |
| Hickory nuts: *see* Pecan nuts | | | | | | |
| Macadamia nuts, salted, 50g | 2.4 | 2.7 | – | 374 | 4 | 2.7 |
| Mixed nuts, 25g | 2 | 1.5 | 0.5 | 152 | 5.7 | 13.5 |
| Monkey nuts: *see* Peanuts | | | | | | |
| Peanuts: | | | | | | |
| *plain, weighed with shells*, 50g | 4.3 | 2 | 2.3 | 195 | 8.9 | 15.9 |
| *plain, kernel only*, 25g | 6.3 | 3.1 | 3.2 | 141 | 6.4 | 11.5 |
| *dry roasted*, 50g | 5.2 | 3.2 | 2 | 295 | 12.8 | 2 |
| *roasted & salted*, 50g | 3.6 | 3 | 0.6 | 301 | 12.3 | 26.5 |
| Pecans, kernel only, 25g | 1.5 | 1.2 | 0.3 | 172 | 2.3 | 17.5 |
| Pine nuts, kernel only, 25g | 1 | 0.5 | 0.5 | 172 | 3.5 | 17.2 |
| Pistachios, weighed with shells, 50g | 2.3 | 1.7 | 0.6 | 83 | 2.5 | 7.7 |
| Poppy seeds, 10g | 1.9 | – | 1.9 | 56 | 2 | 4.4 |
| Pumpkin seeds, 25g | 11.8 | – | – | 143 | 7.3 | – |
| Sunflower seeds, 25g | 4.7 | 3 | 1.7 | 149 | 5.9 | 11.9 |
| Walnuts: | | | | | | |
| *weighed with shell*, 50g | 0.7 | 0.8 | – | 148 | 3.2 | 14.7 |

**TIP:** Store nuts in the dark, at room temperature, and keep them sealed until use or they will go rancid.

| Food type | Carb (g) | Fibre (g) | Net carb (g) | Cal (kcal) | Pro (g) | Fat (g) |
|---|---|---|---|---|---|---|
| Walnuts, contd: | | | | | | |
| *halves*, 25g | 0.8 | 0.9 | – | 172 | 3.7 | 17.1 |
| **Dips** | | | | | | |
| Curry & mango dip (Primula), 100g | 6.1 | – | 6.1 | 334 | 4.5 | 32.4 |
| Doritos Mexican dips, 100g: | | | | | | |
| *guacamole* | 0.6 | 0.1 | 0.5 | 159 | 1.2 | 16 |
| *Mexican bean* | 12.1 | 2.4 | 11.7 | 89 | 2.7 | 3.3 |
| Guacamole, 100g | 6.3 | 2.3 | 4 | 143 | 2.8 | 11.9 |
| Hummus, 100g | 11.6 | 2.4 | 9.2 | 187 | 7.6 | 12.6 |
| Onion & chive dip (Primula), 100g | 2.1 | – | 2.1 | 341 | 4.6 | 34.9 |
| Salsa, 100g | | | | | | |
| *cheese (Old El Paso)* | 9.3 | – | 9.3 | 143 | 2.5 | 10.7 |
| *cool, organic (Meridian)* | 6.3 | 1.2 | – | 141 | 1.2 | 0.4 |
| *hot, organic (Meridian)* | 6.2 | 1.1 | 5.1 | 141 | 1.1 | 0.4 |
| *picante (Old El Paso)* | 4.6 | – | 4.6 | 28 | 1.4 | 0.5 |
| Sour-cream based dips, 100g | 4 | – | 4 | 360 | 2.9 | 37 |

**TIP:** Tapas or mezze tend to be great low-carb restaurant choices (see pages 224-35 for advice on eating out). Choose fresh crudités, grilled cheese and vegetables, olives, hummus and taramasalata to start your meals or to fill you up between meals. Who needs bread and butter?

| Food type | Carb (g) | Fibre (g) | Net carb (g) | Cal (kcal) | Pro (g) | Fat (g) |
|---|---|---|---|---|---|---|
| Spicy Mexican dip (Primula), 100g | 4.8 | – | 4.8 | 324 | 4.7 | 31.7 |
| Taramasalata, 100g | 7.4 | 1.8 | | 523 | 2.7 | 53.6 |
| Tzatziki, 100g | 1.9 | 0.3 | 1.6 | 66 | 3.8 | 4.9 |

**TIP:** Shop-bought salsas often contain sugars. Make your own, using chopped tomatoes, chopped red chillies, chopped red onion and a little basil and olive oil. Set aside for the flavours to infuse.

## SOUP

As all dieters know, clear consommés are the lowest-calorie option. Soups become fattening when thickeners, such as flour, or fats, such as cream, are added. Make your own nutritious, low-carb soups by creating a fish, vegetable, meat or chicken stock and adding vegetables and seasonings. If you want to thicken them, do so with beans, lentils or chickpeas. Read the labels on shop-bought soups to watch for flour or cornflour thickeners, and added gums and sugars, which will all increase the carb count. Instead of adding a swirl of cream on top of soup, try some fresh herbs or flaked almonds as a decorative garnish.

**TIP:** Gazpacho is an easy-to-make, low-carb soup. Just blend tomatoes, cucumber, red pepper, onions, garlic, lemon juice, olive oil and red wine vinegar, and season to taste. Serve cold with fresh basil or chopped black olives sprinkled on top.

| Food type | Carb (g) | Fibre (g) | Net carb (g) | Cal (kcal) | Pro (g) | Fat (g) |
|---|---|---|---|---|---|---|
| Beef broth (Heinz), 200ml | 13.6 | 1.4 | 12.2 | 82 | 4 | 1.2 |
| Beef consommé (Baxter's), 200ml | 1.4 | 0 | 1.4 | 26 | 4.8 | – |
| Beef & tomato Cup-A-Soup (Bachelors), per sachet | 15.5 | 1 | 14.5 | 71 | 1.3 | 0.4 |
| Beef & vegetable soup (Heinz), 200ml | 14.6 | 1.8 | 12.8 | 90 | 4.8 | 1.4 |
| Broccoli soup (Baxters), 200ml | 11.8 | 0.8 | 11 | 90 | 2.6 | 3.6 |
| Broccoli & cauliflower (Baxters): | | | | | | |
| *thick & creamy, per sachet* | 17.2 | 0.6 | 16.6 | 120 | 1.9 | 4.8 |
| *low calorie, per sachet* | 10.3 | 0.4 | 9.9 | 59 | 1.1 | 1.5 |
| Broccoli & potato soup (Baxters organic), 200ml | 11.6 | 1.4 | 10.2 | 62 | 2.6 | 0.6 |
| Cajun spicy vegetable Slim-A-Soup (Batchelors), per sachet | 10.3 | 1.1 | 9.2 | 58 | 1.6 | 1.3 |
| Carrot & butter bean soup (Baxters), 200ml | 15.8 | 3.8 | 12 | 110 | 3.2 | 3.8 |
| Carrot & coriander soup (Heinz), 200ml | 12.4 | 1.2 | 11.2 | 104 | 1.4 | 5.4 |
| Carrot & lentil soup (Weight Watchers), 200ml | 12 | 1.6 | 10.4 | 62 | 2.8 | 0.2 |
| Carrot, parsnip & nutmeg (Baxters organic), 200ml | 11.4 | 2 | 10.4 | 54 | 1.4 | 0.4 |
| Cheese & broccoli Cup-A-Soup, (Batchelors) per sachet | 23.5 | 1.9 | 216 | 160 | 5.2 | 5 |

| Food type | Carb (g) | Fibre (g) | Net carb (g) | Cal (kcal) | Pro (g) | Fat (g) |
|---|---|---|---|---|---|---|
| Chicken broth (Baxters), 200ml | 10.6 | 1.2 | 9.4 | 68 | 2.4 | 1.8 |
| Chicken soup: | | | | | | |
| *Batchelors Cup-A-Soup, sachet* | 12.4 | 0.6 | 11.8 | 98 | 1.5 | 4.7 |
| *Weight Watchers, 200ml* | 8.2 | 0 | 8.2 | 60 | 2.4 | 2 |
| *99% fat-free (Campbell's), 200ml* | 10 | – | 10 | 78 | 3.2 | 1.8 |
| Chicken & ham (Heinz), 200ml | 13.8 | 1.4 | 12.4 | 92 | 4.3 | 2 |
| Chicken & leek Cup-A-Soup, (Batchelors), per sachet | 14.1 | 0.7 | 13.4 | 154 | 2.4 | 3.6 |
| Chicken & mushroom (Batchelors), per sachet: | | | | | | |
| *Cup-A-Soup* | 20.2 | 1.3 | 18.9 | 132 | 3.7 | 4 |
| *Slim-A-Soup* | 8.8 | 0.9 | 7.9 | 59 | 1.1 | 2.2 |
| Chicken & sweetcorn soup: | | | | | | |
| (Batchelors), 200ml | 12.4 | 1.2 | 11.2 | 78 | 3.2 | 1.8 |
| *Slim-A-Soup, per sachet* | 9.2 | 0.3 | 8.9 | 59 | 1.2 | 1.9 |
| Chicken & vegetable soup (Baxters), 200ml | 11.2 | 3.2 | 8 | 62 | 2.6 | 1 |
| Chicken & white wine soup (Campbell's), 200ml | 8 | – | 8 | 98 | 2 | 6.6 |
| Chicken noodle soup: | | | | | | |
| *Batchelors Cup-A-Soup, sachet* | 15.1 | 0.8 | 14.3 | 182 | 7.2 | 3.8 |

**TIP:** French onion soup made with good beef stock and loads of onions is fine on a low-carb diet, so long as you avoid the French bread that frequently accompanies it.

| Food type | Carb (g) | Fibre (g) | Net carb (g) | Cal (kcal) | Pro (g) | Fat (g) |
|---|---|---|---|---|---|---|
| *Weight Watchers, 200ml* | 6.2 | 0.4 | 5.8 | 32 | 1.4 | 0.2 |
| Chicken, noodle & vegetable Slim-A-Soup, per sachet | 10.2 | 0.7 | 9.5 | 59 | 1.6 | 1.4 |
| Chinese chicken Cup-A-Soup (Batchelors extra), per sachet | 19.1 | 2 | 17 | 101 | 3.5 | 1.2 |
| Cock-a-leekie soup (Baxters), 200ml | 8 | 0.6 | 7.4 | 58 | 1.8 | 2 |
| Consommé (Campbell's), 200ml | 1 | – | 1 | 14 | 2.6 | – |
| Cream of asparagus: | | | | | | |
| *Baxters, 200ml* | 11.6 | 0.4 | 11.2 | 132 | 2.2 | 8.6 |
| *Cup-A-Soup, per sachet* | 19.9 | 1.1 | 18.8 | 133 | 2.1 | 5 |
| Cream of celery soup (Campbell's), 200ml | 6.4 | – | 6.4 | 94 | 1.2 | 6.8 |
| Cream of chicken soup (Campbell's), 200ml | 7 | – | 7 | 96 | 2.2 | 7.2 |
| Cream of chicken & mushroom (Campbell's), 200ml | 7 | – | 7 | 112 | 1.8 | 8.8 |
| Cream of chicken & vegetable, *Cup-A-Soup, per sachet* | 18 | 0.6 | 17.4 | 113 | 2.1 | 5.9 |
| Cream of mushroom: | | | | | | |
| *Campbell's, 200ml* | 10.6 | – | 10.6 | 138 | 3.4 | 9 |

**TIP:** 200ml of soup will fill an average bowl three-quarters full. Sachets of instant soup are mixed with boiling water to fill a mug of around 250ml volume.

| Food type | Carb (g) | Fibre (g) | Net carb (g) | Cal (kcal) | Pro (g) | Fat (g) |
|---|---|---|---|---|---|---|
| Cream of mushroom, contd: | | | | | | |
| *Cup-A-Soup, sachet* | 15.4 | 0.7 | 16.7 | 129 | 1.2 | 6.6 |
| Cream of tomato (Baxters), 200ml | 21.2 | 1.4 | 19.8 | 142 | 3 | 5 |
| Cream of vegetable Cup-A-Soup, per sachet | 19.8 | 1.2 | 18.6 | 144 | 1.9 | 6.3 |
| Creamy chicken with vegetables fresh soup (Baxters), 200ml | 11 | 0.8 | 10.2 | 194 | 3.8 | 15 |
| Creamy potato & leek Cup-A-Soup, per sachet | 20.9 | 3.2 | 17.7 | 133 | 2.3 | 4.4 |
| Cullen Skink (Baxters), 200ml | 15.4 | 0.6 | 14.8 | 178 | 12.2 | 7.4 |
| French onion soup (Baxters), 200ml | 8.4 | 0.8 | 7.6 | 44 | 1.4 | 0.4 |
| Garden pea & mint fresh soup (Baxters), 200ml | 12.2 | 3 | 9.2 | 124 | 4.6 | 6.4 |
| Golden vegetable: | | | | | | |
| *Cup-A-Soup, per sachet* | 15.3 | 0.9 | 14.4 | 70 | 1 | 0.5 |
| *Slim-A-Soup, per sachet* | 9.7 | 1.5 | 8.2 | 58 | 1.1 | 1.7 |
| Highlander's broth (Baxters), 200ml | 12.2 | 1 | 11.2 | 86 | 3.2 | 2.8 |

**TIP:** If you choose a packet or tinned soup, go for brands without noodles or rice, which are high in carbs. Consommé or pure vegetable soups are best. Read the labels carefully, though. Many soups are thickened with flour.

| Food type | Carb (g) | Fibre (g) | Net carb (g) | Cal (kcal) | Pro (g) | Fat (g) |
|---|---|---|---|---|---|---|
| Hot & sour Cup-A-Soup, sachet | 18.7 | 1.2 | 17.5 | 91 | 2.5 | 0.7 |
| Italian bean & pasta soup (Baxters), 200ml | 14 | 2.6 | 11.4 | 76 | 3.8 | 0.4 |
| Leek & potato Slim-A-Soup, per sachet | 10.2 | 0.5 | 9.7 | 57 | 0.9 | 1.4 |
| Lentil soup (Campbell's), 200ml | 8.6 | – | 8.6 | 54 | 2.6 | 1.2 |
| Lobster bisque (Baxters), 200ml | 9.4 | 0.4 | 9 | 102 | 6.8 | 4.2 |
| Mediterranean tomato : | | | | | | |
| *Baxters, 200ml* | 13.8 | 1.4 | 12.4 | 66 | 2 | 0.4 |
| *Slim-A-Soup, per sachet* | 9.6 | 0.7 | 8.9 | 58 | 1.1 | 1.7 |
| Minestrone soup: | | | | | | |
| *Baxters chunky fresh, 200ml* | 14 | 2.4 | 11.6 | 84 | 3.4 | 1.6 |
| *Cup-A-Soup, per sachet* | 17.9 | 1.1 | 16.8 | 100 | 1.9 | 2.3 |
| *Slim-A-Soup, per sachet* | 9.3 | 0.7 | 8.6 | 54 | 1.3 | 1.3 |
| Miso, 200ml | 47 | – | 47 | 406 | 26.6 | 12.4 |
| Mulligatawny beef curry soup (Heinz), 200ml | 14.4 | 1 | 13.4 | 120 | 3.6 | 5.4 |
| Mushroom soup: | | | | | | |
| *Weight Watchers, 200ml* | 10 | 0.2 | 9.8 | 64 | 2.6 | 1.4 |
| *Campbell's 99% fat-free, 200ml* | 7 | – | 7 | 48 | 1.2 | 1.8 |

**TIP:** Chop 6 carrots, an onion and a potato, and sauté in butter till soft. Add 750ml of vegetable stock (see page 203) and simmer for 30 minutes. Puree and add the zest and juice of a lemon, with seasoning to taste. A delicious low-carb soup that can be frozen for quick meals.

| Food type | Carb (g) | Fibre (g) | Net carb (g) | Cal (kcal) | Pro (g) | Fat (g) |
|---|---|---|---|---|---|---|
| Oxtail soup: | | | | | | |
| *Campbell's*, 200ml | 10.6 | – | 10.6 | 80 | 2.8 | 3 |
| *Cup-A-Soup, per sachet* | 13.7 | 1 | 12.7 | 76 | 1.5 | 1.7 |
| Parsnip & carrot (Weight Watchers), 200ml | 10.6 | 1.8 | 8.8 | 50 | 1 | 0.4 |
| Pea & ham (Baxters), 200ml | 16.2 | 2.4 | 13.8 | 116 | 5.8 | 3.2 |
| Potato & leek (Baxters), 200ml | 12.6 | 1 | 11.6 | 80 | 2 | 2.4 |
| Royal game (Baxters), 200ml | 11 | 0.8 | 10.2 | 72 | 4.8 | 1 |
| Scotch broth (Baxters), 200ml | 14.2 | 1.8 | 12.4 | 94 | 3.8 | 2.4 |
| Spicy parsnip (Baxters), 200ml | 12.2 | 3 | 9.2 | 102 | 2.2 | 5 |
| Spicy tomato & rice with sweetcorn (Baxters), 200ml | 18.4 | 1.2 | 17.2 | 90 | 2.6 | 0.6 |
| Spicy vegetable Cup-A-Soup Extra, per sachet | 22.3 | 1.2 | 21.1 | 109 | 2.9 | 1 |
| Spring vegetable soup (Campbell's), 200ml | 9 | – | 9 | 42 | 1 | 0.2 |
| Thai chicken with noodles (Baxters), 200ml | 13.6 | 0.6 | 13 | 94 | 3.4 | 0.8 |
| Tomato soup: | | | | | | |
| *Cup-A-Soup, per sachet* | 17.3 | 1.2 | 16.1 | 85 | 0.8 | 1.4 |
| *Weight Watchers*, 200ml | 9.4 | 0.6 | 8.8 | 52 | 1.4 | 1.0 |

**TIP:** For an easy dip to accompany crudités, or as a side dish with meat, fish and poultry, add half a pack of dried French onion soup powder to a small tub of crème fraiche.

| Food type | Carb (g) | Fibre (g) | Net carb (g) | Cal (kcal) | Pro (g) | Fat (g) |
|---|---|---|---|---|---|---|
| *Campbell's 99% fat-free*, 200ml | 16 | – | 16 | 88 | 1.4 | 2 |
| Tomato & vegetable Cup-A-Soup, per sachet | 18.6 | 1 | 17.6 | 109 | 2.6 | 2.7 |
| Vegetable soup: | | | | | | |
| *Campbell's*, 200ml | 12.4 | – | 12.4 | 70 | 1.6 | 1.6 |
| *Baxters chunky fresh*, 200ml | 15.6 | 2.2 | 13.4 | 78 | 3.2 | 0.4 |
| *Weight Watchers*, 200ml | 11.8 | 1.8 | 10 | 62 | 2 | 0.6 |
| Winter vegetable soup | | | | | | |
| *Heinz*, 200ml | 16.4 | 2.2 | 14.2 | 92 | 5.6 | 0.4 |
| *Weight Watchers*, 200ml | | | | | | |

**TIP:** Add fresh sautéed mushrooms to cream of mushroom soup, top with cheese and grill until bubbling, for a nutritious and filling low-carb meal.

## SUGAR AND SWEETENERS

A spoonful of sugar may have made the medicine go down in the Mary Poppins song, but a level teaspoonful contains 5g of carbs that will make your blood sugar level go up. Modern sweeteners have been designed to add the sweetness without the calories or carbs of sugar, but they tend to contain saccharine, which has an unpleasant aftertaste, or aspartame, which has been the subject of several health scares in the US. Nutritionists suggest that you opt for natural sweeteners, like fructose, or a herbal sweetener called stevia, which is available at health food shops. Alternatively, you could try to reduce the sugar you use altogether; if you do it very gradually (quarter of a teaspoon less in tea or coffee every couple of days), you'll re-educate your tastebuds to do without.

| Food type | Carb (g) | Fibre (g) | Net carb (g) | Cal (kcal) | Pro (g) | Fat (g) |
|---|---|---|---|---|---|---|
| Amber sugar crystals, 1 tsp | 4.9 | 0 | 4.9 | 20 | – | – |
| Date syrup, 1 tsp | 3.6 | | 3.6 | 15 | – | – |
| Golden syrup, 1 tsp | 4 | 0 | 4 | 15 | – | 0 |
| Honey, 1 tsp | 5.8 | 0 | 5.8 | 21 | 0 | 0 |
| Icing sugar, 1 tsp | 5 | 0 | 4.9 | 20 | 0 | 0 |
| Jaggery | 4.9 | 0 | 4.9 | 18 | – | 0 |
| Maple syrup, 1 tsp | 3.4 | 0 | 3.4 | 13 | 0 | – |
| Molasses, 1 tsp | 4 | 0 | 4 | 16 | – | – |
| Sugar: | | | | | | |
| *caster*, 1 tsp | 4.9 | 0 | 4.9 | 20 | 0 | 0 |
| *dark brown*, soft, 1 tsp | 4.7 | 0 | 4.7 | 19 | – | 0 |
| *demerara, cane*, 1 tsp | 5 | – | 5 | 20 | – | 0 |
| *granulated*, 1 tsp | 5 | 0 | 5 | 20 | 0 | 0 |
| *light brown*, soft, 1 tsp | 4.8 | 0 | 4.8 | 19 | 0 | 0 |
| *preserving*, 1 tsp | 4.9 | 0 | 4.9 | 20 | 0 | 0 |
| *cube, white*, each | 4.9 | 0 | 4.9 | 20 | 0 | 0 |
| Treacle, black, 1 tsp | 3.4 | 0 | 3.4 | 12.9 | – | 0 |
| **Sweeteners** | | | | | | |
| Canderel, 1 tsp | 0.47 | – | 0.47 | 1.9 | 0.01 | – |
| Hermesetas, 1 tsp | 0.28 | 0.21 | 0.07 | 1.4 | 0.01 | – |
| Splenda, 1 tsp | 0.5 | – | 0.5 | 2 | – | – |

**TIP:** Remember all the other names for added sugar in processed foods: sucrose, glucose, lactose, fructose, galactose, maltose and dextrose, to name but a few.

## SWEETS AND CHOCOLATES

Dark chocolate contains iron and magnesium, so it's not entirely composed of empty calories, but all kinds of sweets will play havoc with your blood sugar. If you over-indulge, you may have to go back to the induction phase of your low-carb diet to normalise your insulin production again. There is some saturated fat in chocolate, but it also contains oleic acid, a mono-unsaturated fat found in olive oil. Chocoholics will be pleased to hear that *The South Beach Diet* offers several recipes using chocolate, including one for dried apricots and chopped pistachios dipped in melted dark chocolate.

| Food type | Carb (g) | Fibre (g) | Net carb (g) | Cal (kcal) | Pro (g) | Fat (g) |
|---|---|---|---|---|---|---|
| Aero (Nestlé Rowntree): | | | | | | |
| *milk chocolate*, 25g | 14.5 | 0.2 | 14.3 | 130 | 1.7 | 7.2 |
| *mint*, 25g | 15.4 | 0.1 | 15.3 | 132 | 1.4 | 7.3 |
| After Eights (Nestlé Rowntree): | | | | | | |
| *original*, 25g | 18.2 | 0.3 | 17.9 | 104 | 0.6 | 3.2 |
| *white chocolate*, 25g | 19.2 | – | 19.2 | 106 | 0.7 | 2.9 |
| American Hard Gums (Trebor Bassett), 25g | 21.4 | 0 | 21.4 | 86.3 | – | 0 |
| Barley Sugar (Trebor Bassett), 25g | 24.3 | 0 | 24.3 | 97.3 | 0 | 0 |
| Black Jack chews (Trebor Bassett), 25g | 28.3 | 0 | 28.3 | 99.8 | 0.2 | 1.5 |
| Blue Riband (Nestlé Rowntree), 25g | 16 | 0.3 | 15.7 | 129 | 1.3 | 6.7 |
| Bonbons, 25g: | | | | | | |
| *buttermints (Cravens)* | 21.5 | 0 | 21.5 | 106 | 0.2 | 2.2 |
| *lemon (Trebor Bassett)* | 21.4 | 0 | 21.3 | 104.3 | 0.3 | 1.9 |
| *strawberry (Trebor Bassett)* | 103.8 | 0.2 | 103.6 | 104 | 0.3 | 1.9 |
| *toffee (Trebor Bassett)* | 20.4 | 0 | 20.4 | 108 | 0.4 | 2.7 |
| Boost (Cadbury), 25g | 15.6 | – | 15.6 | 135 | 1.5 | 7.3 |
| Bounty (Mars) | | | | | | |
| *dark*, 25g | 14.4 | – | 14.4 | 120 | 0.8 | 0.6 |

**TIP:** Dark chocolates usually have less sugar than milk or white chocolates – but not always.

| Food type | Carb (g) | Fibre (g) | Net carb (g) | Cal (kcal) | Pro (g) | Fat (g) |
|---|---|---|---|---|---|---|
| Bounty (Mars), contd: | | | | | | |
| *milk*, 25g | 14.1 | – | 14.1 | 121 | 1.2 | 6.7 |
| Bournville (Cadbury), 25g | 14.9 | – | 14.9 | 124 | 1.7 | 6.4 |
| Breakaway (Nestlé Rowntree), 25g | 14.9 | 1.2 | 13.7 | 124 | 1.7 | 6.4 |
| Butter Mintoes (Cravens), 25g | 21.7 | 0 | 21.7 | 106 | – | 2.2 |
| Buttermints (Trebor Bassett), 25g | 22.2 | 0 | 22.2 | 101 | – | 0.9 |
| Butterscotch (Cravens), 25g | 22.5 | 0 | 22.5 | 103 | – | 1.4 |
| Buttons (Cadbury), 25g | 14.2 | – | 14.2 | 131 | 2 | 7.4 |
| Caramac (Nestlé Rowntree), 25g | 13.6 | 0 | 13.6 | 141 | 1.5 | 9 |
| Caramel (Cadbury), 25g | | | | | | |
| Caramels, milk & plain chocolate (Cravens), 25g | 24.1 | 0 | 24.1 | 123 | – | 0 |
| Chewing Gum (Wrigley): | | | | | | |
| *Airwaves, sugarfree* , 5g | – | 0 | – | 7.6 | 0 | 0 |
| *Doublemint*, 5g | – | 0 | – | 15.4 | 0 | 0 |
| *Extra peppermint*, 5g | – | 0 | – | 8.2 | 0 | 0 |
| *Ice White, sugarfree*, 5g | – | 0 | – | 9.8 | 0 | 0 |
| *Juicy Fruit*, 5g | – | 0 | – | 14.8 | 0 | 0 |
| *Orbit, peppermint, sugarfree*, 5g | – | 0 | – | 9.8 | 0 | 0 |

**TIP:** Sugar-free chewing gums almost all contain aspartame, which many experts advise that we avoid. Some also contain phenylalanine, excess consumption of which can have a laxative effect.

| Food type | Carb (g) | Fibre (g) | Net carb (g) | Cal (kcal) | Pro (g) | Fat (g) |
|---|---|---|---|---|---|---|
| *Orbit, spearmint, sugarfree, 5g* | – | 0 | – | 9.6 | 0 | 0 |
| *PK, all flavours, 5g* | – | 0 | – | 17.6 | 0 | 0 |
| *Spearmint, 5g* | – | 0 | – | 14 | 0 | 0 |
| Chocolate cream (Cadbury), 25g | 17.2 | – | 17.2 | 106 | 0.7 | 3.9 |
| Chocolate éclairs (Cravens), 25g | 18 | 0.1 | 17.9 | 120 | 0.7 | 5 |
| Chocolate limes (Cravens), 25g | 22.7 | 0.1 | 22.6 | 102 | 0.2 | 4.7 |
| Chocolate Orange (Terry's): | | | | | | |
| *dark, 25g* | 14.2 | 1.6 | 12 | 128 | 1 | 7.3 |
| *milk, 25g* | 14.5 | 0.5 | 14 | 132 | 2 | 7.4 |
| Chocolate Truffles (Elizabeth Shaw): | | | | | | |
| *with Cointreau, 25g* | 15.8 | 0.1 | 15.7 | 119 | 1 | 5.6 |
| *with Irish Cream, 25g* | 15.9 | 0.1 | 15.8 | 119 | 1 | 5.6 |
| *with Tia Maria, 25g* | 15.9 | 0.1 | 15.8 | 119 | 1 | 5.6 |
| Chocolate: | | | | | | |
| *milk, 25g* | 14.9 | – | 14.9 | 132 | 2.1 | 7.6 |
| *plain, 25g* | 16.2 | – | 16.2 | 131 | 1.2 | 7.3 |
| *white, 25g* | 14.6 | 0 | 14.6 | 132 | 2 | 7.7 |
| Maya Gold, organic ( Green & Black), 25g | 13.3 | 0 | 13.3 | 139 | 1.9 | 7.0 |
| Coolmints (Trebor Bassett), 25g | 24.7 | 0 | 24.7 | 59 | 0 | 0 |

**TIP:** Melt a few squares of dark chocolate with a little cream for an instant hot-chocolate sauce that is much lower in carbs than shop-bought brands.

| Food type | Carb (g) | Fibre (g) | Net carb (g) | Cal (kcal) | Pro (g) | Fat (g) |
|---|---|---|---|---|---|---|
| Cough Candy (Trebor Bassett), 25g | 23.8 | 0 | 23.8 | 95.8 | 0 | 0 |
| Cream Toffees, assorted (Trebor Bassett), 25g | 18.3 | 0 | 18.3 | 108 | 0.9 | 3.5 |
| Creme Egg (Cadbury), 25g | 17.9 | – | 17.9 | 111 | 0.8 | 4 |
| Crunchie (Cadbury), 25g | 18 | – | 18 | 116 | 1 | 4.5 |
| Dairy Milk (Cadbury), 25g | 14.3 | – | 14.3 | 132 | 2 | 7.5 |
| Dairy Toffee (Cravens), 25g | 18.8 | 0 | 18.8 | 118 | 0.5 | 4.6 |
| Double Decker (Cadbury), 25g | 16.2 | – | 16.2 | 116 | 1.3 | 5.2 |
| Energy Tablets, Lucozade Sport: | 22.3 | – | 22.3 | 90 | 0 | 0 |
| *orange*, 25g | 22.2 | – | 22.2 | 90 | 0 | 0 |
| *lemon*, 25g | 22.2 | – | 22.2 | 90 | 0 | 0 |
| Everton mints (Cravens), 25g | 22.5 | 0 | 22.5 | 103 | 0.2 | 1.4 |
| Flake (Cadbury), 25g | 13.9 | – | 13.9 | 133 | 2 | 7.7 |
| Fruit & Nut (Cadbury), 25g | 13.9 | – | 13.9 | 122 | 2 | 6.6 |
| Fruit & Nut Tasters (Cadbury), 25g | 13 | – | 13 | 126 | 2.3 | 7.3 |
| Fruit Gums (Nestlé Rowntree), 25g | 20.2 | – | 20.2 | 86 | 1.2 | – |
| Fruit Pastilles (Nestlé Rowntree), 25g | 20.9 | 0 | 20.9 | 88 | 1.1 | 0 |
| Fudge (Cadbury), 25g | 18 | – | 18 | 111 | 0.7 | 4.1 |

**TIP:** Dip chunks of fruit into melted dark chocolate. Strawberries, slices of apple and pear all work well.

| Food type | Carb (g) | Fibre (g) | Net carb (g) | Cal (kcal) | Pro (g) | Fat (g) |
|---|---|---|---|---|---|---|
| Fudge (Trebor Bassett), 25g | 17.9 | – | 17.9 | 112 | 0.6 | 4.3 |
| Galaxy (Mars): | | | | | | |
| *chocolate*, 25g | 14.2 | – | 14.2 | 133 | 2.3 | 7.5 |
| *caramel*, 25g | 15 | – | 15 | 122 | 1.3 | 6.3 |
| *double nut & raisin*, 25g | 13.9 | – | 13.9 | 134 | 13.9 | 7.7 |
| *hazelnut*, 25g | 12.1 | – | 12.1 | 143 | 1.9 | 9.7 |
| *praline*, 25g | 13 | – | 13 | 145 | 1.3 | 9.9 |
| Galaxy Caramel Egg, 25g | 15.3 | 0 | 15.3 | 116 | 1.4 | 5.5 |
| Jellies, assorted (Trebor Bassett), 25g | 20.4 | 0 | 20.4 | 77 | 0 | 0 |
| Just Fruit Pastilles (Trebor Bassett), 25g | 20.3 | – | 20.3 | 86 | 1 | – |
| Kit Kat (Nestlé Rowntree) | | | | | | |
| *4-finger*, 25g | 15.4 | 0.3 | 15.4 | 127 | 1.5 | 6.6 |
| *Chunky*, 25g | 15.3 | 0.2 | 15.3 | 129 | 1.4 | 6.9 |
| Lion Bar (Nestlé Rowntree), 25g | 16.9 | – | 16.9 | 122 | 1.2 | 5.6 |
| Liquorice Allsorts (Bassett), 25g | 13.8 | 0.4 | 13.4 | 88 | 0.6 | 1.1 |
| Lockets (Mars), 25g | 24 | 0.3 | 23.7 | 96 | 0 | 0 |
| M&Ms (Mars): | | | | | | |
| *chocolate*, 25g | 17.4 | – | 17.4 | 122 | 1.2 | 5.3 |

**TIP:** Brazil nuts covered in dark chocolate are a good alternative to chocolate bars, and the protein in the nuts helps to slow down the absorption of sugar in the blood. They are also a great source of the antioxidant mineral selenium!

| Food type | Carb (g) | Fibre (g) | Net carb (g) | Cal (kcal) | Pro (g) | Fat (g) |
|---|---|---|---|---|---|---|
| M&Ms (Mars), contd: | | | | | | |
| *peanut*, 25g | 14.3 | – | 14.3 | 128 | 2.6 | 6.8 |
| Maltesers (Mars), 25g | 15.4 | – | 15.4 | 124 | 2.5 | 5.8 |
| Marble (Cadbury), 25g | 13.7 | – | 13.7 | 134 | 4.1 | 7.8 |
| Mars Bar, 25g | 17.3 | – | 17.3 | 112 | 1 | 4.4 |
| Matchmakers, all varieties (Nestlé Rowntree), 25g | 17.4 | 0.2 | 17.2 | 119 | 1.1 | 5 |
| Minstrels (Galaxy), 25g | 17.4 | – | 17.4 | 123 | 1.5 | 5.3 |
| Milk Tray (Cadbury), 25g | 15 | – | 15 | 124 | 1.3 | 6.5 |
| Milky Way (Mars), 25g | 17.9 | – | 17.9 | 113 | 1.1 | 4.2 |
| Mint Crisp (Cadbury), 25g | 17.6 | – | 17.6 | 126 | 1.6 | 5.6 |
| Mint crisp chocolates (Elizabeth Shaw), 25g | 17 | 0.4 | 16.6 | 115 | 0.5 | 5.2 |
| Mint humbugs (Cravens), 25g | 22.4 | 0 | 22.4 | 103 | 0.2 | 1.5 |
| Mint imperials (Trebor Bassett), 25g | 24.5 | – | 24.5 | 99 | 0.1 | – |
| Munchies (Nestlé Rowntree), 25g | 15.9 | 0.1 | 15.8 | 123 | 1.2 | 6 |
| *mint*, 25g | 16.9 | 0.4 | 16.5 | 108 | 1 | 4.1 |
| Murray Mints (Trebor Bassett), 25g | 22.6 | 0 | 22.6 | 102 | 0 | 1.3 |
| Nuts about Caramel (Cadbury), 25g | 14.5 | – | 14.5 | 124 | 1.4 | 6.7 |

**TIP:** Choose sweets and chocolates made for diabetics. They contain no sugar and are, therefore, much lower in carbohydrates.

| Food type | Carb (g) | Fibre (g) | Net carb (g) | Cal (kcal) | Pro (g) | Fat (g) |
|---|---|---|---|---|---|---|
| Old Jamaica (Cadbury), 25g | 14.7 | – | 14.7 | 116 | 1.4 | 5.7 |
| Orange Cream (Cadbury), 25g | 17.2 | – | 17.2 | 106 | 0.7 | 3.9 |
| Peanut Lion Bar (Nestlé Rowntree), 25g | 14.2 | – | 14.2 | 131 | 1.8 | 7.4 |
| Pear Drops (Trebor Bassett), 25g | 23.9 | 0 | 23.9 | 96 | 0 | 0 |
| Peppermints, 25g | 25.6 | 0 | 25.6 | 98 | 0.1 | 0.2 |
| Peppermint Cream (Cadbury), 25g | 17.2 | – | 17.2 | 106 | 0.7 | 3.9 |
| Picnic (Cadbury), 25g | 14.9 | – | 14.9 | 119 | 1.9 | 5.7 |
| Pineapple chunks (Trebor Bassett), 25g | 23.8 | 0 | 23.8 | 96 | 0 | 0 |
| Polos (Nestlé Rowntree): | | | | | | |
| *mints*, 25g | 24.6 | – | 24.6 | 101 | 0 | 2.5 |
| *sugar-free*, 25g | 24.8 | 0 | 24.8 | 60 | 0 | 0 |
| *smoothies*, 25g | 22.1 | 0 | 22.1 | 103 | – | 1.7 |
| Pontefract cakes (Trebor Bassett), 25g | 16.7 | 0.6 | 16.7 | 70 | 0.6 | 0.1 |
| Poppets (G. Payne & Co): | | | | | | |
| *peanut*, 25g | 9.3 | – | 9.3 | 136 | – | 9.3 |
| *raisins*, 25g | 16.5 | – | 16.5 | 102 | – | 3.5 |

**TIP:** Chocolate contains some healthy minerals – including copper, zinc, iron and magnesium – from its source as cocoa beans that grow on the cocoa tree *Theo bromacacao*.

| Food type | Carb (g) | Fibre (g) | Net carb (g) | Cal (kcal) | Pro (g) | Fat (g) |
|---|---|---|---|---|---|---|
| Refreshers (Trebor Bassett), 25g | 22.6 | 0 | 22.6 | 94 | – | 0.1 |
| Revels (Mars), 25g | 16.4 | – | 16.4 | 124 | 1.6 | 5.8 |
| Ripple (Galaxy), 25g | 14.2 | – | 14.2 | 133 | 2.3 | 7.5 |
| Rolo (Nestlé Rowntree), 25g | 17.1 | 0.1 | 17 | 118 | 0.8 | 5.1 |
| Sherbet Lemons (Trebor Bassett), 25g | 23.5 | 0 | 23.5 | 96 | 0 | 0 |
| Snickers (Mars), 25g | 13.8 | – | 13.8 | 128 | 2.6 | 6.9 |
| Softfruits (Trebor Bassett), 25g | 22 | 0 | 22 | 92 | – | 0.3 |
| Softmints (Trebor Bassett), 25g | 22 | 0 | 22 | 94 | – | 0.6 |
| Spearmints, Extra Strong (Trebor Bassett), 25g | 24.7 | 0 | 24.7 | 99 | 0.1 | – |
| Starbar (Cadbury), 25g | | | | | | |
| Starburst (Mars), 25g | 21.3 | – | 21.3 | 103 | 0.1 | 1.9 |
| *Sourburst*, 25g | 18.2 | – | 18.2 | 77 | 1 | 0 |
| Sugared Almonds (Cravens), 25g | 19.5 | 0.6 | | | | |
| Sweet Peanuts (Trebor Bassett), 25g | 20 | 0.4 | 19.6 | 107 | 0.8 | 0.4 |
| Sweets, boiled, 25g | 21.8 | 0 | 21.8 | 82 | – | – |
| Toblerone (Terry's), 25g | 14.8 | 0.6 | 14.2 | 131 | 1.4 | 7.4 |
| Toffees, mixed, 25g | 17.8 | – | 17.8 | 108 | 0.5 | 4.3 |

**TIP:** If you can't overcome cravings, buy 'treat-sized' packs of your favourite sweets or chocolates. Eat one and freeze the rest so you won't be tempted to have more.

| Food type | Carb (g) | Fibre (g) | Net carb (g) | Cal (kcal) | Pro (g) | Fat (g) |
|---|---|---|---|---|---|---|
| Toffee Crisp (Nestlé Rowntree), 25g | 15.1 | 0.2 | 14.9 | 128 | 1.1 | 7 |
| Toffo (Nestlé Rowntree), 25g | 17.5 | – | 17.5 | 113 | 0.6 | 4.6 |
| Topic (Mars), 25g | 14.2 | – | 14.2 | 123 | 1.2 | 6.7 |
| Trebor Mints (Trebor Bassett), 25g | 24.5 | 0 | 24.5 | 100 | 0.2 | 0.1 |
| Tunes (Mars), 25g | 24.5 | – | 24.5 | 98 | 0 | 0 |
| Turkish Delight (Cadbury), 25g | 18.3 | – | 18.3 | 91 | 0.5 | 1.8 |
| Twix (Mars), 25g | 15.9 | – | 15.9 | 124 | 1.5 | 6 |
| Vanilla Fudge (Cravens), 25g | 19.4 | – | 19.4 | 117 | 0.3 | 4.3 |
| Walnut whip, vanilla (Nestlé Rowntree), 25g | 15.2 | – | 15.2 | 124 | 1.5 | 6.4 |
| Wholenut (Cadbury), 25g | 12.2 | – | 12.2 | 138 | 2.3 | 8.8 |
| Wine gums (Trebor Bassett), 25g | 19 | – | 19 | 84 | 1.5 | – |
| Yorkie (Nestlé Rowntree): | | | | | | |
| *milk chocolate*, 25g | 14.7 | – | 14.7 | 131 | 1.6 | 7.4 |
| *raisin & biscuit*, 25g | 15.1 | – | 15.1 | 122 | 1.5 | 6 |

**TIP:** Check the weight of a chocolate bar or tube of sweets on the packaging. The breakdowns given here are for 25g, which is the smallest size of many varieties.

## VEGETABLES

All vegetables are not created equal when it comes to net carb counts (or the glycaemic index). Green vegetables, salad leaves, mushrooms, onions and aubergines are all low in net carbs (and low on the glycaemic index), so can be eaten on all the low-carb diets. Carrots, tomatoes and green peas are slightly higher on the glycaemic index but they contain important nutrients, so earn their place on your plate. Starchy root vegetables are higher in carbs so should be eaten more sparingly; these include beets, squash, parsnip, and all kinds of potatoes. You are advised to keep portion sizes of these higher-carb vegetables small.

**TIP:** Portion sizes given in the Vegetables section are roughly half a cup, unless otherwise stated. Gram weights are given here, though, because many vegetables are difficult to fit in a cup!

| Food type | Carb (g) | Fibre (g) | Net carb (g) | Cal (kcal) | Pro (g) | Fat (g) |
|---|---|---|---|---|---|---|
| Artichokes, 1 globe | 2.7 | – | 2.7 | 18 | 2.8 | 0.2 |
| Artichoke, Jerusalem, boiled, 90g | 9.5 | – | 9.5 | 37 | 1.4 | 0.1 |
| Asparagus, 6 spears, boiled | 3.8 | 1.5 | 2.3 | 21 | 2.4 | 0.3 |
| Aubergine, half medium, fried | 1.4 | 0.5 | 0.9 | 151 | 0.6 | 16 |
| Avocado, half | 8 | 3.4 | 4.6 | 160 | 1.9 | 14 |
| Bamboo shoots, raw, 75g | 0.5 | 1.3 | 0.8 | 8.2 | 1.1 | 0.5 |
| Beans, broad, boiled, 75g | 4.2 | 4.0 | 0.2 | 36 | 3.8 | 0.6 |
| Beans, French, 100g boiled | 2.9 | 2.4 | 0.5 | 22 | 1.8 | 0.5 |
| Beans, runner, 50g, trimmed, boiled | 1.1 | 1.5 | 0.4 | 9 | 0.6 | 0.2 |
| Beansprouts, mung, 25g: | | | | | | |
| raw | 2 | 0.75 | 1.25 | 7.8 | 0.7 | 0.1 |
| *stirfried in blended oil* | 0.6 | 0.2 | 0.4 | 18 | 0.5 | 1.5 |
| Beetroot, 90g: | | | | | | |
| *pickled* | 5.0 | 1.5 | 3.5 | 25 | 1.1 | 0.2 |
| *boiled* | 8.6 | 1.7 | 6.9 | 41 | 2.0 | 0.1 |
| Broccoli, florets, boiled, 60g | 0.6 | 1.4 | 0.8 | 14 | 1.9 | 0.5 |
| Brussels sprouts, 6 trimmed, boiled | 10.9 | 3.3 | 7.6 | 49 | 3.3 | 0.6 |

**TIP:** Canned vegetables have a lower vitamin and mineral content than fresh – but they still have more nutrients than a hunk of French bread or a plate of spaghetti.

| Food type | Carb (g) | Fibre (g) | Net carb (g) | Cal (kcal) | Pro (g) | Fat (g) |
|---|---|---|---|---|---|---|
| Cabbage (Savoy, Summer), 75g: | | | | | | |
| *trimmed* | 3.1 | 1.8 | 1.3 | 20 | 1.3 | 0.3 |
| *shredded & boiled* | 1.9 | 1.6 | 0.3 | 14 | 0.6 | 0.4 |
| *Spring greens, raw* | 2.3 | 2.5 | – | 25 | 2.3 | 0.7 |
| *Spring greens, boiled* | 1.2 | 1.9 | – | 15 | 1.4 | 0.5 |
| *white* | 3.7 | 1.6 | 2.1 | 20 | 1.0 | 0.2 |
| Carrot: | | | | | | |
| *1 medium, raw* | 7.9 | 2.4 | 5.5 | 35 | 0.6 | 0.3 |
| *1 medium, raw (young)* | 6.9 | 2.7 | 4.2 | 34 | 0.8 | 2.7 |
| *grated,* 40g | 3.2 | 0.9 | 2.3 | 15 | 0.2 | 0.1 |
| *boiled (frozen),* 80g | 3.8 | 1.8 | 2.0 | 18 | 0.3 | 0.2 |
| *boiled (young),* 80g | 3.5 | 1.8 | 1.7 | 18 | 0.5 | 0.3 |
| Cassava, 100g: | | | | | | |
| *baked* | 40.1 | 1.7 | 38.4 | 155 | 0.7 | 0.2 |
| *boiled* | 33.5 | 1.4 | 32.1 | 130 | 0.5 | 0.2 |
| Cauliflower, 100g: | | | | | | |
| *raw* | 3.0 | 1.8 | 1.2 | 34 | 3.6 | 0.9 |
| *boiled* | 2.1 | 1.6 | 0.5 | 28 | 2.9 | 0.9 |

**TIP:** Try to include three different-coloured vegetables at each meal. Dark green ones, like broccoli and kale, contain cancer-fighting phytochemicals. Yellow and orange ones, such as carrots and summer squash, help to keep your eyes healthy. Garlic and onions are good for the blood. Tomatoes (strictly a fruit) contain anti-cancer lycopene.

| Food type | Carb (g) | Fibre (g) | Net carb (g) | Cal (kcal) | Pro (g) | Fat (g) |
|---|---|---|---|---|---|---|
| Celeriac, 100g: | | | | | | |
| *flesh only*, raw | 2.3 | 3.7 | – | 18 | 1.2 | 0.4 |
| *flesh only, boiled* | 1.9 | 3.2 | – | 15 | 0.9 | 0.5 |
| Celery, 100g: | | | | | | |
| *stem only, raw* | 0.9 | 1.1 | – | 7 | 0.5 | 0.2 |
| *stem only, boiled* | 0.8 | 1.2 | – | 8 | 0.5 | 0.3 |
| Chicory, 100g | 2.8 | 0.9 | 1.9 | 11 | 0.5 | 0.6 |
| Corn-on-the-cob | | | | | | |
| *boiled, 1 medium cob* | 22.4 | 2.5 | 19.9 | 127 | 4.8 | 2.6 |
| *mini corncobs, boiled, 100g* | 2.7 | 2.0 | 0.7 | 24 | 2.5 | 0.4 |
| *See also:* Sweetcorn | | | | | | |
| Courgettes (zucchini): | | | | | | |
| *trimmed, 50g* | 0.9 | 0.4 | 0.5 | 9 | 0.9 | 0.2 |
| *trimmed, boiled, 75g* | 1.5 | 0.9 | 0.6 | 14 | 1.5 | 0.3 |
| *trimmed, sliced, 75g* | | | | | | |
| *fried in corn oil, 75g* | 1.9 | 0.9 | 1.0 | 47 | 1.9 | 3.6 |
| Cucumber, trimmed, 75g | 1.1 | 0.4 | 0.7 | 7.5 | 0.5 | 0.1 |
| Eggplant: *see* Aubergine | | | | | | |
| Fennel, Florence | | | | | | |
| *boiled, 75g* | 1.1 | 1.7 | – | 8 | 0.7 | 0.1 |

**TIP:** Blend a packet of Boursin cheese with a small tub of crème fraiche and spoon over raw, chopped cauliflower. Top with cheese and bake for 30 minutes at medium heat for a brilliant low-carb cauliflower cheese.

| Food type | Carb (g) | Fibre (g) | Net carb (g) | Cal (kcal) | Pro (g) | Fat (g) |
|---|---|---|---|---|---|---|
| Garlic, half tsp purée or | | | | | | |
| 1 clove, crushed | 1.9 | 0.9 | 1 | 60 | 0.1 | 5.7 |
| Gherkins, | | | | | | |
| *pickled*, 75g | 1.9 | 0.9 | 1 | 10 | 0.7 | 0.08 |
| Ginger root, half tsp, chopped | | | | | | |
| or grated | 1 | – | 1 | 5 | 0.2 | – |
| Greens, spring: *see* Cabbage | | | | | | |
| Gumbo: *see* Okra | | | | | | |
| Kale, curly, 40g: | | | | | | |
| *raw* | 0.6 | 1.2 | – | 13 | 1.4 | 0.6 |
| *shredded, boiled* | 0.4 | 1.1 | – | 10 | 0.9 | 0.4 |
| Kohlrabi, 85g: | | | | | | |
| *raw* | 3.1 | 1.9 | 1.2 | 20 | 1.4 | 0.2 |
| *boiled* | 2.6 | 1.6 | 1.0 | 15 | 1.0 | 0.2 |
| Lady's Fingers: *see* Okra | | | | | | |
| Leeks: | | | | | | |
| *trimmed*, 60g | 1.7 | 1.3 | 0.4 | 13 | 1.0 | 0.3 |
| *chopped, boiled*, 100g | 2.6 | 1.7 | 0.9 | 21 | 1.2 | 0.7 |
| Lettuce, 1 cup (30g): | | | | | | |
| *green* | 0.5 | 0.3 | 0.2 | 4 | 0.2 | 0.1 |
| *iceberg* | 0.6 | 0.2 | 0.4 | 4 | 0.2 | 0.1 |

**TIP:** For easy ratatouille, blend chopped courgettes, onions, peppers and aubergines with chopped tomatoes, a finely chopped red chilli, fresh basil, a clove of garlic, salt and pepper.

| Food type | Carb (g) | Fibre (g) | Net carb (g) | Cal (kcal) | Pro (g) | Fat (g) |
|---|---|---|---|---|---|---|
| *mixed leaf* | 0.8 | 0.8 | – | 5 | 0.4 | 0.03 |
| *Mediterranean salad leaves* | 0.8 | 0.3 | 0.5 | 4.5 | 0.3 | 0.1 |
| Mange-tout, 50g: | | | | | | |
| *raw* | 2.1 | 1.6 | 0.5 | 16 | 1.8 | 0.1 |
| *boiled* | 1.6 | 1.1 | 0.5 | 13 | 1.6 | 0.05 |
| *stir-fried* | 1.8 | 1.2 | 0.6 | 36 | 1.9 | 2.4 |
| Marrow: | | | | | | |
| *flesh only, 50g* | 1.1 | 0.2 | 0.9 | 6 | 0.2 | 0.1 |
| *flesh only, boiled, 75g* | 1.2 | 0.5 | 0.7 | 7 | 0.3 | 0.1 |
| Mooli: *see* Radish, white | | | | | | |
| Mushrooms, common, 40g: | | | | | | |
| *raw* | 0.2 | 0.4 | – | 5 | 0.7 | 0.2 |
| *boiled* | 0.2 | 0.4 | – | 4 | 0.7 | 0.1 |
| *fried in oil* | 0.1 | 0.6 | – | 63 | 1 | 6.5 |
| *canned* | – | 0.2 | – | 4 | 0.8 | 0.2 |
| Mushrooms, oyster, 30g | – | – | – | 2 | 0.5 | 0.06 |
| Mushrooms, shiitake, 40g: | | | | | | |
| *boiled* | 4.9 | N | 4.9 | 22 | 0.6 | 0.1 |
| *dried* | 25.6 | N | 25.6 | 118 | 3.8 | 0.4 |
| Neeps (England): *see* Swede | | | | | | |

**TIP:** Baked potatoes are a bad choice all round on low-carb diets, as the baking breaks down the starches and makes them more easily absorbed. You'd be better off with chips, as the fat would impede absorption to an extent. Neither are recommended, though.

| Food type | Carb (g) | Fibre (g) | Net carb (g) | Cal (kcal) | Pro (g) | Fat (g) |
|---|---|---|---|---|---|---|
| Neeps (Scotland): *see* Turnip | | | | | | |
| Okra (gumbo, lady's fingers): | | | | | | |
| *raw*, 25g | 0.8 | 1.0 | – | 8 | 0.7 | 0.2 |
| *boiled*, 30g | 0.8 | 1.0 | – | 8 | 0.7 | 0.2 |
| *stir-fried*, 30g | 1.3 | 1.9 | – | 81 | 1.3 | 7.8 |
| Olives, quarter cup (25g), | | | | | | |
| pitted, in brine | – | 0.7 | – | 26 | 0.2 | 2.7 |
| Onions: | | | | | | |
| *raw, flesh only*, 30g | 2.4 | 0.4 | 2.0 | 11 | 0.4 | 0.1 |
| *boiled*, 40g | 1.5 | 0.3 | 1.2 | 7 | 0.2 | – |
| *cocktail/silverskin,* | | | | | | |
| *drained*, 40g | 1.2 | N | 1.2 | 6 | 0.2 | – |
| *fried in vegetable oil*, 40g | 5.6 | 1.2 | 4.4 | 66 | 0.9 | 4.5 |
| *pickled, drained*, 40g | 2.0 | 0.5 | 1.5 | 10 | 0.4 | 0.1 |
| Parsnips, trimmed, peeled, | | | | | | |
| boiled, 80g | 10.3 | 3.8 | 6.5 | 53 | 1.3 | 1.0 |
| Peas: | | | | | | |
| *no pod*, 75g | 8.5 | 3.5 | 5.0 | 62 | 5.1 | 1.1 |
| *boiled*, 90g | 9.0 | 4.0 | 5.0 | 71 | 6.0 | 1.4 |
| *canned*, 90g | 12.2 | 4.6 | 7.6 | 72 | 4.8 | 0.8 |
| Peas, mushy, canned, 100g | 13.8 | 1.8 | 12 | 81 | 5.8 | 0.7 |

**TIP:** Olives are carbohydrate-free and a great addition to many dishes. Try stuffing a chicken breast with chopped olives, feta cheese and sundried tomatoes.

| Food type | Carb (g) | Fibre (g) | Net carb (g) | Cal (kcal) | Pro (g) | Fat (g) |
|---|---|---|---|---|---|---|
| Peas, processed, canned, 100g | 17.5 | 4.8 | 12.7 | 99 | 6.9 | 0.7 |
| *See also*: Petit pois | | | | | | |
| *See also under: Beans, Pulses and Cereals* | | | | | | |
| Peppers: | | | | | | |
| *green, raw, 40g* | 1.0 | 0.6 | 0.4 | 6 | 0.3 | 0.1 |
| *green, boiled, 50g* | 1.3 | 0.9 | 0.4 | 9 | 0.5 | 0.2 |
| *red, raw, 40g* | 2.6 | 0.6 | 2.0 | 13 | 0.4 | 0.2 |
| *red, boiled, 50g* | 3.5 | 0.9 | 2.6 | 17 | 0.6 | 0.2 |
| *yellow, raw, 40g* | 2.1 | 0.7 | 0.4 | 10 | 0.5 | 0.1 |
| *chilli, 15g* | 0.1 | N | 0.1 | 3 | 0.4 | 0.1 |
| *jalapeños, 15g* | 0.5 | – | 2 | 3.3 | 0.2 | 0.04 |
| Petit pois: | | | | | | |
| *fresh, 75g* | 13.1 | 3.1 | 10 | 75 | 5.2 | 0.6 |
| *frozen, boiled, 100g* | 5.5 | 4.5 | 1.0 | 49 | 5 | 0.9 |
| **Potatoes, Chips and Fries** | | | | | | |
| Chips (French fries), 150g: | | | | | | |
| *crinkle cut, frozen, fried* | 50.1 | 3.3 | 46.8 | 435 | 5.4 | 25 |

**TIP:** Oven-roasting brings out the flavour of vegetables. Cut a selection into bite-sized chunks and drizzle them with olive oil then bake till tender. Courgettes, squash, peppers and red onions all work well. Add whole cloves of garlic – they lose their sharpness when cooked.

| Food type | Carb (g) | Fibre (g) | Net carb (g) | Cal (kcal) | Pro (g) | Fat (g) |
|---|---|---|---|---|---|---|
| Chips, 150g, contd: | | | | | | |
| *French fries, retail* | 51 | 3.2 | 47.9 | 420 | 4.9 | 23.2 |
| *homemade, fried* | 45.2 | 3.3 | 41.9 | 284 | 5.8 | 10 |
| *microwave chips* | 48.2 | 4.4 | 43.8 | 332 | 5.4 | 14.4 |
| *oven chips* | 44.7 | 3 | 41.7 | 243 | 4.8 | 6.3 |
| *straight cut, frozen, fried* | 54 | 3.6 | 50.4 | 410 | 6.2 | 20.2 |
| Croquettes, fried in oil, 100g | 21.6 | 1.3 | 20.3 | 214 | 3.7 | 13.1 |
| Hash browns, 100g | 24 | – | 24 | 190 | 3 | 9.8 |
| Mashed potato, instant, 125g: | | | | | | |
| *made with semi-skimmed milk* | 18.5 | 1.2 | 17.3 | 88 | 3 | 1.5 |
| *made with skimmed milk* | 18.5 | 1.2 | 17.3 | 82 | 3 | 1.2 |
| *made with water* | 16.9 | 1.2 | 15.7 | 71 | 1.9 | 1.2 |
| *made up with whole milk* | 18.5 | 1.2 | 18.3 | 95 | 3 | 1.5 |
| Potato fritters, 100g | 17.2 | 1.3 | 15.9 | 174 | 2.2 | 10.7 |
| Potato waffles,100g | 30.3 | 2.3 | 28 | 200 | 3.2 | 8.2 |
| Potatoes, new, 100g: | | | | | | |
| *boiled, peeled* | 17.8 | 1.1 | 16.7 | 75 | 1.5 | 0.3 |
| *boiled in skins* | 15.4 | 1.5 | 13.9 | 66 | 1.4 | 0.3 |
| *canned* | 15.1 | 0.8 | 14.3 | 63 | 1.5 | 0.1 |

**TIP:** Remove the filling from baked potatoes, dust the skins in paprika and a little sea salt and drizzle with olive oil. Serve with guacamole. Potato skins do contain carbs but less than the fillings and they are rich in fibre.

| **Food type** | Carb (g) | Fibre (g) | Net carb (g) | Cal (kcal) | Pro (g) | Fat (g) |
|---|---|---|---|---|---|---|
| Potatoes, old, 90g: | | | | | | |
| *baked, flesh & skin* | 28.5 | 2.4 | 26.1 | 122 | 3.5 | 0.2 |
| *baked, flesh only* | 16.2 | 1.3 | 14.9 | 69 | 2.0 | 0.1 |
| *boiled, peeled* | 15.3 | 1.1 | 14.2 | 65 | 1.6 | 0.1 |
| *mashed with butter & milk* | 13.9 | 1.0 | 12.9 | 94 | 1.6 | 3.9 |
| *roast in oil/lard* | 23.3 | 1.6 | 21.7 | 134 | 2.6 | 4.0 |
| Southern-style skins (McCain), 100g | 17.8 | – | 17.8 | 147 | 2.2 | 7.4 |
| Pumpkin, flesh only, boiled, 75g | 1.6 | 0.8 | 0.8 | 10 | 0.4 | 0.2 |
| Radicchio, 30g | 0.5 | 0.5 | – | 4 | 0.4 | 0.1 |
| Radish, red, 6 | 1.1 | 0.5 | 0.6 | 7 | 0.4 | 0.1 |
| Radish, white/mooli, 20g | 0.6 | N | 0.6 | 3 | 0.2 | 0.02 |
| Ratatouille, canned, 115g | 7.4 | 1.1 | 6.3 | 55 | 1.1 | 2.3 |
| Salad: *see* Lettuce | | | | | | |
| Salsify: | | | | | | |
| *flesh only, raw*, 40g | 4.1 | 1.3 | 2.8 | 11 | 0.5 | 0.1 |
| *flesh only, boiled*, 50g | 4.3 | 1.8 | 2.5 | 11 | 0.6 | 0.2 |
| Shallots, 30g | 1.0 | 0.6 | 0.4 | 6 | 0.4 | 0.2 |
| Spinach: | | | | | | |
| *raw, one cup*, 30g | 0.5 | 0.6 | – | 7 | 0.8 | 0.2 |
| *boiled*, 90g | 0.7 | 1.9 | – | 17 | 2.0 | 0.7 |
| *frozen, boiled*, 90g | 0.4 | 1.9 | – | 19 | 2.8 | 0.7 |

**TIP:** Sprinkle nuts and seeds on salads to add 'good' fats as well as interesting textures. Try sesame seeds, flaxseeds or pumpkin seeds.

| Food type | Carb (g) | Fibre (g) | Net carb (g) | Cal (kcal) | Pro (g) | Fat (g) |
|---|---|---|---|---|---|---|
| Spring onions, bulbs & tops, | | | | | | |
| quarter cup, 30g | 0.9 | 0.4 | 0.5 | 7 | 0.6 | 0.2 |
| Sprouts: *see* Brussels Sprouts | | | | | | |
| Squash: | | | | | | |
| *flesh only*, 50g | 1.1 | 0.2 | 0.9 | 6 | 0.2 | 0.1 |
| *flesh only, boiled*, 75g | 1.2 | 0.5 | 0.7 | 7 | 0.3 | 0.1 |
| Swede, flesh only, boiled, 90g | 2.0 | 0.6 | 1.4 | 10 | 0.3 | 0.1 |
| Sweet potato, boiled, 90g | 18.4 | 2.0 | 16.4 | 76 | 1.0 | 0.3 |
| Sweetcorn, kernels, 80g: | | | | | | |
| *canned, drained, re-heated* | 21.3 | 1.1 | 20.2 | 97 | 2.3 | 1.0 |
| *canned, no salt, no sugar* | | | | | | |
| *(Green Giant)* | 13.4 | 2 | 11.4 | 62 | 2 | 0 |
| Tomatoes: | | | | | | |
| *1 medium* | 4.7 | 1.1 | 4.1 | 26 | 1 | 0.4 |
| *canned, whole*, 100g | 3 | 0.7 | 2.3 | 16 | 1 | 0.1 |
| *cherry*, 6 | 5.2 | 1.6 | 4.6 | 31 | 1.2 | 0.8 |
| *1 medium, fried in oil* | 7.8 | 1.4 | 6.4 | 137 | 1 | 10.3 |
| *sun-dried*, 30g | 3.3 | 1.9 | 1.4 | 63 | 1.3 | 4.9 |
| *paste*, 2 tbsp | 6 | 1 | – | 30 | 2 | 0 |
| *passata*, 200g | 9 | 0.4 | 8.6 | 50 | 2.8 | 0.2 |
| *chopped, canned*, 200g | 5 | – | 5 | 30 | 2.4 | – |

**TIP:** Squash is cholesterol-free, and high in antioxidant vitamins A and C. Grill with a little olive oil, sea salt and pepper, adding fresh herbs of your choice. Serve with a little crème fraiche.

| Food type | Carb (g) | Fibre (g) | Net carb (g) | Cal (kcal) | Pro (g) | Fat (g) |
|---|---|---|---|---|---|---|
| Turnip, flesh only, boiled, 60g | 2.8 | 1.4 | 1.4 | 7 | 0.4 | 0.2 |
| Water chestnuts, canned, 40g | 3.0 | N | 3.0 | 12 | 0.4 | – |
| Yam, flesh only, boiled, 90g | 29.7 | 1.3 | 28.4 | 120 | 1.5 | 0.3 |
| Zucchini: *see* Courgettes | | | | | | |

**TIP:** Add water chestnuts to curries and stir-fries to add flavour and texture. They are relatively low in carbs, and fat-, cholesterol- and sodium-free. Or wrap them in bacon and grill as a starter.

## VEGETARIAN

In the US, the Food and Drug Administration has recently advised that everyone eats 25g of soya protein a day, because of its all-round health benefits. There are no such recommendations in the UK yet, but cardiologists think it's a good idea to use soya proteins instead of meat ones at a few meals a week, because they are lower in fat and contain better kinds of fat, as well as antioxidant vitamins. See Barry Sears' *The Soy Zone* for loads of recipe ideas, or just substitute soya or tofu in your normal family recipes, such as shepherd's pie, 'Bolognese' sauce, casseroles and stir-fries.

| **Food type** | Carb (g) | Fibre (g) | Net carb (g) | Cal (kcal) | Pro (g) | Fat (g) |
|---|---|---|---|---|---|---|
| Baked beans with vegetable sausages (Heinz), 200g | 24.2 | 5.8 | 18.4 | 204 | 11.2 | 7 |
| Burgers: | | | | | | |
| *vegetable burger (Linda McCartney)* | 21 | 1.7 | 19.3 | 179 | 2.3 | 9.5 |
| *vegetable quarter pounder (Birds Eye)* | 23 | 1.8 | 21.2 | 190 | 4.3 | 9.1 |
| Carrot, peanut & onion burgers (Cauldron), each | 23.5 | 4.0 | 19.5 | 251 | 8.9 | 13.5 |
| Cauliflower cheese (Birds Eye), 100g | 22 | – | 22 | 365 | 18 | 23 |
| Cornish pasty (Tamarfoods Cornish Pride), each | 37.3 | 2.0 | 35.3 | 452 | 11 | 28.9 |
| Hummus, 2 tbsp | 6.2 | 1.6 | 4.6 | 53 | 1.5 | 2.6 |
| Lentils, 115g: | | | | | | |
| *green/brown, boiled* | 19.3 | 4.3 | 15 | 120 | 10 | 0.8 |
| *red, split, boiled* | 20 | 2.2 | 17.8 | 114 | 8.7 | 0.5 |
| Macaroni cheese, individual (Birds Eye) | 47 | – | 47 | 375 | 13 | 15 |

**TIP:** Vegetarian cheeses are manufactured using rennet from either fungal or bacterial sources. Advances in genetic engineering processes mean they may now also be made using chymosin produced by genetically altered micro-organisms. Its worth ensuring that non-GM sources are used in your brand.

| Food type | Carb (g) | Fibre (g) | Net carb (g) | Cal (kcal) | Pro (g) | Fat (g) |
|---|---|---|---|---|---|---|
| Onions & garlic sauce | | | | | | |
| (Ragu), 100g | 9.2 | – | 9.2 | 58 | 2.3 | 1.3 |
| Pâté, 50g: | | | | | | |
| *herb (Tartex)* | 3.0 | – | 3.0 | 83 | 3.5 | 8 |
| *herb & garlic (Vessen)* | 5.0 | – | 5.0 | 165 | 3.5 | 9 |
| *mushroom (Tartex)* | 3.5 | – | 3.5 | 100 | 3.5 | 8 |
| *red & green pepper (Vessen)* | 4.5 | – | 4.5 | 111 | 3 | 9 |
| Polenta, ready-made, 100g | 15.7 | – | 15.7 | 71.9 | 1.6 | 0.3 |
| Quorn, myco-protein, 100g | 2 | 4.8 | – | 86 | 11.8 | 3.5 |
| Ravioli in tomato sauce, | | | | | | |
| meatfree (Heinz), 200g | 28.8 | 1 | 27.8 | 150 | 4.8 | 1.6 |
| Red kidney beans: | | | | | | |
| *small can* (200g) | 35.6 | 17 | 18.6 | 200 | 13.8 | 1.2 |
| *boiled,* 115g | 19.8 | 10.3 | 9.5 | 118 | 9.6 | 0.6 |
| Rice drink (Provamel), 240ml: | | | | | | |
| *calcium enriched* | 24 | – | 24 | 120 | 0.2 | 2.6 |
| *vanilla* | 24 | – | 24 | 118 | 0.2 | 2.4 |
| Roast vegetable & tomato | | | | | | |
| pasta, 97% fat-free (Birds | | | | | | |
| Eye), each | 56 | – | 56 | 300 | 10 | 3.7 |
| Sausage rolls (Linda | | | | | | |
| McCartney), 100g | 23.1 | 1.6 | 21.5 | 260 | 10.9 | 14.5 |

**TIP:** Check that prepared foods carry a vegetarian V symbol, to be sure no meat products have been used in them.

| Food type | Carb (g) | Fibre (g) | Net carb (g) | Cal (kcal) | Pro (g) | Fat (g) |
|---|---|---|---|---|---|---|
| Sausages (Linda McCartney), 100g | 8.6 | 1.2 | 7.4 | 252 | 23.2 | 13.8 |
| Soya bean curd: *see* Tofu | | | | | | |
| Soya chunks: | | | | | | |
| *flavoured*, 100g | 35 | 4 | 31 | 345 | 50 | 1 |
| *unflavoured*, 100g | 35 | 4 | 31 | 345 | 50 | 1 |
| Soya curd: *see* Tofu | | | | | | |
| Soya flour: | | | | | | |
| *full fat*, 100g | 23.5 | 11.2 | 12.3 | 447 | 36.8 | 23.5 |
| *low fat*, 100g | 28.2 | 13.5 | 15.6 | 352 | 45.3 | 7.2 |
| Soya milk: | | | | | | |
| *banana flavour*, 240ml | 25.2 | 2.9 | 22.3 | 180 | 8.6 | 5 |
| *chocolate flavour*, 240ml | 23 | 3.6 | 19.4 | 173 | 8.6 | 5 |
| *strawberry flavour*, 240ml | 18.5 | 2.9 | 15.6 | 154 | 8.6 | 5 |
| *sweetened*, 240ml | 6 | – | 6 | 103 | 8.9 | 5 |
| *unsweetened*, 240ml | 1.2 | 0.5 | 0.7 | 62 | 5.8 | 3.8 |
| Soya mince: | | | | | | |
| *flavoured*, 100g | 35 | 4 | 31 | 345 | 50 | 1 |
| *unflavoured*, 100g | 35 | 4 | 31 | 345 | 50 | 1 |
| Spaghetti bolognese, meatfree (Heinz), 200g | 26.2 | 1.4 | 24.8 | 172 | 6.2 | 4.8 |

**TIP:** *The Carbohydrate Addict's Diet* contains recipes for soya flour bread, muffins, pancakes and even a coffee cake, which can be included in their complementary meals.

| Food type | Carb (g) | Fibre (g) | Net carb (g) | Cal (kcal) | Pro (g) | Fat (g) |
|---|---|---|---|---|---|---|
| Sweet pepper sauce (Ragu), 100g | 6 | 2.3 | 3.7 | 54 | 1.7 | 2.6 |
| Tofu (soya bean curd): | | | | | | |
| *steamed*, 100g | 0.7 | – | 0.7 | 73 | 81 | 4.2 |
| *steamed, fried*, 100g | 2 | – | 2 | 261 | 23.5 | 17.7 |
| Vegetable biryani (Birds Eye), each | 74 | – | 74 | 690 | 12 | 38 |
| Vegetable burgers, organic (Linda McCartney), 100g | 27.7 | 2.3 | 25.4 | 238 | 3.1 | 12.7 |
| Vegetable granulated stock (Knorr), 30g | 11.9 | 0.3 | 11.6 | 60 | 2.5 | 0.3 |
| Vegetable gravy granules, 50g | 29.8 | 0.5 | 29.4 | 158 | 4.2 | 2.5 |
| Vegetable sauce, 100ml | 7 | 2.5 | 5 | 59 | 2 | 2.6 |
| Vegetable stock cubes, each | 4.6 | 0.2 | 4.4 | 28 | 1.2 | 0.5 |
| *organic (Knorr)*, each | 2.2 | 0.1 | 2.1 | 31 | 0.7 | 2.2 |
| Vegetarian Double Gloucester cheese, 25g | 0.25 | – | 0.25 | 102 | 6.2 | 8.5 |
| Vegetarian mild Cheddar cheese, 25g | 0.25 | – | 0.25 | 103 | 6.4 | 8.6 |
| Vegetarian Red Leicester cheese, 50g | 0.25 | – | 0.25 | 100 | 8.1 | 8.4 |
| Vegetable pasty, each | 29.9 | 1.8 | 28.1 | 188 | 4.4 | 5.7 |

**TIP:** If you are worried about eating genetically modified foods, check the labels on all soya products.

| Food type | Carb (g) | Fibre (g) | Net carb (g) | Cal (kcal) | Pro (g) | Fat (g) |
|---|---|---|---|---|---|---|
| Yofu organic yoghurt (Provamel), 100ml: | | | | | | |
| *peach & mango* | 20.5 | 1.5 | 19 | 128 | 4.8 | 2.8 |
| *red cherry* | 20.1 | 1.5 | 19 | 125 | 4.8 | 2.8 |
| *strawberry* | 19.5 | 0.3 | 19.2 | 135 | 4.8 | 0.3 |

**TIP:** For a light, easy-to-prepare vegetable stock, finely chop 6 leeks, 4 Spanish onions, 8 stalks of celery and 2 celery roots. Sauté in a little olive oil with garlic, if desired. Place the vegetables in a large pot. Cover with cold water and bring to a boil. Simmer for 1 hour, skimming away any impurities that rise to the top. Strain and reduce to about 1.5 litres. Salt, pepper and herbs can be added to taste.

## FAST FOOD

Being on a low-carb diet doesn't mean you can't eat in fast food restaurants, but you have to be selective. If there's a salad bar, that's your best option. If you really want a burger or grilled chicken sandwich, throw away the white flour bun and eat the meat with the salad. If the chicken comes with a bread coating, cut it off. Avoid hot dogs, bologna and pepperoni, which could contain nitrates (see page 138). Watch out for ketchup and brown sauce, which are full of sugar, but mustard, pickles, salsa and Tabasco sauce are all fine. Choose thin-crust pizzas with lots of vegetables on top to stop the carbs in the pizza base being absorbed so quickly.

| Food type | Carb (g) | Fibre (g) | Net carb (g) | Cal (kcal) | Pro (g) | Fat (g) |
|---|---|---|---|---|---|---|
| **McDonald's** | | | | | | |
| Big Breakfast, each | 39.8 | 4 | 35.8 | 591 | 26.2 | 36.3 |
| Big Mac, each | 44 | 5.3 | 38.7 | 493 | 26.7 | 22.9 |
| Cheeseburger, each | 33.1 | 2.5 | 30.6 | 299 | 15.8 | 11.5 |
| Chicken McNuggets (6) | 11.5 | 2.1 | 9.4 | 253 | 18.6 | 14.8 |
| Filet-O-Fish, each | 40.8 | 1.2 | 39.6 | 389 | 16.6 | 17.7 |
| French Fries, regular, per portion | 28.3 | 2.8 | 25.5 | 206 | 2.9 | 9 |
| Hamburger, each | 32.8 | 2.5 | 32.8 | 253 | 13.1 | 7.7 |
| Hash Browns | 15.8 | 1.7 | 14.1 | 138 | 1.4 | 7.7 |
| McChicken Sandwich, each | 38.6 | 3.8 | 38.6 | 375 | 16.5 | 34.8 |
| Milkshake, vanilla, regular, each | 62.7 | – | 62.7 | 383 | 10.8 | 10.1 |
| Quarter Pounder, each | 37.1 | 3.7 | 33.4 | 423 | 25.7 | 19 |
| *with cheese* | 37.5 | 3.7 | 33.8 | 516 | 31.2 | 26.7 |
| **Wimpy** | | | | | | |
| All day breakfast | 46.2 | 3.8 | 42.4 | 710 | 31.4 | 44.3 |
| Bacon & egg in a bun | 32.3 | 1.7 | 30.6 | 400 | 23.5 | 19.9 |
| Bacon Classic Cheeseburger | 33.3 | 2.4 | 30.9 | 455 | 26.2 | 23.1 |
| Bacon in a bun | 32.3 | 1.7 | 30.6 | 290 | 15 | 11.2 |
| Bacon/Cheeseburger | 32.3 | 1.7 | 30.6 | 375 | 21.4 | 18.1 |
| BBQ Pork Rib in a Bun | 68.9 | 3.4 | 65.6 | 515 | 25.1 | 16.2 |

**TIP:** Most burger-style restaurants now offer grilled chicken sandwiches, which have a much lower carb count. Eat without the bun and ask for extra salad and mayonnaise.

| Food type | Carb (g) | Fibre (g) | Net carb (g) | Cal (kcal) | Pro (g) | Fat (g) |
|---|---|---|---|---|---|---|
| Bender: | | | | | | |
| *in a bun* | 33.5 | 2.2 | 31.3 | 410 | 21.8 | 22.4 |
| *in a bun with cheese* | 33.5 | 2.2 | 31.3 | 455 | 21.8 | 25.9 |
| *egg & chips* | 32.5 | 2.7 | 29.8 | 490 | 20.8 | 30.6 |
| Cheeseburger | 32.3 | 1.7 | 30.6 | 315 | 16.7 | 13.1 |
| Chicken chunks & chips | 68.3 | 4.2 | 64.1 | 645 | 21.4 | 31.6 |
| Chicken in a bun | 42 | 1.9 | 40.1 | 435 | 16.3 | 22.2 |
| Chips | 42.4 | 3.5 | 38.9 | 295 | 3.7 | 12.1 |
| Classic Kingsize | 33.3 | 2.4 | 30.9 | 550 | 36.2 | 30.3 |
| Fish 'n' Chips | 43.5 | 3.9 | 39.6 | 465 | 27.5 | 20.1 |
| Fish in a bun | 62.8 | 3.4 | 59.4 | 510 | 34.2 | 13.5 |
| Halfpounder | 42.3 | 6.7 | 35.6 | 840 | 51.2 | 51.5 |
| Hamburger | 32.3 | 1.7 | 30.6 | 270 | 13.7 | 9.6 |
| Hot 'n' Spicy Chicken in a bun | 45.7 | 2.4 | 43.3 | 430 | 18.5 | 19.7 |
| International grill | 46.4 | 3.9 | 42.5 | 770 | 36.7 | 49.1 |
| International grill deluxe | 46.4 | 3.9 | 42.5 | 970 | 50.4 | 63.5 |
| Quarterpounder | 42.3 | 6.7 | 35.6 | 550 | 28.2 | 30 |
| *with cheese* | 42.3 | 6.7 | 35.6 | 595 | 31.2 | 33.5 |
| Spicy Beanburger | 68.7 | 15.9 | 52.8 | 535 | 16.1 | 22 |
| Toasted Tea Cake & butter | 35.3 | 1.2 | 34.1 | 250 | 5.8 | 9.9 |
| Wimpy Classic | 33.3 | 2.4 | 30.9 | 340 | 19.6 | 14.5 |
| *special grill* | 46.2 | 3.7 | 42.5 | 820 | 39.2 | 53.3 |

**TIP:** The average burger is high in saturated fat, so don't make it a regular indulgence.

| Food type | Carb (g) | Fibre (g) | Net carb (g) | Cal (kcal) | Pro (g) | Fat (g) |
|---|---|---|---|---|---|---|
| *with cheese* | 33.3 | 2.4 | 30.9 | 385 | 22.6 | 18 |
| Wimpy special grill | 46.2 | 3.7 | 42.5 | 690 | 30.2 | 42.7 |
| **Burger King** | | | | | | |
| Cheeseburger | 30.1 | 1.8 | 28.3 | 331 | 19.6 | 14.2 |
| Chicken Whopper | 45 | 2.5 | 42.5 | 548 | 39.4 | 23.4 |
| Chicken Whopper Lite | 28.9 | 1.7 | 27.2 | 289 | 25 | 7.5 |
| Hamburger | 30 | 1.8 | 28.2 | 290 | 17.2 | 10.8 |
| Regular King Fries | 43 | 2.9 | 40.1 | 400 | 3 | 16 |
| Veggie Burger | 55.4 | 7.6 | 47.8 | 432 | 14.7 | 16.9 |
| Whopper | 47.6 | 3.6 | 44 | 646 | 30.6 | 37.9 |
| **Pizza Hut** | | | | | | |
| BBQ Dip, portion | 7.3 | n/a | n/a | 31 | 2.8 | 0 |
| Cheesy Bites: | | | | | | |
| *Cheddar* | 28.7 | n/a | n/a | 319 | 8.5 | 18.9 |
| *Tomato & Cheddar* | 26.9 | n/a | n/a | 308 | 8.2 | 18.6 |
| Chicken Wings (Take Away), portion | 3 | 2.3 | 0.7 | 466 | 40 | 32.7 |
| Dippin' Chicken, portion | 26.3 | 0 | 26.3 | 329 | 24.2 | 14.3 |
| Garlic & Herb Dip, portion | 6.21 | n/a | n/a | 280 | 1.29 | 27.75 |

**TIP:** Most pizzerias now have salad bars. All you need to avoid there are the potato salads and sweetcorn.

| Food type | Carb (g) | Fibre (g) | Net carb (g) | Cal (kcal) | Pro (g) | Fat (g) |
|---|---|---|---|---|---|---|
| Garlic Bread with Cheese, portion | 49.5 | 3.3 | 46.2 | 618 | 25.6 | 35.3 |
| Garlic Bread, portion | 44.3 | 2.5 | 41.8 | 386 | 8 | 19.6 |
| Garlic Mushrooms, portion | 22.1 | 3.8 | 18.3 | 215 | 6.6 | 11.1 |
| Hawaiian Medium Pan, per slice | 28 | 1.3 | 26.7 | 241 | 12.1 | 8.9 |
| Jacket Skins, portion | 51.4 | 4.7 | 46.7 | 570 | 7.6 | 37.1 |
| Lasagne, portion | 62.4 | 9.3 | 53.1 | 669 | 39.4 | 29.2 |
| Margherita Medium Pan, per slice | 26.3 | 1.8 | 24.5 | 238 | 10.7 | 10 |
| Meat Feast Medium Pan, per slice | 27.8 | 1 | 26.8 | 324 | 16.6 | 16.2 |
| Ranch Dip, portion | 3.8 | n/a | n/a | 489 | 3.2 | 51 |
| Spicy Chicken Bake, portion | 80.7 | 0 | 80.7 | 499 | 18.5 | 12.4 |
| Stuffed Crust Original Margherita, per slice | 35.7 | 1.3 | 34.4 | 328 | 18.7 | 12.3 |
| Supreme Medium Pan, per slice | 14.6 | 0.5 | 14.1 | 291 | 26.5 | 1.3 |
| Tangy Tomato Bake, portion | 92.9 | 5.5 | 87.4 | 653 | 27.1 | 21.6 |
| The Edge, per slice: | | | | | | |
| *Meaty* | 14.9 | n/a | n/a | 206 | 10.6 | 11.6 |
| *The Veggie* | 14.8 | n/a | n/a | 136 | 6.9 | 5.6 |
| *The Works* | 14.1 | n/a | n/a | 161 | 8.25 | 8 |

**TIP:** Chicken nuggets have a breaded coating over a little meat and they are often cooked in trans fats as well. Go for chicken kebabs or satays, which are much lower in carbs and fat.

| Food type | Carb (g) | Fibre (g) | Net carb (g) | Cal (kcal) | Pro (g) | Fat (g) |
|---|---|---|---|---|---|---|
| The Italian Medium, per slice: | | | | | | |
| *Ham & Mushroom* | 34 | n/a | n/a | 269 | 13 | 10.2 |
| *Margherita* | 37.5 | n/a | n/a | 291 | 14.4 | 10.2 |
| *Meat Feast* | 27.8 | n/a | n/a | 324 | 16.6 | 16.2 |
| *Supreme* | 26.5 | n/a | n/a | 297 | 13.7 | 14.6 |
| Tomato & Herb, portion | 38.4 | n/a | n/a | 154 | 1.1 | 0.1 |
| Twisted Crust: | | | | | | |
| *Margherita* | 31.5 | n/a | n/a | 256 | 13.5 | 8.5 |
| *Meat Feast* | 28 | n/a | n/a | 266 | 13 | 11.3 |
| *Supreme* | 29.6 | n/a | n/a | 257 | 13.1 | 9.6 |
| Vegetarian Original Medium Pan, per slice | 26.2 | 1.8 | 24.4 | 225 | 10.5 | 8.8 |
| **Domino's Pizza** | | | | | | |
| Cheese & Tomato 9.5″, per slice | 18.2 | 1.7 | 16.5 | 126 | 6.7 | 2.9 |
| Chicken Dunkers | 1.5 | 0.5 | 1.0 | 220 | 23.5 | 13.3 |
| Chicken Strippers | 13.4 | 1 | 12.4 | 219 | 23.3 | 8 |
| Deluxe 9.5″, per slice | 19.2 | 1.6 | 17.6 | 171 | 8.4 | 6.7 |
| Full House 9.5″, per slice | 18.9 | 1.3 | 17.6 | 183 | 9.3 | 7.8 |
| Garlic Pizza Bread, per slice | 16.4 | 0.9 | 15.5 | 117 | 4.7 | 3.6 |
| Mighty Meaty 9.5″, per slice | 18.1 | 2 | 16.1 | 177 | 9.9 | 7.2 |

**TIP:** The thinner the crust, the lower the carbs in your pizza. Choose plenty of toppings and eat as little of the crust as you can!

| Food type | Carb (g) | Fibre (g) | Net carb (g) | Cal (kcal) | Pro (g) | Fat (g) |
|---|---|---|---|---|---|---|
| Mixed Grill 9.5″, per slice | 19.6 | 1.7 | 17.9 | 177 | 9 | 6.9 |
| Pepperoni Passion 9.5″, per slice | 20.6 | 1.4 | 19.2 | 187 | 9 | 7.6 |
| Tandoori Hot 9.5″, per slice | 18.7 | 1.9 | 16.8 | 138 | 8.2 | 3.5 |
| Vegetarian Supreme 9.5″, per slice | 19.3 | 1.7 | 17.6 | 140 | 7.7 | 3.3 |
| **Pizza Express** | | | | | | |
| American, per pizza | 87.3 | n/a | n/a | 753 | 35.3 | 32.4 |
| American Hot, per pizza | 87.4 | n/a | n/a | 758 | 35.9 | 32.6 |
| Cannelloni, per portion | 38.7 | n/a | n/a | 556 | 20.9 | 35.4 |
| Fiorentina, per pizza | 88.4 | n/a | n/a | 740 | 38.22 | 27.5 |
| La Reine, per pizza | 87.4 | n/a | n/a | 665 | 34.9 | 22.8 |
| Lasagne Pasticciate, per portion | 29.9 | n/a | n/a | 579 | 26.4 | 39.5 |
| Margherita, per pizza | 87.3 | n/a | n/a | 621 | 29.3 | 20.4 |
| Mushroom, per pizza | 87.5 | n/a | n/a | 627 | 30.1 | 20.6 |
| Pollo, per portion | 32.5 | n/a | n/a | 573 | 41.1 | 31.8 |
| Quattro Formaggi, per pizza | 87.2 | n/a | n/a | 636 | 29.4 | 22.1 |
| Salade Nicoise, per portion | 65 | n/a | n/a | 729 | 40 | 37 |
| Sloppy Giuseppe, per pizza | 97 | n/a | n/a | 783 | 41 | 33 |
| Tortellini, per portion | 91.9 | n/a | n/a | 1116 | 26.9 | 71.3 |

**TIP:** If you are going to blow your low-carb diet on pizza, try to choose one with good-quality ingredients and lots of vegetables. Better still, ask for a chicken Caesar salad, now available at many pizzerias (but forego the croutons).

| Food type | Carb (g) | Fibre (g) | Net carb (g) | Cal (kcal) | Pro (g) | Fat (g) |
|---|---|---|---|---|---|---|
| **Fish and chips** | | | | | | |
| Cod, in batter, fried | 11.7 | 0.5 | 11.2 | 247 | 16.1 | 15.4 |
| Plaice, in batter, fried | 12 | 0.5 | 11.5 | 257 | 15.2 | 16.8 |
| Rock Salmon/Dogfish, in batter, fried | 10.3 | 0.4 | 9.9 | 295 | 14.7 | 21.9 |
| Skate, in batter, fried | 4.9 | 0.2 | 4.7 | 168 | 14.7 | 10.1 |
| Chips, fried in oil | 30.5 | 2.2 | 28.3 | 239 | 3.2 | 12.4 |
| **Sandwiches (Boots Shapers)** | | | | | | |
| Cheese & Pickle, per pack | 51 | 3.8 | 47.2 | 341 | 16 | 8.1 |
| Cheese, Tomato & Spring Onion, per pack | 43 | 3.6 | 39.4 | 306 | 21 | 5.5 |
| Chicken & Ham Sandwiches, per pack | 34 | 3.2 | 30.8 | 294 | 25 | 6.4 |
| Chicken Fajita Salad Wrap, per pack | 46 | 3.2 | 42.8 | 307 | 18 | 5.7 |
| Chicken Triple Sandwiches, per pack | 58 | 5.3 | 52.7 | 414 | 29 | 7.3 |
| Chicken, Egg & Cheese Triple, per pack | 55 | 6.7 | 48.3 | 434 | 31 | 10 |

**TIP:** Deep-fried fish isn't a particularly healthy option, but it isn't as high in carbs as you might think. Remember to cut off the batter and try to avoid the chips, which will set you back at least 30g in carbs!

| Food type | Carb (g) | Fibre (g) | Net carb (g) | Cal (kcal) | Pro (g) | Fat (g) |
|---|---|---|---|---|---|---|
| Chicken, Prawn & BLT, per pack | 49 | 5.1 | 43.9 | 412 | 27 | 12 |
| Egg Mayonnaise & Cress, per pack | 39 | 4.2 | 34.8 | 305 | 15 | 9.9 |
| Egg Salad, per pack | 44 | 2 | 42 | 304 | 13 | 8.4 |
| Flatbread: | | | | | | |
| *chicken tikka* | 24 | 1.4 | 22.6 | 172 | 11 | 3.6 |
| *fajita* | 20 | 2.6 | 17.4 | 138 | 9 | 2.4 |
| *feta cheese* | n/a | n/a | n/a | 172 | n/a | n/a |
| *Italian chicken* | 21 | 1.7 | 19.3 | 191 | 11 | 7 |
| *Moroccan chicken* | 26 | 1.7 | 24.3 | 176 | 9.6 | 3.7 |
| *Peking duck* | 29 | 1.9 | 27.1 | 169 | 7.4 | 2.6 |
| *spicy Mexican* | 23 | 3.7 | 19.3 | 156 | 7 | 4 |
| *Thai chicken* | 22 | 4.3 | 17.7 | 178 | 10 | 5.4 |
| *tuna* | 19 | 1.3 | 17.7 | 123 | 8.8 | 1.3 |
| Ham & Double Gloucester, per pack | 35 | 4.5 | 30.5 | 307 | 20 | 9.7 |
| Ham, Cheese & Pickle, per pack | 33 | 5 | 28 | 296 | 22 | 8.4 |
| Ham, Cream Cheese & Chive Bagel, per pack | 45 | 2.4 | 42.6 | 319 | 19 | 7 |
| Just Salad Wrap, per pack | 43 | 3.7 | 39.3 | 289 | 10 | 8.6 |
| Lemon Chicken, per pack | 40 | 2.6 | 37.4 | 315 | 14 | 11 |

**TIP:** Flatbreads and wraps are a good alternative to bread; better still, look for your favourite sandwich fillings in a tub, and use them as a topping for a fresh green salad.

| Food type | Carb (g) | Fibre (g) | Net carb (g) | Cal (kcal) | Pro (g) | Fat (g) |
|---|---|---|---|---|---|---|
| Mini Sushi Selection, per pack | 53 | 4.1 | 38.9 | 293 | 9.6 | 4.7 |
| Oriental Chicken Triple, per pack | 53 | 5.3 | 47.7 | 440 | 30 | 12 |
| Paprika Chicken, per pack | 35 | 4.3 | 30.7 | 297 | 20 | 8.6 |
| Prawn Cocktail Salad, per pack | 30 | 4.9 | 25.1 | 296 | 17 | 12 |
| Prawn Mayonnaise, per pack | 37 | 5.1 | 31.9 | 320 | 16 | 12 |
| Prawn, Salmon & Ocean Triple, per pack | 53 | 5.7 | 47.3 | 404 | 21 | 12 |
| Roast Chicken Salad, per pack | 37 | 4.4 | 32.6 | 284 | 21 | 5.8 |
| Roast Chicken, per pack | 31 | 2.4 | 26.6 | 288 | 24 | 7.5 |
| Salmon & Cucumber, per pack | 39 | 3.5 | 35.5 | 327 | 18 | 11 |
| Tuna & Cucumber, per pack | 43 | 3 | 40 | 323 | 20 | 7.9 |
| Tuna & Sweetcorn,per pack | 48 | 3.4 | 44.6 | 317 | 19 | 5.4 |
| Tuna Melt Swedish, per pack | 33 | 2.6 | 30.4 | 258 | 21 | 4.7 |

**TIP:** If you can't resist sandwiches, at least choose one with a wholegrain wrap or bun. They are higher in fibre, which slows down the transit of sugars in your blood.

## SAMPLE LOW-CARB MENUS

You could easily devise your own low-carb menus by checking the net carb column for foods in the listings, and avoiding the foods that contain more than a certain number of net carbs per portion – say 10. Or, if you want to allow yourself a high-fibre cereal for breakfast, or a pizza for dinner, you could cut back to very low carb foods for the rest of the day. Here are a few low-carb meal suggestions:

*Breakfast*

- Low-fat yoghurt blended with seasonal fruits and flaked almonds
- Scrambled eggs and smoked salmon
- Crab and brie omelette
- A cheese and cold meat platter
- Grilled lean bacon and tomato

*Lunch*

- Chicken Caesar salad
- Japanese sashimi takeaway
- Greek salad with feta and olives
- Ratatouille topped with melted cheese
- Hummus and roasted vegetables
- Homemade vegetable soup
- Niçoise salad with tuna, anchovies, boiled egg and green beans
- A packed lunch of cottage cheese, pineapple and Chinese cabbage salad

*Dinner*

- Chicken breast roasted with peppers, artichokes, tomatoes and red onions
- Salmon with homemade salsa, and stir-fried mixed vegetables
- Sirloin steak with al dente carrots, broccoli, green beans, in a coriander, soy sauce and lime juice dressing
- Spicy tuna steaks with Chinese-style vegetables
- Thai curry with courgette 'noodles'
- Tofu and mixed vegetable stir-fry with Asian spices
- Cauliflower cheese, made with skimmed milk and mustard
- Peppers stuffed with feta cheese, olives, onions and mushrooms, topped with cheese and pine nuts

*Snack*

- An apple and a chunk of cheese
- A low-fat yoghurt drink
- Tzatziki or hummus with cucumber and raw carrot crudités
- Ham and low-fat cream cheese, rolled together and cut into slices
- Grapes and brie
- Green or black olives in garlic olive oil
- Nuts and seeds

### Atkins diets

Recipes for the dishes listed here and menus for several different daily net carb counts can be found in *The New Diet Revolution* and *Atkins for Life*, along with all the other Dr Atkins books (see page 237). Atkins low-carb breads, cereals and pasta, used in many of his menus, will soon be available in UK supermarkets. Read pages 36-40 for a short explanation of the main principles of the Atkins diets.

*Breakfast choices*

- ½ cup Fiber 1 cereal with low carb soy milk and ½ cup blueberries
- Flatbread with egg salad
- Spinach and feta omelette with small tomato and 1 slice low-carb bread
- 1 slice Lemon Zucchini bread and a soft-boiled egg

*Lunch choices*

- Hamburger with green salad and Macaroni and Cauliflower Salad
- Panini and Greek Salad
- Spicy Turkey Club with mushroom salad
- Eggplant, Mushroom and Goat Cheese Sandwich with chicken consommé
- Chicken and Sun-dried Tomato Quesadilla with cucumber salad

*Dinner choices*

- Miso-Soy Glazed Salmon and green vegetable stir-fry
- Sesame Tofu with Snow Peas and Peppers, ½ cup low carb pasta
- Braised Ribs with Horseradish Sauce, mashed cauliflower and green salad
- Lamb chops with tomatoes and olives, courgettes and mushrooms, served with ½ cup low carb pasta
- Broiled steak with flavoured butter and a mesclun salad

*Dessert choices*

- Brown Rice Pudding
- ½ cup mixed berries
- Almond Flan and ½ cup pineapple
- 1 Chocolate Chip Oatmeal Cookie
- 2 poached apricots with toasted almonds

*Snack choices*

- 1oz macadamia nuts with 2oz cheese
- ½ Haas avocado with turkey and ham roll-ups
- 1 celery stick stuffed with cream cheese
- Hard-boiled egg
- ½ cup broccoli florets with a sour cream dip

### The Carbohydrate Addict's Diet

Recipes for the dishes listed here and more daily menus can be found in *The Carbohydrate Addict's Diet* and other books by the Hellers (see page 237). Read pages 41-44 for a short explanation of the main principles of the diet.

*Breakfast choices*

- Carbohydrate Addict's Complementary French Toast
- Salami and eggs
- Cottage cheese (full or low fat) with cucumber slices
- Scrambled eggs with bacon or low-fat pork sausage
- Carbohydrate Addict's Complementary Cinnamon Coffee Cake
- Onion-Cheese Omelette and sausage links

*To drink:* Cappuccino Slush, coffee, tea or diet drink

*Lunch choices*

- Baked Fish with Lemon and Herbs, served with steamed cauliflower or spinach and Carbohydrate Addict's Complementary Bread
- Sliced turkey with cucumber, radishes, olives and dill pickle

- Chicken Paprikash served with celery stuffed with cream cheese (full fat or low fat) and a tossed salad
- Lamb chops with green beans and Cool Summer Dip
- Fresh Seafood Salad served with celery, green pepper and cucumber in Creamy Herb Dressing
- Cheese-covered Mixed Vegetables and Spinach Salad
- Hot dogs, sauerkraut and tossed salad

*To drink*: coffee, tea, iced tea (sugarless) or diet drink

*Dinner choices* Reward meal – anything you like eaten or drunk within an hour. You can dine out in restaurants or cook favourite recipes, but you should try to eat your reward meal at the same time every day.

### The Zone Diet

To remain in 'the Zone', every meal and snack must be Zone-balanced. Read *The Zone Diet*, or any of Barry Sears' other books (see page 237) to make sure you understand the rules, and to find the recipes for these dishes and many others. Read pages 45-48 for a short explanation of the main principles of the diet.

*Breakfast choices*

- Spicy Ham and Cheese Omelette
- Yoghurt-topped Apple
- Florentine Filled Crêpes
- Fruity-nut Cottage Cheese with Raspberry Sauce
- Coriander Egg Salad

*Lunch choices*

- German Turkey Salad
- Stir-fried Scallops with Mixed Vegetables
- Pork and Vegetable Pitta Pocket
- Spicy American Turkey Burger
- Beef Italiano
- Native American Chicken with Vegetables

*Dinner choices*

- Spiced Beans with Mushrooms
- Prawn Gumbo
- Stir-fried Salmon with Mangetout

- Tuscan Pork Cutlet
- Devilled Steak with Mixed Vegetables
- Baked Chicken and Italian Vegetable Parcel

*Dessert choices*
- Frozen Yoghurt Alaska Jubilee
- Peaches with Almond and Apple Topping
- Blushing Pear
- Tangy Fruit Fluff
- Fruit Smoothies

*Snack choices*
- 30g low-fat mozzarella, 85g grapes, 6 peanuts
- 40g crabmeat, 1 tsp low-fat mayonnaise in ½ mini pitta bread
- 15g tortilla chips, 1 tbsp salsa, 30g low-fat cheese, 1 tbsp avocado
- 115g blueberries, 30g low-fat cheese, ½ pecan nut
- 4 slices low-fat ham, ½ apple, 1 macadamia nut

## The South Beach Diet

Read Dr A. Agatston's book, *The South Beach Diet*, so that you understand the principles. He gives many more sample daily menus, along with the recipes for dozens of delicious and exotic dishes. See pages 48-51 of this book for a short explanation.

### Phase 1

*Breakfast choices*
- Easy Asparagus and Mushroom Omelette with vegetable juice cocktail
- Baked eggs with low-fat bacon strips
- Artichokes Benedict

*Lunch choices*
- Dilled Prawn Salad with Herb-Dill Dressing
- Red pepper stuffed with cottage cheese and chopped vegetables
- Crab Cobb Salad

*Dinner choices*
- Sirloin steak with broccoli, tomatoes and Surprise South Beach Mashed 'Potatoes'
- White Fish in Spring Onion and Ginger Sauce with mangetout and cabbage
- Fish Kebabs with Spaghetti Squash

*Dessert choices* Different flavours of Ricotta Crème

*Snack choices*
- 1-2 Turkey Roll-ups with Coriander Mayonnaise
- Cherry tomatoes stuffed with low-fat cottage cheese

**Phase 2**

*Breakfast choices*
- High-fibre cereal with skimmed milk and strawberries
- 1 slice grilled low-fat Cheddar on wholemeal toast

*Lunch choices*
- Greek Salad
- Roast beef open sandwich
- Lemon Couscous Chicken

*Dinner choices*
- Meat Loaf with asparagus, mushrooms and tomato and onion salad
- Asian-style Chicken Packets with Vegetables and Oriental Cabbage Salad
- Cod en Papillote and salad

*Dessert choices*
- Fresh pear with ricotta cheese and walnuts
- Chocolate-dipped Strawberries

*Snack choices*
- Apple with 1 tbsp peanut butter
- Baba Ghannouj with raw vegetables

## EATING OUT

Just because you're trying to lose weight, you needn't deprive yourself of lunches and dinners out in restaurants. The guidelines for low-carb diets are fairly clear-cut, so it will be much easier to make choices from menus than if you were calorie counting, or trying to follow a low-fat diet. In the following pages, you will find some suggestions about dishes that should be safe for low-carb dieters, and others that will blow your daily totals. They are arranged in alphabetical order according to the nationality of the cuisine. These guidelines aren't foolproof, though, as different chefs use different cooking methods and ingredients. If in doubt, ask the waiter!

### British

British restaurants should be easier for those aiming to cut their carbs, because the dishes are familiar and the names are in English. Ask for an extra green vegetable or salad instead of the ubiquitous potatoes and chips, and opt for fresh grilled meats and fish without elaborate sauces.

LOW-CARB OPTIONS
Potted shrimps, jellied eels, oysters
Smoked haddock with a poached egg on top
Dover sole
Roast beef or rack of lamb
Game dishes – venison, pheasant, pigeon, rabbit
Calf's liver and bacon

HIGH-CARB OPTIONS
Full English breakfast, with fried bread or toast
Kedgeree
Pies made with pastry, such as steak and kidney pie, toad in the hole
Pies made with potato, such as shepherd's pie, fish pie
Yorkshire pudding
Bubble and squeak
Sausages and mash
Haggis and neeps
Most desserts – steamed puddings, jam roly-poly

### Chinese

Many of the sauces in Chinese dishes contain monosodium glutamate (MSG), made from beets, which has a high carb count. They also tend to serve processed white rice, but you could try asking if they can substitute it with brown rice, or just order an extra vegetable dish instead.

LOW-CARB OPTIONS
Clear soups, such as hot and sour
Steamed, baked or grilled fish and seafood dishes
Stir-fried meat or chicken dishes without sauces
Steamed bean-curd dishes
Chinese greens, beansprouts, mangetout, sugar snaps
Soy sauce

HIGH-CARB OPTIONS
Dim sum (dumplings)
Pancake or spring rolls
Sesame prawn toasts
Rice dishes, especially egg fried rice
Noodle dishes, especially chow mein
Sweet and sour dishes (high-carb sauce, and they tend to come in batter)
Oyster sauce, black bean sauce, lemon sauce
Chop suey
Crispy duck with pancakes

### French

The heavy butter-and-cream dishes that many people associate with French cuisine might be acceptable on an Atkins diet, but they are bad news for your heart. Meats or chicken cooked in wine should be fine, as they tend to thicken these sauces by reducing them, rather than adding flour.

LOW-CARB OPTIONS
French onion soup or consommé (without croûtons)
*Moules marinière*
*Coq au vin* (chicken in wine)
Entrecôte or Tournedos in Beaujolais, or with cracked pepper (*au poivre*)
*Fruits de mer* (seafood) – although coquilles St Jacques are scallops in a heavy cream sauce
Bouillabaisse (seafood casserole)

HIGH-CARB OPTIONS
Anything *en croûte* (in pastry)
Anything with *pommes* (potatoes)
Vichysoisse soup (cream of potato)
Quiche Lorraine
Béchamel or Beárnaise sauces
Sole Véronique (with grapes and cream)
*Canard* (duck) with fruit sauces
Crêpes Suzette (pancakes with flaming liqueur)

### Greek

There are plenty of great low-carb options in Greek restaurants. Avoid the dishes that contain pastry, rice or potatoes and opt for fish, chicken and meat cooked in olive oil, garlic, tomatoes and wine.

LOW-CARB OPTIONS
Taramasalata, hummus and tzatziki served with crudités instead of pitta bread
Halloumi – grilled cheese
Greek salad – with feta cheese and black olives
*Kleftiko* – slow-roasted lamb on the bone
*Stifado* – a wine-based meat or vegetable stew
*Souvlaki*, or shish kebab – meat grilled on a skewer
*Sheftalia* – minced and seasoned lamb
Grilled fish and seafood dishes

HIGH-CARB OPTIONS
Dolmades – vine leaves stuffed with rice
*Gigantes* – haricot beans in tomato sauce
Moussaka, if made with Béchamel sauce
Meatballs (*keftédes*), sausages (*loukánika*) and rissoles (*soutzoukákia*) could have added filler
*Spanakopitta* – spinach and feta pies
*Kalamari* – squid deep-fried in batter
*Fasolia plaki* – a bean casserole
Baklava and Greek pastries

**Japanese**

You'd think Japanese restaurants would be ideal for those on low-carb diets, with all their fresh fish dishes, but it's important to understand the terms used to avoid the ones that contain rice, batter, pastry or noodles.

LOW-CARB OPTIONS
Clear soups without noodles, including miso (soya bean) soup
Sashimi – raw fish
*Shabu shabu* – beef and vegetables cooked in broth
*Teppanyaki* – beef, fish and vegetable slivers cooked on a hot plate
Grilled fish or chicken with shoyu (soy sauce)

HIGH-CARB OPTIONS
*Donburi* – rice with beef, chicken or egg
*Gyoza* – rice pastry dumplings filled with minced pork
*Katsu* – means the dish will be breaded and deep-fried
Noodles – varieties include ramen, udon, soba and somen
Sushi – raw fish, seafood or vegetables with rice
Tempura – fish, seafood or vegetables deep-fried in light batter
Teriyaki sauce – full of sugar or corn syrup

## Indian

All curries are not created equal. The calorie and fat counts of creamy ones, such as kormas and pasandas, will be much higher than those that are simply cooked in spices. If you're carb-counting, there are many danger areas on Indian menus, and it's not so satisfying to eat curry without bread or rice.

LOW-CARB OPTIONS
Tandoori chicken, prawns or lamb with salad
Tikka dishes – meat cut into cubes and marinated
Fish, meat, chicken and vegetable curries cooked in herbs and spices
Vegetable dishes – *bhindi bhaji* (ladies fingers), *saag* (spinach and onions), *gobi* (cauliflower), *raita* (cucumber and yoghurt)
Paneer – curd cheese

HIGH-CARB OPTIONS
Dosas, pakora, samosas, uppatham, vadai – all deep-fried with batter or pastry
Rice dishes, including birianis and pilau rice
Breads – nan, chapatis, poori, paratha, roti
Dishes containing *aloo* (potato)
Dishes containing *dahl* (lentils)
Dishes containing *chana* (chickpeas)
Most sweets, including gulab jamun, kulfi, faloodi

### Italian

Pasta and pizza are both high-carb options, but if you can't resist, why not order a starter portion of pasta with tomato sauce or share your pizza with a friend? Alternatively, there are plenty of low-carb antipasti and main courses in Italian restaurants.

LOW-CARB OPTIONS
Clear soups
Antipasti of roasted vegetables or cold meats
Salads – rocket and parmesan, or tricolore (mozzarella, tomatoes and avocado with basil)
Grilled fish or seafood, meat or chicken
*Pollo alla Romana* – chicken with peppers and onions
*Agnella al Rosmarino* – lamb with rosemary

HIGH-CARB OPTIONS
Garlic bread
Pasta, especially with cream sauces
Risotto
Polenta
Pizza (see pages 208-10 for the carb counts of some fast-food pizzas)
Deep fried vegetables, or mozzarella sticks
*Scaloppa alla Milanese* – veal in breadcrumbs
Most desserts, such as tiramisu, profiteroles, panna cotta, ice cream

## Mexican

All those great Mexican tortilla dishes will be off-limits on a low-carb diet, as well as the rice and refried beans. Chili con carne has kidney beans in it, and is invariably served with rice.

LOW-CARB OPTIONS
Grilled chicken wings
Salads – such as taco or fajita salads
Salsa, sour cream and guacamole, with crudités instead of tortilla chips
Fajitas – griddled meat, chicken or prawns with peppers and onions, eaten without the tortillas
Grilled meats, chicken or fish
Seafood dishes – *camarónes, pescado, marisco* – with garlic and chili

HIGH-CARB OPTIONS
Chili con carne
Refried beans, pinto beans, rice, nachos
*Quesadillas* – pan-fried tortillas
Tacos – fried tortilla folded into a roll
*Burritos* – tortilla folded over a minced filling
*Enchilados* – soft tortillas
*Chimichangas* – larger filled tortillas
*Mole* – a chocolate-based sauce
*Torta* – a filled bread roll

**Middle Eastern**

This is one of the healthiest types of cuisine, but they use a lot of pulses – chickpeas, broad beans, cracked wheat, lentils and rice – that could present a problem on a low-carb diet.

LOW-CARB OPTIONS
*Sabzi* – herb leaves with feta
Shanklish salad – with peppery cheese
Baba ganoush – puréed aubergines with lemon juice
Kebabs, with salad rather than pitta bread or rice
*Shashlik* – marinated meat or vegetables on a skewer
*Shish taouk* – grilled chicken with lemon and garlic
Stews with preserved lemons and olives
Most meat and fish dishes

HIGH-CARB OPTIONS
Falafel – chickpea balls, served with hummus or tahini
*Fatayer* – pastry with cheese, spinach and pine kernels
*Kibbeh* – minced lamb, cracked wheat and onion
Salad olivieh – contains chopped potatoes
Tabbouleh – cracked wheat, parsley, lemon juice
Couscous, rice and breads
Rice-stuffed vine leaves
*Batata hara* – spicy potatoes
*Fuul* – broad beans with seasonings
Baklava and pastries, cakes

### Spanish

There are plenty of low-carb options in Spanish restaurants, but several of the classic dishes, such as paella, are off limits. Watch out for stews that contain potatoes, battered fish and seafood dishes, and sausages, like chorizo, that may contain filler.

LOW-CARB OPTIONS

Seafood and fish, grilled, with olive oil and garlic, such as *Pulpo a la gallega* (octopus)
*Pincho moruno* – a small kebab
*Escalivada* – peppers, onions and Mediterranean veg
*Salpicón* – cold chopped salad with shellfish
*Zarzuela* – a fish and seafood stew
Most tapas, meat and chicken dishes

HIGH-CARB OPTIONS

*Chocolate con churros* – the classic Spanish breakfast of chunks of sweet batter dipped in thick hot chocolate
*Fabada* – a stew with butter beans and chorizo
Paella – rice with seafood, chicken and meat
*Fideos* – noodles (*Fideuà* is a noodle paella)
*Tortilla española* – omelette with potatoes and onions
*Patatas bravas* – spicy potatoes
*Merluza a la gallega* – hake poached with potatoes, peppers and shellfish
*Crema catalana* – custard with burnt sugar on top

**Thai**

If you're carb-counting, the main problem you will have in Thai restaurants is the rice and noodles that crop up in many dishes. Green and red curries made with coconut milk may be high-calorie, but they are fine on the carb scale. Satays with peanut sauce are also high-calorie but reasonable-carb.

LOW-CARB OPTIONS

Clear soups without noodles – *tom yam, poh tak* or *tom kha gai*
Salads, such as *som tam* (with green papaya) or *yam nua* (hot/sour beef)
Steamed fish or seafood with lemongrass and spices
Stir-fried chicken, meat, fish or seafood dishes
Thai curries – except *massaman*, which contains potato
Sliced duck, beef or chicken cooked with spices

HIGH-CARB OPTIONS

Spring rolls (*popia*) or dumplings, like *ka nom geeb*
*Kratong thong* – crispy batter cups with filling
*Khao soi* – chicken curry soup with egg noodles
Fish or crab cakes with sweet chilli sauce
*Pad thai* – fried noodles with egg and beansprouts
*Mee krob* – crispy fried vermicelli in sweet sauce
Rice dishes – *khao, kow* or *khow* is rice
Noodle dishes – *sen mee, sen yai, sen lek, woon sen* etc

# FURTHER READING

## General Advice on Nutrition

*Aspartame (NutraSweet): Is it Safe?*, H.J. Roberts M.D., Charles Press, 1990

*Before the Heart Attacks*, H. Robert Superko, Rodale Press, 2004

*Clinical Evaluation of a Food Additive: Assessment of Aspartame*, Christain Tschanz, CRC Press, 1996

*Collins Gem Calorie Counter*, HarperCollins, 2003

*Collins Gem Diet and Exercise*, HarperCollins, 2002

*Collins Gem Healthy Eating*, HarperCollins, 1999

*Daily Telegraph Encyclopedia of Vitamins, Minerals & Herbal Supplements*, Dr Sarah Brewer, Robinson, 2002

*Fat is a Feminist Issue*, Susie Orbach, Arrow, 1998

*Fats That Heal, Fats That Kill*, Udo Erasmus, Alive Books, 1998

*Food Pharmacy*, Jean Carper, Pocket Books, 2000

*Good Fat, Bad Fat: Lower Your Cholesterol and Reduce Your Odds of a Heart Attack*, P. Castelli, Glen C. Griffin, 1997

*Healthy Eating for Life to Prevent and Treat Diabetes*, Physicians Committee for Responsible Medicine with Patricia Bertron RD, John Wiley & Sons, 2002

*New 8-Week Cholesterol Cure*, Robert E. Kowalski, HarperCollins, 2001

*Nutrients A to Z, A User's Guide*, Michael Sharon, 1999

*Optimum Nutrition Bible*, Patrick Holdford, Piatkus, 1998

*Prescription for Nutritional Healing*, Phyllis and James

F. Balch, 2002
*Principles of Nutritional Therapy*, Linda Lazarides, Thorson's, 1996

**Atkins' diets**

All books by Dr Robert C. Atkins
*Dr Atkins' New Diet Revolution*, Vermilion, 2003
*Dr Atkins' Quick and Easy New Diet Cookbook*, Pocket Books, 2003
*Dr Atkins' New Carbohydrate Counter*, Vermilion, 2003
*Atkins for Life: The Next Level*, Macmillan, 2003
*Dr Atkins Vita-Nutrient Solution: Nature's Answer to Drugs*, 2003

**The Zone**

All books by Barry Sears, Ph.D.
*The Zone Diet*, Thorsons, 1999
*Mastering the Zone*, 1997
*A Week in the Zone*, 2000
*The Soy Zone*, 2001

**The Carbohydrate Addict's Diet**

All books by Drs Rachael and Richard F. Heller
*The Carbohydrate Addicts' Diet*, Vermilion, 2000
*The Carbohydrate Addict's Calorie Counter*, Signet, 2000
*The Carbohydrate Addict's Healthy Heart Programme*, Vermilion, 1998

**The South Beach Diet**

All books by Dr A.Agatston

*The South Beach Diet*, Headline, 2003

*The South Beach Diet Cookbook*, Random House, 2004

**Other Low-carb Diet and Recipe Books**

*500 Low-Carb Recipes*, Dana Carpenden, Fair Winds Press, 2002

*The Complete Scarsdale Medical Diet*, Herman Tarnower, MD and Samm Sinclair Baker, Bantam Books, 1995

*The Formula: A Personalized 40-30-30 Fat-Burning*, Gene and Joyce Doust

*The Good Carb Cookbook*, Sandra C. Woodruff, Avery Publishing Group, 2001

*Lose Weight the Smart Low-Carb Way*, Bettina Newman and David Joachim, Rodale Books, 2002

*The Low-Carb Comfort Food Cookbook*, Michael R. Eades, John Wiley & Sons, 2003

*The New Glucose Revolution*, Jennie Brand-Miller et al, Publishers Group West, 2003

*The New High Protein Diet*, Charles Clark, Vermilion, 2002

*The No-Grain Diet*, Joseph Mercola, Hodder, 2004

*Protein Power: The High Protein, Low-Carbohydrate Way to Lose Weight, Feel Fit and Boost Your Health*, Michael R. Eades and Dr Mary Dan Eades, HarperCollins, 2000